TEN YEARS OF TURBULENCE

A PUBLICATION OF THE GRADUATE INSTITUTE
OF INTERNATIONAL STUDIES,
GENEVA

Also published in this series:
The United States and the Politicization of the World Bank
Bartram S. Brown

Trade Negotiations in the OECD
David J. Blair

World Financial Markets after 1992
Hans Genberg and Alexander K. Swoboda

Succession Between International Organizations
Patrick R. Myers

TEN YEARS OF TURBULENCE

The Chinese Cultural Revolution

Barbara Barnouin
Yu Changgen

KEGAN PAUL INTERNATIONAL
London and New York

First published in 1993 by
Kegan Paul International Ltd
PO Box 256, London WC1B 3SW, England

Distributed by
John Wiley & Sons Ltd
Southern Cross Trading Estate
1 Oldlands Way, Bognor Regis
West Sussex, PO22 9SA, England

Routledge, Chapman & Hall Inc
29 West 35th Street
New York, NY 10001-2291, U.S.A.

© The Graduate Institute of International Studies 1993
Phototypeset in Palatino by Intype, London
Printed in Great Britain by
TJ Press Ltd, Padstow, Cornwall

All rights reserved. No part of this book may be reprinted or reproduced or utilized in any form or by any electronic, mechanical or other means, now known or hereafter invented, including photocopying and recording, or in any information storage or retrieval system, without permission in writing from the publishers.

British Library Cataloguing in Publication Data
Barnouin, Barbara
Ten Years of Turbulence: Chinese Cultural
Revolution. – (Publication of the
Graduate Institute of International
Studies, Geneva)
I. Title II. Yu Changgen III. Series
951.05

ISBN 0-7103-0458-7

Library of Congress Cataloging-in-Publication Data
Barnouin. Barbara.
Ten years of turbulence: the Chinese cultural revolution/Barbara Barnouin. Yu Changgen.
360pp. 120cm. – (Publication of the Graduate Institute of International Studies, Geneva)
Includes bibliographical references and index.
ISBN 0-7103-0458-7
1. China – History – Cultural Revolution, 1966–1976. I. Yu. Changgen. II. Title. III. Title: 10 years of turbulence.
IV. Series: Publications de l'Institut universitaire de hautes études internationales, Genève.
DS778.7.B37 1993   951.05'6 – dc20
92-2352   CIP

CONTENTS

Introduction	vii
1 ORIGINS	1
Ideological origins	2
Political origins	25
2 BACKDROP	51
The purge of the group of five	51
The May 16 circular	71
3 THE CASE OF LIU SHAOQI	73
The beginning	73
The 11th Plenum of the 8th Central Committee	78
The fall of Liu Shaoqi	86
4 THE GREAT CHAOS	93
The emergence of mass organisations	94
The seizure of power	108
The February Adverse Current	115
Escalation of the chaos	120
The role of the military	124
5 FLUCTUATIONS BETWEEN ORDER AND DISORDER	153
From great alliances to revolutionary committees	153
Twists and turns from right to left	163
The 9th Party Congress	171
The campaign to purify class ranks	178
6 THE LIN BIAO AFFAIR	199
The way to Lushan	199
The fall of Lin Biao	222

7 FINAL POWER STRUGGLES	247
The criticism of Lin Biao and Confucius	247
The last succession crisis	273
The elimination of the gang of four	289
CONCLUSION	298
NOTES	301
Note on Chinese Sources	336
Bibliography	344
Glossary of Chinese Names	357
Index	367

INTRODUCTION

The Cultural Revolution (CR) was undoubtedly one of the most tumultuous and dramatic periods of China's modern history. It was marked by violence, factionalism and economic disruptions. The cataclysm it created had traumatic effects on the majority of the Chinese people, both in their private and professional lives.

A myriad of literature about this period has been published in the West and in China. Without denigrating the value of these contributions, we believe that most of the Western books are often theoretical, and written from a distance; Chinese writings – which we will discuss in more detail in the Note on Chinese Sources – are, with a few exceptions, fragmented and inspired by official policy. It is one of the objectives of this study to integrate Western and – after careful evaluation – Chinese literature. The evaluation has been substantiated by extensive informal conversations with people who were politically active during the Cultural Revolution, and by the experiences of the Chinese co-author who lived through this period with a critical mind.

In this study, we emphasise the primordial role of Mao Zedong in instigating and prolonging the Cultural Revolution. It was a phenomenon directly linked to Mao's theoretical, political and social perceptions, his status among the Chinese leadership, and his personality. It is our hypothesis that, without him, the CR would not have occurred.

Mao's motivations in instigating the CR were both ideological and political, in varying degrees of importance. On the ideological front, he perceived a constant danger of capitalist restoration. With his paranoic sense of grandeur Mao used the

CR as a means to eliminate those he considered, rightly or wrongly, to be his political adversaries. His overwhelming power status allowed him to impose his political designs among his peers. But the CR, once unleashed, developed into a phenomenon which he was unable to control completely, opening the way for violent factional strifes and power struggles.

Factionalism, which penetrated the entire Chinese society and revealed a deep cleavage among the Chinese people, was perhaps the most salient feature of the CR. It developed at two levels. At grassroot level the country was divided into conservative and radical factions with the former defending the party apparatus Mao had set out to destroy, and the latter participating in the destructive process which Mao had proclaimed – at least temporarily – as the principal prerogative of the CR. Both factions claimed ideological allegiance to Mao, but, in fact, ideology played a relatively small role in their rivalries in comparison to personal inclinations and conflicts, which determined the integration of people into one faction or another. But another important factor which determined factionalism was manipulation by the leadership, primarily by Mao himself.

The second level of factionalism occurred at leadership level. A major purpose of this book is to show that Mao himself was not involved in power struggles, but was, in fact, a figure towering above the rest of the leadership and, as such, the only person able to dominate the political situation to a degree which allowed him to manipulate other leaders as well as the population.

Among the leaders below him, conflicting interests developed and shifted over the period of the CR. Throughout the entire period, Mao acted as a ruler who followed the principle of 'divide and rule', never allowing any faction to gain uncontested power, while vicious power struggles and personal bickering often dominated the activities of the leadership below his level.

1
ORIGINS

The CR engulfed the entire country in a destructive political movement which shook the very foundation of Party and state, and which persecuted millions of people from all strata of the Chinese society. In the moderate language of the 1981 Resolution on Party History, it brought about 'the most serious setback and heaviest losses suffered by the party, the state and the people since the founding of the People's Republic.'[1] The Resolution attributed the immediate cause of the CR to Mao's 'entirely erroneous appraisal of the . . . political situation in the Party and the state', since he believed that the socialist society at all levels was undermined by capitalist and revisionist agents whose purpose it was to restore capitalism in China. The Resolution further affirmed the inaccuracy of Mao's perceptions and argued that they 'conformed neither to Marxism-Leninism nor to Chinese reality'.[2] If this was the case, where did Mao's ideas originate and why were they so vital that they unleashed such a powerful movement as the Cultural Revolution? The Resolution does not offer an answer to this question. It also papers over the cooperation the Chinese leadership had willingly extended to Mao and his policies and thus offers no explanation why the leadership supported Mao's policies, often to the point of self-destruction.

Part of the answer lies with the very nature of communist parties and socialist systems which promote the establishment of a ruling caste headed by a supreme leader with vast powers of decision making and immense political authority in his hands. History is replete with such examples. In China, with its millenarian tradition of autocratic imperial rule, this phenomenon was particularly rampant. Mao, the revolutionary leader, overcame numerous obstacles on the way to final victory of his policies. The success of his strategies and of his policies leading to China's unification contributed significantly to the development of his charisma. Mao was viewed as the principal architect of the Chinese revolution which changed the face of the country. These achievements established him in a position comparable only to China's most powerful emperors.

Mao's decision to launch the CR can be attributed to a number of factors. The first was the radicalisation of his thinking – partly due to societal developments since the late 1950s; the second was his charismatic leadership and the cult of personality; and the third was Mao's alienation from other national leaders who, although they basically supported him, were unable fully to conform to his ideas in the implementation of policies.

It can be safely assumed that without Mao's ideological evolution and without his supreme power status, the CR would not have occurred. Clearly, he was the principal force behind it. The extent of his involvement can be gauged from the fact that he himself declared that he had only two major achievements to his credit: the first was to have defeated the Guomindang and to have unified the country; and the second was to have implemented the CR and assured the continuity of socialism.[3]

Ideological origins

As a socialist leader, Mao was deeply immersed in his own ideological thinking. Whenever his ideas took form, he would consider them as the ultimate truth.[4] His thoughts were accepted as the principal guiding line for all major political decisions. Already in 1945, Mao Zedong Thought was enshrined in the Party constitution and became accepted as a sacred creed on which the leadership based the ideological and political control over the Chinese people.

Over the decade before the CR, Mao's thinking evolved in several phases and finally culminated in a radicalised version of his theory on class struggle and continuous revolution, which provided the ideological justification and framework for the CR. During the first phase, Mao came to believe that, even after the establishment of a socialist system, the process of complete socialisation of a vast country like China would lead to ideological conflicts. These conflicts could be solved only by firmly resisting – through class struggle – any tendencies of reversal to a capitalist system. During the second phase, Mao considered that the socialisation of society was a slow process, hampered by bureaucracy and revisionist tendencies, which could be completed only through a continuous revolution. Later, Mao became convinced that not only society, but the Party itself was vulnerable to the dangers of revisionism, so that class struggle within the Party had become a necessity. Finally, his views about revisionism within the Party became increasingly radical. During the early 1960s, he began to perceive a strong presence of a bourgeois class within the Party, and in particular, among the Party leadership, which aimed at the restoration of a capitalist system in China. To eliminate this class and to assure the continuity of socialism, Mao developed the concept of a Cultural Revolution whose purpose it was to overthrow the protagonists of capitalism and to establish an ideal socialist order.

1957–1958: from contradictions among the people to class struggle

Within a few years after the establishment of the People's Republic, the Chinese leadership was able to look back to the socialist transformation of the backward society they had inherited in 1949. The land reform of the early 1950s had eliminated the landlords,[5] the socialisation of private industry and commerce had liquidated the capitalists, and the extermination of class enemies was considered to have been successfully terminated in 1956. In September of that year, the 8th Party Congress had officially declared that the socialist system had been basically established,[7] though there still remained some remnants of the old system.[8] It was therefore now the main task of the party to concentrate its efforts on the development of overall socialist production and on the industrialisation of the economy.[9]

In principle, Mao shared the views of the 8th Congress about the fading class struggle in Chinese society. He made this explicit in a letter to Huang Yanpei – the leader of one of the democratic parties – written on 4 December 1956 where he repeated the Congress's view that 'in our country, class contradictions have been basically solved'. But he nonetheless added a reservation to this statement by adding: 'That is to say, they have yet to be completely resolved, and ideological contradictions will continue to exist for a long time to come'.[10] Some months later, on the occasion of the 3rd Plenum of the 8th Central Committee, he went even further and categorically argued that 'the contradiction between the proletariat and the bourgeoisie, between the socialist and the capitalist roads is undoubtedly the principal contradiction in contemporary Chinese society'.[11]

This change of mind was essentially due to the 'Hundred Flowers' movement. In the mid 1950s, despite some success in the economic sector, Mao was preoccupied with the slow pace of economic progress in China. He was particularly disturbed by the backwardness of rural areas and the lack of education of the peasantry.[12] In early 1956, he expressed the view that the contribution of intellectuals was essential to the revolution. 'An adequate number of excellent scientists and technicians were needed', he said, 'to wipe out China's economic, scientific, and cultural backwardness within a few decades and rapidly get abreast of the most advanced nations in the world'.[13] In an effort to encourage intellectuals to participate more actively in the development of Chinese society and economy, Mao, at a Politburo meeting on 28 April 1956, introduced a 'Double Hundred' policy, where a hundred flowers should bloom and a hundred schools of thought contend. This policy emphasised independent thinking and free discussion and promised intellectuals the freedom to express their opinion on science, literature and art.[14] While politics was still excluded from debate, it was permitted to criticise bureaucracy within the Party and the attitude of officials, so that the efficiency of the Party could be improved. A national propaganda conference in March 1957 and a *People's Daily* (PD) article of 11 April urged the implementation of this policy. At the end of the month a nationwide campaign to rectify Party cadres at all levels was announced for the following year with the recommendation that it be carried out in an atmosphere of free discussion.[15]

Mao's decision to launch the 'Hundred Flowers' movement

was partly influenced by events within the international communist movement. The 20th Congress of the Soviet Communist Party and the ensuing political relaxation as well as the upheavals in Eastern Europe had given him much ground to reflect on this issue. He believed that the unrest had been at least partially caused by the isolation of the communist Party from the people and by the repression of the intellectuals in these countries. On 27 February 1957, he delivered a speech 'On the Correct Handling of Contradictions Among People' in which he presented his theory on non-antagonistic contradictions between the leaders and the led. He argued that these contradictions among the people had not been correctly handled by the Communist Party of Hungary. 'If one persists in using methods of terror in solving internal contradictions, it may lead to transformations of these contradictions into antagonistic contradictions as happened in Hungary.'[16] To avoid similar outbreaks in China, Mao wanted such contradictions to be openly discussed and resolved by 'democratic methods' of reasoning and critical debate.[17] Based on this theory, Mao attempted to increase the dialogue between Party officials and intellectuals. He believed that previous indoctrinations had sufficiently remoulded the vast majority of the intellectuals who were, by that time, 'red in their hearts'.[18]

When intellectuals began to respond to Mao's call, a great deal of disatisfaction about Party policies and officials came out into the open. As the movement gathered momentum, the most outspoken critics sharply decried the represssiveness, dogmatism and sectarianism of the Party, the despotism of Party leaders at different levels, and the interference of incompetent Party cadres in professional work. A number of social scientists even questioned the validity of Mao Zedong Thought in history and social sciences. 'Mao does not have the time', one historian said, 'to solve these problems for us. . . . Academic problems should be solved by the scholastic world.'[19] The young writer Liu Shaotang rejected the application of Mao's Yanan talks to contemporary literature and art. He wrote:

> Works now created to serve politics and lacking a high level of artistic excellence can no longer fulfil the needs of the people. To insist on the same old theories and

thought and the same old manner of leadership is a regressive rather than a progressive act.[20]

Although the critics appeared not to have questioned the legitimacy of Marxism and communist rule, the expressions of discontent went far beyond the limits the leadership had set – though not clearly defined – for the campaign.

At the beginning of June, the Hundred Flowers movement was abruptly stopped. If Mao had expected the large majority of the intellectuals to be 'red', he was now convinced that they were 'bourgeois rightists' who had abused the Party and socialism.[21] Under the pretext of attacking dogmatism in the Party – which had been declared permissible within the framework of the campaign – they had, in Mao's view, attacked Marxism itself.[22] While they had feigned to support democratic dictatorship of the proletariat, they were, in fact, opposed to it.[23] Thus, Mao had found 'proof' that more than half a million class enemies existed in the society who, under the pretext of helping the Party to reform, had waged violent attacks on socialism. Mao initiated an anti-rightist campaign against intellectuals which labelled more than half a million 'rightists' as enemies of the people.

From 1957 onward, Mao stigmatised intellectuals as untrustworthy and disloyal. He remained vindictively opposed to them and denigrated them with such statements as 'Intellectuals are most ignorant' and 'young people without much learning' had founded new schools of thought.[24]

The wave of criticism which had surfaced during the Hundred Flowers movement catalysed a major change in Mao's thinking. His theory on the non-antagonistic nature of contradictions was transformed into one where contradictions became antagonistic and could be solved only through class struggle. Although he still believed that the process of socialisation had eliminated class struggle in the production sector, he expected it to continue in the political and ideological fields. Mao presented his new appraisal of the situation in a substantially revised version of his February speech which was published on 19 June. It concluded that:

> although the large-scale turbulent class struggles of the masses characteristic of times of revolution have in the main come to an end . . . class struggle is by no means

over. The class struggle between the proletariat and the bourgeoisie, between the various political forces, and between the proletariat and the bourgeoisie in the ideological field will be protracted and tortuous and at times even very sharp. The proletariat seeks to transform the world according to its own world outlook, and so does the bourgeoisie. In this respect, the question of which will win out, socialism or capitalism, is not really settled yet.[25]

1958: revolution as a permanent phenomenon

Mao continued to be concerned with the slow pace of economic development. He began to envision an acceleration plan – the Great Leap Forward (GLF)[26] – that would be part of an overall pattern of continuous revolution defined in the 'Sixty Articles on Work Methods' of January 1958:

> Our revolutions follow each other, one after another. Beginning with the seizure of power on a nationwide scale in 1949, there followed first the anti-feudal land reform; as soon as land reform was completed, agricultural collectivisation was begun. . . . The three great socialist transformations, that is to say the socialist revolution in the ownership of the means of production, were basically completed in 1956. Following this, we carried out last year's socialist revolution on the ideological and political fronts. . . . But the problem is still not resolved and for a fairly long period to come, the method of airing of views and rectification must be used every year to solve the problems in this field. We must now have a technical revolution, in order to catch up with and overtake England in fifteen years or a bit longer.[27]

After denigrating the intellectuals as useless bookworms of empty words, Mao began to emphasise the role of the masses in the process of economic construction. Manpower, in his view, was China's greatest asset, and technical progress and mass mobilisation therefore had to be linked. 'China's 600 million people', he said in April 1958, 'have two remarkable peculiarities; they are, first poor, and secondly, blank. That may seem like a bad thing, but it is really a good thing . . . a clear sheet of paper has no blotches and so the newest and most beautiful pictures can be painted on it'.[28] Mao clearly had full confidence in his ability and that of his colleagues to manipulate the Chinese people. Not only do precedents of docility of population abound in China's history, but Mao's own inherent voluntarism gave him the conviction that 'there is no such thing as poor land, but only poor methods for cultivating the land', and that 'the subjective creates the objective'.[29]

The Chinese revolutionary movement between 1927 and 1949 was based on such premises. It was carried out against major adversities and was successful precisely because it disregarded objective factors. It is therefore not surprising that Mao intended to use the same approach in his attempt to solve the seemingly insurmountable problems relating to China's economic social and cultural backwardness.

Before the GLF was inaugurated, tens of millions of peasants were mobilised during the winter of 1956–7 to participate in gigantic projects of water conversation and other public works. During the GLF, Mao received the enthusiastic support of the local leadership who functioned like the rural gentry of imperial times and, who, in a mixture of national and self-serving duty, often went to extremes in the implementation of official policies.[30]

When Mao, with the general support of the leadership, launched the Great Leap Forward in 1958, he based himself on political and ideological premises rather than on a realistic assessment of the economic situation. For him, it was not enough to lay stress only on 'production' as, in his view, the Soviets did. They 'are concerned only with the relations of production', he said, 'they do not pay any attention to the superstructure, they do not pay any attention to politics and to the people'.[31] Mao perceived the GLF as only a part of a more complex movement termed the 'Three Red Banners' which he defined in terms of three major objectives: the 'General Line' of 'going all out, aiming high and achieving greater, faster, better and more economical results in building socialism';[32] the establishment of People's Communes; and the improvement of industry, agriculture, culture, education and public health.

The single most important measure in this programme was

the establishment of the People's Communes. Mao viewed them as the last stage of collectivism in the agricultural sector. The first step had been the establishment of agricultural producers cooperatives (APC) at the peasant household level. A second, higher stage, extended the APC to the village level; and the third and final stage grouped village APC's into People's Communes functioning as independent administrative units according to strict egalitarian principles. Egalitarianism was implemented through a system of free supply of food and daily necessities and of sharing all raw material, resources, tools, machinery and labour.[33]

According to the slogan to 'achieve greater, faster and more results', a campaign of unprecedented intensity called on the people to prepare themselves for three years of hard work, 'to be followed by a thousand years of happiness'.[34] It was predicted that agricultural output would double in 1958 and again in 1959 and thus would solve, once and for all, China's millenary problem of food shortage. Simultaneously, in a campaign to first double then triple steel production, 90 million people in rural and urban areas were mobilised to participate in steel smelting with backyard furnaces, but mostly without raw material. An immense hunt for scrap material, including pots and pans, spread throughout the country. After half a year, the project had to be abandoned, having cost over 2 billion yuan in subsidies and another 2 billion in work costs.[35]

Within two years after the launching of the GLF, the economy collapsed. Agricultural and industrial output decreased, with a drastic effect on activities in the finance, trade and capital construction sectors.[36]

In the People's Communes, the indiscriminate transfer of manpower, land, animals, farm tools, and funds between production brigades,[37] which took place in the name of egalitarianism, undermined any attempt at efficient operation. The free supply of food and daily necessities to the peasants went far beyond the Communes' financial capacities. And the transfer of millions of agricultural workers to steel production in backyard furnaces left only women, children and old men to harvest the exceptionally abundant crop of 1958. The wastage due to the inefficient harvesting was enormous, but output statistics were grossly exaggerated by the local leaders.

Class struggle within the Party

When some of the disastrous consequences of the GLF became evident to the leadership, Mao called a forum of discussion at Lushan in July, 1959, to assess the situation. During the discussions, a number of critical issues were raised. Even the most optimistic supporters of the Great Leap, and that included Mao himself, began to see the impossibility of doubling grain output on a yearly basis, of increasing industrial output 'by leaps and bounds', of introducing a viable system of free supply in the countryside, and of overtaking 'England in 15 years' and soon thereafter 'catch up with the United States'.[38]

While these errors of appreciation and other specific problems of the GLF were open to critical discussion, Peng Dehuai's criticism of the GLF[39] crucially influenced Mao's attitude towards his senior colleagues as well as the substance of his thought. The discussions at Lushan inspired Mao to further develop his theories of class and class struggle in socialist society. He saw Peng Dehuai and others who had expressed doubts about the GLF, as representatives of the bourgeoisie and believed that the struggle between bourgeoisie and proletariat had moved from society as a whole into the Party which nurtured bourgeois elements in its midst. In 1959 he wrote:

> The struggle at the Lushan conference is a class struggle, a continuation of the life and death struggle between the two major antagonistic classes – the bourgeois and the proletarian classes – which had gone on throughout the socialist revolution in the last ten years. It seems that this kind of struggle will continue in China and in our party for at least 20 years and possibly half a century.[40]

Mao's assumption that antagonistic classes existed within the Party is a major step in the evolution of his thinking on class struggle. It ushered in the first important purge within the ranks of the party and paved the way for inner-party conflicts which were to reach unprecedented heights during the CR.

In the wake of the Lushan conference, a campaign against rightist deviation began to unfold, focusing on critics of the GLF, of the People's Communes and of the 'General Line of Socialist Construction'. It is noteworthy that, in contrast to the anti-rightist campaign of 1958, whose targets had been intellectuals outside the Party, the present campaign was focused on rightist deviation within the Party itself.

The immediate consequence of the campaign was the continuation of the GLF in 1960 and the further deterioration of the economic situation. Between 1960 and 1962, both agricultural and industrial output fell drastically.[41] The most dramatic consequence of this decline was starvation which began to appear in the second half of 1959 and accelerated during 1960. The entire country was faced with such an acute food shortage that a strict rationing system had to be introduced. City residents lived in a state of half starvation. Peasants in the countryside, particularly those living in traditionally poor areas or in provinces where the local leadership had been particularly enthusiastic about the GLF, were left to die in millions.[42] The starvation in the countryside was to a large degree the result of the political climate prevailing at that time. Ambitious local officials at all levels vied for maximum achievement, with the result that they over-estimated their own production capabilities and set greatly exaggerated production quotas for themselves. When they failed to reach their targets, they were reluctant to admit it, turned in the part of the production they had promised to the state and were often left with nothing for local consumption.[43]

Mao, though he refused to accept Peng's criticism, was not indifferent to the disaster created by the GLF. He realised that official reports from rural areas did not reflect realities and that during his own visits to the countryside, he was presented with embellished pictures of the situation. Already in the spring of 1959, Mao addressed a letter to rural cadres from county to provincial level urging them to report facts and not to exaggerate results.[44]

In order to be able to make a more realistic assessment about the situation in agriculture, Mao began to use members of his personal guard to inspect the situation on his behalf. His guard was composed of soldiers from rural areas of all provinces. He sent them to their villages and counties with instructions to investigate and to report to him their experiences about life in the countryside without embellishment. They were also ordered to return with samples of the food available to the peasants. The results of this investigation were devastating. Mao reportedly was so shocked that he abstained from eating meat for several months, and insisted on consuming only coarse food. His feet, like those of many other citizens, became swollen from malnutrition.[45]

The deterioration of the economy, which was compounded by the withdrawal of all Soviet aid in June 1960, forced the leadership to assess the situation realistically and to think in terms of self-reliance in economic policy. At the end of 1960, the GLF was terminated and the 'General Line' was replaced by a policy of readjustment.[46] After a disastrous harvest in 1960, the leadership adopted a series of urgent measures to remedy the situation. State requisitions from Communes were considerably cut, and substituted by imports. The transfer of manpower, material and funds between production brigades was abolished. This meant that the richer brigades were allowed to keep their benefits and the poorer ones were encouraged to rely on themselves.[47] Parallel to these measures, a production contract system, based on households, was practised in some provinces. Generally speaking, local leaders exercised considerable latitude in the interpretation of the new policies and tended to adopt the measures they saw fit.[48]

1962: 'Never forget class struggle'

Mao recognised the need for such policies and initially supported them. On several occasions, he even criticised his own mistakes in directing agricultural policies.[49] But he also disapproved of the manner in which his instructions had been carried out. In his speech to a Central Committee working conference held in December 1960 and January 1961, he criticised the way egalitarianism, of which he approved in principle, had been operated by the People's Communes. This practice, in his view, had led to the tendency to prematurely realise the transition to communism, which he condemned as the 'communist wind'.[50]

But despite such signs of moderation, Mao remained firmly anchored in his belief in collective economy and was alarmed by the developments in the rural areas where, in an atmosphere of relaxation, private economy began to spread and prosper. From 1962 onward Mao's thinking about class and class struggle became increasingly radical.[51] He continuously discovered signs of class enemy offensives in society and in the Party, and he invented new measures to counteract them. During the period from 1962 to 1965, he became more and more convinced that China was in great danger of turning revisionist, and that capitalist restoration was imminent.

His views were, at least partly, inspired by the Sino-Soviet conflict. Ever since the 20th Congress of the Soviet Communist Party, he suspected that revisionism had taken root in the Soviet Union. Though his disagreement with Moscow centred on several issues, the most unacceptable were Khrushchev's denial of the existence of class struggle within a socialist society, and his assertion that the Soviet state was 'a state for all people' and that the Soviet party was 'a party for all people'.[52] Talking about the differences in the socialist camp, Mao said that the problem is 'in fact very simple. There is only one principle involved: the problem of class struggle'.[43] He was determined to prevent in China what, in his view, had occurred in the Soviet Union: the revival of a bourgeois class compounded with revisionism and capitalist restoration.

The internal situation had even greater impact on Mao's thinking. He was alarmed by the deterioration of collectivism and by the pockets of market economy which had emerged in the rural areas. In August, 1962, he criticised the tendency of returning to individual farming and castigated embezzlement, theft and speculation among lower-level cadres, the revival of superstition and of such ancient practices as keeping a concubine.[54] But his major concern was the peasants' inclination to favour individual farming which he designated as 'polarisation' (*liang ji fen hua*) or 'do it alone' (*dan gan*). In contrast to 'egalitarianism', which was the essence of socialism, and which had to take the form of collective farming, 'polarisation' represented capitalism. Since the founding of the People's Republic, Mao had worked towards the elimination of 'polarisation' by first implementing the land reform, then organising cooperatives and, finally, establishing the People's Communes. With the revival of *dan gan*, Mao's achievements in the rural areas seemed to be in a process of reversal. In his view, this was an attack by capitalism on socialism, which called for a counter-offensive.

Mao's concern over the threat to socialist society became even more evident at the 10th Plenum of the 8th Central Committee (September 1962) where he further developed his thinking on class and class struggle. He emphasised that during the long historical period of socialism, class and class struggle were inevitable, and that there was a consistent danger of capitalist restoration. He urged his audience to 'never forget class struggle' which had to be kept in mind 'every year, every month, every day'.[55] He announced that the following year, a nationwide counter-offensive against 'the frenzied attack of the capital and feudal forces' would be launched in the form of a rural socialist education movement.[56]

The launching of the movement was confirmed at a conference held in May 1963, in Hangzhou which made the alarming assessment that more than one-third of the People's Communes were not in the hands of the Marxists. Thus, 'a serious and acute situation of class struggle has emerged in Chinese society' where the capitalist and feudal forces were 'launching a wild attack'. It was imperative to 'reorganise revolutionary class ranks' to overcome the attack of the class enemies.[57]

The campaign on socialist education which began to unfold in the rural areas, became known as the 'Four Clean Ups'. It was planned to last from three to seven years and aimed at the rectification of rural cadres politically, economically, organisationally and ideologically – hence the 'Four Clean-ups'. It reached its peak during the years of 1964 and 1965 and was subsequently abandoned.

In the cities the 'Five Antis' campaign was to be inaugurated. It was directed against embezzlement and stealing; against speculation with unlawfully obtained property and illegal trading; against extravagance through the misuse of public funds; against deviations from the Party's political line; and against a bureaucratic style of work. This campaign, however, never went beyond its experimental stage, which was carried out at Beijing University in 1964.[58]

Mao was dissatisfied with the results of these campaigns. Revisionism and bourgeois ideology, he believed, continued to be present in many areas of society. Using symbolic numbers to exemplify what he considered realities, he stated in

May 1964, that 'one-third of all grassroot-level units are not in our hands'.[59] This applied to the rural as well as to the industrial sectors. To Mao, it was clear, that the People's Communes did not all 'belong to us'. In a commentary on a report to the Central Committee of December 1964, Mao questioned the socialist fidelity in the production sector: 'How many of our industries are directed by capitalist management? One-third? One-half? Or perhaps more? Only by examining them all one by one can this question be answered. Only by reforming them one by one can the situation be changed'.[60] In the same month, he emphasised the existence of a 'bureaucratic class' within the Party,[61] a concept which he reiterated at a working conference of the Politburo in January 1965 where he stated that 'the main target of the present movement (rural education) is "those Party persons in power" who were travelling the capitalist road.'[62]

Class struggle in the superstructure

The second factor contributing to Mao's concern about the broad evolution of the Chinese society pertained to the developments in the cultural and academic sectors, or, in Mao's terms, the superstructure. During the early 1960s the political atmosphere in China was generally relaxed. It would indeed have been difficult to pursue political movements in the climate of starvation in the countryside and of severe malnutrition in the cities which kept the authorities fully occupied with the task of redressing the economic situation.

After the official abandonment of GLF policies, they were open to criticism and became the major subject of political study sessions in the country. Although the fundamental principle of the GLF had to be formally acknowledged, people criticised its absurdities and excesses.[63]

The intellectual atmosphere also became more open, and different schools of thought emerged in the cultural field. In fact, another 'Hundred Flowers' movement, though not officially announced as such, began to develop and was allowed to flourish until the start of the CR.[64] In 1962, more than three million Party members, who had been accused of rightist deviation, were rehabilitated after Zhou Enlai and Chen Yi had made major speeches declaring that the intellectuals were no longer considered 'bourgeois' but 'an integral part of the working class'.[65] The relieved intellectuals forged the expression: *'tuo mao jia mian'*: 'remove the hat of a bourgeois intellectual, receive the crown of a proletarian intellectual'.[66]

In the literary field, satire became a great fashion during the early 1960s. Essays (*za wen*) deriding the utopia, voluntarism and commandism of the GLF were widely read. Deng Tuo, secretary of the Beijing municipal Party committee, who was responsible for culture and education took the lead in this form of literature. As early as in 1961, he started a column in *Beijing Evening News* entitled 'Evening Talks at Yanshan' with a series of short sketches which enjoyed great popularity.[67]

Another series of satirical essays, *Notes from the Three-family Village*, were published in the journal *Frontline* under the common authorship of Deng Tuo, Wu Han, a noted historian of the Ming Dynasty and vice mayor of Beijing, and Liao Mosha, head of the propaganda department of the municipal Party committee.[68] Writers in other cities and in several provinces followed these examples and also began to publish *za wen* about the absurdities of the GLF. These essays were written at a time when the GLF was abandoned and when daily life was dominated by famine or at least severe under-nourishment.

The *Evening Talks at Yanshan* and *Notes from the Three-family Village* provided the starving citizens with welcome mental food. Written in a language different from the revolutionary *langue de bois* of the previous years, they told ancient stories and anecdotes replete with conventional wisdom. Written in simple but elegant Chinese, they attracted wide audiences. Their satirical style amused the readers and contributed greatly to their popularity.

There is widespread consensus in Western literature that Deng Tuo, Wu Han and Liao Mosha were opposed to Mao's style of leadership and used Aesopian language – understood only by a small intellectual elite – to criticise Mao and his policies.[69] This view corresponds to the interpretation offered by Mao himself on these essays on the eve of the CR. An article in *Evening Talks at Yanshan* entitled 'Special Treatment for Amnesia' has been quoted as an example for such criticism. The article contains a passage stating that 'amnesia made people to quickly forget what they have seen and said.' They 'go back on their own words and fail to keep faith.' The best way to cure this disease was 'to hit the patient over the head with a special club to induce a state of shock.'[70] This was later condemned in Yao Wenyuan's article of November 1965 as 'a most venomous anti-Communist article' which 'used exactly the same language as the Right opportunists to slander the Central Committee of the Party which they hated.'[71] It was interpreted in Western writings as an allusion to Mao's mental state which was conducive to irrational behaviour and decisions.[72] Another example is Deng Tuo's article 'Is Wisdom Reliable?' which suggested that even an emperor should 'seek advice from all sides' and 'one need not plan everything oneself'.[73] Later, this article was construed as an attack against Mao himself.

However, at the time when these essays were published, they were not regarded as a veiled criticism of Mao.[74] If anything, they reflected Mao's own statements on similar subjects. Mao referred to Party secretaries as 'tyrants' if they did not discuss all important matters collectively and failed to seek the advice of others.[75] He drew on historical examples of emperors who refused to listen to their advisors and perished in the end. In his talk at an enlarged working conference (the 7,000 Cadres conference) on 30 January 1962, he told the story of the Western Chu emperor Xiang Yu 'who hated listening to opinions which differed from his',[76] and he pointed out that Xiang was finally defeated by the Han emperor Gao Zu who 'was a hero whom the historians of the feudal period called a straightforward, open-minded man, who listened to advice and was relaxed as a flowing river'.[77] Moreover, Mao presented himself as the prime example of someone who had made mistakes and was ready to bear responsibility for them.[78]

In the field of literary criticism, theories emerged about 'truthful writing', which depicted realities rather than socialist utopia, and about the 'broad path to socialism', which did not deny the principle of socialism but aimed at a greater scope in the interpretation of this concept. Some writers and critics advocated the description in literary works of 'middle characters' who were neither revolutionary heroes nor anti-revolutionary villains, and criticised 'the smell of gunpowder' in Chinese films which depicted heroic revolutionary wars.[79]

Writers and film makers rediscovered Chinese classics and

literary works of the early twentieth century and began to neglect revolutionary themes. Even some foreign films appeared in the cinemas. A great variety of traditional Chinese opera was played, and some Western operas such as Verdi's *La Traviata* and Puccini's *Madame Butterfly* could even be seen in Beijing.[80]

A series of unorthodox interpretations began to surface in several academic fields. Historical studies examined the nature of peasants' uprisings in past dynasties, which in Maoist interpretation, were revolutionary acts.[81] The noted historian Jian Bozan held the view that after a new dynasty had been established, suppression of the peasants temporarily relaxed. The new dynasty usually made concessions to the peasants in the form of tax reductions and distribution of new plots. These actions were not revolutionary but contributed to the amelioration of the peasants' conditions. This concept became known as the 'concession theory'. Jian also argued that peasants tended to be rather conservative and lacked class consciousness. When they revolted, they meant to take over the landlords' position and not to change the society. Other historians' argument that peasant uprisings of the past should not be regarded as revolutionary movements, but rather as spontaneous uprisings against oppressors, also became a target of criticism.[82]

The role of some of the peasant leaders like Li Xiucheng, the hero of the Taiping uprising, was debated. The play-wright Yang Hansheng depicted him as a hero who defied the leadership, while the radical intellectual Qu Benyu later described him as a traitor to the revolutionary cause.[83]

In 1964, in a major philosophical debate about the interpretation of Marxist dialectics, Mao's views about the essence of dialectics, summarised in the principle that 'one divides into two' were questioned. In his essay 'On Contradiction', Mao had written: 'the universality or absoluteness of contradiction has a twofold meaning. One is that contradiction exists in the process of development of all things, and the other is that in the process of development of each thing a movement of opposites exists from beginning to end.'[84] In other words, every entity consists of two opposing elements. This thesis served as the theoretical basis for his views about class and class struggle. A society is divided into two opposing classes of exploiters and exploited. Their antagonism is the driving force for progress within society.[85] The philosopher Yang Xianzhen, president of the Central Party School, argued that this was only one side of the problem. Two opposites can also form an entity. This was expressed as 'two combine into one'.[86] Yang believed that differences, opposing views and ideologies were not necessarily incompatible with each other but could also complement each other. They could exist side by side without threatening the unity of the country.

Critical articles focusing on economic policies and, in particular on the GLF also made their appearance. The noted economist Sun Yefang, Director of the Economics Institute of the Academy of Sciences criticised the management system in industrial enterprises that stressed quantity of production at the expense of production cost and economic results. He suggested the introduction of certain market structures rather than further centralisation, and emphasised the importance of profits and material incentives for workers as means to improve economic efficiency.[87]

Mao was alarmed by the expression of liberal ideas and by the relaxed atmosphere prevailing in politics and economy. If in his 30 January 1962 speech, he had eloquently attempted to induce the party leadership to speak the truth and to listen to diverging opinions, he had mainly referred to the tendency of local and provincial leaders to act like the demiurge and to falsify facts about the economic situation. A few months later, in his speech to the 10th Plenum in September 1962, his tone changed considerably. Focusing his attention on literary trends in society, he warned that literature had become an anti-Party activity. 'Writing novels is popular these days,' he said. 'The use of novels for anti-Party activity is a great invention. Anyone wanting to overthrow a political regime must create public opinion and do some preparatory ideological work. This applies to counter-revolutionary as well as to revolutionary classes.'[88] After the Plenum, Peng Zhen, the mayor of Beijing who had participated in the meeting, asked Deng Tuo, Wu Han and Liao Mosha to stop producing their satirical columns.[89]

Mao believed he had solved the theoretical problems of literature and arts already during the Yanan Forum on literature and arts in 1942. He had pointed out that 'all literature and art belong to definite classes and are geared towards definite political lines. There is, in fact, no such thing as art for art's sake, art that stands above classes, art that is detached from or independent of politics.[90] Socialist art should serve proletarian politics. It should be geared to workers, peasants and soldiers.[91] The task of revolutionary writers and artists, Mao wrote, was to extol the masses and to portray the bright side of the people, to castigate the enemy and to expose the dark forces.[92] Since 1942, when he first exposed these views until 1962 when he spoke to the 10th Plenum, his thinking on literature and art had not evolved. In late 1963 and in 1964, Mao went beyond criticising certain forms of art such as novels and classical opera (of which he himself was a well-known amateur) and began to focus his attention on the cultural authorities, the 'superstructure', itself.[93]

His apprehension and disparagement of intellectuals became apparent when he pointed to the 'negative' role intellectuals had played in history. 'In the Jia Qing reign (1522–67), when intellectuals had power, things were in a bad state, the country was in disorder,' he declared, adding that 'it is evident that to read too many books is harmful.'[94] This seems to have been an astonishing statement from a man who was himself an avid reader of innumerable books and articles covering a broad range of subjects. Mao was widely respected for his vast knowledge about Chinese history and culture and admired for his ability to quote from historical and classical literary sources.

Based on Mao's critical comments, a group of radical intellectuals, some of them based at the philosophy and social sciences departments of the Chinese Academy of Sciences, began to contest the academic establishment. This group belonged to a younger generation of well-trained intellectuals who were thoroughly versed in Marxist theory and who defended the class character of philosophical and social theories. Among them was the philosopher Guan Feng who became prominent in the late 1950s and early 1960s for criticising his senior colleague Feng Yaolan who, in Guan Feng's, view had neglected class concepts in his philosophy. Two other radical scholars, Qi Benyu and Lin Jie, strongly disagreed with the historian Jian Bozan's views on peasant uprisings, the nature of which, they declared, was a revolutionary class struggle.[95]

Philosophy, history and economics as well as literature and art became targets of severe criticism from Mao and the circles of leftist intellectuals. In the educational field, the situation, in Mao's view, was even more threatening. Education at all levels – he felt – was dominated by the 'dictatorship of the bourgeoisie' rather than by that of the proletariat because the old values of bourgeois education had not been superseded by revolutionary thought.

During the years of 1963 and 1964, Mao, on several occasions, criticised the literary establishment where he perceived a predominance of 'feudal and backward things, while socialist things are negligible . . . If nothing is done', Mao declared, 'the Ministry of Culture should be changed into the Ministry of Emperors, Kings, Generals, Ministers, Scholars, and Beauties, or the Ministry of Foreign Things and the Dead.'[96] On 12 December 1963, he generalised his criticism declaring that:

> problems abound in all forms of art. . . . In many departments very little has been achieved so far in socialist transformation. . . . The social and economic base has changed, but the arts as part of the superstructure, which serves this base, still remain a serious problem. Hence, we should proceed with investigation and study and attend to this matter in earnest. Isn't it absurd that many communists are enthusiastic about promoting feudal and capitalist art, but not socialist art.[97]

A year later, on 27 June 1964, Mao went a step further in his criticism of the cultural establishment. The literary and artistic associations and most of their publications, he declared:

> have not carried out the policies of the Party. They have acted as high and mighty bureaucrats, have not gone to the workers, peasants, and soldiers and have not reflected the socialist revolution and socialist construction. In recent years they have slid right down to the brink of revisionism.[98]

Mao's declarations gave rise to a wave of criticism in the cultural sphere. A rectification campaign was launched in the literary and art circles during which a number of well-known writers became the target of vicious criticism. For example,

Shao Quanlin, the Party secretary of the All China Writers Federation, was reprimanded for his acceptance of the 'middle character' in literature, while a number of such fiction writers as Zhao Shuli, Zhou Lipo and Ma Feng were criticised for depicting these characters instead of 'revolutionary heroes' or 'bad elements'. In July, Yang Xianzhen's philosophy of 'two combines into one' was stigmatised by the *People's Daily* who accused Yang of spreading 'an erroneous theory of class conciliation'. As a consequence, Yang was removed from his post.[99]

In July, the Party centre approved and distributed a report from the Shanxi Province propaganda department emphasising 'noteworthy manifestations of serious and acute class struggle can be detected in the fields of education, science, literature and art, journalism, broadcasting, publicatiorn, public health and sports'.[100]

But all the denunciations and criticism voiced against relatively liberal academic and cultural works, though they led to the purge of a few officials, did not satisfy Mao. In most cases, they remained an exchange of view taking place in an academic atmosphere, between the academic and the literary establishment and a group of radical intellectuals who were thoroughly versed in Marxist theory and who defended the class character of philosophical and social theories. Most of these discussions had no major political impact. In July 1964, Mao had established the group of five headed by Peng Zhen, Mayor of Beijing to direct a campaign of rectification in literary and artistic circles, but the campaign, in Mao's view, was deliberately moderate.[101]

The purpose of the CR

All this undoubtedly was far from corresponding to Mao's sensitivity about the threat of revisionism and capitalist restoration. He therefore developed the concept of a Cultural Revolution whose purpose was tersely summarised in a sentence: 'combat and prevent revisionism' (*fan xiu fang xiu*). Behind this simplification was the idea of a three-dimensional transformation of society. The first was the achievement of three immediate objectives: (1) the removal of power holders who were travelling the capitalist road; (2) the repudiation of bourgeois and reactionary academic authorities; (3) the transformation of the superstructure 'which did not correspond to the socialist economic base'.[102]

This formulation reflects the dogmatism and radicalisation of Mao's thinking in his later years. But it also has deep roots in the power struggles which had shaken the Chinese Communist Party (CCP) since its very begining. In Mao's view, some leaders refused to accept the Leninist opinion that the transition from capitalism to communism requires a full historical period, during which the exploiting class inevitably cherishes hopes of restoration and makes attempts at restoration. These leaders, Mao argued, disagreed with his concepts about the existence of class, class struggle and the danger of a capitalist revival in socialist society. He therefore concluded that they were not true Marxist revolutionaries but representatives of the bourgeoisie 'who had sneaked into the Party' and who were in a process of transforming socialism into revisionism, as Khrushchev had done in the Soviet Union. It was thus the prime object of the CR to expose those enemies hidden within the Party and to eliminate them politically.

The history of the CCP is replete with examples of inner-Party struggles against rightist or leftist deviation of every description. The CR had many features in common with previous inner-Party conflicts, but, this time, they were taking place on an unprecedented scale; and Mao's uncontested authority enabled him to dominate with ease the power struggles accompanying the political liquidation of senior leaders.

In Mao's view, it was not enough to expose and to overthrow the 'capitalists' among the power holders, since they were supported by a 'social stratum', composed of 'former landlords, rich peasants, and capitalists, and by intellectuals, journalists, writers and artists, as well as some of their children . . . willing to take the path of revisionism.'[103] The most formidable representatives of this stratum were the 'bourgeois reactionary academic authorities' who were in a position to publicise their erroneous views and thus to lead people astray. They were the second target of the CR. Mao considered that intellectuals, whether Party members or not, were bound to have a bourgeois outlook, and only a small number of them had become true proletarian intellectuals.

Mao believed that the elimination of capitalist power holders within the Party, and of reactionary intellectuals would pave the way for the proletariat to transform the superstructure of the society which was his third short-term objective.

After achieving these immediate targets, Mao aimed at a more far-reaching goal, which was to establish a society dominated in all spheres by the dictatorship of the proletariat. At the eve of the CR, Mao perceived many social inequalities typified by such phenomena as a 'commodity system' with money exchange, small units of production and an unequal wage system.[104] In his view, such a situation promoted the emergence and growth of new capitalist and bourgeois elements in society. If they were eliminated in some areas, they would inevitably spring up in others, unless an all-round dictatorship in all spheres of life could be achieved. To transform the basic system and to establish a classless and egalitarian society was the second dimension of Mao's objectives. To attain the degree of equality Mao considered as fundamental, each unit should become a self-sufficient entity, where every member should be able to function as a worker, a peasant, a soldier and a teacher, assuming each role whenever circumstances required it. In such a world, the concept of professional specialisation would have no place, since it would only lead to another type of inequality.[105]

The transformation of society should be paralleled by the remoulding of peoples' minds. Mao expressed this third dimension of the CR in the following terms: this is 'a great revolution which touches people to their very souls and aims at changing their world outlook'.[106] The most important requirement for the change in world outlook was 'to combat self-interest', to substitute concern for one's own interest by the concern for others, thus favouring collectivism over individualism.

If the last two targets of the CR were visionary and utopian, the meaning of the first objective was inconclusive, since there was no clear definition of terms such as 'capitalist roader' or 'reactionary academic authority'. In fact, the CR became a witch hunt of those whom Mao perceived as his political enemies, and a power struggle amongst different factions, all of whom considered themselves as the true representatives of Mao Zedong Thought.

Political origins

Mao's theoretical thinking provided the conceptual basis for the CR. But it was Mao's position in the Chinese power structure which allowed him to effectively launch it.

In the historical evolution of power structure within the CCP until the eve of the CR, two phases can be clearly distinguished. From the time of the establishment of the CCP in 1921 until the end of the Long March in late 1930, the Party was periodically shaken with power struggles at leadership level which brought about frequent changes of leaders and leading organs. After the Long March until the eve of the CR, power structure at the apex remained relatively stable, and the changes that did occur were of secondary importance. This stability at leadership level was assured by the rising power status of Mao Zedong who was surrounded by a group of senior cadres recognising him as their undisputed leader. This situation prevailed until the early 1960s when Mao decided to break off with the establishment represented by Liu Shaoqi.

Once established in the base area, Mao's political prestige continued to rise. He devoted a lot of time to political writings and to proposing solutions for problems faced by the revolution. He, more than any other leader, shaped the party's strategies and tactics during the anti-Japanese war, and his formulations of political lines became more and more accepted.[107]

The year 1943 marked the beginning of Mao's rise to unchallengeable leadership within the Party. A year earlier, Mao had initiated a rectification campaign to review the history of the Party. Mao's criticism of past errors committed during the fifth anti-encirclement campaign, which had forced the communists to abandon the red base areas, and his version of Party history were officially accepted. He was recognised as the representative of the 'correct' political line and was elevated to top leadership of the Party: he was elected chairman of the Politburo and of the Central Committee's secretariat. But the leadership made another vital decision which was to exercise great influence on the future of the Party. It gave Mao the final veto on decisions of the secretariat which at that time was the leading organ of the Party,[108] thus investing him with a degree of power which none of his predecessors had been able to wield.[109]

The secretariat's two other members were Liu Shaoqi and Ren Bishi. Liu, who had given strong support to Mao during several policy disputes during the anti-Japanese war, was also appointed to deputy chairmanship of the Central Military Commission (CMC). The propaganda department and the organisational department under the Politburo were directed respectively by Mao and Liu Shaoqi. This marked the beginning of the Mao-Liu system of leadership, in which Mao, nonetheless, maintained a superior status to Liu.[110]

With the recognition of Mao Zedong Thought as the supreme ideology of the Party and the beginning of Mao's personality cult in 1945, Mao's political status was even further consolidated. The term Mao Zedong Thought was used for the first time in connection with Marxism-Leninism by Wang Jiaxiang who, on the occasion of the 22nd anniversary of the CCP in 1943, published an article in which he wrote: 'Today and in coming times, the correct road is the Thought of Comrade Mao Zedong, what Comrade Mao Zedong has laid down in his writings and manifested in action. The Thought of Mao Zedong is Chinese Marxism-Leninism; it is Chinese Bolshevism; it is Chinese Communism.'[111]

Deng Xiaoping embraced the same idea at a Central Committee Plenum in March 1945 and urged every Party member to learn from 'Marxism-Leninism and Mao Zedong Thought'.[112] In the following month, the meeting passed a resolution eulogising Mao's thinking as 'the integration of the universal truth of Marxism-Leninism with the actual practice of the Chinese revolution'.[113] The 7th Party Congress introduced Mao Zedong Thought into the constitution as a 'guide to all work'.[114] At the congress, Liu Shaoqi made the most flattering observations about Mao Zedong Thought. In his report about the amendment of the Party constitution, Liu referred to Mao Zedong Thought no less than 105 times.[115] In Liu's words, Mao Zedong Thought incarnated the Chinese brand of communism and Marxism. It had developed and matured over a time span of twenty-four years and its validity had been tested in countless struggles by thousands of people. It had stood all tests and proven to be objective truth and the only correct theory and policy capable of saving China. Liu observed that theory can only be created by the representatives of the proletariat and that Mao was the most outstanding among them. He argued that it should be an obligation for each and every Party member to learn Mao Zedong Thought and to work under its direction.

In Liu's analysis, Mao Zedong Thought contained nine major aspects: it was a complete analysis of the current world and Chinese situation, it provided the theoretical and political basis for new democracy, peasant emancipation, the revolutionary united front, the revolutionary war, the base areas, for the establishment of a new democratic republic, for Party construction and for general culture.[116] Thus there was practically no problem area which the CCP had to tackle, for which Mao had not already provided concepts for solutions and guidelines for action. The next four years of war against the Guomindang proved the validity of Mao's strategies, and he emerged on the eve of the People's Republic, not only as the most powerful and prestigious national leader in China's modern history but also as the legendary saviour of China's 600 million people.

The 7th Party Congress established the basic pattern of power structure at the leadership level for the next twenty years. Thereafter, only minor changes were introduced at leadership level. The Congress elected Mao as the Chairman of the Central Committee, the Politburo and the new secretariat which also included Liu Shaoqi, Zhou Enlai, Zhu De and Ren Bishi. Since Politburo members were scattered throughout different areas during the years of the civil war, the secretariat which theoretically functioned under the direction of the Politburo, became, in fact, the leading organ at that time. It remained as such until the 8th Congress in 1956 when a standing committee composed of Mao, Liu, Zhou, Zhu and Chen Yun, nominated after Ren Bishi's death in 1950, was established and the Secretariat resumed its role as the executive of the Central Committee.[117] At the foundation of the People's Republic, Mao became head of state with Liu Shaoqi as his deputy and Zhou Enlai as the third man in hierarchical order.

From the founding of the People's Republic (PR) to the eve of the CR, China's top leadership structure remained basically stable. The only exception was in 1953 when Gao Gang, vice chairman of the state and member of the Politburo, and Rao Shushi, director of the Central Committee's organisation department, and a number of others, who according to the official version, had attempted to overthrow Liu Shaoqi and Zhou Enlai, were removed from their posts.

Cult of Mao's personality

One of the most striking features of the post-revolutionary years was the evolution of the cult of Mao's personality and its spread from within the Party to the entire nation. To cultivate Mao's personality to such a level was not an isolated phenomenon. It was, in fact, the tip of an iceberg from which the entire leadership structure at all levels gained considerable advantage. Party leaders at all levels claimed respect from their subordinates and their cooperation to 'build up and safeguard the prestige' of the leaders in the name of Party discipline and in the interest of the revolutionary cause. Several thousand years of imperial tradition deeply rooted in China's peasant population provided fertile ground for such a cult. The achievements of the PR in its early years also nourished the popularity of and the respect for the Party and its leadership.

Imperial morality was so deeply ingrained in Chinese society that even the revolutionary leadership did not escape from this tradition, and they readily accepted Mao as the greatest emperor in Chinese history. Mao himself was convinced about this superiority. As he wrote in one of his poems:

> Alas! Emperors Qin Huang, Han Wu
> Weren't bred enough in liberal arts,
> And Emperor Tang Zhong and Song Zu
> were lacking in poetic parts.
> And Genghis Khan, Proud Son of Heaven
> But good at shooting hawks with darts.[118]

Mao, allowed himself to be compared with Qin Shihuang, the founder of the Qin Dynasty. A number of comparisons have indeed been made between him and the Qin emperor. Qin Shihuang was the first emperor to unify the country and to establish a centralised state in China. Mao's achievements of unification and centralisation were generally viewed as a comparable accomplishment.

Qin Shihuang and Mao Zedong developed similar concepts of continuity of their respective empires. Qin Shihuang wanted his kingdom to be passed on through his sons for thousands of years. Mao's ambition was similar. The societal concept he had devised was a long-term historical one to be implemented by 'thousands upon thousands of successors over thousands of years' on the basis of a protracted revolution ending in a permanent classless society. In this respect, however, he was even more ambitious than the Qin emperor. He believed that China's revolutionary struggle would be an example to the entire world; and China's classless society would only be perfect if all bourgeois and capitalist impediments would be 'banished from the earth so that it will be impossible for the bourgeoisie and all other exploiting classes to exist or for new ones to arise'.[119]

Qin Shihuang standardised weights and measures, coinage, the axle width of vehicles, and script. He also strove to standardise thought by issuing orders to prohibit philosophical disputation which had been flourishing during the Warring States era (475–221 BC). All works on subjects other than official Qin historical chronologies and utilitarian treatises on divination, the practice of agriculture and medicine were collected and burnt. As a warning against defiance of his orders, he executed 460 scholars.[120]

Mao also perceived intellectuals as a fundamental threat to the disciplined and homogeneous society he wanted to create. As Qin Shihuang, he feared spiritual independence and the impact of intellectual criticism on the whole of the society he wanted to create. Mao remarked that, while Qin Shihuang had burnt books and had buried intellectuals alive, he had eliminated only five hundred of them. Mao was proud to announce that, during the anti-rightist campaign, though not physically killing them, he had buried many more.[121]

The image and the prestige Mao enjoyed may well have surpassed those of the most powerful Chinese emperors. The organisational facilities of the Chinese Communist Party and the powerful impact of modern organisational techniques, which were widely and efficiently used by the Chinese official media, were at his disposal. It was therefore possible to develop a cult of personality centring around Mao, until it turned, as the *Guangming Ribao* later pointed out, into a 'god-building' movement.[122] Systematic efforts were made to transform the thought process of people and, in particular, of many intellectuals whom the leadership believed to be deeply immersed in traditional thinking. Official propaganda incited the whole nation to unite in the eulogy paying tribute to the glorification of the 'great saviour of the nation'. Special efforts were made to propagate Mao Zedong Thought. In the early 1950s, Mao's selected works began to be published and a campaign to remould intellectuals was started. Political studies to learn Mao Zedong Thought became part of daily life.[123]

By the time the 8th Party Congress was convened in September, 1956, the Chinese leadershp seemed to take Mao's role for granted, for they did not consider it necessary to make additional efforts to add to Mao's prestige. Liu Shaoqi's report to the Congress, unlike the one he had presented to the 7th Congress, dealt mainly with questions of national economy and did not mention Mao Zedong Thought. A paragraph in the report paid tribute to Mao's 'role of helmsman in our revolution', his talent to 'integrate the universal truth of Marxism-Leninism and the actual practice of the Chinese revolution', 'his firm belief in the wisdom and the strength of the masses', 'his upholding of the mass line in the work of the Party and of the Party's principles of democracy and collective leadership'.[124]

The 8th Party Congress was held in September 1956, after Khrushchev's repudiation of Stalin's personality cult at the 20th Congress of the Soviet Communist Party in February 1956 and the ensuing process of de-Stalinisation. Khrushchev's new policies were an inconclastic blow to Mao and the Chinese leadership. Their apprehension was compounded by the chain reaction of events that took place in Eastern Europe in the autumn of 1956. In the Chinese view, these events and the posthumous disparagement of Stalin's authority and personality were clearly linked. But the official Chinese reaction was to formally condemn personality cult as such and to declare that the CCP was immune to such malpractice. In an editorial in the *People's Daily*, personality cult was rejected as 'a decadent legacy left over by the long history of humanity'. Opposition to personality cult, the article read, 'was a great and heroic struggle waged by the Soviet Communists and the Soviet peole in cleaning up ideological obstacles on their way to progress'.[125]

At the 8th Party Congress, Deng Xiaoping emphasised the

importance of collective leadershp which the Party had practiced since the Yanan days. Deng differentiated between Mao and Stalin pointing out that 'Love for the leader (Mao) is essentially an expression of love for the interests of the Party, the class and the people, and not the deification of an individual (Stalin).'[126] He reminded his audience of a decision by the Party centre taken at Mao's suggestion in 1949 which prohibited the celebration of Party leaders' birthdays and the use of their names to designate places, streets and enterprises.[127]

A significant change was the omission of reference to Mao Zedong Thought in the Party constitution. It has been suggested that the removal of this reference had been the result of a concession made to the international communist movement which rejected the notion of personality cult.[128] It has also been construed that the omission of this clause represented a political set back for Mao Zedong.[129] According to recent Chinese publications, Mao, as early as 1953, had made several statements to the effect that the expression ' "Mao Zedong Thought" should be deleted wherever it appears and be replaced by "Comrade Mao Zedong's writings".'[130] In December 1954, the question was again raised in an internal document which stated that, 'according to Comrade Mao Zedong's instructions, the term "Mao Zedong Thought" should henceforth not be used, so that misunderstandings can be avoided'. The document emphasises that Mao Zedong Thought 'is nothing else but Marxism-Leninism', and that 'such misunderstandings that they may differ in content, has to be avoided'.[131]

The reference to a possible misunderstanding and the emphasis on the equality of Mao Zedong Thought and Marxism-Leninism can be explained by two factors. One, during the period of close cooperation between the Soviet Union and China in the early 1950s, Mao and the Chinese leadership did not want to take the risk of alienating Stalin by establishing a different doctrine of socialism than that officially accepted by the international communist movement. Two, Mao himself wanted to avoid the impression that he intended to divorce himself from Marxism-Leninism. It is, therefore, not surprising that during the preparatory work for the amendment of the Party constitution to be presented to the 8th Congress, references to Mao Zedong Thought were also not present. The first draft of the Party constitution which was produced in October, 1955 and followed by four others, all written under Mao's direction, omitted to mention Mao Zedong Thought.[132] The Party constitution voted at the Congress finally replaced the reference to 'Marxism-Leninism and Mao Zedong Thought' as the guiding principle for all party work by the formula of 'Marxism-Leninism as the guiding principle of the Party's activities.[133]

Although the 8th Congress seemed to stress collective over individual leadership, Deng affirmed the supremacy of Mao's role saying: 'Our Party also owes its victories to the leading personnel of the Party organisations at all levels, particularly to the leader of our Party, Comrade Mao Zedong'[134] and he instructed Party organs at all levels to be 'conscientious about educating the vast new members more effectively, to take part in practical measures to organise and guide their studies of Marxism-Leninism and Comrade Mao Zedong's writings.' Mao Zedong's writings, of course, embedded his Thought.[135]

By no means did the 8th Congress inaugurate a decline in the cult of Mao. He declared at a Central Committee meeting in March 1958 that one had to differentiate between a 'correct' and a 'wrong' personality cult. It was 'correct' to enhance the position of Marx, Engels, Lenin and Stalin, since they represented the truth. Whoever held the truth, Mao said, can be placed on a pedestal. The wrong cult was blind faith in an individual.[136] Since it can be safely assumed that Mao considered himself as the holder of truth, there could be no doubt that the cult of his own personality was justified.

The early 1960s witnessed a new upsurge in the cult of Mao's image. It was initiated by Lin Biao in the People's Liberation Army (PLA) who emphasised that 'Marxism-Leninism in its present form is our Chairman Mao's Thought. It is the summit of thinking of our era.' 'All political ideology', he said, 'is class ideology and ideology of class struggle. Chairman Mao's Thought is about class struggle and the emancipation of the proletariat.'[137] A conference of the Military Commission (MC) in September 1960 acclaimed Mao as 'the greatest Marxist of our era'. His Thought was not only considered as 'the guide for revolution and socialist construction' but also as 'the strongest ideological weapon against imperialism, revisionism and dogmatism'. The entire army was called upon 'to read

Chairman Mao's books, listen to Chairman Mao's words, do everything according to Chairman Mao's directives and to be Chairman Mao's good soldiers'.[138]

Had there been no implicit encouragement from Mao to Lin's initiatives, the movement of deification might not have gained much momentum. But a positive response was quick to come. Mao declared that Lin Biao had gone to the grassroot level of the army 'to do investigation and study . . . to discover a number of important problems in the work of our army and to put forward a few very good measures for the building up of the army'.[139] This was exceptional praise. For years, the chairman had abstained from complimenting any high-level leader. Lin Biao, impressed by the unexpected praise, increased his efforts to develop the trend of studying Chairman Mao's works and of 'putting politics in command' in the army. He responded to Mao's encouragement by ordering the *Liberation Army Daily* at the beginning of 1964, to publish Mao's quotations in every one of its issues. The collection of these quotations later became 'the little red book'. With the publication of the little red book, Lin also devised a method to learn Mao Zedong Thought. It consisted of studying and applying Mao's works to specific problems 'in a creative way, combine study with application, first study what must be urgently applied so as to get quick results, and strive hard to apply what one is studying'.[140]

At the 7,000 Cadres conference of 1962, which was mainly an assessment of the results of the GLF, Lin Biao made a speech recalling Mao's great achievements during the entire period of the Chinese revolution and socialist construction. His concluding remarks emphasised that, whenever Mao's directives had been followed conscientiously, victory had been won. Conversely, whenever Mao's directives had been ignored, there was failure. Disregard for Mao's directives, Lin asserted, was the root cause for the failure of the GLF.[141]

Lin's campaign which was initiated in the army, spread through the entire society. In 1964, the 'little red book' or 'Quotations from Chairman Mao Zedong' was published in almost 1 billion copies. Its foreword presented Mao as 'the greatest Marxist-Leninist of our era' and Mao Zedong Thought as 'Marxism-Leninism of the era in which imperialism is heading for total collapse and socialism is advancing to worldwide victory'.¹⁴² A movement to study Mao Zedong's selected works was launched which required those with higher education to read thoroughly the four volumes of his works within a fixed period of time. Those with less education were expected to read a shorter selection of the volumes. Illiterates, mostly peasants, were summoned to reading sessions where some of Mao's simpler essays such as 'In Memory of Norman Bethune', 'Serve the People', and 'The Foolish Old Man Who removed the Mountains' were read to them. They were required to memorise important statements from Mao's works. Study sessions which previously had been devoted to different political issues, now concentrated on this subject. A new type of person, the 'activist of learning Chairman Mao's works' emerged among those who excelled in their study, and it became a common practice to invite such activists to meetings where they explained how they had studied and applied Mao's works 'in a creative way'. Mao's quotations began to appear everywhere. Even bicycles would carry small wooden boards (*yu lu pei*, or quotation plates) with quotations written on them which had to be periodically replaced by new ones.¹⁴³

Edgar Snow remarked about the 'immoderate glorification of Mao Zedong' during his visit to China in the winter of 1964–5.¹⁴⁴ Mao himself believed in the need for such a cult. In December 1970, Mao suggested to Edgar Snow that Khrushchev's fall from power might well be attributed to the fact that Khrushchev had no cult at all. He added that some scientific studies on primitive societies, such as Lewis Henry Morgan's research confirmed that people had a 'need to worship' and that such worship 'lent support to historical materialism and concepts of class struggle'.¹⁴⁵

During the CR, the cult of Mao was infused with religious symbolism. As Maurice Meissner wrote: 'Just as Chinese emperors of old were "Sons of Heaven" whose virtue linked the social order with the cosmic order, so "heaven" became the symbol of Mao and he was identified with the forces of the cosmos, the "Mao-sun" was hailed as "the reddest of all suns" whose radiance dwelt in the hearts of all true revolutionaries.'¹⁴⁶ Exhibition halls commemorating Mao's revolutionary deeds were built across the country. They were exposed towards east, the source of light and referred to as 'sacred shrines'.¹⁴⁷

Whereas in the beginning of the CR, the cult of Mao was integrated in a genuine and spontaneous mass movement with the red army as its vanguards, it became a formalistic ritual in its later days. The practice, loaded with religious overtones, of asking Chairman Mao's instruction every morning in front of his picture, and confessing one's 'mistakes' to him in the evening, was one such ritual, which symbolised the attribution of political and moral virtue to Mao alone.

Mao's alienation from the leadership

In 1958, Mao decided to relinquish his post as the head of state and to retain his position as chairman of the Party so that he could 'concentrate his energies on dealing with questions of the direction and policy line of the Party and the state . . . and to set aside more time for Marxist-Leninist theoretical work'.[148] This decision which was officially accepted by the 6th Plenum of the Central Committee had been announced by Mao some years earlier (the exact date is unknown) when he declared that the leadership was to be divided into a first and a second line. The front line leaders, i.e. the members of the Politburo's Standing Committee headed by Liu Shaoqi were in charge of the day-to-day work of Party and state while Mao retired into the second line to concentrate on major policy and theoretical issues.

Mao's withdrawal to the second line has often been interpreted as a demotion and a loss of prestige related to the policies of the GLF. It is difficult to estimate the extent to which Mao's prestige was damaged by the disastrous consequences of the GLF. In rural areas, dissatisfaction with overly zealous rural cadres had become widespread among the peasants, but the prestige of the Party, of its leadership and particularly of Mao Zedong remained intact despite the failures of the GLF. According to official propaganda, the Party was not to be blamed for the debacle, which was caused by natural calamities, the economic pressure of the Soviet revisionists, and the wrong working style of low-level rural cadres. It appears that these explanations were generally accepted, and the Party encountered no difficulties in imposing harsh austerity measures and a strict rationing system.[149] In the wake of the GLF, as a demonstration of the great improvement of people's livelihood in comparison to the situation before liberation, work units in rural areas organised 'recall bitterness meals' at which food consisting of bitter herbs would be offered to remind people of the harshness of their lives before liberation. During these meals which took place in unlit meeting halls as a reminder of the darkness of the past, the participants would listen to accounts of tragic personal experiences from the past. These accounts would be discussed, and people would express their grief over the bitterness of the past and their gratitude to Chairman Mao.[150]

The Lushan conference and the ensuing purge of Peng Dehuai, Huang Kecheng, Zhang Wentian and Zhou Xiaozhou demonstrated that Mao's retirement to the second front had not weakened his authority. If he accepted criticism of the GLF and the People's Communes on some concrete issues such as 'the communist wind', issuing blind directions, exaggerating the results and relying on 'commandism', he would not tolerate systematic criticism of policies to which he was deeply committed. This was amply illustrated in the case of Peng Dehuai who, in his letter to Mao, had made a general and honest evaluation of the GLF and analysed the major causes for its failure. He attributed the exaggerations and the 'miracles' of the movement to 'Left' inclinations,[151] and to the lack of competence of the party leadership in economic construction.[152] His communication was moderate in tone and it was neither a challenge to Mao nor an attempt to charge him with the responsibility for the disaster.[153] But it expressed overall criticism of GLF policies.

Mao in fact had criticised himself at the Lushan conference. Since he had 'applied himself essentially to the revolution', he said, he was 'not really competent' in the fields of economic and industrial development.[154] But he condemned Peng Dehuai as the representative of rightist deviation who had exhibited 'bourgeois vacillation', and called Peng's letter an anti-Party programme.[155]

From Lushan onwards, Mao's sensitivity to criticism from others reached a high level of intolerance and he regarded his own views as the only valuable interpretation of Marxism-Leninism.[156] This also reflected the millenarian tradition that the patriarch of the family would not be criticised by his sons or any other family member subordinated to him.

Mao had denounced Peng Dehuai without consulting any of his colleagues. This personal and arbitrary decision undermined the pattern of decision making based on consensus among the leadership. Even though Mao always had the final word, before the Lushan conference he had not used the procedure of surprise attack to impose his will. Nonetheless, on this occasion he obtained full support from Liu Shaoqi, Zhou Enlai, Zhu De and Lin Biao and other leaders all of whom were also deeply committed to the basic policies of the party and to the defence of Mao in the face of criticism, however justified it may have been. Criticising Mao, who epitomised Mao Zedong Thought would have been equivalent to attacking the basic political line of the Party and to jeopardising their own political credibility. Since they all had contributed to the establishment of a totalitarian regime with Mao at its peak, their own political survival was inseparable from Mao.

During the 7,000 Cadres conference in January 1962, which was to draw lessons from the GLF, Mao's prestige was faced with another test. The Party leadership again came out in Mao's defence. In his written report to the conference, Liu Shaoqi declared that 'Mao always has the most profound understanding and far-reaching insight' on revolution and economic construction.[157] Mao is always the first to discover and to remind others of shortcomings and mistakes when they occur. Liu concluded that if Mao's guidance had been followed more diligently, many mistakes could have been avoided or more easily corrected.[158]

In 1961, Mao told Field Marshal Montgomery that Liu Shaoqi's status as his successor had been firmly established since the 7th Party Congress in 1945 and that he continued to think that Liu should take his place after his death.[159] But only a few years later, in 1966, Mao purged Liu and drove him to his death.

What were the factors leading to Mao's gradual alienation from his long-standing comrade in arms which culminated in his belief that Liu had established a 'bourgeois headquarters' within the Party which was undermining socialist transformation in China? At least part of the answer can be found in the radicalisation of Mao's political outlook which focused increasingly on problems related to class and class struggle. Although Liu and other leaders accepted his theories, they did not follow them as closely as Mao desired. His emperor mentality was more and more characterised by intolerance towards what he considered negligence in the implementation of his policies. This perception was compounded by his strong will power which commanded success, and his paranoic sense of grandeur, which made him sensitive and suspicious about real or imagined threats to his authority.

Formally, the members of the Standing Committee of the Politburo Mao Zedong, Liu Shaoqi, Zhou Enlai, Zhu De, Chen Yun, Lin Biao and Deng Xiaoping were equal in status. But, in fact, Mao, instead of conforming to the majority of the Standing Committee, had been elevated above its ranks. In spite of the factual inequality, the relations among the top leaders had been relatively harmonious over a long period of time, although on several occasions in the past, Mao had voiced his discontent with some of the leaders. In 1953, he criticised Liu Shaoqi for having issued documents without his approval.[160] In 1957, he accused Zhou Enlai and Chen Yun of 'opposing adventurism' in economic planning at a time when Mao wanted to accelerate the process of collectivisation. In 1961, he reproached Deng Xiaoping for having drafted a document for a conference without consulting him beforehand. These problems remained without major consequences. It was only in 1962 that Mao began to point to serious differences which had surfaced between him and other leaders on a number of issues.

The 7,000 Cadres conference had come to the conclusion, that the economic decline had reached its nadir and that, from then on, the situation could only improve. A month later, during an enlarged meeting of the Standing Committee which discussed the state budget, the earlier prognosis appeared to have been unrealistic. A closer look at the economic situation revealed a large budget deficit and a huge gap between the supply of commodities and the purchasing power in society. Liu Shaoqi, after analysing the economic problems of that period, concluded that the economy was in a state of crisis.[161]

To deal with these issues, a central finance and economic group headed by Chen Yun was established. It suggested a series of remedial measures which were discussed at a central working conference in May. On this occasion, Liu Shaoqi pointed out that serious economic difficulties continued to persist and that it was time to assess realistically those problems which, for many years, had been deliberately under-rated. Deng Xiaoping spoke of the necessity to rehabilitate those cadres who had been wrongly accused during the anti-rightist campaign in 1959. The vice prime minister in charge of agriculture and head of the Central Committee (CC) rural work department, Deng Zihui, argued for the need to promote the peasants' enthusiasm for work by providing private plots to Commune members. This was particularly important, he contended, in remote rural areas where *dan gan* should be encouraged.[162]

Encouraged by the discussions on rehabilitation, Peng Dehuai wrote a long letter of 80,000 characters to Mao in which he contested the accusation brought forward against him after the 1959 Lushan conference, that he had formed 'an anti-Party clique' and had 'maintained illicit relations with a foreign country'.[163]

Although he approved the measures proposed by the central working conference, Mao expressed his disagreement with Liu Shaoqi and other leaders on a number of fundamental issues three months later at another central working conference in August at Beidaihe. Firstly, he did not appreciate their pessimistic assessment of the economic situation which, in his view, was depicted 'as dark as night'. Accusing the leadership to 'blow the dark wind' (*heian feng*), he contended that their assessment led to the conclusion that socialism did not work.[164]

Secondly, he condemned the policy of allotting private plots to peasants at the expense of the People's Communes. This *dan gan feng* ('to blow the wind of going alone'), according to Mao, was a matter so serious that it posed the problem of whether to follow the capitalist or the socialist road. Thirdly, he referred to the problem of rehabilitation of many of the victims of the 1959 campaign. In his view, this amounted to saying that the 1959 anti-rightist campaign had been unjustified and should be written off at one stroke, an idea which he considered a 'wind to reverse the verdict' (*fanan feng*). As a consequence, he opposed the rehabilitation of Peng Dehuai.[165]

Mao's denunciation of the 'three winds' served him as a basis to elaborate on his theory of class and class struggle at the 10th Plenum of the 8th CC in 1962 in Beijing. At the same time, he accused the CC rural work department of promoting capitalism and its head, Deng Zihui, of lacking the mentality for socialist revolution. He also condemned Peng Dehuai for attempting 'to reverse the correct verdict concerning himself' and blamed Xi Zhongxun, Jia Taofu and others for trying to reverse the verdict on Gao Gang.[166]

At the Plenum, Mao again demonstrated his unchallengeable authority. The Plenum accepted his theory about class struggle as the guiding principle for the work of the Party. It deprived Deng Zihui of his post and dissolved the CC rural work department. Furthermore it established two special investigation groups to examine the cases of Peng Dehuai and Xi Zhongxun. The group in charge of the latter condemned him as the leader of an anti-Party clique.[167]

Mao's differences with other leaders, and especially with Liu Shaoqi, increased during the rural socialist education movement. The first CC document concerning this movement – 'The first ten points' – drafted under Mao's direction in May 1963 sought 'to organise revolutionary class ranks and to wage a large-scale mass movement to fend off the attack of capitalist and feudalist forces'.[168] It presented a programme of action which centred on problems of corruption and embezzlement among grassroot-level cadres and which should investigate their handling of accounts, storage and assets.

The central leadership dispatched work teams to the rural areas to examine production teams and brigades for their political, economic, organisational and ideological 'cleanliness' which earned the movement the title 'the four cleanings'.

The results of the initial investigations were far from encouraging. Liu Shaoqi, who had probed into selected rural areas himself and had sent his people and especially his wife Wang Guangmei to live in the countryside for a time reached the conclusion that the situation in the rural areas was extremely serious. Many cadres at all levels were corrupt and practised a 'double-faced counter revolutionary regime'.[169] Based on this assessment, Liu believed that this 'major form of opposition' against socialist construction, which proved that in many areas the landlord class was still present and influential, had to be removed. He summed up Wang's experiences in a document which was widely distributed among Party members. The 'Taoyan experiences' held that corruption in the country side was so serious that the method of 'investigation and study' advocated by Mao was insufficient to cope with the situation.[170] Liu recommended the method to 'squat on the spot' (*dun dian*) followed by his wife who had spent several months in the village to examine local cadres and instructed Central Committee members to follow the example of *dun dian* declaring it as an experience needed by all CC members.

Liu developed his concepts in September 1963 in a document referred to as the 'later ten points'. This and the former document both specified that rural cadres at the level of production brigade and production team leaders should be viewed as the main targets of the campaign. But the 'first ten points' held that most of the cadres at these levels were 'good', the second started from the premise that practically all bottom-level cadres had fallen under the influence of vicious class enemies and were basically corrupt.[171] Liu's document thus greatly broadened the scope of investigation.

At a Politburo meeting held from mid December 1964 to mid January 1965, Mao expressed different views about the targets and the methods of the campaign. Contrary to Liu who considered that corruption and other problems in the rural areas were rampant at all levels inside and outside the Party, Mao refuted this view as 'non-Marxist' and insisted that the major contradiction existed between 'the party persons in power taking the capitalist road' and the broad masses of the people. He reproached the 'later ten points' for targeting grassroot level cadres in general who in his view, could not be 'all bad'. His main concern were 'Party persons in power taking the capitalist road'. Mao wanted to narrow the scope of criticism to power holders. But Liu was concerned that Mao's definition of the targets of the campaign would involve too wide an array of higher cadres. He suggested that the term 'capitalist elements' should be used to define the targets. The discussion did not seem to bring them closer. Instead, a few unpleasant exchanges took place, and, at one point, Liu interrupted Mao when he spoke. In that instance, Mao put the draft of his 23 points on the table and demanded approval without any further discussion.¹⁷²

The 23 articles were accepted unanimously. But the atmosphere of the meeting became tense again after Deng Xiaoping suggested that – since matters of principle had already been solved with the adoption of Mao's proposals – Mao might prefer not to attend the next day's meeting which was to discuss practical details. After all, Mao had retired to the second front and expressed the desire to be relieved from daily routine work.

Mao appeared at the next day's meeting with copies of the Party constitution and the national constitution in hand. Taking the floor, he declared: 'I am a member of the Party, I am a citizen. But one of you wanted to stop me from coming to this meeting, another prevented me from speaking.'¹⁷³ Mao's angry outbreak stunned all of those present at the meeting. Liu was compelled to condemn his own attitude towards Mao. But he was convinced that the open clash with Liu signalled a growing challenge to his supreme leadership which he attributed to the division of the leadership into a front and a second line. A year later, at a working conference on 24 October 1966, Mao explained that the purpose of the division had been 'to establish their prestige before I die', so that China would not suffer from the kind of succession problems that had occurred in the Soviet Union. In Mao's view, Stalin had not been attentive to this issue and had failed to build up a prestigious successor thus enabling Khrushchev to usurp power. Now he felt that, contrary to his expectations, 'things had moved in the opposite direction', that 'independent kingdoms' had emerged, and that 'there are many things I have not been consulted about'. His voluntary relinquishment of responsibility for day to day work became the source of his feeling that front line leaders, and especially Liu Shaoqi, ignored him and had put him on the shelf like an 'old buddha'.¹⁷⁴

Liu Shaoqi's stature had indeed gained unprecedented heights. In the early 1960s, it was generally accepted that China was ruled by two chairmen. Since his appointment as the head of state, Liu's and Mao's pictures appeared side by side and in equal size on the newspapers' front page on National Day and other formal occasions. Liu's prestige and the respect in which he was held, became a source of increasing irritation to Mao. It was a manifestation of his growing emperor mentality that he contradicted his professed intention of building up other leaders' prestige.

Moreover, Mao had become increasingly disillusioned with the other leaders at the apex. Among the members of the Politburo standing committee, Zhou Enlai was indispensable as the administrator of the country. But though Zhou was Mao's faithful follower, his political outlook was clearly too moderate. Zhu De was a ceremonious figure. Chen Yun had too often demonstrated his 'rightist' tendencies in economic policy.[175] And Deng Xiaoping, who had for a long time been Mao's favourite, was blamed by Mao for not having 'sought my instructions or reported to me since 1959'.[176] This left only Lin Biao who had demonstrated enough revolutionary spirit to satisfy the Chairman.

Among the 18 full and 6 alternate members of the Politburo elected by the 8th Congress, there were only two full members, Lin Biao and Ke Qingshi, and two alternate members, Chen Boda and Kang Sheng, who had been able to follow the radicalisation of Mao's thinking to the full. In the Central Secretariat headed by Deng Xiaoping, there was again only Kang Sheng whom Mao thought capable of fully implementing his policies.[177] The powerful heads of the Central Committee departments, too, were not trusted by Mao. In due course, he considered many of them as men of Liu Shaoqi who had established a bourgeois headquarters under his direction within the Party.[178]

The grouping of the left

As Mao's alienation with the majority of the front-line leaders grew, he grouped around himself a coterie of followers who appeared to be sensitive to his own radical appraisal of the situation. With the exception of Lin Biao, their ascension to power was almost imperceptible. But when the CR began they suddenly emerged as authoritative leaders fully in command of the situation.

Lin Biao was the most important representative of that group. After his nomination as minister of defence, Lin became increasingly active politically. The increase in his political stature was due principally to his 'holding up high the red banner of Mao Zedong Thought', as Liu Shaoqi had done in the early 1940s. Lin took over from Liu by initiating and developing new stages in the movement to deify Mao.

In September 1960, when front-line leaders began to implement practical measures to remedy the debacle of the GLF, Lin Biao was preoccupied with political indoctrination of the army. In a conference of the MC he criticised Peng Dehuai's military policy as being pure militarism and summarised his own guidelines for the army's political work as the 'four firsts'.[179]

In November 1963, Mao issued a written comment complimenting Lin for his work in the army and pointing out that the 'four firsts' and the 'three-eight work styles' had yielded positive results, since thanks to them, 'the ideological-political work of the liberation army, as well as its military work have developed remarkably, have become more concrete and at the same time have been raised to a higher theoretical plane than in the past'.[180]

Mao's comment not only consolidated Lin's position as the leader of the army, but it also gave strong impetus to the campaign to 'learn from the PLA' and to practise the 'four firsts' and the 'three-eight work styles'. The army was extolled as being 'revolutionised' and 'proletarianised'.

Next in importance to Lin Biao was perhaps Kang Sheng. In the second half of the 1950s, he became a fervent supporter of Mao Zedong Thought. At a conference on propaganda in March 1957, he lectured extensively on the new developments of Mao Zedong Thought. 'Since 1956, he pointed out, 'Chairman Mao has set forth a series of new theories which neither Marx, Engels or Lenin had previously thought of. Stalin had touched on the subject but had not developed it thoroughly.'[181] With this statement, he referred to Mao's theories on contradictions in a socialist society. Echoing Lin Biao, he pointed out that 'Mao Zedong Thought is the highest peak of Marxism-Leninism.'[182]

In the course of reorganising the Party centre shortly after the 8th Party Congress, a number of study or advisory groups under the Central Committee were established. In March 1957, two of them, the Central Cultural and Educational Group and the Central Theoretical Group were placed under Kang's direction. This appointment signalled Mao's approval of Kang's activities. In 1959, Mao further increased his responsibilities by appointing him as deputy director of the editorial board of *Mao Zedong's Selected Works*, of which Liu Shaoqi was the director, and to the direction of the Central Party School, two prestigious posts which gave him a power base and allowed him to rally a group of leftist theoreticians around him. Since theoretical work was one of Mao's major preoccupations, Kang's involvement with it greatly facilitated his access to him.[183]

In 1958, at a CC meeting which was convened to prepare the GLF, Mao criticised Zhou Enlai and Chen Yun for their 'anti-adventurous' approach to economic policy in 1956.[184] Kang seized the opportunity to make a sharp speech condemning the 'right deviation' of that time. At the Lushan conference, he wrote to Mao concerning Peng Dehuai's letter expressing his indignation about Peng's 'anti-Party and anti-socialist behaviour'.[185]

From 1962 onwards Kang Sheng became increasingly involved in the implementation of Mao's policies against revisionism in the academic and literary fields. When Mao was preoccupied with the 'evil wind of reversing verdicts', Kang Sheng reported to him that a novel attempting to 'reverse the verdict' on Gao Gang, who had been purged in 1955, had been published. The novel was about Liu Zhidan who, together with Xie Zichang and Gao Gang, had been a leader of the Shaanxi-Gansu guerilla group in the early 1930s.[186] This book which described Liu Zhidan's merits as a guerilla leader, according to Kang Zheng, was also an implicit praise of Gao Gang whose name had been eliminated from official party history. It also attempted to rival Mao's own deeds as a leader in the Jiangxi base area. Kang coined the cynical expression that 'to use novels to attack the Party is a great invention'. These words Mao repeated in a speech about the subject of literature in September 1962.[187]

As a result, the author and others who had worked with Liu Zhidan in the 1930s and had provided the author with material about Liu Zhidan were purged. They were Xi Zhongxun, a vice premier, Jia Paofu, deputy director of the Economic commission of the State Council and Ma Wenrui, minister of labour.[188] Kang Sheng, who was in charge of the purge, was again promoted. From 1962 on, he headed the CC international liaison department in charge of relations with foreign communist parties, and the CC investigation department which was, in some ways, the equivalent of the Soviet KGB.

In the following years, Kang Sheng continued to denounce moderate thinkers. In 1964, he initiated the criticism of Yang Xianzhen, president of the Central Party School, for his philosophical views. It was also Kang Sheng who convinced Mao that Wu Han's play *Hai Rui Dismissed from Office* established a parallel between Hai Rui and Peng Dehuai and was an attempt to 'reverse the verdict' on Peng Dehuai. He cited Wu Han's play as another attempt to use literature as a 'disguise for anti-Party activities'.[189] When Mao, in July 1964, set up the Five Men Cultural Revolution Group composed of Peng Zhen, Lu Dingyi, Zhou Yang, Wu Lengxi and Kang Sheng, the latter was the only leftist among the veteran leaders who participated in the group, and perhaps the only one whom Mao fully trusted. Kang Sheng's career flourished during the CR when he became a formidable organiser of persecution and purges within the Party system. He reached the peak of his career in 1973 when he was appointed vice chairman of the Party. He died in 1975.[190]

Closely associated with Kang Sheng was Jiang Qing, Mao's wife. She occupied a unique position in Mao's entourage and played a special role during the entire period of the CR, for which she was later condemned to death. In 1981 her sentence was suspended.[191] As a political figure, Jiang Qing remained relatively obscure until the 1960s when she gradually became Mao's most convenient ally in the implementation of his cultural policies. But already in the early 1950s, Jiang Qing, on a number of occasions, began to play a more active role in the cultural field. She was instrumental, for example, in protesting against the film *Wu Xun* in 1951, and in the debates about the Chinese classical novel *A Dream of Red Mansions* in 1954. In the course of these campaigns, Jiang Qing who was arrogant, pedantic and sometimes hysterical, had a number of confrontations with leading members of the Party establishment responsible for ideological and literary affairs which left her bitter at being deliberately slighted.[192]

In the early 1960s, as Mao began to pay increasing attention to culture, Jiang Qing became more and more involved in politics. In her capacity as Mao's secretary in charge of literature and art, she monitored the events in these areas. She found, that:

> what appeared on stage and screen was lavish, foreign and ancient. There were films from Hong Kong, from US imperialism, from Soviet revisionism, and from capitalist nations . . . On the whole, they only propagated capitalism and feudalism instead of serving the workers, peasants, and soldiers.[193]

In May 1963, Jiang Qing sponsored an article written by *Wenhui Bao* criticising the staging of 'ghost operas' which ushered in the campaign of criticising art and literature.[194]

When Mao charged Jiang Qing with the task of reforming classical Beijing opera, the reform produced eight 'revolutionary model operas' which were widely performed during the CR excluding all traditional classical operas from the scenes.

Jiang Qing collaborated closely with Kang Sheng in the campaign and together they often succeeded in forming Mao's opinion about the revisionist nature of literature and art. Their cooperation became particularly intense during the organisation of the campaign against Wu Han's play *Hai Rui Dismissed from Office* which ushered in the Cultural Revolution.

Another important figure in Mao's entourage was Chen Boda who, after the establishment of the People's Republic, became vice president of the prestigious Academy of Marxism-Leninism in Beijing where he continued to propagate Mao Zedong Thought and to develop theoretical justification for official policies. Since the mid 1950s, he acted as Mao's first political secretary with the rank of a vice minister.[195] As Kang Sheng was appointed to head the CC groups on literature and art established after the 8th Congress, Chen Boda headed the newly established CC political research group. In 1958, he became chief editor of *Red Flag* and deputy minister of the CC propaganda department. During the Great Leap Forward he was closely associated with Mao's agricultural policies whose theoretical foundation he propagated.[196] Later, he was in charge of or took part in the drafting of most of the important Party documents on internal affairs as well as of the polemics against the Soviet Union.[197] Chen Boda had the habit of observing Mao closely, noting every book Mao read and every change in his theoretical thinking. Nicknamed the 'old scholar' (Lao Fuzi), he was widely accepted as the foremost interpreter of Mao Zedong Thought and was to play an important role during the early stages of the CR.

Zhang Chunqiao, who was a local Party official in Shanghai, attracted Mao's attention with an article which recalled the 'pattern of military-communist life' characterised by a 'free supply system' in the communist ruled areas before the founding of the PR.[198] This noble tradition, Zhang argued, was soon to be replaced by a 'grade level system' with its resulting inequalities which he believed, was a manifestation of 'bourgeois rights' referred to by Marx in his writings. Zhang concluded that though inequalities could not be eliminated overnight, they should be restricted and gradually phased out.[199]

To restrain and eventually eliminate bourgeois rights was one of Mao's most cherished ideas. Mao ordered Zhang's article to be reprinted in *People's Daily*. In addition, he gave the article an unusual endorsement by writing a complimentary introductory note to it which declared that Zhang's article was 'basically correct', was 'written in popular style' and 'therefore easy to understand'.[200] This note made Zhang Chunqiao's name known to the entire Party. Mao mentioned him again two months later when he received a report from Henan province stating that thanks to the GLF, one of its counties would 'enter into communism' in two years' time. Mao laughed at this ambition and wrote a comment on the report saying: 'As beautiful as a poem! Perhaps our scholars Boda and Chunqiao should go there and have a look?' It was an unusual honour to be favourably mentioned by the 'great leader' twice within two months.[201]

When Jiang Qing came to Shanghai to start her theatre reform, Zhang Chunqiao provided her with all the necessary facilities. Consecutively, they transformed the Shanghai local operas *The Red Lantern, Shajiabang*,[202] and *On the Docks* into revolutionary Beijing operas. But it was during the preparations to criticise Wu Han and his play, that Zhang's fate became inseparable from Jiang Qing and the CR.

Yao Wenyuan was the most junior both by age and by rank in Mao's leftist group. He attracted Mao's attention through one of his articles criticising the Shanghai Wenhui Bao for its 'liberal orientation'.[203] To launch his attack against liberal intellectuals, Mao welcomed voices from leftist intellectuals. He ordered the *People's Daily* to reprint it on the front page with an approbatory editorial note entitled 'The Bourgeois Orientation of *Wenhui Bao* over a Period of Time'.[204] Over night, Yao became a national hero of the anti-rightist campaign and soon afterwards, was recruited by Zhang Chunqiao as a literary critic at Shanghai's *Liberation Daily*. Keeping himself closely informed about Mao's intentions concerning literature and art, he wrote a number of articles reflecting Mao's trends of thought which won him the reputation as the 'stick' (*gunzi*) in literature and art. With his famous article condemning Wu Han's play *Hai Rui Dismissed from Office* he became instrumental in ushering in the preliminary purges of the Cultural Revolution.

There were still a few other persons who had joined Mao's leftist group. Among them were Wang Li, Guan Feng and Qi Benyu. Wang Li was a journalist for the PLA newspaper and, since 1958, deputy chief editor of *Red Flag*. Like Chen Boda, he was considered as one of the most competent writers of Party documents. He drafted the 'first ten points' and the '23 articles' for the rural education campaign. He participated in the drafting of most of the articles in the Sino-Soviet ideological polemics. In 1963, he was appointed as deputy head of the CC International Liaison Department. In 1966, he became a member of the CCRG.[205]

Guan Feng was a journalist at *Red Flag* who became well known for his critical articles against revisionist trends in society during the preparatory stage of the CR. Qi Benyu, a staff member of the CC general office, in December 1965, published an article entitled 'Study History for Revolution', which paralleled Yao Wenyuan's attack on Wu Han.[206]

Unlike the already established moderate leaders, all these persons had one idea in common: to follow closely the evolution of Mao's radical views about Chinese society and to faithfully adopt his leftist ideas. When they suddenly emerged at the beginning of the CR, they represented the increasingly radical tendencies which Mao tried to promote within society. Their position of power was attained by most of them, without following the established channels that lead to the height of a political career. In effect, with Mao's support they leaped to power. Kang Sheng and Chen Boda were the only ones of this leftist group who had long years of established political standing.

2
BACKDROP

The purge of the group of five

The 1981 resolution on Party history divided the CR into three stages. The first began in May 1966 with the adoption of the 'May 16th Circular' by the Politburo and ends with the 9th Party Congress in April 1969. This was the most turbulent period which focused on the purge of Liu Shaoqi and a large number of senior revolutionary leaders. The second stage, from the 9th to the 10th Congress in August 1973, was dominated by the Lin Biao affair. The final phase from 1973 to the downfall of the 'gang of four' in October 1976 was characterised by a complex struggle for Mao's succession.[1]

This division ignores the period between the criticism of Wu Han in November 1965 and the purge of Peng–Luo–Lu–Yang in May 1966 – a period which was crucial to the launching of the CR. In addition, there were other issues during this period which were linked to the commencement of the CR – the problem of the 'February Outline Report',[2] the formation of the alliance between Lin Biao and Jiang Qing in the field of literature and art against the establishment,[3] the denunciation of the *Three-family Village*[4] and the adoption of the May 16th circular by the Politburo in May 1966.[5]

These events, initiated by Mao, were the beginning of a major offensive against the Party establishment in Beijing which Peng Zhen tried to resist but to which he was forced to yield step by step.

The choice of Wu Han's play *Hai Rui Dismissed from Office* and soon afterwards of Deng Tuo's *The Evening Talks at Yanshan* as a target of attack symbolised the changing political climate of the mid 1960s. The historical figure of Hai Rui was first discovered and used by Mao as an example of uprightness to be emulated by the entire Party in the face of power. In 1959, when Mao was preoccupied by the endless false reports which grossly exaggerated the rates of production of People's Communes during the GLF, he saw a performance of a classical opera *Tablets of Life and Death* in which Hai Rui, a minister during the Ming Dynasty, risked his life by telling the truth about the miserable conditions of peasants' life to his emperor. Impressed by the play, Mao asked for a book on the history of the Ming Dynasty which he read overnight. Mao, convinced that the Party was badly in need of some of Hai Rui's spirit, told his story to the 7th Plenum of the CC held in Shanghai in April 1959 and encouraged the participants to 'learn from Hai Rui's uprightness and tenacity'.[6]

In his letter of April 1959 to local cadres at six levels (province, prefectorate, county, people's commune, production brigade, production team) Mao emphasised the grave problem of exaggeration and falsification of production statistics and appealed to the cadres to report the real facts. 'Honest men who dare to tell the truth' he wrote, 'serve the interests of the people, and will not suffer themselves in the end. Those who like to tell lies, can only do harm to the people and to themselves, and they will suffer in the end.'[7]

After the Shanghai meeting, Hu Qiaomu, who was then one of Mao's five political secretaries, approached Wu Han, a noted expert on Ming Dynasty history, to write about Hai Rui.[8] On 16 June 1959, and on 21 September, he published two articles on the subject entitled 'Hai Rui Scolds the Emperor' and 'On Hai Rui'. Since Peng Dehuai was purged at the Lushan conference a month earlier, Hu Qiaomu, who was to clear Wu Han's article, added a paragraph about 'right opportunists' which made a distinction between Hai Rui who was dismissed by his emperor and Peng Dehuai who was dismissed by Mao, clearly stating that right opportunists were 'not at all Hai Rui'.[9]

A year later, Wu Han produced his play *Hai Rui Dismissed from Office*, which was published in January 1961 in *Beijing Literature and Art*.[10] When the play came to Jiang Qing's attention, she was immediately convinced that it was an attempt to use historical parallels to satirise the present. In 1962, she communicated her views to Mao. But Mao, remembering his own remarks about Hai Rui, was not impressed and told her to 'read more books if you have time!'[11] Jiang Qing discussed her views with Kang Sheng who advised her to be patient and to wait for another opportunity.[12]

Following Mao's repeated critical comments on literature and art, a movement to repudiate bourgeois ideas in almost all intellectual areas developed in 1964. At that time, Kang Sheng thought that this wave of criticism provided the right opportunity to bring the subject of Wu Han's play again to Mao's attention, insinuating that *Hai Rui Dismissed from Office* was linked to Peng Dehuai and the 1959 Lushan conference, and that the description of the injustice against Hai Rui had been submitted to really defend Peng Dehuai's cause.[13] The time appeared to have been well chosen. Since Mao, preoccupied as he was with class struggle in the literary field, had approved the criticism of the novel *Liu Zhidan* as a reversal of the verdict on Gao Gang, Wu Han's play could also be considered a reversal of the verdict on Peng Dehuai.[14]

Mao, who had invited Peng Dehuai to a talk on 23 September, 1965, had told him in reference to the Lushan conference, that 'perhaps the truth is on your side', but had nonetheless maintained his condemnation of Peng Dehuai.[15] By the end of the year, after leaving for the south, Mao was convinced that Wu Han's case was a political issue which he could use to attack the Beijing Party establishment. 'The crux of *Hai Rui Dismissed from Office* is "dismissed from office",' Mao pointed out to Kang Sheng and Chen Boda on 21 December in Hangzhou. 'The emperor dismissed Hai Rui. . . . In 1959, we dismissed Peng Dehuai from office. And Peng Dehuai is Hai Rui, too.'[16]

Jiang Qing, who had assumed the task of organising the new campaign, asked Li Xifan, a literary critic at *People's Daily*, to write an article against Wu Han. Li Xifan had made a name for himself by criticising Yu Pingbo, a well-known expert on the classical novel *A Dream of Red Mansion* in the early 1950s.[17] But for unknown motives, he declined. Perhaps he did not want to challenge Wu Han whom he knew to be close to Peng Zhen and Deng Xiaoping or, perhaps he did not share Jiang Qing's views about the play.[18] Jiang Qing who approached several other writers in Beijing unsuccessfully, finally decided to take her cause to Shanghai where she could count on the assistance of its mayor Ke Qingshi.[19]

Ke Qingshi put Zhang Chunqiao and Yao Wenyuan at her disposal. Working for several months, they produced about ten drafts before Jiang Qing was satisfied with the final version. During the entire period, Mao remained behind the scenes and never mentioned Wu Han. But at a session of the Standing Committee during a CC working conference in September and October, 1965, where Mao emphasised the need to attack bourgeois reactionary ideas, he asked Peng Zhen whether Wu Han could be rebuked.[20] Peng Zhen reportedly replied, that some of Wu Han's ideas may be criticised.[21] For the first time, he became aware of the fact that Wu Han might be in danger. But the publication of Yao Wenyuan's article 'On the New Historical Play *Hai Rui Dismissed from Office*' in Shanghai about a month later [22] both angered and bemused Peng Zhen and the Beijing Party Committee. Although the attack on Wu Han was not unexpected, its vehemence was. According to established practice, an attack on such a well-known figure as the vice mayor of Beijing, a noted intellectual and a popular writer should not have been published without prior consultation with the Party centre or the Central Propaganda department. The fact that the Shanghai Party committee had failed to proceed according to this rule, provoked angry reactions in Beijing, where the viciousness of the attack was considered entirely without foundation.[23]

However, the very fact that such an article could have been published by a relatively unknown and junior writer implied that its author had received high-level political backing. It was soon discovered in Beijing, that Jiang Qing had played a role in promoting the publication. It seemed unlikely that Jiang Qing, at that time, would have been able to provoke such an attack without Mao's approval. But Mao originally had not only instigated the play, he had also, not long ago, called upon the entire Party to take Hai Rui's uprightness and courageous spirit as an example. If Mao had changed his mind then what were his reasons? This question could not be answered, since nobody at the Party centre had been informed about Mao's intentions. Even attempts by Liu Shaoqi to reach the chairman and to enquire about the matter failed.[24]

Without mentioning Mao's earlier praise of Hai Rui and its call to the nation to learn from him, Yao's article divested him from all virtues and merits described in Wu Han's play. He linked the publication of the play in 1961 with class struggle emphasising that in that year, China was suffering from 'temporary economic difficulties', a situation of which class enemies inside and outside the country took advantage by launching a wild attack on the Chinese socialist system. 'Return of land' and 'redressing grievances' were the 'focal point of bourgeois opposition to the dictatorship of the proletariat and the socialist revolutionary struggle at that time.' Since in Wu Han's play, Hai Rui requested landlords to return land to the peasants from whom it had previously been seized, and since Hai Rui, in the presence of the emperor, asked for the redress of peasants' grievances, Yao concluded that the play represented the interests of the overthrown class and sympathised with their resistance to the dictatorship of the proletariat. *Hai Rui Dismissed from Office* is a form of reflection of such class struggle, Yao Wenyuan concluded.[25]

Although Peng Zhen was aware that Mao supported the criticism of Wu Han, he nonetheless attempted to protect him and, at the same time, his own stronghold in Beijing. It was unthinkable to launch a direct counter-attack against Yao Wenyuan since this would imply a challenge to Mao. But it was possible to attempt to soften the impact of Yao's attack. Using his position at the CC Secretariat and the Beijing municipal Party committee, Peng gave instructions not to reprint Yao's article in Beijing.[26] It is not known whether other leaders like Liu Shaoqi and Deng Xiaoping gave their approval to Peng's decision. But there also is no evidence to suggest that they tried to pressure Peng to act differently.

The Beijing authorities' failure to publish Yao's article in the capital contributed another element to Mao's conviction that Beijing was so tightly controlled by the mayor and the municipal Party committee that 'not even a needle could slip through or a drop of water trickle down'.[27] With mounting anger against the Beijing authorities, Mao decided to personally intervene and ordered a Shanghai printing house to reprint Yao's article in pamphlet form and to distribute it within the country through Xinhua book stores. Peng Zhen who was unaware that Mao had issued this instruction himself, ordered the Beijing Xinhua book store not to subscribe to the pamphlets.[28]

Seventeen days after the distribution of Yao's article in pamphlet form, Mao increased the pressure and instructed Zhou Enlai to have the article published in all major newspapers. Zhou Enlai called Peng Zhen, a number of officials from the propaganda department, and the heads of the major Beijing newspapers to a meeting on 28 November to discuss the reprint of Yao's article. Although publication of Yao's article could no longer be avoided, angry and sarcastic views were expressed about it during the meeting. Deng Tuo, for instance, called it 'a typical example of abuse and blackmail'.[29] Peng Zhen emphasised that the debate about Hai Rui should remain non-political and academic in nature and that the article should be preceded by an editorial note which would provide guidelines for future discussions.[30]

On 29 and 30 November, the *Beijing Daily*, the *Liberation Army Daily* and the *People's Daily* all reprinted Yao Wenyuan's article with an introductory note. The *People's Daily*'s note, carefully revised by Zhou Enlai, stated that the:

> correct approach to *Hai Rui Dismissed from Office* was to consider how to look at historical figures and plays and how to study history.... We hope to promote debates and mutual criticism of different views through discussions. Our policy is to allow the freedom of criticism and counter-criticism; even to erroneous views we should reply with reasoning, by seeking truth from facts and by convincing people by sound argument.[31]

This was a very moderate introduction, the aim of which was to encourage academic discussions rather than to transform the controversy about Wu Han's play into a political and ideological issue. The *Beijing Daily* followed the same line, emphasising that criticism should 'promote the views of historical materialism through discussion'. The editorial note of the *Liberation Army Daily*, however, expressed a different opinion. Under Lin Biao's direction, it stated categorically that Wu Han's play 'is an anti-party, anti-socialist and anti-Mao Zedong Thought poisonous weed which should be criticised.[32]

The question whether Wu Han's play should be commented within the framework of an academic discussion or condemned as an ideological misfit, became an important issue over the next few months. As the criticism against Wu Han's play at the political level unfolded, Peng Zhen's concern to protect Wu Han and, by the same token, his own fief, also increased. Under Peng's directives, Party officials in the central propaganda department and the Beijing Party committee attempted to come to Wu Han's rescue by publishing long articles under pseudonyms where they criticised *Hai Rui* but kept the issue within the confines of an academic discussion. Many scholars who resented Yao Wenyuan's arbitrary accusations against Wu Han followed suit and went as far as to vigorously refute him.

As the criticism against Wu Han escalated, Peng then advised Wu Han to admit his mistake.[33] This attempt to rescue Wu Han from political condemnation and to confine his case to a cultural and ideological level epitomises the nature of Chinese politics where defence did not consist in providing rational explanations and self-justification but in self-accusations and in pleading guilty of political mistakes.

Wu Han produced a lengthy public self-criticism[34] where he declared that his acknowledgement of Hai Rui's virtues was due to his incapacity of clearly distinguishing between proletarian and feudal ideals. His greatest mistake was to have emphasised that, albeit with certain qualifications, feudal morality could still be valid. Referring to the political conclusion Yao Wenyuan had drawn about his play, Wu Han said that under the circumstances prevailing in 1961, its publication had produced 'serious and bad effects'.[35] Wu Han omitted the fact that Mao had encouraged him to write the play.

In the wake of Wu Han's self-criticism the *People's Daily* and *Beijing Daily* published a number of accusatory articles on the same subject, most of them written by high-ranking Party officials under pseudonyms. But the authors continued to take great care to attack Wu Han from a theoretical angle and to avoid drawing political conclusions about him. Wu Han's colleague and close friend, Deng Tuo, writing under the pen name of Xiang Yangsheng, refuted Wu Han's 'theory of inheriting old ethical values'; Li Qi, the head of the Beijing Party committee's propaganda department, writing under the pen name of Li Dongshi, refuted Wu Han's historical analysis; and a group of writers from the central propaganda department, under the pseudonym of Fang Qiu, discussed the ideological trend represented by Wu Han's play. At the same time, the central propaganda department refused to publish articles by Qi Benyu and Guan Feng which attacked the 'reactionary essence' of Wu Han's play.[36]

The February outline report vs. summary of the forum on literature and art

Wu Han and his play about Hai Rui were not the only targets of leftist criticism at that time. A number of well-known historians, philosophers, economists, novelists, dramatists and theoreticians also came under open scrutiny. In order to provide a political orientation to these debates, Peng Zhen, as the head of the Group of Five, decided to formulate a number of principles which could serve as their guidelines.

Under his direction, an 'Outline Report on the Current Academic Discussion' was drafted. Its basic features had been discussed at a meeting on 3 February 1966, of the Group of Five and another seven officials from the central propaganda department and the Beijing Party committee, including Kang Sheng and Wang Li.[37] The meeting entrusted Xu Liqun and Yao Zhen, both deputy ministers of the central propaganda department, to produce a draft of the report. On 5 February, Peng Zhen presented the report to the Standing Committee which accepted it and sent it to Mao for his comments. Three days later, the group of five, headed by Peng met with Mao in Wuhan to discuss the report and hear his views. Mao made a few remarks about it saying that in the movement of criticising historical studies, scholars like Guo Moruo and Fan Wenlan should be protected. But he seemed to be more concerned with the Wu Han problem, and he repeated that 'the key question concerns the dismissal from office'.[38] He casually asked Peng Zhen whether he thought that Wu Han was opposing the party and socialism. Peng Zhen, who neither wanted to affront the chairman nor accuse his friend of a political crime, replied that Wu Han 'sided with the man dismissed from office by the People's Republic'.[39]

Since Mao did not raise any objections to the draft of the Outline Report, Peng Zhen, after his return to Beijing, reported to Liu Shaoqi and Deng Xiaoping that Mao had approved the text. On 13 February, the Outline Report was issued as a CC directive to Party committees at all levels to serve as a guideline for the current academic discussions. Since Mao did not discuss his views with the front-line leaders, neither before or after the publication of Yao Wenyuan's article, they had no knowledge about Mao's underlying purpose in the campaign, launched by radical writers, against Wu Han. The outline report represented their common understanding that the present situation called for academic discussions and not for politicisation.

The outline report thus de-emphasised the political nature of the debate and demanded that 'all people express their opinion freely', since 'everyone is equal before the truth'. In an implicit reference to Yao Wenyuan, the report condemned the behaviour of 'scholar tyrants who are always acting arbitrarily and trying to overwhelm people with their power'. In its attempt to dilute the political content of the campaign, the report called upon the press not to confine the discussions 'to political questions but to go fully into the various academic and theoretical questions involved'.[40] While it was necessary to co-operate with 'left academic workers' who were the main force in uncovering bourgeois ideologies, the outline report warned against their 'arrogance' and the danger that they may turn into 'bourgeois experts and scholar – tyrants'.[41]

Since Yao Wenyuan's article against Wu Han was generally unpopular, the February Outline Report was well received and the discussions in newspapers and journals were well under control with a tone that was more academic than political. As a result, the use at random of such epithets as 'anti-party elements' and 'anti-socialist elements' was largely avoided.

But Peng Zhen was fighting a losing battle. Mao, still away from Beijing, was forging his own plans for a cultural revolution that had hardly anything in common with the policies pursued by the front-line leaders in the capital. While Peng Zhen was preparing the Outline Report, Mao forged an alliance between the leftist revolutionaries of his entourage and Lin Biao, chief of the army, to launch an offensive against the establishment in the fields of literature and arts. Under his instructions, a forum on literature and art within the armed forces, directed by Jiang Qing, took place in Shanghai between the 2 and 20 February 1966. Four military officers, headed by Liu Zhijian, deputy director of the PLA's general political department, were instructed to formulate a summary of the discussions. In Jiang Qing's view, the document they produced was entirely inadequate. Mao then entrusted Chen Boda, Zhang Chunqiao and Yao Wenyuan, none of whom had participated in the forum, with the drafting of a new document.[42] Mao himself examined and revised their draft three times, before it was sent to the central military commission to be officially issued on 10 April.[43]

The document represented a significant change in Mao's thinking on literature and art. In his comments in 1963 and 1964 on the subject, he had said that 'very little had been achieved so far in socialist transformation' in these areas which had 'slid down to the brink of revisionism'.[44] The document declared that 'the last sixteen years have witnessed sharp class struggles on the cultural front' and that 'we have been under the dictatorship of a black anti-party, anti-socialist line which is diametrically opposed to Chairman Mao's thought'.[45] Clearly, under the circumstances, an academic discussion as Peng Zhen had hoped was not possible. But since the Party establishment was unwilling to co-operate in a real Cultural Revolution, it was necessary to seek the help of the PLA. In Jiang Qing's words, 'In January and February, 1966, I found myself incapable of coping with the situation. I had to ask the "holy gods" of the PLA.'[46]

The escalation of the campaign

Peng Zhen, reassured by Mao's apparent endorsement of the Outline Report began to question the attitude of the Shanghai Party committee in the Wu Han affair. On 11 March, he ordered Xu Liqun, deputy minister of the central propaganda department to call Yang Yongzhi, head of the Shanghai Party committee propaganda department to enquire why they had failed to report the publication of Yao Wenyuan's article to the central propaganda department in Beijing. Where had the 'Party spirit' of the Shanghai committee gone, he asked.[47]

This inquiry came to Kang Sheng's ears who reported it to Mao. Mao was indignant and made a number of angry remarks about the cultural and political establishment in Beijing. Since the central propaganda department, he said, did not ask to be informed when Wu Han wrote his reactionary articles, why should they be informed about Yao Wenyuan's writings? Those who suppressed articles written by leftists and shielded anticommunist intellectuals were scholar–tyrants. 'The Central Propaganda Department,' Mao said, 'was a palace of the King of Hell. We must overthrow the palace of the King of Hell and set the little devils free.'[48] Referring specifically to Wu Han and the historian Jian Bozan, Mao designated them as scholar–tyrants who were protected by a 'big party-tyrant' from above.[49] The Beijing Party committee, in his view, should be dismantled if it continued to shield such people as Wu Han and Deng Tuo.

On the same occasion, Mao also attacked the Outline Report as a 'reversal of the relations between the enemy and ourselves, putting one into the position of the other.'[50] These were the most fierce condemnations, Mao had as yet pronounced against the Party apparatus. It was clearly a declaration of war against the Beijing Party establishment.

From 9 to 12 April, the Central Secretariat held a meeting during which Kang Sheng briefed the participants about Mao's latest views on cultural activities.[51] In the wake of the briefing, the secretariat was compelled to change the course of its previous policies and, on 16 April, the *Beijing Daily* and *Frontline* published large excerpts from *Evening Talks at Yanshan* and *Notes from the Three-family Village* with an editorial note declaring that it had been a mistake to publish these essays. The note emphasised that the editorial board, by allowing the publication of these papers, 'did not put proletarian politics in command and that our minds were influenced by bourgeois and feudal ideas. Hence, in this serious struggle, we lost our vigilance.'[52] It also claimed that the essays had 'distorted Party directives', misinterpreted the policy of the Hundred Flowers movement, advocated complete freedom of thought, idealised all aspects of the feudal system and used 'ancient things' to satirise the present and to launch attacks by innuendo.[53] The readers were invited to join in the criticism.

Further assaults on the *Three-family Village* were soon published by leftist writers. The *Liberation Daily* brought out an article inspired by Jiang Qing and written under the pseudonym Gao Ju. Entitled 'Open fire on the anti-party, anti-socialist black line', the article declared that Deng Tuo, Wu Han and

Liao Mosha had not only spread feudalist and bourgeois ideas, but had also 'attacked the Party and socialism'. It condemned them as 'anti-Party, anti-socialist elements'. As for *Beijing Daily* and *Frontline*, they were protecting the writers and, 'under the signboard of struggle they were actually harbouring them'.[54]

Guan Feng launched an attack along the same lines in *Guangming Daily*. But the most devastating blow was dealt again by Yao Wenyuan who produced a lengthy and detailed analysis of Deng Tuo's, Wu Han's and Liao Mosha's writings condemning them as the 'most vicious attacks on the Party, socialism and Mao Zedong Thought' and concluding that they spread 'poisonous fog and blinding dust'. The *Beijing Daily*, the *Beijing Evening News* and *Frontline* were accused of conniving with the writers at treason against Mao Zedong's socialist values.[55] Other articles along the same lines appeared in *People's Daily* and *Red Flag*.[56] They were reprinted in all of China's important newspapers and provoked the publication of a host of similar articles. A nationwide campaign to denounce the *Three-family Village* soon engulfed the entire country. Even children in kindergarten learned to sing a rhyme to denounce the three writers as enemies of socialism:

> Wu Han Deng Tou Liao Mosha
> yi gan teng shang san hei gua
> da da da
> women jianjue da dao ta
>
> Wu Han Deng Tuo Liao Mosha
> one stem three black melons
>
> beat, beat, beat
> we will resolutely overthrow them[57]

The wave of criticism focusing on writings published in the early 1960s went well beyond the framework of an academic discussion which Peng Zhen had attempted to maintain. It was another class struggle against intellectuals followed by political liquidation, imprisonment and death. Deng Tuo became the first fatal victim of the CR. He committed suicide on 18 May, one month after he was publicly denounced. In his last letter to his wife, he wrote that it had never been his intention to criticise Chairman Mao through his writings and wished him a long life. Wu Han was imprisoned and died in captivity. Liao Mosha, who was also imprisoned, was the only one among the three to survive. He was rehabilitated after the CR.[58]

The campaign against the *Three-family Village* had nationwide repercussions on all writers who, in the early 1960s, had published similar critical articles. They were condemned as anti-Party and anti-socialist elements. Even university students, who had published similar essays in school publications, became victims of the campaign which labelled them as 'small Deng Tuo, Wu Han and Liao Mosha'.

The Peng–Luo–Lu–Yang anti-party clique

While every unit in China was mobilised to denounce 'counter-revolutionary publications', a ruthless power struggle, as yet unknown to the public, was waged at leadership level involving what was later known as the 'Peng–Luo–Lu–Yang anti-Party clique'.[59]

Peng Zhen became the most prominent victim of these purges. His position had become increasingly insecure and his attempts to protect Wu Han began to backfire. The February Outline Report and the revelation of the so-called 'Chang Guan Lou Event' were used as the basis for the accusations against him. This event refers to a meeting held in a building named Chang Guan Lou in Beijing's summer palace. In 1961, Peng had instructed Deng Tuo to review all Central Committee documents pertaining to the GLF. Peng's purpose was to analyse and to draw proper conclusions from this movement. At the meeting at Chang Guan Luo, Deng Tuo submitted a report revealing a series of erroneous decisions which had contributed to the disastrous results of the campaign.[60] Peng's initiative was now construed as a treachery to Mao personally and to the Party.

At the April meeting of the CC Secretariat, Kang Sheng and Chen Boda who had just returned with Mao's latest instructions from his retreat in Hangzhou, extensively criticised Peng Zhen. While Kang Sheng concentrated on Peng's recent mistakes since the publication of Yao' article on Wu Han's play, Chen Boda reviewed Peng's entire revolutionary career and accused him of a series of 'crimes' he had committed in the past. After the meeting, Peng Zhen disappeared from public view.[61]

In mid-April, Mao intervened personally in the condemnation of Peng Zhen. Presiding over an enlarged meeting of the Politburo's Standing Committee, he severely denounced Peng's anti-party crimes exemplified by the Outline Report which, according to Mao, Peng had fabricated behind the back of the other members of the group of five.[62]

Mao, bypassing the official line of command, asked Kang and Chen to transmit orders to the Secretariat to draft a document revoking the February Outline Report. He also instructed the Politburo to hold an enlarged meeting, including Mao's coterie who were not members of that body, to adopt the new circular and to 'solve the problem of Peng, Luo, Lu, Yang'.[63]

Mao did not attend the enlarged Politburo meeting, held from 4 to 26 May. Liu Shaoqi, who presided over the meeting, was completely taken by surprise by these developments. Having been travelling on a state visit to Pakistan, Afghanistan and Burma from 25 March to 20 April, he found, on his return, that Peng Zhen, one of his closest collaborators, was in the process of being purged. The meeting he was to chair was intended to ratify the decision. Since neither Liu nor any other of the Politburo members had the courage to oppose the chairman, Peng Zhen's fate was sealed. He was not only condemned for his 'mistakes' but also accused of having formed an anti-Party clique with Luo Ruiqing, Lu Dingyi and Yang Shangkun. All four were hitherto referred to as the 'Peng – Luo – Lu – Yang anti-Party clique'.

The May Politburo meeting took an unusual course. It was dominated by speakers who were not members of the Politburo but belonged to Mao's leftist coterie. It had five items on its agenda.[64] The first was a general discussion which in fact amounted to an eight-hour speech delivered by Kang Sheng, who was only an alternate member of the Politburo. Kang expounded Mao's thinking about class and class struggle from 1962 onwards, the evolution of Mao's views since November 1965 about the necessity of launching a CR and, in particular, Mao's instructions issued between 18 to 30 March during Kang's visit to Hangzhou. Kang also explained the process of drafting the document which was to be called the 'May 16th

Circular' and which was to be adopted by the conference as the guideline for the CR.[65]

The next speaker to take the floor in the afternoon of 6 May, was Zhang Chunqiao who was not even a member of the Central Committee. He also emphasised class struggle in the cultural field, especially during the period since the publication of Yoao's article about Wu Han. His declarations were followed by Chen Boda's speech which lasted the whole morning of 7 May and was entirely devoted to analysing Peng Zhen's mistakes throughout his political career. Peng was accused of having given priority to the cities over the countryside during the civil war instead of following Mao's principle that the countryside should encircle the cities. As mayor of Beijing he had failed to 'put politics in command' and had given priority to production. He had harboured bourgeois anti-Party and anti-socialist elements in all areas of cultural and political life.[66]

All speeches were dominated by references to Mao's thinking and to his instructions. During the ensuing discussions, the Politburo members all avoided expressing any opinion different from that of the leftist speakers.

The next topic on the agenda was the adoption of the May 16 circular as a CC document. It revoked the February Outline Report, dissolved the group of five and announced the establishment of a new Central Cultural Revolution Group (CCRG) under the Standing Committee of the Politburo.[67] The conference, aware of the fact that Mao had examined and revised the circular several times and finally written the largest part of the document himself, adopted the circular without changing a word.

The May 16 circular repeated Mao's accusation that the Outline Report 'is actually an outline report by Peng Zhen alone' and that it was 'concocted ... according to his own ideas behind the back of Comrade Kang Sheng'. It declared that Peng 'did not make it clear that it was being sent to the CC for examination as an official document' and that it did not 'get the approval of Comrade Mao Zedong'.[68]

These accusations clearly ran counter to the facts that Kang Sheng had participated in the meeting preparing the Outline Report, that the draft had been approved by the Standing Committee and that Peng had sought to obtain Mao's approval of it. Since Mao had not expressed any objections, Peng and all other Standing Committee members had presumed that

Mao was in agreement with the text. But none of the Standing Committee members dared to confront the truth, and even less to defend Peng Zhen. They all accepted Mao's distortion of the facts and supported the purges he had decided to carry out. Had there been more solidarity among the front line leaders and some real opposition to Mao's conspicuous stance, politics in the country might have run a different course. As it was, the leadership continued to co-operate in building up a demi-god and a system supporting him.

The other three members of the 'anti-Party clique' met with a similar fate. Lu Dingyi, alternate member of the Politburo, member of the Central Secretariat and head of the CC propaganda department had closely cooperated with Peng Zhen in his attempts to limit the scope of the CR to an academic discussion. Since ideological indoctrination was Lu's responsibility, he was accountable for the developments Mao perceived as revisionist trends in the Party. In Mao's view, Lu's diligence and efficiency during the rectification campaigns of the 1960s left much to be desired. Mao's accusation that the Propaganda Department was 'the palace of the King of Hell' was Lu's political death sentence.

Lu was accused of three major mistakes: opposition to Chairman Mao and Mao Zedong Thought; opposition to the CR; and opposition to and persecution of Lin Biao and his family.

Since the early 1960s Lu Dingyi had, on several occasions, made sarcastic remarks about Lin Biao's panegyric of Mao Zedong Thought. ' To learn Mao Zedong Thought', he said, 'does not mean to make him an idol.' He regarded it as 'philistinism' to make Mao ominscient. The use of Mao Zedong Thought as an invocation reminded him of the Boxers who believed that they could not be harmed by rifles and swords if they said an incantation. Lu suggested that it was 'boastful to say that some problems can be solved by reading an article by Chairman Mao.'[69]

While the CC propaganda department was warning against the 'philistinism of Mao Zedong Thought,' Lin Biao was preaching Mao Zedong Thought asking everyone to 'memorise important statements and to study and apply them repeatedly'.[70] It was thus the PLA political department and not the CC propaganda department which became the channel to spread Mao Zedong Thought – a clear and obvious signal that

Lu had lost Mao's confidence. As the deputy head of the group of five, Lu was accused of having closely cooperated with Peng Zhen in his opposition to the CR. Like Peng, he was charged of having shielded a large number of anti-socialist writers and was co-responsible for the failure to publish articles written by leftists during the campaign against Wu Han and for the February Outline Report.

The third accusation of having persecuted Lin Biao's family involved Lu Dingyi's and Lin Biao's wives, Yan Weibin and Ye Qun. Both women had known and disliked each other since the 1940s, when they took part in the rectification campaign in Yanan. In the course of this campaign, which closely scrutinised a large number of people living at the Yanan base, Ye Qun's declaration that she had joined the Party in Beijing at the age of sixteen caused a lot of suspicion. She was also suspected of having had a number of love affairs while she lived in Beijing.

From March 1960 onward, Yan Weibin began to write anonymous letters to Ye Qun[71] first accusing her of maltreating Lin Biao's eldest daughter, a child of his earlier marriage, then criticising Ye's decadent lifestyle, implying that Ye had had several affairs before her marriage to Lin Biao. Finally, Yan expressed doubts about Ye's Party membership, stating that she was a sham Party member. Ye Qun received such letters for a number of years before the security department found the identity of the writer.[72] The discovery of Yan's authorship occurred at the same time as Lu Dingyi had expressed his opposition to Lin Biao's laudations of Mao and Mao Zedong Thought. Lu denied any knowledge about his wife's anonymous letters, but he was nonetheless accused of having persecuted Lin's family. Since the letters were to be made public at the enlarged Politburo meeting in May, Lin Biao considered it necessary to write a few words to defend Ye Qun's innocence. On 20 May, the date of Lu's self-criticism, each participant received a printed paper stating: 'Ye Qun was a virgin,' signed, Lin Biao.[73]

The purge of Luo Ruiqing had little to do with the CR.[74] It involved a power struggle within the PLA leadership. Luo had been working under Lin Biao's command for many years. When Lin commanded the 1st Red Army Group in the base area in Jiangxi in the 1930s, Luo was the director of Lin's security bureau. During the anti-Japanese war, Lin Biao was the president of the military and political university in Yanan with Luo as his deputy. When Lin became minister of defence in 1959, he nominated Luo general chief of staff to replace Huang Kecheng who was purged with Peng Dehuai.

When Lin began to develop his role as the heraldic exponent of Mao Zedong Thought in the army, a fundamental disagreement surfaced between the two military leaders about the role of politics in the army. While Lin emphasised the overall importance of political and ideological indoctrination of the PLA, his chief of staff insisted that military training and political education should at least have equal status. But Luo went further than that. On several occasions, he had expressed sarcastic dissent with Lin Biao's high praise of Mao Zedong Thought as 'the highest and most lively Marxism – Leninism' and the 'peak of Marxism – Leninism.' If Mao Zedong Thought was the highest, he argued, then it could not go higher. And if it was already at a peak, then it could not develop further.[75]

But more important than ideological squabbles clearly was Luo's powerful position in the army and in the state security apparatus. By the mid 1960s, Luo had accumulated a number of important posts: general secretary of the central military commission, general chief of staff of the PLA, member of the secretariat of the Central Committee in charge of military affairs, vice premier of the State Council and minister of public security. Lin Biao, a sick man without much energy, felt threatened by the bright and vital Luo Ruiqing who was able to wield widespread influence over large section of the army.

Luo was charged on four counts: the first was his opposition to Mao Zedong Thought on the grounds that he had openly challenged Lin Biao's statements on the matter. Secondly, he was accused of having intentions to take over Lin Biao's position as minister of defence. This charge was brought forward by Lin Biao's wife, Ye Qun, who testified that Luo Ruiqing entrusted the former air force commander, Liu Yalou, shortly before his death in February, 1965, to convey the following message to her:

> Everybody has to retire from politics sooner or later. This applies to Lin Biao, too, Ye Qun should take care of Lin's health. Lin Biao should concentrate more on his work at

the centre, and Luo would take care of the army. Luo would reward Ye Qun, if she performed this service for him.⁷⁶

The third accusation pertained to Luo's implementation of a bourgeois military line by advocating military training more than political education.⁷⁷ Fourthly, Luo was accused of collaborating with He Long to usurp power within the army and to seize power in the navy over which he had little influence.⁷⁸

In November, 1956, Lin sent his wife Ye Qun to Hangzhou where Mao was residing to report to Mao about Luo's reluctance to give priority to political work in the army and especially about his apparent lack of respect for Mao Zedong Thought. On 2 December, Mao, convinced by Ye Qun's report, wrote a comment on Luo's case stating that 'everybody should be on the alert against those who have no faith in, but feign compliance with, bringing politics to the fore, and who disseminate a set of eclecticism (i.e. opportunism) themselves.'⁷⁹

From 8 to 15 December, Lin convened an enlarged meeting of the Standing Committee in Shanghai for the sole purpose of repudiating Luo Ruiqing for his 'sins of opposing the party and usurping the army.' The participants began by reiterating Mao's statement about Luo's failure to give priority to politics and spreading eclecticism. Ye Qun made the major speech – it lasted ten hours – to repudiate Luo, accusing him of promoting a 'bourgeois military line' by spreading such eclectic fallacies as 'military affairs are politics' and 'equal emphasis should be given to military affairs and politics.'⁸⁰

But her major accusation pertained to Luo's alleged ambitions to take over Lin's post as minister of defence: Luo had omitted to inform Lin about military matters and had attempted to force Lin Biao to retire.

After Ye's speech had revealed his 'problems' to the enlarged Standing Committee, Luo, who was travelling on an inspection tour in south-west China, was ordered to Shanghai to make a confession⁸¹ and to be notified that he was removed from all his posts.

The procedure was repeated a few months later (4 March to 8 April) in Beijing where Ye Qun, Wu Faxian and other army officers made speeches to repudiate him. In addition to the accusations brought forward against him at the December meeting, it was declared that he was a 'bourgeois careerist' and a 'conspirator'. During the anti-Japanese war he had allegedly followed the right opportunist line represented by Wang Ming and Peng Dehuai. He was also accused of having conspired with Peng Zhen and Lu Dingyi against Mao and Lin Biao.[82] On 18 March Luo attempted to kill himself by jumping from the top of the building. His suicide attempt failed but he broke both his legs.[83] Luo was purged and rehabilitated only in 1975.

Little is known about the reasons for the purge of Yang Shangkun, the head of the CC General Office, who, on 10 Novemeber 1965, became the first victim of the Peng-Luo-Lu-Yang anti-Party clique. He was accused of having installed listening devices in Mao's office for the purpose of collecting information for Peng Zhen.[84] The problem of the Peng Luo Lu Yang anti-party clique was officially disposed of at the May meeting of the Politburo. On 18 May, Lin Biao made the major speech to the conference. His first point was to draw attention to the threat of a coup d'état, citing many historical examples to the effect that 'Coup d'état is prevalent in the world.'[85] He emphasised that in China, too, there existed a real danger of a counter-revolutionary coup d'état, as exemplified by the anti-Party clique of Peng, Luo, Lu, Yang who wanted to overthrow Mao.[86]

A major item on the agenda was the criticism of Peng Zhen and Lu Dingyi. Peng Zhen made a short self-criticism admitting his mistakes in directing the CR as the head of the group of five. But he disavowed any allegations of being anti-socialist and of having planned to topple Mao. 'As for attempting a coup and subversion of the Centre, and having illicit relations with foreign countries, even in a dream,' he said, 'I could not have thought of such things. Concerning the question of having developed anti-Party relations with Luo Ruiqing and Lu Dingyi, the Centre may investigate.'[87]

However, the Centre had no intention to further investigate Peng's case, and the meeting, on 23 May, passed a unanimous decision to purge Peng, Luo, Lu and Yang. Peng, Luo and Lu were deprived of their membership in the central secretariat and Yang lost his post as an alternate member. Peng was removed from his posts as first secretary of the Beijing municipal Party committee and mayor of Beijing, and Lu was removed from the Central Propaganda Department.

Li Xuefeng, head of the CC north China bureau, was appointed first secretary of the Beijing Party committee with Wu De, then first Party secretary of Jilin Province, as his deputy. Tao Zhu (first secretary of the CC south-central China bureau) replaced Peng as responsible secretary of the central secretariat and Lu Dingy as the director of the central propaganda department. Ye Jianying, one of the ten Marshalls replaced Luo Ruiqing as general secretary of the CMC.[88] The reorganisation of the Beijing Party committee and the CMC was made public on 4 June. A new Central Cultural Revolution Group (CCRG) was established under the leadership of Chen Boda, with Jiang Qing as one of his deputies and Kang Sheng as an advisor.

The May 16th circular

The fundamental differences which existed between Mao and the front-line leaders regarding the purpose of the CR, emerged clearly in the so-called 'May 16th Circular' issued by the meeting and whose major points had been drafted by Mao personally. It focused heavily on the repudiation of the February Outline Report which had emphasised that the CR was an academic discussion where different views should be freely debated. To Mao, the CR was a 'sharp class struggle' the purpose of which was to criticise and repudiate the 'considerable number' of 'anti-party and anti-socialist representatives of the bourgeoisie.' It explicitly condemned the Outline Report for its attempt to 'channel the political struggle in the cultural sphere into the so-called pure academic discussion'[89] and accused it of having put forward such 'bourgois slogans' as 'everyone is equal before the truth' with the aim of 'protecting the bourgeoisie and opposing the proletariat.'[90]

The circular argued that in class struggle, there was no equality between bourgeoisie and proletariat. The proletariat was fully entitled to 'overwhelm and eradicate' the bourgeoisie. The Outline Report was a document of 'bourgeois liberalisation' . . . 'directing its spearhead against the proletarian Left.' Its intention was clearly to 'label the (true) Marxist –Leninists as "scholar–tyrants" and thus to support the real bourgeois scholar–tyrants and prop up their tottering monopoly position in academic circles.' The May 16th Circular defines the real issue of the debate as one 'of implementing or of resisting Comrade Mao Zedong's line on the Cultural Revolution.' It then proceeds to instruct 'the whole Party' to:

> thoroughly expose the reactionary bourgeois stand of the so-called academic authorities who oppose the Party and socialism, thoroughly criticise and repudiate reactionary bourgeois ideas in the sphere of academic work, education, journalism, literature and art and publishing, and seize the leadership in these cultural spheres.[91]

This statement defines one of the objectives of the CR. But it had another more fundamental purpose which later became the theoretical basis for the purge of Liu Shaoqi and other senior leaders. It was contained in a paragraph drafted by Mao himself in which he referred to 'those representatives of the bourgeoisie who had sneaked into the Party, the government, the army and various cultural circles' and who:

> are a bunch of counter-revolutionary revisionists. Once conditions are ripe, they will seize political power and turn the dictatorship of the proletariat into a dictatorship of the bourgeoisie. Some of them we have already seen through, others we have not. Some are still trusted by us and are being trained as successors, persons like Khrushchev, for example, who are still nestling beside us.[92]

3

THE CASE OF LIU SHAOQI

The beginning

The purge of Liu Shaoqi appears to have been shrewdly and systematically premeditated. Through a process of escalating criticism, Liu's popular image was destroyed and he was projected as the major revisionist in the country whose aim was to restore capitalism.

To begin with, Mao purposefully kept Liu Shaoqi and the front-line leaders in the dark regarding the unfolding of the Cultural Revolution drama. It was discussed exclusively with his newly formed coterie. By the time the May Politburo meeting was held, Mao had broken contact with Liu and had appointed Kang Sheng to maintain the liaison between himself and the Politburo. His next step was to launch a general frontal attack against the Party establishment.

Kang Sheng, who was fully aware of Mao's intentions, chose Beijing University (Beida) to 'kindle the flames' of a new mass movement.'[1] (Kang sent his wife, Cao Yion, to Beida to contact her friend Nie Yuanzi and to encourage her to launch an attack against the university's Party committee. At the outset, the movement at Beida was thus manipulated by the CCRG.[2] Nie, a Party secretary of Beida's philosophy department in her forties, wrote, in collaboration with six of her colleagues, a big character poster accusing the university authorities of sabotaging the CR by introducing a number of regulations which were designed to dampen it. The poster also claimed that Beida was controlled by bourgeois elements and agents of capitalism and was pursuing a bourgeois line in education.[3]

Such an attack on a Party committee was almost inconceivable in China at that time. In the past, hostile campaigns had always been initiated and organised by the authorities. Under the circumstances, an apparently spontaneous attack on the Party establishment at Beida could be considered a political crime. Far milder statements which had been voiced against the Party and its cadres in 1957, had been a cause of professional and political disarray to their authors who were labelled 'rightists' and condemned to be 'remoulded' through forced labour. It was therefore not surprising that Nie's provocative poster incited a great deal of critical response, and hundreds of wall posters written by Party members, teachers, and students appeared in defence of the Party.[4]

Kang Sheng sent Nie's poster to Mao who was still sojourning in Hangzhou. Mao praised it as the 'first truly Marxist-Leninist big character poster' and ordered it to be 'broadcast at once and published in the newspapers'.[5] It was broadcast on 1 June and was published the next day on the front page of *People's Daily*. Preceded by a vituperative editorial under the title 'Hail to a Poster at Beida' it was announced that 'anyone who opposes Chairman Mao, no matter how old or how prominent, must be overthrown'.[6]

The publication of Nie Yuanzi's poster was an opening volley. It had an immediate impact on other universities and schools where the students began to attack Party committees and teachers whose activities they considered incompatible with Mao Zedong Thought. Lu Ping, president of Beijing University was labelled as a member of Peng Zhen's 'black gang'. A number of other university presidents in Beijing, Shanghai and Nanjing were condemned as 'black gangsters'. The red guard movement, which surfaced about the same time, reinforced these activities. As a result, Party committees in schools and universities became increasingly paralysed.[7]

This initial and widely publicised campaign generated considerable confusion and disarray within the central leadership. What should they do and how should they handle the explosive situation; they were apparently not certain. Their first reaction was to send work teams to Beida and other universities to replace the paralysed Party committees. But since Mao continued to be absent from Beijing, Liu Shaoqi and Deng Xiaoping were even more unsure if they could take this step without clearance from the Chairman. Since it was politically imprudent to take any initiative on their own, they flew to Hangzhou on 9 June, to ask Mao to return to Beijing and to personally take charge of the CR.[8] But Mao refused and insisted that Liu should continue with the responsibility of running the Party centre.[9] On the same occasion, the question of the dispatch of work teams was also discussed. Both Liu and Deng were in favour of using this procedure since this was an accepted organisational practice which had become the standard response in many previous campaigns. Chen Boda, who was present during the discussion, was opposed to it. Mao, however, remained ambivalent and simply said: 'they may be sent, they may not be sent. But they should not be dispatched hastily.'[10]

Interpreting Mao's ambivalent statement as an acceptance of work team policies, Liu, after his return to Beijing, convened an enlarged meeting of the Standing Committee which, in view of the spreading organisational disorder at schools and universities, unanimously decided to dispatch work teams to them. Other major cities and provincial authorities followed Beijing's example and a large number of work teams began to operate in universities, schools and other institutions where Party committees were unable to function.

Liu Shaoqi perceived the CR as a political movement similar to previous political campaigns. Therefore, he used the same methods to lead the movement, relying on the leading role of Party committees at different levels, and, if they were not operational, to replace them by work teams. He favoured regulations and order over disorder and chaos. While Mao wanted to 'kindle the flames', Liu emphasised that the role of work teams was one of fire brigades dispatched to put the fire out.[11]

The work teams at the universities were usually composed of cadres from ministries and provincial government institutions. At the schools they were mostly members from youth league organisations.[12] They operated in a similiar way as in previous political movements. Their mission was to bring the situation under control and to carry out the CR in an orderly manner. They tended to act in much the same way as the Party committees they had come to rescue, and suppressed students who had opposed these committees. With this procedure, the work teams met with considerable resistance from radical students who accused them of 'shielding the black gang and of suppressing the revolution'.[13]

In the view of the leadership, opposition to work teams was equivalent to opposing the Party, and they characterised opponents as 'ghosts and monsters', a political phraseology to denominate class enemies. On 22 June, Liu Shaoqi instructed the work teams in the following terms:

> When the ghosts and monsters come out one after another, do not hit back hurriedly. We should tell the leftists to brace themselves and bear with it. The leaders should watch out for the opportune moment. Once the ghosts and monsters have exposed themselves, we should promptly launch a counterattack.

Concerning secondary school teachers whom Liu considered particularly suspect, he said in the middle of July: 'The major tasks of the CR in secondary schools is to carry out a political examination of the teachers.'[14]

Based on this instruction, the new Beijing Party committee under Li Xuefeng declared that those who opposed work teams were rightists and should be exposed. He called upon Party members to come out in defence of the Party[15] and decided to start an 'anti-disruption' campaign to restore order in universities and colleges. The campaign lasted until mid July and condemned more than 100 students as counter-revolutionaries in Beijing alone. Others were labelled as 'sham leftists and real rightists', and many more were examined, dragged to struggle sessions and denounced.[16] Numerous secondary school teachers were detained and asked to make confessions about their impure political thinking and attitude.[17]

For more than fifty days Liu directed the CR in a manner which was fundamentally contrary to Mao's intentions. When Mao, in the May 16th Circular defined the purpose of the CR as one which was to remove 'those representatives of the bourgeoisie who have sneaked into the Party, the government, the army and various cultural circles (and who) are a bunch of counter-revolutionary revisionists',[18] the persons he had in mind were, in fact, Liu Shaoqi and other veteran leaders who had adopted the Circular without being aware of Mao's true intentions.

Mao had been absent from Beijing since late November 1965. From his retreat in the provinces, he had manoeuvred and observed events in Beijing and led the leadership into the trap he had set for it. Adroitly hiding his cards, he opened the way for him to strike at those he perceived as his opponents.

When he considered that the time was ripe, he returned to Beijing with the intention, revealed in his letter of 8 July 1966 to Jiang Qing, to 'create great disorder under heaven' to achieve 'great order under heaven' by arousing 'the broad masses to expose our dark aspects openly, in an all-round way and from below'.[19]

On 16 July, Mao made his spectacular swim in the Yangtze River where he reportedly covered 9 miles in 65 minutes.[20] Across the nation, newspapers published the picture of Mao in a swimming suit, and the entire country was congratulating him for his extraordinary performance and his excellent health.[21] After this upsurge in the cult of Mao's personality, he returned to Beijing on 18 July where he finally involved himself personally in the direction of the CR.

From 19 to 23 July, Liu Shaoqi convened several meetings to discuss work-team policies. Although members of the CCRG criticised this approach to the CR, the Standing Committee insisted that work teams were necessary and should continue to operate.[22]

This time, Mao took a clear stand on this point. On 24 July, he called a meeting of the Standing Committee and the members of the CCRG where he stated that the CR should be led by revolutionary committees composed of leftist students and teachers and not by work teams.[23] The following day, in a talk to the secretaries of the CC bureaus and the CCRG, he declared that work teams had 'played a negative role and had obstructed the movement'. The work-team policy had been an 'error of orientation and political line'. Mao announced that work teams would be withdrawn immediately.[24]

Mao's undisputed authority asserted itself again. Liu Shaoqi and other front-line leaders, although they had put their full weight behind this policy, did not offer any resistence. On 29 July, at a meeting of students and teachers, Li Xuefeng flatly announced the withdrawal of the work teams on Mao's behalf. Deng who spoke after him, was more subtle in his presentation of the work-team policies. He drew attention to the fact that work teams had been dispatched by the Beijing Party committee according to a decision taken by the Party centre. Now that 'it revoked the work teams according to instructions from

Chairman Mao and the party centre', some comrades said that 'the veteran revolutionaries are confronted with new problems'.[25] Zhou Enlai also referred to the 'new problems' faced by the leadership and informed the meeting about the three objectives of the CR as defined by Mao: 'struggle-criticism-transformation'.[26] Liu Shaoqi who was the last to speak, said that the Party centre warmly supported the revolutionary students and teachers who carried out the CR. But he also declared that he had been unable to understand the CR. He stated:

> As for how to conduct the CR you are not quite clear, you do not quite know. You ask us to tell you how to proceed. I tell you frankly, I do not know either. I believe that many comrades at the party centre and the members of the work teams to do not know it either.

He also emphasised that work-team policies had been decided by the centre. But now, work teams 'do not suit the needs of the CR, so the centre decided to revoke them'.[27]

The 11th Plenum of the 8th Central Committee

The adoption by the Politburo of the 'May 16 Circular' marked the beginning of the CR. But specific policies regarding its course still needed to be formulated. Mao therefore convened the 11th Plenum of the 8th Central Committee which met from 1 to 12 August 1966. He later reminisced about this meeting in talk with a visiting Albanian delegation. He told the visitors that before the meeting, there was a majority among the leadership who did not agree with him. Sometimes he almost stood alone. Therefore, he was forced to take his views to the 11th Plenum of the 8th Central Committee. After the meeting had discussed Mao's views, he obtained the support of a little more than half of the participants.[28]

Mao sometimes made such statements to pretend that his position was not as powerful as people were inclined to believe. It did, however, not reflect the real events at the 11th Plenum. If it was true that the overwhelming majority among the members and alternate members of the Central Committee did not share his views about the CR it might have been for the simple reason that they did not fully comprehend them.

Mao often expressed himself in vague and ambiguous language. He was usually more inclined to emphatically criticise tendencies he disliked than to suggest concrete alternatives. This was again the case before the plenary session, when Mao had been very cryptic about his real intentions towards anybody but his inner circle.

The participants in the conference were 141 members and alternate members of the Central Committee and 47 other persons including members of the CCRG. Four items were on the agenda: to pass a resolution on the CR; to endorse the major decisions made since the meeting of the 10th Plenum of the 8th Central Committee in September 1962; to pass a communique about the present meeting; to ratify the purge of the 'Peng-Luo-Lu-Yang anti-Party clique'.

However, the most important event of the Plenum, which was not even on the agenda of the conference, was the reorganisation of the leadership on a scale unparalleled since more than twenty years.

During the first few days, the meeting proceeded according to schedule. On the first day, Deng Xiaoping, in his capacity as the General Secretary of the Party, presented the agenda. Liu Shaoqi followed with the main speech during which he described all the major decisions taken by the party centre since the 10th Plenum and submitted them for endorsement. He also talked extensively about work teams and the errors he had committed while he was in charge in Beijing during Mao's absence.[29]

Chen Boda, the head of the CCRG also presented a statement severely attacking the leadership's work team policies. During the next two days other speakers continued to talk about the same issue and some of them, following Liu Shaoqi's example, criticised themselves. But among other participants, doubts about the decision to withdraw the work teams lingered on.

This implicit but evident adherence to work-team methods caused Mao to change the course of the Plenum and to escalate his attacks on Liu Shaoqi. On the fourth day of the Plenum, Mao unexpectedly convened a enlarged meeting of the Politburo's Standing Committee where he vented his mounting anger with the front line leaders and sharply censured their political outlook. In particular, he accused them of having suppressed the students. Recalling the history of the students' movements which, he said, had been suppressed first by the late Qing Dynasty, then by the northern war lords and finally by the Guomindang, he deplored that the communist party had also joined in the suppression. Work teams had introduced rules prohibiting contacts among students from different classes, departments and schools which severely restricted their activities. This, according to Mao, was suppression and terror, and they had originated at the centre. Mao pointed out that the centre had reversed its own decision. It had closed universities and schools for half a year to allow students to carry out the CR. But when the student movement had gathered momentum, the centre suppressed it. This, in Mao's words, did not conform to Marxism; it represented an error of line and it proved that too many people favoured the bourgeoisie and opposed the proletariat.[30]

In face of such sharp accusations, Liu Shaoqi declared that he was ready to assume full responsibility for these mistakes, since he had been in Beijing at the time. But Mao responded ironically: 'You were exercising dictatorship in Beijing. You did a fine job!'[31]

Mao ordered the distribution of his statement to the Standing Committee and to all participants in the Plenum for discussion. The Plenum, which, according to the original plans, should have ended on 5 August, was prolonged in order to allow for the study of Mao's words.

On 5 August, Mao made the unusual gesture of writing a big character poster himself. The poster, entitled: 'Bombard the Headquarters', referred to the poster written by Nie Yuanzi and the *People's Daily* commentary about it emphasising that they were 'superbly written'. Mao noted that:

> In the last fifty days or so, some leading comrades from the central levels down to the local levels have acted in a diametrically opposite way (to what Nie Yuanzi's poster had suggested). Having adopted the reactionary stand of the bourgeoisie, they have enforced a bourgeois dictatorship and struck down the surging movement of the Great Proletarian Cultural Revolution. They have stood facts on their head and juggled black and white, encircled and suppressed revoluntionaries, stifled opinions different

from their own [and] imposed a 'white terror'. They have puffed up the arrogance of the bourgeoisie and deflated the morale of the proletariat.

The poster concluded by asking the question whether 'viewed in connection with the rightist deviation in 1962 and the wrong tendency of 1964 which was "leftist" in form but rightist in essence, should this not prompt one to deep thought?'[32]

Mao's poster brought two issues into the open: his differences with Liu and other leaders about the guidelines for the CR which appeared as a continuation of their divergences in 1962 and 1964; and Mao's perception of the existence of another headquarters in the Party which was later referred to as 'the bourgeois headquarters headed by Liu Shaoqi'. The poster marked the final breaking point between Mao and the head of state.[33]

The Plenum was again prolonged to allow for the study of Mao's poster in group meetings where Kang Sheng, Jiang Qing, Zhang Chunqiao and others, including Xie Fuzhi, vice premier and minister of public security, elaborated further on it and multiplied their attacks on Liu Shaoqi.[34] Liu Shaoqi later stated that only after reading Mao's poster he began to understand the magnitude of his mistakes. 'Before that, I did not know I had committed such grave error.'[35]

The majority of the Central Committee members who, without hesitation, had expressed their full support to the series of high level decisions taken over the last four years, were unable to give their sincere support to this unforeseeable new policy. Mao's poster which was distributed to all the participants of the meeting on 7 August had a deep effect on most of them. By its fierceness, it created a state of bemusement and even fear in the minds of those who were 'leading comrades from central to local levels' and who had approved of and executed Liu's policies. None of them was able to clearly assess, to what extent their own actions propelled them into the group of cadres who had taken 'the reactionary stand of the bourgeoisie'. But there was no explicit disagreement either. Even those who might not have been so deeply involved in Liu's 'mistakes' were simply stunned by the indignation of their 'great leader'.

On 8 August, the Plenum adopted unanimously the 'Decision of the Central Committee of the CCP concerning the Great Proletarian Cultural Revolution', a document which had been drafted in July by a group of writers headed by Chen Boda and revised by Mao. This decision became known as 'the 16 points'.[36] It defined the CR as a 'struggle against . . . those Party persons in authortity who are taking the capitalist road' and to 'crush' them:

> to criticise and to repudiate the reactionary bourgeois academic 'authorities' and the ideology of the bourgeoisie and all other exploiting classes; to transform education, literature and art and all other parts of the superstructure that do not correspond to the socialist economic base, so as to facilitate the consolidation and development of the socialist system.[37]

This was summarised as the process of 'struggle-criticism-transformation' (*dou pi gai*). In diametric opposition to the methods advocated by Liu Shaoqi who believed that the masses should be guided by the Party or by work teams, the decision stated that 'in the Great Cultural Revolution, the only method is for the masses to liberate themselves . . . Trust the masses, rely on them and respect their initiative'.[38]

Mao's ideological radicalisation and his denunciation of Liu Shaoqi had important organisational consequences. He suggested to reshuffle the Party leadership structure and proposed candidates for the Politburo's Standing Committee which were all elected by the assembly. The new Standing Committee was increased by four members and was now composed of eleven persons who were in order of importance: Mao Zedong, Lin Biao, Zhou Enlai, Tao Zhu, Chen Boda, Deng Xiaoping, Kang Sheng, Liu Shaoqi, Zhu De, Li Fuchun and Chen Yun. The four new members were Tao Zhu, Chen Boda, Kang Sheng and Li Fuchun. The number of Politburo members was also increased by the inclusion of Xu Xiangqian, Nie Rongzhen and Ye Jianying.[39]

The upgrading of Lin Biao to the second rank and the demotion of Liu Shaoqi from the second to the eighth rank in the Standing Committee marked the beginning of Liu's tragic fall. Only one vice chairmanship, namely that of Lin Biao, was maintained. This transformation replaced the Mao-Liu system, by the Mao-Lin system of leadership and terminated the division between the first and the second front.

The promotion of Chen Boda and Kang Sheng from alternate members of the Politburo to the Standing Committee epitomised the enhancement of the status of the CCRG within the hierarchical structure of leadership. Moreover, the CCRG who theoretically operated under the jurisdiction of the Politburo, began to overshadow it by taking over the direction of the CR which hitherto dominated the political life in the country.

After the Plenum, the CR was expected to take the form of a campaign to reverse Liu Shaoqi's previous policies and to cleanse the Party apparatus of 'bourgeois elements' who had followed Liu's political line. However, the practical implementation of this new orientation encountered numerous obstacles. The major cause for these obstructions was the relative weakness of the radicals. If students in universities and schools were ready to condemn 'reactionary academic authorities', they differed greatly in their response to Party committees and work team policies. A radical minority was ready to oppose them, while the majority of students and teachers were reluctant to participate in this movement of repudiation.[40] In other institutions and work units, the radical faction was even weaker. In most cities other than Beijing and in the provinces, the CR was controlled by municipal and provincial Party committees. The basic issue was again whether the CR should be an orderly movement led by the Party or a revolt against the Party establishment. The major cause of contention between Mao and the veteran leaders was not the CR itself but the way it should be directed since the Party leadership at all level had an ingrained aversion against Mao's intentions to destroy the Party establishment and to promote anarchism. The leaders were used to a high status, and it became a matter of self-preservation to resist the unfamiliar instructions issued by Mao and the CCRG. Mao thus faced increasing difficulties in the manipulation of the movement. He needed additional support from the 'masses' and thus appealed to the entire nation to launch an attack on the Party establishment. In the view of the CCRG, the movement therefore had to escalate to ensure greater support for the radicals.[41]

The first step in the process of escalation was the publication, on 1 October, of a *Red Flag* editorial which for the first time pointed out to the general public the existence of two opposing political lines: the proletarian revolutionary line represented by Mao, and a bourgeois reactionary line whose representative the article did not identify. 'The bourgeois reactionary line must be thoroughly criticised and repudiated', the article stressed, since 'only then can the struggles, criticisms and repudiations and transformations be carried out . . . only then can there be a clear cut idea of whom to rely on in waging the struggles, carrying out the criticisms and the transformations.'[42]

The call to repudiate the bourgeois reactionary line was followed by an 'urgent instruction' on 5 October to rehabilitate those whom Party committees and work teams had labelled counter-revolutionaries, anti-Party elements, rightists and sham leftists during the 50 days of 'white terror'. The material collected against them was ordered to be destroyed, and Party committees were no longer entitled to lead the CR.[43]

To implement the decision to 'thoroughly criticise and repudiate the bourgeois reactionary line', Mao, in October 1966, convened a CC working conference which was attended by leading members of the Party central bureau, of provincial and municipal Party committees and representatives of Party committees of ministries and CC departments.[44] In their reports about the state of the CR in the areas under their jurisdiction, most speakers expressed neither enthusiastic support for the movement nor resistance to it. Mao considered this lukewarm resonse to the campaign, which was of utmost importance to him, as 'not very normal.'[45]

Chen Boda and Lin Biao made the major speeches to the conference. Focusing on 'the two lines of the Great Cultural Revolution' Chen Boda criticised Liu Shaoqi and Deng Xiaoping, holding them responsible for the formulation of the bourgeois reactionary line.[46] Lin Biao stressed the necessity of the CR and the methods to be used to carry it out.[47] Zhou Enlai, whose political outlook could hardly be considered different from that of Liu Shaoqi and Deng Xiaoping, admitted that he could have never imagined such a large-scale movement and accused himself of 'always lagging behind the Chairman'.[48] Lin Biao's and Chen Boda's speeches were printed in pamphlet form and distributed throughout the country as a guideline to the CR.

On 23 October, Liu Shaoqi and Deng Xiaoping criticised themselves at the conference. Liu's statement closely followed the standard pattern established for such recantations. Elaborating on Mao's poster, Liu first focused on the mistakes he had committed during the fifty days. Then he provided the reasons for his errors. They were not accidental, he said, but linked to mistakes of principle and line he had committed during earlier periods of his life. He enumerated all the mistakes he had made between 1946 and 1964, his erroneous assessment of the political and ideological situation, his bourgeois outlook which he had not been able to completely abandon, and finally his failure to thoroughly study Mao Zedong Thought.[49] Deng's statement followed the same pattern.

Mao's views on both Liu's and Deng's self-criticism which, as was customary, he had read and approved before they were presented to the conference, were, on the whole, favourable. Mao wrote a comment on each of the texts which stated that Liu's self-criticism was 'basically well written and very earnest', and that Deng would mend his mistakes and stand up again.[50]

The following day, Mao expressed various grievances regarding Liu and Deng, accusing them especially of having too high an opinion of themselves and over-estimating their own competence. But he also made a few conciliatory remarks. 'People should be allowed to make some mistakes,' Mao said. When Lin Biao tried to establish a link between Liu and Deng on the one hand and Peng Zhen on the other, Mao objected: 'Liu and Deng acted openly, not in secret,' he said. 'They are not like Peng Zhen.'[51] On 25 October, he told the conference again that 'Comrade Liu Shaoqi and Comrade Deng Xiaoping should not be entirely blamed. They had responsibility. The centre, too had its responsibility,'[52] and 'not everything comrade Shaoqi has done is bad. If they (Liu and Deng) have made mistakes they can probably correct them. When they have corrected them it will be alright, and they should be allowed to come back and go to work with fresh spirit.'[53]

The conference officially defined Liu's mistakes as errors of line, which, in the traditional hierarchy of political mistakes established by the CCP, constituted the most serious of them.

Liu had formulated a bourgeois reactionary line. But Liu was still not considered an enemy of the people, since, 'the contradictions between those comrades who have committed the error of line and the Party and the masses is still a contradiction among the people'.[54] Liu was to be criticised but not yet overthrown and he continued to appear in public until the end of the year.

The fall of Liu Shaoqi

In the autumn of 1966, Mao's main concern was not the removal of Liu from leadership. Since Liu had been forced to accuse himself of having initiated the bourgeois reactionary line in the CR as well as of his errors in principle and line over the past two decades, his removal from power was a foregone conclusion. But a more tortuous and tragic fate was in store for him. He became not only a target of attack, but a scapegoat and a symbol of opposition against which the CR was waged. For the following two years, he epitomised the escalating polemics of the CR.

After the October conference, the campaign against Liu was waged on three levels. At the political level the criticism of the bourgeois reactionary line became a campaign of 'down with Liu Shaoqi'. Not only was he deemed responsible for having formulated the line, but he was accused of being a revisionist, the number one Party person in power taking the capitalist road, and a Chinese Khrushchev. Mao, at the October conference, had been reluctant to the use of large character posters criticising Liu and Deng in the open. 'It is not a good thing to put up large character posters against Liu and Deng in the streets,' Mao had said. According to Jiang Qing, he had sent Chen Boda to Beijing and Qinghua universities to prevent the appearance of posters against Liu and Deng.[55] But in spite of Mao's reservations, such posters began to appear in ever-greater numbers.

The campaign against Liu was manipulated by the CCRG who used radical red guards for its escalation. In December, several members of the CCRG made statements to red guard organisations which encouraged them to intensify their attacks against Liu and Deng. On 18 December, Zhang Chunqiao summoned Kuai Dafu, leader of the radical red guards at

Qinghua University to Zhongnanhai informing him that Liu Shaoqi and Deng Xiaoping 'still refused to capitulate' and suggested that the red guards should 'unite, bring their spirit of thorough revolution into full play and relentlessly beat the dog in the water'.[56] On 24 December Qi Benyu made a speech to the red guards at the Beijing Mining Institute in which he stated that 'Liu and Deng were the biggest Party persons in power taking the capitalist road'.[57] Two days later, Kang Sheng told the trade union rebels that Liu Shaoqi was China's Khrushchev and the chieftain of the revisionists.[58]

Jiang Qing, at a meeting with red guards on 27 December, stated that Mao, 'a few months ago', had been against the use of posters against Liu. But 'now you can do anything, but do not try to drag him out.'[59]

In contrast to the CCRG, Zhou Enlai tried to moderate the red guards. At a meeting with red guard and rebel representatives on 8 January 1967, he expressed dissatisfaction with the slogan 'down with Liu Shaoqi and Deng Xiaoping'.[60] But his efforts to restrain the radicals remained fruitless, mainly because the remarks of CCRG members were unequivocal and authoritative. To receive such instructions was a privilege reserved only to the true left revolutionary red guards. To them the message was clearly that Liu should be overthrown. They knew how to react and how to accelerate the movement against Liu.

Qinghua University red guards took the lead in staging a demonstration of six thousand people on 25 December who shouted the slogans 'down with Liu Shaoqi' and 'thoroughly smash the bourgeois headquarters headed by Liu Shaoqi'. Two days later, a hundred thousand university and college red guards held a mass rally in Beijing to denounce Liu as the most prominent capitalst roader within the Party. This was followed by all other rebel and red guard organisations in Beijing and in other cities who, at huge demonstrations, demanded that Liu should be overthrown.[61]

The criticism of the bourgeois reactionary Liu–Deng line soon began to spread to other targets, as radical red guards and rebels accused Party committees at various levels of having followed the Liu–Deng line. By the end of the year, the entire Party establishment came under fire in a campaign which was raging throughout the country.

Clearly, Liu's status had changed. If earlier, Mao considered that Liu's case was one of 'contradictions within the people', he was now viewed as 'an enemy of the people' and a counter-revolutionary revisionist.

By the end of 1966, many of the 'so-called academic authorities opposing the Party and socialism' had been criticised and repudiated. But the Party appartus was slow to change. To protect themselves, power holders skilfully used their organisational resources and, in many areas cooperated with the local and provincial PLA to guard the premises of the Party against the assults of radicals who, although aggressive, still remained a minority. The Party establishment's strategy of survival appeared to have been successfully implemented at that time.

A clear definition of who were 'representatives of the bourgeoisie who have sneaked into the Party, the government, the army and various cultural circles' was still outstanding. Only a few such persons as the Peng, Luo, Lu, Yang group, Deng Tuo, Wu Han and Liao Mosha had hitherto been officially condemned as anti-Party elements and enemies of the people. But Mao, who viewed the following year as one 'of all-round development of class struggle throughout China',[62] intended to instigate a thorough purge of the establishment. The escalation of the attacks on Liu would serve this purpose and Liu would be used as a symbolic figure for 'those Party persons in power travelling the capitalist road'.

Jiang Qing and Kang Sheng were both keen to work in this direction. They suggested to Mao that Liu should not only play the role of the number one capitalst roader but also of a renegade of the Party. For this purpose, a special case group directed by Jiang Qing, Kang Sheng and Xie Fuzhi was established in December 1966, to investigate Liu's wife. The group was to provide 'proof' that Wang Guangmei was an American spy. Wang Guangmei was born into a rich family, had attended an American school in Beijing and had acted as interpreter for one of the American mediation teams who attempted to reconcile the CCP and the Guomindang in the 1940s. Sixty-four persons who had some connections with Wang at that time, were forced to accuse her of spying.[63] A few months later, in March 1967, another group was established to provide proof that Liu had capitulated to the Guomindang after his arrest in Shenyang in 1929 when he was the leader of CCP underground activities in the area.[64] Four hundred persons were dispatched to read through 2.5 million documents in different archives to find evidence that Liu had apostatised the Party while under arrest. The search did not yield the desired results. Liu's betrayal was established only after a veteran communist was coerced into writing a testimony to this effect.[65]

At ideological level, a large-scale campaign of criticism and repudiation against Liu Shaoqi, in line with Mao's strategy of 'struggle-criticism-transformation', was launched in the spring of 1967. Mao considered that the 'January Storm' which broke out in Shanghai in early 1967, marked the stage of 'seizing power' politically from the revisionists, whereas 'criticism and repudiation' was 'the power seizure from revisionists ideologically'.[66] The struggle of the January Storm was to establish Liu and other Party leaders as capitalist roaders and to encourage rebels to seize their power. In the campaign to criticise and repudiate Liu, he was to be exposed as the chief representative of revisionist theories, so that Mao Zedong Thought in general and his theory of continued revolution under the dictatorship of the proletariat in particular could be popularised without obstacle. Another factor was Mao's desire to promote alliance, through their common attack on Liu, among red guard and rebel groups hostile to each other.[67]

The campaign started on 30 March 1967 with the publication of a long article in the *Red Flag* written by Qi Benyu but revised and approved by Mao.[68] This was the first time that the official media announced that Liu was 'the top party person in power taking the capitalist road'. The article described Liu's political 'crimes' in eight points:

Preaching a capitulationist and a traitor's philosophy and directing some people to make confessions and surrender to the Guomindang in the eve of the outbreak of the War of Resistance against Japan.
Advancing the capitulationist line of 'new stage of peace and democracy' after the war of resistance.
Opposing the socialist transformation of capitalist industry and commerce, opposing agricultural cooperation after the founding of the PRC.

Propagating the dying out of class struggle and advocating class collaboration in 1956.
Advocating a revisionist line in rural areas and in foreign relations in the three difficult years in the early 1960s.
Publishing his deceitful book on self-cultivation of communists which opposed Marxism-Leninism and Mao Zedong Thought.
Putting forward and pushing through the opportunist line which was 'left' in form but right in essence in the socialist education movement in 1964.
Putting forward and carrying out the bougeois reactionary line in the Cultural Revolution.[69]

Mao attached special importance to the repudiation of Liu's influential book *How to Be a Good Communist* which was generally referred to as 'on self-cultivation'. The book which had been widely used as a textbook for Party members in the 1950s and 1960s, was now condemned not so much for its contents but for what it did not contain. In February 1967, Mao pointed out that the book was 'deceitful' because it did not advocate revolution, class struggle, the seizure of power and the dictatorship of the proletariat.[70] In May, a joint editorial of the *Red Flag* and the *People's Daily* called upon the entire nation to criticise and repudiate the book in discussion meetings and through the publication of articles and papers.[71] Numerous articles were published and read in meetings which emphasised the 'erroneous theories and views' Liu had allegedly promoted: the theory of 'the dying out of class struggle', the theory that 'social development results only from productive forces', the theory of 'inner-Party peace' in handling inner-Party relations, the emphasis on profit and material incentives in the management of the economy; the principle of giving priority to intellectual development in schools and to technical and vocational approach at the work place; the 'merger of private and public interest'.[72]

After the 11th Plenum in August 1966, Liu was relieved of his responsibilities at the Party centre. For some months, he continued to perform occasional ceremonial duties as the head of state. By the end of the year when attacks against him escalated, he disappeared from the public view. Liu continued to live in his courtyard at Zhongnanhai in isolation from the commotion created by the struggle against his line.

THE CASE OF LIU SHAOQI

In early January, revolutionary rebels of the Zhongnanhai staff began to attack Liu on a personal level by organising the first struggle meeting against him in which he was directly involved.[73]

Another such session took place at Zhongnanhai on 6 April, during which Liu was questioned about the eight points mentioned in Qi Benyu's article 'Patriotism or National Betrayal' and was asked to turn in written answers to the Zhongnanhai rebels on 14 April.[74] Wang Guangmei attempted to defend herself and her husband against the accusations stating that she herself was 'absolutely not a bad woman' and that Liu Shaoqi could not be considered 'a sham revolutionary or counter-revolutionary'.[75]

In the summer of 1967, the campaign against Liu reached a peak. Until then, struggles against him had been confined to Zhongnanhai. Now, more and more red guards and rebels were surrounding the government compound demanding that Liu should be 'dragged out' for a face-to-face confrontation.[76] This request was ignored, as were all the subsequent ones. But Liu was submitted to two more struggle meetings at Zhongnanhai after which he wrote that he refused to accept accusations of being against the Party, against socialism and Mao Zedong Thought.[77] He was separated from his wife and children and held in custody in his courtyard. This deprived him of his freedom of movement. In September, his wife was arrested and imprisoned.[78]

From early 1968 on, Liu suffered from pneumonia, diabetes and high blood pressure. On his sick bed, Liu learned from a radio broadcast on 24 November, that the 12th Plenum of the CC had passed a resolution expelling him from the party 'forever'. His physical condition deteriorated sharply, and from then on, he never spoke again.[79]

After the armed clashes at the Sino-Soviet border in early 1969, Mao was convinced of an imminent Soviet attack on China. He believed that the Soviets would use the talks on the border question which were to take place between the two countries in October 1969, as a smoke-screen to divert Chinese attention from their real intentions which was to launch a surprise attack on China. He decided to evacuate most leaders of the Party and the state from Beijing to other localities.[80] Liu

Shaoqi who was critically ill, was flown to Kaifeng in Henan on 17 October where he was kept in a room without furniture in an isolated, heavily guarded building and deprived of medical treatment. He died there on 12 November at the age of 71.[81]

4
THE GREAT CHAOS

The most striking feature of the period between the summer of 1966 and the summer of 1967 was disorder and confusion. This was not entirely accidental, since Mao himself had defined the creation of disorder which should later lead to the establishment of a new order, as the basic strategy of the CR at that time.[1] Disorder, to Mao, was the major means of effectively implementing the criticism of the bourgeois reactionary line promoted by Liu Shaoqi, and of promoting the 'revolutionary left' which, in Mao's view, had been suppressed by Liu's political line, a line which had been followed by most Party committees.

The invitation to create disorder was echoed by Lin Biao, who explained to members of the CCRG on 8 August, 1966, that it should have a dimension which would 'turn sky and earth upside down'.[2] Mao reiterated this policy at a central working conference on 23 August:

> The principal question is, what policy should we adopt regarding the so-called disturbances in various areas. My view is that we should let disorder reign for a few months. . . . Even if there are no provincial Party committees, it does not matter; aren't there still prefectural and county committees?[3]

The new mass organisations formed by the red guards in middle schools and universities, which emerged principally during the second half of 1966, and the revolutionary rebels who established themselves during the winter of 1966-7, became the instruments for the creation of disorder. They served Mao 'to expose our dark aspects openly, in an all-round way and from below'.[4] But they were by no means homogeneous organisations. As we shall see, deep cleavages existed among them reflecting fundamental divisions in society as a whole. The turbulence they created was not only a result of their opposition to revisionist policies but, in many cases, it mirrored violent factionalism in their midst.

The emergence of mass organisations

The emergence of mass organisations of red guards and rebels in the early stages of the CR was a phenomenon which was entirely new in Chinese politics and deeply interrelated with this movement. These mass organisations were fundamentally different from those already existing in China, such as the Youth League, the trade unions, the Women's Association and a limited number of 'democratic parties' which were established after the founding of the PR and functioned under the CCP's direct control. Red guard and rebel organisations not only escaped the control of the Party but aimed at the destruction of the Party apparatus. While they emerged as spontaneous organisations, with Mao's encouragement, they were soon flourishing.

The red guard and rebel movement was relatively short lived. But during its height, it developed its own momentum, quickly outlasting its usefulness for Mao. Red guards and rebels became the scapegoats for the disorder they had been encouraged to create and ended up as victims of the CR.

The veteran red guards

During May 1966, attacks against the *'Three-family Village* anti-Party clique' were raging everywhere in criticism meetings. At the same time, Mao's personality cult was promoted by the official media, and the enlarged meeting of the Politburo – the purpose of which was to purge Peng Zhen, Yang Shangkun, Luo Ruiqing and Lu Dingyi – was in full action.

But skirmishes at leadership level could not be kept entirely secret. A small group of students at one of Beijing's most prestigious high schools,[5] attended primarily by the offspring of high-ranking cadres, had discovered that a serious political struggle was taking place behind the scene. According to their understanding, not only people like Deng Tuo, Liao Mosha, and Wu Han but some other high-ranking Party officials were equally opposed to Chairman Mao. In the heady wave of mass hysteria, created by the personality cult of Mao, the youngsters held a meeting on 29 May where they pledged actively to defend Mao Zedong Thought and the cause of the proletariat. The date of their meeting was later projected as the birthday of the red guard movement.[6]

On 2 June, a big character poster entitled 'Red Guards' appeared in the Qinghua middle school proclaiming: 'We are the red guards to safeguard the Red political power. The Party centre and Chairman Mao are our mainstay.' . . . 'We will shed our last drop of blood to protect the party centre and our great leader Chairman Mao' and 'we shall carry the Great Proletarian Cultural Revolution resolutely to its end.'[7] The Qinghua middle-school poster, since it was the first response to Nie Yuanzi's poster at Beijing University, attracted widespread attention. While more than one hundred middle-school students signed their names to it, many others went to Beida and Qinghua middle schools to read the posters. The middle schools attached to Beida, the Geological Institute, the Petroleum Institute, the Mining Institute, the August 1 School and the Beijing 25 Middle School followed Qinghua's example, and also set up red guards organisations. This initiated a wave of movements, throughout Beijing's schools, for establishing similar organisations.

The first issue with which the red guards preoccupied themselves was educational reform. Mao had made a series of statements to this effect since 1964, the central theme of which was that the education system was 'divorced from reality', that there were too many subjects on the syllabus, and that examinations were 'a surprise attack'. In his 7 May letter to Lin Biao, Mao suggested that 'the school term should be shortened, education should be revolutionised, and the domination of our schools by bourgeois intellectuals should not be allowed to continue'.[8]

In response to Mao's call, the middle-school students began to criticise the school authorities who were following established educational standards, and demanded thorough changes in the school system. Since in the course of the rebellion, excesses had occurred – excesses that had seriously hampered the normal functioning of the schools – work teams were dispatched to the middle schools. They condemned red guard activities as illegal and some of the organisations, suspected of underground counter-revolutionary activities, were forced to dissolve.[9]

A large number of red guards refused to be intimidated. On 24 June, a big character poster appeared at Qinghua middle school which, under the title of 'Long Live the Proletarian Revolutionary Spirit', proclaimed their authors' determination 'to smash the old world to pieces'. On 4 July, they put up another poster entitled 'More on the proletarian revolutionary spirit' in which they emphasised Mao's teaching on rebellion.[10] The two posters came to the attention of Mao, who felt that the red guard organisations would serve his purpose of creating 'great disorder under heaven'. After his invalidation of work-team policies, he adopted a series of measures to promote the red guard movement. On 1 August, Mao wrote a letter to the Qinghua middle-school red guards saying: 'It is justified to rebel against reactionaries. I offer you my warm support.' This letter and the two Qinghua posters were distributed as official documents at the 11th Plenum of the CC which was in session during the month of August.[11] The 16 points adopted by the 11th Plenum on 8 August, also contained a statement in support of the red guards which emphasised that 'large numbers of revolutionary young people, previously unknown, have become courageous and daring path breakers'.[12]

But it was the official sanctioning of the red guard organisations at Tiananmen Square on 18 August that gave an important impetus to their movement. At the mass rally, initiated by Mao to celebrate the successful conclusion of the 11th Plenum, the movement received the green light to mobilise the country for the CR. The rally at which a million people had gathered, acted as a catalyst to the proliferation of the red guard movement. Flanked by a group of jubilant young students, Mao allowed them to put a red guard arm band on his arm. This symbolic gesture was the supreme mark of recognition which resulted in the establishment of red guard organisations throughout the country. But this important event also became a demarcation line within the red guard movement. Those who had already established their organisations before 18

August, called themselves veteran red guards to distinguish themselves from those who joined the movement after that date. The veteran red guards remained the most influential group within the movement and, during its tidal wave, took the lead in most of its operations.[13]

The veteran red guards, a small number among the millions of rank-and-file red guards, were born around the date of the founding of the PR. At the beginning of the CR, they were about sixteen to eighteen years old. Their families belonged to the 'five red categories' of workers, peasants, revolutionary cadres, revolutionary soldiers and revolutionary martyrs. But most veteran red guards were really the offspring of high-ranking Party, government and army officials, and thus represented the elite within the social strata of society.

To demonstrate their superiority, veteran red guards invoked the 'theory of blood lineage' which they expressed through the rhyme: 'if the father is a hero, the son will be a brave man; if the father is a reactionary, the son will be a scoundrel' (*laozi yingxiong er haohan, laozi fandong er hundan*).[14] This couplet which first appeared in the middle school attached to the Beijing Aeronautical Engineering Institute on 29 July 1966, became a central issue of debate among the students, driving them into two opposing groups formed on the basis of family background.[15]

Considering themselves as the vanguard of the CR, the red guards, led by the 'veterans', took to the streets and started a wave of 'red terror' that shook the country and that attracted the attention of the whole world. Following Lin Biao's call at the mass rally to 'strike down all ghosts and monsters' and to 'eradicate all old ideas, old culture, old customs and old habits of the exploiting classes', they focused their attention on the eradication of the 'four olds', the meaning of which was interpreted at random. At first, red guards began to destroy name plates of streets and stores which reminded them of the 'four olds' and replaced them by new ones. The main street in the former Legation Quarters was renamed 'anti-imperialist road' (*fandi lu*); the street housing the Soviet Embassy became the 'anti-revisionist road' (*fanxiu lu*), the old Dongan (eastern peace) market became the Dongfeng (east wind) market, since the east wind represented socialism and the west wind capitalism. The middle school, attached to Qinghua university, received the name of 'red guard militant school'.[16]

The *People's Daily* congratulated the red guards for these actions in a front-page article[17] and complimented 'the young red guard fighters' who 'are sweeping away the dust of all the old ideas, culture customs and habits of the exploiting classes'.[18] This explicit official encouragement of vandalism led the red guards to destroy historical monuments and cultural relics. In Beijing, which has 6,843 classified historical sites, 4,922 of them were damaged or destroyed during the months of August and September, 1966. Numerous valuable old books, paintings and other cultural relics were burnt to ashes. In Beijing, in a little more than one month, 33,695 households were ransacked by red guards who destroyed everything they believed to be a symbol of bourgeois and feudal ideas. In Shanghai, the number of households attacked was even higher, amounting to 84,222. In Beijing, the imperial palace had to be closed to avoid destruction.[19]

In response to the call to 'strike down all ghosts and monsters' issued on 1 June 1966, red guards began to single out the 'five black category elements',[20] whom they believed to be 'ghosts and monsters'. Their aim was to drive them out of the city so that Beijing could become a 'clean' socialist capital. A total of 85,198 persons were declared undesirable and forced to live in the countryside.[21] During this movement, violence escalated. People were beaten with belt buckles, sometimes to their death. In Beijing's suburbs, incidents of violence appeared to be more ruthless than in the city. In Daxing county, 'undesirable elements' were simply killed. In a few days between late August and early September, 325 persons, the oldest 80 years old, the youngest only 38 days old, met their death at the hands of red guards.[22]

On 29 August, the *People's Daily* published another editorial entitled 'Salute to Our Red Guards' legitimising once more the red guards' atrocities. It pointed out that 'none of the old parasites hidden in dark corners can escape the sharp eyes of the Red Guards' who 'are pulling out the bloodsuckers, these enemies of the people one by one'.[23]

This type of official encouragement added more fuel to the already over-heated mass hysteria of the red guards who soon began to expand the scope of their witch hunt beyond the 'five black categories' to people who belonged to the 'grey zone' between the 'five black' and the 'five red' categories. Many intellectuals and artists became victims of this phase of the 'red terror'. Well-known writers, scholars, painters, singers, dancers and actors were condemned as revisionists and subjected to severe humiliation. According to statistics (which remain incomplete), in the 17 provinces and municipalities, 140,000 people working in the educational sector were persecuted. A total of 7,682 died under torture or due to maltreatment. In the ministry of culture alone, 2,600 persons were persecuted to death. In the medical colleges attached to the Ministry of Public Health, 556 of 674 professors and assistant professors were persecuted, and 36 died under torture.[24]

The destruction of feudal and bourgeois culture was only a part of the aim Mao wanted to achieve with the mass movement. The second, and to him the most important, was class struggle which implied the confrontation and the denunication of revisionist officials. The struggle against Party representatives who were following revisionist policies did not, however, proceed with the vigour Mao expected. Most Party leaders in the provinces resisted the red guard movement in the areas under their jurisdiction. After its legitimacy had been established, local Party leaders switched tactics and encouraged the formation of red guard organisations supporting the local Party establishment. As part of the strategy to create a viable mass movement that would efficaciously carry out the class struggle, the central leadership encouraged travels to and from Beijing of red guards, a policy which was called 'exchange of revolutionary experiences'. A major purpose of this policy was to break the control by the local leadership over the mass movements they had themselves promoted.[25]

Mao himself had fuelled this policy by declaring in June, that students who wanted to go to Beijing should be allowed to do so and should have free trips. Chen Boda at a meeting with students from outside Beijing on 16 August, confirmed this. On 5 September, the CC and the State Council sent out a joint circular to inform the entire country that all university and college students and representatives of middle-school students (one out of ten) could come to Beijing. Their expenses for travel, food and accommodation, they were informed, would be covered by the state.[26] Millions of students followed the call. Middle-school students did not send representatives; they arrived themselves in Beijing. From August 18 to 26 November, the 73-year-old Mao reviewed 13 million red guards and teachers from all over the country which pushed the red guard movement to a peak.

After visiting the capital, the red guards travelled to other areas of their choice to exchange revolutionary experiences. The massive flow of students to and from Beijing not only strained the transportation system but also created logistical problems such as housing and feeding them. In Beijing, schools, universities and public buildings were periodically transformed into dormitories and their canteens were ordered to feed the red guards. The situation became more serious as the winter approached, since heating and especially additional bedding had to be provided. The authorities tried to put a halt to these massive movements and issued orders to this effect. But students, though in decreasing numbers, continued to roam around the country until 1968.[27]

University red guards

University red guards established their organisations after Mao had officially sanctioned the movement of the middle-school red guards at Tiananmen Square on 18 August. From the very beginning they were factionalised. Family background played an important role in determining the rifts that existed among them. As in the case of the veteran red guards, the faction which later was referred to as conservative, was composed mainly of people who, due to their family background, belonged to the privileged strata of Chinese society. Many persons among that faction were sons and daughters of high- or medium-ranking cadres. Many were already Party members or, alternatively, if they had not reached this stage – were youth league members – a stepping-stone towards Party membership. Their social origins gave them great advantage over other persons of their age. As their families represented the vested interests within society, they were not prepared to accept the destruction of the prevailing order through social upheaval. Transformation of society threatened their very existence and that of their family.[28]

The radicals looked at things differently. They did not have a 'good' family background and enjoyed no particular privileges. Most of them were not members of the youth league or the Party – clearly a serious disadvantage in a society which had erected an invisible wall between those who were Party members and those who were not and which considered non-Party members as second-class citizens. Their response to Mao's call to the masses to liberate themselves, to think for themselves and to repudiate reactionary academic authorities was different. They saw in it as an unexpected opportunity to express their resentment against a social order which they considered repressive.[29]

The issue that decisively caused the rift between conservatives and radicals was Liu Shaoqi's decision to use work teams to stabilise and bring under control the increasingly disruptive situation engendered by the radical students. The conservative faction supported the work teams actively and often cooperated with them to single out 'sham leftists and real rightists'.

Why was it that after the official condemnation of work teams policies, radicals remained a minority, and a large number of university red guards continued to defend work teams and school authorities and to attack those who followed Mao's instructions according to which 'to revolt was justified'? The major reason was that the general norm of conduct was to obey the Party, not to oppose it, a norm that had become deeply ingrained by many years of indoctrination. Moreover, in July and August, the majority of the students were unaware of the extent of the attacks Mao was planning against Liu Shaoqi, Deng Xiaoping and a large number of other high-ranking cadres.[30]

By the end of August and during the autumn of 1966, Mao's intentions became much more evident. He and his proletarian headquarters clearly encouraged the middle-school red guards to rampage the streets, and gave continuous support to the radicals minorities in universities and other institutes of higher learning.[31] Official criticism of work teams who were accused of having organised 'counter-attacks against the masses' continued with increased emphasis.[32] A *People's Daily* editorial warned the authorities at local and unit level not to try to protect themselves by hoodwinking workers and peasants to struggle against revolutionary students.[33] This strengthened the position of the minority considerably.

Encouraged by the official support, the radical minority escalated their attacks against the work teams, requesting that the material collected during the 'white terror' be restored and that work-team leaders return to the schools to make self-criticism.[34] The ministerial authorities were reluctant to allow their people, usually high-ranking cadres, to return to the students who intended to subject them to humiliating and often violent struggle meetings. But the students persevered in their demands and staged sit-ins in front of the ministries or attempted to break in to abduct the person they wanted. Students from the Beijing Institute of Geology, for example, broke into the ministry of geology four times between late August and October with the intention to capture Zhou Jiayu, a vice minister who, as the work-team leader at their institute, had condemned a number of students. They finally succeeded in abducting him and staged struggle sessions against him.[35] The minority students at the Beijing Aeronautical Engineering Institute held a 28-day sit-in before the National Defence Commission to claim Zhao Ruzhang, a bureau director within the commission. The situation created such a stalemate that it was brought to Mao's attention. Mao intervened in favour of the students and Zhao was finally turned over to them.[36]

The emergence in August and September of three headquarters marked the organisational division of the red guards at university level. While the first and second headquarters belonged to the majority or conservative faction, the third represented the minority or radicals, most of whom had been suppressed by the Liu-Deng line.[37]

When Lin Biao, on the occasion of the National Day of 1 October 1966, issued a call on behalf of Mao to criticise and repudiate Liu Shaoqi's bourgeois reactionary line, the third headquarters and other radical red guard organisations were the first to respond to his appeal. On 6 October, the third headquarters held a rally with 100,000 people to start the attack on the bourgeois line. Zhou Enlai, Chen Boda, Kang Sheng, Jiang Qing and a number of other leaders extended official recognition and support to the third headquarters by participating in the rally.[38] As a result, the ranks of the radical red guards increased considerably. In some cases, organisations under the first and second headquarters were dissolved and its members joined the ranks of the third headquarters, in others, they tried to adapt to the changing situation and to follow the third headquarters as closely as possible.

As the radical organisations grew, five leaders emerged among them: Nie Yuanzi, head of the New Beida Commune; Kuai Dafu, leader of the Qinghua University Jinggangshan Red Guard Corps; Han Aijing, leader of the Beijing Aeronautical Engineering Institute Red Flag Militant Brigade; Wang Dabing, leader of the Beijing Institute of Geology East is Red Commune; Tan Houlan, leader of the Beijing Teachers' University Jinggangshan Militant Corps.[39] These five leaders, considered as the vanguard of the CR, became blind instruments in the hands of leading radicals in their goal of eliminating their political opponents. They were in direct contact with the CCRG who guided their activities. On several occasions, the CCRG sent them on special missions. Jiang Qing and Zhang Chunqiao sent Nie Yuanzi to Shanghai where she was to take part in the organisation of the radicals' attack on the Shanghai Municipal Party Committee in November 1966. Kuai Dafu was chosen to lead the attack on Liu Shaoqi.[40] Tan Houlan was given the mission to destroy the Confucius Temple in Shandong province and to launch an attack on the State Council and on Zhou Enlai who had decreed that the temple was a historical monument which should be protected. Other red guard organisations in Beijing and elsewhere closely observed the movements of the five leaders who personified the policy trend to be followed.[41]

The CCRG also manipulated red guard organisations outside Beijing. The red guards of Nankai University in Tianjin, for example, received specific instructions to cooperate with those from the Beijing Aeronautical Engineering Institute to uncover 'renegades' among high Party officials.[42] Radical red guards from Beijing were dispatched to other localities in order 'to kindle the flames of the CR'. Their major task was to incite local radical red guards to rebel against the authorities. Local radicals tended to treat them like 'imperial envoys' from the capital.[43]

The 'December black wind'

The CCRG's outspoken support of the radical factions and the escalation of the campaign to criticise the bourgeois reactionary line in the fall of 1966, left the conservatives in an awkward position. The campaign soon developed into an indiscriminate attack on Party officials at all levels. As this affected the families of the majority of conservative red guards, they began to revolt against the campaign and to openly protest against the activities of the CCRG whom they accused of 'serious mistakes of orientation and line' and of 'splitting the ranks of the masses'. In numerous Beijing colleges, big character posters appeared carrying the titles: 'Questioning the CCRG'; 'the CCRG's erroneous line must be criticised'; 'Kick away the CCRG, follow Chairman Mao'; 'Drag out the real bourgeois conspirators around Chairman Mao', etc.[44]

In December 1966, the attacks against the CCRG reached a culmination point with the activities of the 'Committee of United Action of Beijing Red Guards' (Lian Dong), the most aggressive among the conservative red guard groups. This organisation was established on 5 December, by veteran red guards from Qinghua middle school. These young people, 16 to 17 years of age, had been the vanguard of the red guard movement and the CR since the summer. They had been instrumental in destroying the 'four olds' and in attacking the 'five black categories'. But, since the evolution of the campaign against the bourgeois reactionary line threatened their families, they, with the support of the veteran cadres and, implicitly that of Zhou Enlai, began to oppose all attacks on the veteran revolutionaries.[45] They rallied behind them some five hundred red guard organisations in Beijing, Shanghai and other major cities to oppose 'the new form of bourgeois reactionary line' which they believed was threatening the achievements of the Chinese revolution.[46] They challenged the third headquarters, whose members were older and much more numerous, in a series of debates questioning the criticism of veteran cadres. In protest at the arrest of some of their members, they attacked the building of the Ministry of Public Security three times. They became increasingly aggressive against the CCRG, who, in their view, 'did neither represent Chairman Mao . . . nor the party centre'. In early January they even began to cast some doubt on Mao's present policies stating that they were 'loyal to Marxism-Leninism and to pre–1960 Mao Zedong Thought'.[47]

Lian Dong developed into a spearhead of resistance to the CR. At first, it was called the 'defending Dad and Mum faction'. Later, the Maoist leadership took them more seriously and Xie Fuzhi, the Minister of Public Security, condemned them as a counter-revolutionary organisation having fanned the 'December black wind'. On 21 January, Beijing middle-school red guards held a mass rally to 'thoroughly criticise and repudiate Lian Dong'. Their bases in a number of middle schools were destroyed by red guards loyal to the CCRG, and core members of Lian Dong were arrested. Examples of 'Lian Dong crimes' committed during the months of 'red terror' were shown in a public exhibition. The vanguard of the red guards collapsed after only a few months of existence.[48]

The revolutionary rebels

After Mao's legitimisation of the red guard movement at the rally at Tiananmen Square on 18 August 1966, red guard organisations began to appear everywhere in China. They emerged not only in schools but also among workers and office personnel. Persons with a family background of the 'five red categories', irrespective of their age, felt particularly encouraged to put on an arm band and to become self-appointed red guards. At a time when the 'theory of blood lineage' determined a person's social prestige, they felt certain of being able to play a significant role in the CR. But before long, the authorities decided that red guards had to be confined to schools and universities and that all red guard organisations in factories and other institutions should be dissolved.[49]

However, with the evolution of the mass criticism against Liu and Deng, the need for an organisational form to channel the movement within work units, governmental and non-governmental organisations became increasingly apparent. The call, in October, to repudiate bourgeois power holders in the Party, induced at first a timid, then an increasingly vociferous response and, in late 1966 and early 1967, gave rise to groupings of 'revolutionary rebels' in different work units.

Unlike the veteran red guards, the first groups of rebels neither had a distinguished class background nor a sense of political superiority. In the past, they had often failed to demonstrate political zeal.[50] The majority were not Party members, and many of them were considered 'politically inferior' before the CR. In many cases, they had been under investigation during Liu Shaoqi's June campaign to 'wipe out all ghosts and monsters' although they were neither 'Party persons in power travelling the capitalist road', nor 'reactionary academic authorities' which were the official targets at that time.

There were also a few 'progressive' Party members and cadres among the early rebels. The major motives for their participation in the rebellion were often personal conflicts with, or resentment against, the authorities in their own work units.[51] All these groups, in joining the ranks of the rebels, for the first time, were able to vent their grievances against a system they considered bureaucratic, authoritarian and at times even repressive.

The rebels, encouraged by the widening campaign against Liu Shaoqi's bourgeois policies, individually or in groups, wrote posters to denounce what they considered as the reactionary line implemented by the leadership of their units. But as their number was small and, until the end of 1966, had not received much official support, they did not represent a serious threat to Party committees.

It was only after the establishment, on 9 November 1966, of the general headquarters of Shanghai workers' revolutionary rebels headed by Wang Hongwen, that the rebel movement gathered momentum.[52] The general headquarters defined opposition of the municipal Party committee as its major objective. Since the municipal Party committee refused to recognise their organisation,[53] the workers general headquarters, on 10 November sent a delegation to Beijing to plead their case and to establish their legitimacy. At Anting, a locality in the outskirts of Shanghai, the municipal authorities stopped the train in which the delegation was travelling. The incident led to serious clashes between the rebels and their opponents which interrupted the Shanghai-Nanjing railroad for more than 30 hours.[54]

The 'Anting event' added fuel to the CCRG's determination to support the rebel workers against the Shanghai Party committee. Using the Anting event as an example of suppression of the revolutionary masses, the group, on 16 November, obtained Mao's approval to recognise the workers general headquarters as a 'legitimate revolutionary organisation'.[55]

Mao's decision ushered in a debate on the question of establishing mass organisations in the industrial and communication sectors, which took place at a meeting of Party and government leaders engaged in industrial and communicational planning at central and provincial levels from the middle of November to early December in Beijing. Many participants expressed their opposition to the establishment of such organisations which, they feared, might bring about disruptions of the production process. But the members of the CCRG, eager to accelerate the CR within the industrial and communication sectors, insisted on the workers' right to their own organisations. Mao's final decision, on 22 November, that workers should be supported in their attempt to establish organisations, paved the way not only for workers but also for employees of all trades, including the government sector, to establish mass organisations, to which they gave colourful revolutionary names.[56]

All of these organisations claimed their loyalty to Mao Zedong Thought, but were, from the very beginning, characterised by factionalism which divided them into radical and conservative sections respectively referred to as 'revolutionary rebels' and 'proletarian revolutionaries'. This choice of names implied a subtle difference indicating that proletarian revolutionaries could look back on the history of the Chinese revolution whereas to rebel was a new phenomenon.

Among the numerous mass organisations that had emerged at the end of 1966, the two most famous were the Shanghai general headquarters of rebels (radical) and the Shanghai workers scarlet guards defending Mao Zedong Thought (conservative) who supported the municipal Party committee. The same basic pattern emerged throughout China. By the end of 1966, rebels were battering against Party, government and military organs criticising cadres at all levels. Because of the criticism of power holders, the broad ranks of the people, for the first time, were able to give vent to their pent-up grievances against their superiors who had hitherto been protected from all criticism by a system which did not permit the questioning of decisions of leaders at any level. The conservatives, on their part, maintained a cautious attitude towards Party organisations, but expressed reservations against the CCRG who gave firm support to rebel organisations.

The CR brought thus out into the open a deep cleavage in society between those who had a vested interest in the system and those who felt oppressed by it. Confrontations between radicals and conservatives aggravated during the phase of 'power seizure' in January 1967 which, during the months to follow, evolved into a nationwide civil war like strife which reached its peak during the summer. The rebels had indeed created the 'great disorder' which Mao had desired. When Mao decided to re-establish order, the political tide turned against the rebels who became the targets of most of the ensuing campaigns.

The seizure of power

The seizure of power in January 1967 undoubtedly was a unique event in the history of the People's Republic. It was a nationwide movement, which called on people of all walks of life to overthrow the existing organs of power and to seize power for themselves. But at the same time, Mao also had defined the form of a new order to be established. After the process of seizing power was completed, Mao's strategy was to realise 'great alliances' in the form of revolutionary committees representing a 'three-in-one combination' of mass organisations, veteran cadres and the military. These committees were expected to be the centre of the mass criticism of revisionism represented by Liu Shaoqi. The seizure of power, in Mao's view, represented the organisational and political overthrow of Liu's line, while the continuation of mass criticism of Liu's line would be its ideological overthrow. In the course of this process, disorder would give way to order, and Mao would be able to convene the 9th Party Congress sometimes in 1968 to wind up the CR.

The concept of power seizure was inspired by the events in Shanghai where revolutionary mass organisations had overthrown the municipal Party committee and government. In Mao's view, the actions of the Shanghai rebels were an example to be emulated, and he declared seizure of power as a decisive battle of the CR, fought by the 'great alliance' of revolutionary mass organisations.

Mao's major reason for adopting such a daring and unorthodox policy was his dissatisfaction with the manner in which the CR had hitherto evolved. Several months had elapsed since the CR was officially launched. Though the movement unfolded on a grand and spectacular scale – with the destruction of the 'four olds' and the paralysis of Party structures, particularly at schools and universities – it encountered firm resistance from most Party committees. In Mao's view, red guards alone were not able to implement the policy of recrimination against the bourgeois reactionary line, and revolutionary rebels among workers and employees needed to be strengthened to give the movement the necessary impetus. Power seizures by revolutionary rebels in their respective work units were expected to provide the necessary basis for reform of society which Mao considered to be characterised by excessive bureaucracy and privileges of the power holders. In his view, 'the Marxist principle of smashing the existing state machine must be put into practice in the struggle for the seizure of power'.[57] And he believed that an entirely new state machine would be built up on the debris of the old one.

The concept of power seizure was a relatively recent one. It was not mentioned in the May 16 circular which provided the guidelines for the CR. The circular stated that 'those representatives of the bourgeoisie who had sneaked into the Party, the government, the army and all spheres of culture' should be discovered and 'some of them' should be 'transferred to other positions'.[58] The 16 points ordered the dismissal 'from their leading posts of all those in authority who are taking the capitalist road and to make possible the recapture of the leadership by the proletarian revolutionaries'.[59] Both documents refer to the removal of individuals, not to an overall seizure of power.

The first attempt to seize power took place in Shanghai, where radical workers were well represented and where they had already begun to engage in intense controversies with the Party establishment. On 30 December 1966, the radical 'workers' headquarters' defeated the conservative faction, the 'scarlet guards' in an armed fight during which 240 core members of the scarlet guards were captured. In protest, a large number of them went on strike.[60]

Their strike action spread out to other workers who, in addition to the two large organisations, had established more than 70 smaller organisations, among them organisations of contract workers, of workers returning to Shanghai from the countryside, and of apprentices, all of them concerned with their own immediate economic benefits. Contract workers demanded to be fully state employed; workers who had been sent to the countryside in the early 1960s demanded their reintegration into the city; and apprentices insisted on the right to be accepted as regular workers. Entering municipal offices by force, these different groups demanded compensation for the economic losses they had endured over the years.[61]

On the eve of the New Year, vast sectors of industry and communications were paralysed by the striking workers. On the Shanghai-Nanjing railroad, 57 cargo and passenger trains were blocked with more than a thousand passengers suffering from hunger and cold. In the Shanghai harbour, about a hundred ships waited for unloading. More than a thousand factories functioned with limited capacity or stopped working altogether. The city's coal reserves were so low that a general stoppage of the power supply was expected within days.[62]

Under the mounting pressure, the municipal authorities finally agreed to grant wage increases, allowances and subsidies. But in spite of their concessions, the municipal Party committee and government were unable to control the situation, and helplessly stood by as rebellious workers took over public buildings, and the two largerst workers organisations continued to clash in the streets.

The revolutionary rebels construed the strikes initiated by the conservative faction and the inability of the municipal authorities to resist the workers as a coalition between persons in power taking the capitalist road and conservative forces sabotaging production, and demanded the overthrow of the municipal Party committee.

On 3 January, Zhang Chunqiao and Yao Wenyuan met Wang Hongwen, the leader of the Shanghai workers' headquarters in Beijing. According to Zhang, Shanghai was at a historical turning point. It was the opportunity to achieve 'great order through great disorder'. He added, 'Chen Pixian (first secretary of the Shanghai Party committee) is not able to bring the chaos in Shanghai under control. January 1967 will be the historical moment for the Shanghai revolutionaries to seize power from the capitalist roaders.'[63]

Zhang and Yao flew to Shanghai on 4 January to transmit to the municipal Party committee a directive Mao had issued on the 2nd of the month. According to this document, 'the fall of Chen Pixian and Cao Diqiu (Mayor of Shanghai) had been decided by the general course of events. A new political authority will be established in Shanghai'. Zhang announced that 'the rebels from the municipal party offices would be the working group for the new authorities'.⁶⁴

On 4 January radical rebels of the *Wen Hui Bao* declared in their newspapers that they had seized power. The following day, rebels of the *Shanghai Liberation Daily* followed suit and took over their paper.⁶⁵ Zhang and Yao supported these initiatives and pointed out to leaders of the workers' headquarters that 'to seize power from the leadership is the fundamental problem. Persons in power taking the capitalist road should be singled out and overthrown.'⁶⁶ On the same day (January 5) 11 rebel organisations headed by the workers' general headquarter published a 'message to all Shanghai people' in *Wen Hui Bao*, which attributed the responsibility for the economic chaos to the Shanghai authorities who had enticed the scarlet guards to 'undermine production and sabotage transport and communications' and to 'cut off water and electricity supply and bring public transport to a standstill'. The message demanded that the scarlet guards return to their work.⁶⁷ On 6 January, the rebel organisations mobilised 100,000 people in a mass rally where they made three announcements. Firstly, the Shanghai revolutionary rebels and revolutionary masses no longer recognised Chen Pixian and Cao Diqiu as the secretary of the Party committee and the mayor of Shanghai.⁶⁸ Secondly, they intended to submit a note to Chairman Mao and the Party centre suggesting that Cao be dismissed from all his posts and subjected to manual labour under the 'supervision of the masses'. Chen Pixian should confess his crimes of resisting and sabotaging the CR. Thirdly, a report should be submitted to the Party centre suggesting the reorganisation of the Shanghai Party committee, pending which all members of the Party committee other than Chen and Cao should remain at their posts.⁶⁹

The rally of 6 January, generally considered the day of the power seizure in Shanghai, was followed by other actions.⁷⁰ On 9 January, 32 rebel organisations issued an 'urgent notice' in ten points to combat economism and promote production. According to the notice, all strikes should terminate; government and enterprises should freeze their funds except for the expenditure needed for production and for the normal functioning of offices; matters related to readjustment of wages and material benefit would be dealt with at a later stage; seizure of public buildings was prohibited.

At a Politburo meeting on 8 January, Mao, who closely observed the events in Shanghai, referred to the power seizure at the two major Shanghai newspapers as an example of 'one class overthrowing another' and a 'great revolution'. He emphasised that revolution could not be made without promoting production, and predicted that 'since the revolutionary forces in Shanghai have arisen, the entire country has a future. This event will influence not only the East China region, but all provinces and municipalities in the country.'[72]

Mao gave instructions to reprint the 'message to all Shanghai people' in the *People's Daily* along with an editorial note cleared by him. The editorial emphasised the 'great importance' of the message which 'resolutely responds to Chairman Mao's great call to take firm hold of the revolution and prompt production', the 'key question in the Great Proletarian CR'. Referring to the power seizure at *Wen Hui Bao* and the *Liberation Daily*, the editorial repeated Mao's views, stating that 'this is a great revolution. This great event will certainly play a tremendous role in pushing ahead the development of the movement of the Great Proletarian CR throughout east China and in all the cities and provinces in other parts of the country.'[73]

The 'urgent notice' of 9 January, also caught Mao's attention. The fact that the conservatives had deserted their posts and that the rebels seemed determined to avoid economic disruptions convinced him that the CR could be carried out while simultaneously ensuring the functioning of the economy. As a result, he expressed even more support for the Shanghai rebels by instructing the *People's Daily* to reprint the 'urgent notice' and by sending, on 11 January, a 'message of greetings to revolutionary rebel organisations in Shanghai', which was signed by the CC, the State Council, the Military Commission and the CCRG. This official message complimented the Shanghai rebels for 'having formulated a correct policy in accordance with Chairman Mao's principle of "taking firm hold of the revolution and promoting production" and opposing economism'.[74]

This message of greetings was a most unusual endorsement of the Shanghai rebel activities. Mao's explicit support of the

Shanghai rebels demonstrated his desire to maintain order in the economic sector which, at the end of 1966, had begun to show signs of deterioration. Praising the Shanghai rebels as the 'path-breakers in production',[75] he projected them as the model to be emulated by revolutionary rebels throughout the country.

Mao's endorsement of the seizure of power in Shanghai paved the way for attacks on other municipal authorities. Paraphrasing an ancient Chinese proverb, Mao told Politburo members and the CCRG on 8 January: 'Do not think that, if butcher Zhang dies, we will have to eat pork meat with hair' (*Shi le Zhang tufu, jiu chi hun mao zhu*). In simple words, it meant that Party committees can be dispensed with.[76] On 16 January, Mao went a step further; he authorised the publication of a *Red Flag* article which, in effect, was an unequivocal official call to red guards and radical rebels to seize power throughout the country.[77] According to the article, 'to wrest power from these persons means the revolution of one class to overthrow another class . . . i.e. a revolution of the proletariat to overthrow the bourgeoisie'.[78] The call was repeated on 22 January in an editorial in the *People's Daily* which emphasised that the 'great call of Chairman Mao' to all people was 'to form a great alliance to seize power from those who are taking the capitalist road'.[79]

These 'instructions' were rather vague, for they neither contained guidelines about how to recognise those who travelled the capitalist road, nor did they indicate where power should be seized. Also they failed to specify the mass organisation that had the right to seize power. How to form great alliances was also not made explicit. The radical red guards perceived themselves to be the only group with real understanding of Mao's revolutionary line, and began to seize power everywhere in schools and in those Party and government organs accessible to them. Inspired by a *People's Daily* article which claimed that 'the great alliance requires a clear cut stand' and was not a 'hodge podge', they refused all cooperation with other factions.[80] Zhou Enlai also encouraged this trend by emphasising that 'those who seize power, must represent the real revolutionary left, must be revolutionary rebels. It should not be a sham seizure of power by the right, the conservatives or the middle-of-the-roaders.'[81]

The movement of power seizure expanded greatly. Red guards and revolutionary rebels attempted to overthrow the authorities and Party committees in their work units throughout the country. The first power seizures at provincial level took place in Shanxi on 14 January, in Guangdong and Jiansu on 22 January, in Guizhou on 25 January, in Anhui on 26 January, in Beijing on 28 January in Heilongjiang on 31 January.[82]

Power seizures also occurred at central government level. After the Shanghai events, revolutionary rebels in the ministries under the State Council and in CC departments announced their intention also to seize power. Since power seizures was officially sanctioned, this could hardly be avoided. However, to minimise disruptions that accompanied such seizures, Zhou Enlai issued a number of strict guidelines.

The power seizures were to be confined to the execution of the CR. The professional work of the ministries must not be interfered with though it could be supervised by the rebels. Zhou emphasised that the majority of the ministers and vice ministers would continue their work, though some perhaps with their title suspended; besides, supervision would stop at minister level. In order to minimise red guard influence, it was further stipulated that power could be seized by rebels from the ministries' staff with outsiders playing a subordinate role. Outside interference in the ministries of foreign affairs and of finance was to be completely avoided.[83]

When the movement reached its peak, red guard organisations from the ministerial systems made several attempts to participate in the power seizures in the ministries. For instance, the red guards from the Beijing Petroleum Engineering Institute and from the Chemical Engineering Institute broke into the ministry of petroleum industry and the ministry of chemical industry to assist in the power seizure. The Beijing Institute of Law and Political Science dispatched its red guards to seize power in the Beijing Public Security Bureau. In these and other cases of interference, the rebels of the ministerial staff resisted the attempts at outside involvement. In a few instances, as in the case of the ministry of higher education where rebel organisations were too weak to control the red guards, military control was imposed.

The Party newspaper hailed these actions as 'an extremely

great pioneering undertaking', a 'great event without precedent in mankind's history, a great event which has bearing on the future of the world and the destiny of mankind'.[84] It is, however, doubtful that the red guards and rebels understood it that way. Their actions were influenced by two major factors. One was that such action – encouraged by Mao and his proletarian headquarters – gave credibility to their position as proletarian revolutionaries and denied it to the conservatives. Secondly, most radicals were eager to destroy bureaucracy and totalitarianism which, in their view, was characteristic of the rule of the party.

The February Adverse Current

The political ramifications of the power seizures were indeed significant. The disruptions and conflicts spilled over to the top of the Party hierarchy. Liu Shaoqi, Deng Xiaoping and large numbers of other moderate Party leaders were increasingly denigrated.

The marshal Zhu De and He Long came under vicious attacks of red guard organisations, especially those attached to the military colleges. Zhu De who, at the beginning of the CR, was already 80 years old, had been Mao's life-long comrade-in-arms as the commander-in-chief of the red army and the PLA. He Long was also a legendary army general. Both had maintained great influence and prestige in the PLA, a major cause of resentment for Lin Biao, who, in cooperation with the CCRG, instigated red guards to attack them. Only after Zhou Enlai's interference, Zhu De barely escaped a face-to-face struggle with the red guards.[85] With Mao's consent, He Long was arrested and was refused proper medical treatment; he died of diabetes on 9 June 1969.[86]

At the same time, a number of moderates within the CCRG also came under attack. Tao Zhu, one of its advisors, was among them. Of the four deputy heads, Jiang Qing and Zhang Chunqiao were radicals, while Wang Renzhong, secretary of the Hubei provincial Party committee and Liu Zhijian, deputy director of the PLA general political department and of the all army CRG were moderates. The differences between them and the radicals became so acute, that in January 67, all three were purged.[87] Also during January, a number of high-ranking Party leaders died due to the CR. The minister of coal, Zhang Linzhi, was beaten to death by revolutionary rebels.[88] The secretary of the Shanxi Party committee, Wei Heng, committed suicide after having been imprisoned and tortured by rebels. Yan Hongyan, secretary of the Yunnan provincial Party committee also killed himself when he was under attack by revolutionary red guards and rebels.[89]

The CR had taken a course which was bound to meet with some resistance among high-ranking leaders. In spite of their devotion to Mao, it could hardly be expected that they would passively consent to a policy which threatened their political and physical survival. In January and February, a number of military and government leaders expressed their anger with the policies implemented in the name of the CR. Although none of them would dare to affront Mao directly, they clearly articulated their disagreement with the activities of the CCRG. Their protest became known as the February Adverse Current. Mao referred to this event as the 'two uproars', the 'uproar at the Jingxi guest house' and the 'uproar at Huairentang', a meeting hall of the Politburo in Zhongnanhai.[90]

In January and during the first half of February, an enlarged meeting of the Military Commission was held at the Jingxi guest house. On 19 and 20 January, Marshall Nie Rongzhen and Marshall Xu Xiangqian, both vice chairmen of the military commission protested against the attempts of the CCRG to introduce the CR into the army. Marshal Ye Jianying, general secretary of the commission accused Jiang Qing and Zhang Chunqiao of encouraging red guards to attack high-ranking military cadres. During his speech, he banged the table with such anger that he broke his finger![91]

A Politburo meeting on 11 February at Huairentang, attended also by the CCRG, developed into a sharp dispute between Ye Jianying and Xu Xiangqian on the one side and Kang Sheng and Chen Boda on the other, over the issue of maintaining stability in the army. Zhou Enlai who presided over the meeting, succeeded in cutting their quarrel short by pointing out that the subject of the dispute was not on the agenda. At another Politburo meeting, on 16 February, the dispute escalated into a major clash between Politburo members and the CCRG. The meeting, again chaired by Zhou Enlai, was convened to discuss the economic situation. Present at the meeting were the Standing Committee members Chen Boda, Kang Sheng and Li Fuchun, the Politburo members Chen Yi and Li Xiannian, and Tan Zhenlin, Ye Jianying and Xie Fuzhi from the Central Secretariat. Yu Qiuli, vice premier in charge of economy and Wang Li, Zhang Chunqiao, Yao Wenyuan, members of the CCRG also participated.[92]

Regardless of the agenda, and before Zhou even declared the meeting open, the veteran cadres poured out their grievances against the CR which centred around three issues: should the CR be directed by the Party? Was it right to submit so many cadres, and especially veteran revolutionaries to attacks and humiliation? Should order and stability be maintained in the army?[93]

Tan Zhenlin, speaking with emotion and anger, took the lead in the debate. He emphasised that the CR should be conducted under the leadership of the Party and shouted 'To hell with the masses'. He accused the CCRG of 'wanting to overthrow all veteran cadres' emphasising that 'the 40 years of their revolutionary career end with a broken family, their wives and children separated from them'. He said that 'the present struggle is the most cruel that had ever taken place in the history of the Party', and added that he had to 'hide his tears from his secretary and his children'. Ready to leave the meeting, he stood up and shouted at the members of the CCRG: 'Do whatever you like. I have had enough of you. I quit. Cut off my head, put me into prison, expel me from the Party, I will fight to the end.'[94]

Li Xiannian followed suit wondering who would administer the country if all veteran cadres were overthrown. He pointed out that the practice of obtaining confessions by coercion was widespread and that the situation had been out of control since the publication of the *Red Flag* issue 13, which had encouraged criticism and repudiation of the bourgeois reactionary line.[95] At this point Zhou Enlai asked why an editorial of such importance had not been submitted to the Politburo prior to publication.[96]

Chen Yi pointed out that people like Liu Shaoqi, Peng Zhen, Bo Yibo, Liu Lantao and An Ziwen all had supported Mao. He said: 'They never opposed Chairman Mao'. Referring to the Yanan rectification campaign, he said sarcastically. 'We were the ones who opposed the Chairman at that time and needed to be reformed. Was the Premier not also reformed? Now history has proved who opposed the Chairman. [None of us did.] It will continue to prove it. Stalin gave power to Khrushchev who in the end, became a revisionist.'[97] Ye Jianying and Yu Qiuli spoke according to the same line. The members of the CCRG listened to the accusations without uttering a word. Zhou Enlai finally adjourned the meeting which had lasted three hours without coming to the issues on the agenda.

As soon as the meeting was adjourned, Zhang Chunqiao, Yao Wenyuan and Wang Li reported to Jiang Qing about the events. Jiang Qing decided to inform Mao who, the same evening, listened to their report. Hearing about the outbursts of the veteran cadres, he began to smile. 'Some old soldiers just spoke some angry words', he said. 'I have not heard them, you also have not heard them.' But his attitude changed when Chen Yi's remarks about the Yanan rectification campaign and his references to Khrushchev were reported to him.[98] At midnight on the 18th, he called a meeting with Zhou Enlai, Ye Qun (who represented Lin Biao), Kang Sheng, Li Fuchun, Ye Jianying, Li Xiannian and Xie Fuzhi. Mao firmly declared that some people had finally shown their true colours with regard to the CR. 'What does it mean', he asked, 'when you say the CR rejects the leadership of the Party? What kind of leadership do you want? Should Wang Ming be invited to come back? The CCRG is following the resolution of the 11th Plenum. They have made some mistakes, but they amount to 1, 2, or 3 per cent. Ninety-seven per cent of their actions were correct.' He accused the leaders of having attempted to reverse the verdict of the Yanan rectification campaign. His anger intensified when he declared that there were people who wanted to denigrate the CR, and that, to create an uproar at Huairentang, was to restore capitalism, to restore Liu Shaoqi and Deng Xiaoping. In that case, the 74-year-old chairman declared, he would go back to Jinggangshan with Lin Biao to start another guerilla war.

> 'You want to execute Chen Boda and Jiang Qing, to exile Kang Sheng, to reorganise the CCRG. Let Chen Yi be its head and Tan Zhenlin his deputy. If that is not enough, Wang Ming and Zhang Guotao should be invited to come

back. Even the United States and the Soviet Union should be invited to participate.'

After this outburst of anger, he left the meeting room.[99]

The most outspoken veteran cadres, Tan Zhenlin, Chen Yi and Xu Xiangqian were given leave to prepare their self-criticism. All others were criticised at a series of enlarged Politburo meetings which took place between February 25 and 18 March under the chairmanship of Zhou Enlai. The meetings formally condemned the February Adverse Current.[100]

The February Adverse Current had profound repercussions on the future course of the CR. Firstly, all reprobation of the CR and its excesses were muted, since Mao condemned all opposition to it as a 'note worthy counter-revolutionary restoration'.[101]

Secondly, the Politburo ceased to function while the status of the CCRG was greatly enhanced. The Politburo's responsibilities were taken over by the CCRG which was increasingly controlled by Jiang Qing. Zhou Enlai, who also had made self-criticism reproaching himself to be slow and obtuse in matters of political line, was permitted to attend the CCRG meetings.[102]

Thirdly, during the second half of March, the CCRG informed Beijing red guard organisations about the events at the Jingxi guest house and at Huairentang and about Mao's reaction to them. As a result, a mass campaign to attack the February Adverse Current developed during which not only Tan Zhenlin, Chen Yi and Xu Xiangqian, but also Li Fuchun, Ye Jianying, Li Xiannian, Nie Rongzhen and Yu Qiuli were condemned as 'black generals' (*hei gan jiang*) of the February Adverse Current.[103] Zhou Enlai, since he had failed to take a clear stand on the issue, became the target of attack of a few radical red guard organisation who accused him of being the 'back-stage boss' of the February Adverse Current.[104]

Fourthly, the condemnation of the February Adverse Current boasted the morale of the radicals especially in the provinces where they had been suppressed by the leadership of the military regions. In many areas, radicals attacked local military leaders as 'Tan Zhenlinists'.[105]

In March and April, Mao tried to intensify the campaign against Liu Shaoqi within the mass organisations. Most of these organisations were, however, deeply involved in activities related to the seizure of power and in factional fighting. The condemnation of the February Adverse Current further distracted them from Liu Shaoqi's case whose fall from power was already a foregone conclusion.

Mao, aware of these developments, tried to play down the importance of the February Adverse Current. On 30 April he summoned the marshals and vice premiers involved in the Current to a 'meeting of unity', during which he had a relaxed chat with them, telling them, that since they had openly aired their grievances about the CR, they had not secretly plotted.[106] Though the meeting brought about some relaxation of the tensions between Mao and the veteran leaders, the damage had been done; for the impact of all this high-level political infighting had already filtered down to the grassroot level and generated an even more chaotic situation – a situation that even Mao had difficulty in controlling.

Escalation of the chaos

During the unprecedented struggle to seize power, factional fighting became so rampant, that alliances could be achieved only with great difficulty which in turn slowed down the process of establishing 'three-in-one' combinations and revolutionary committees. In order to promote great alliances, Mao intensified the campaign against Liu Shaoqi's revisionism in the hope that mass organisations would unite over this issue.[107] The escalation of the campaign against Liu Shaoqi started with the publication, on 1 April, of Qi Benyu's article on 'Patriotism or National Betrayal?' where he criticised Liu Shaoqi's entire revolutionary career. The response of radical red guards and rebels to this attempt was at the most lukewarm. They, who had only a few months early participated enthusiastically in the criticism of Liu Shaoqi, now preferred to oppose the February Adverse Current in Beijing and the crackdown on radicals by the military authorities in the provinces.

In Beijing, some one hundred thousand red guards staged a demonstration against all leaders involved in the February Adverse Current. Within the government system, radical rebels and red guards formed alliances at the level of administrative systems[108] and established 'liaison stations' which organised the proceedings of criticising the vice premiers involved in the Current. There was a 'criticising Chen Yi liaison station' in the foreign affairs system, a 'criticising Tan Zhenlin liaison station' in the agricultural system and a 'criticising Yu Qiuli and Gu Mu liaison station' in the industrial and communications system.[109] Gu Mu, although he had not been present at the February Politburo meetings, was included in the campaign since, in his dealings with red guards, he had expressed reservations about the CR. The marshals became targets of students at military schools and other units. All were confronted with the slogan 'down with . . .' which in the terminology of the CR meant that they should be removed from their posts and subjected to fierce mass criticism. The conservative factions in the systems were opposed to the usage of 'down with . . .' and preferred that the vice premiers and marshals should simply be censured, a difference which added to the cleavages opposing the moderate and the radical factions.

Some radicals included Zhou Enlai in their criticism of the February Adverse Current. Apparently inspired by the CCRG who disliked Zhou's moderate attitude towards the CR, they claimed that Zhou was the 'back-stage boss' of the February Adverse Current. In late March, the first posters attacking Zhou, appeared in the streets. As the attacks intensified in May, Mao instructed Chen Boda to publicly declare that Zhou belonged to the 'proletarian headquarters' and thus could not be criticised.[110] The question whether Zhou Enlai should be criticised or not, became another cause of dissent between some of the radicals and the conservatives.

In the provinces, the cleavage between radicals and moderates was even more pronounced. The military involvement in the CR and the support they extended to conservative factions further complicated the situation.[111] Several incidents of repression of radical red guards by the military in February, and, later, the rehabilitation of the suppressed organisations contributed to the hostility of the factions. From April onward, their controversies took the form of violent armed fighting, where weapons from sticks to firearms were used. When Mao learned in July, that the military had secretly provided weapons to conservative mass organisations, he ordered that radical factions should also be armed.[112] Jiang Qing, in a talk to revolutionary rebels in Henan province on 22 July, supported the principle of 'attacking with non-violence, but defending with force' (*wen gong wu wei*) which implied that the radicals, in their dealings with the conservatives, should debate and use reasoning. But if the other side counter-attacked with violence, they should respond in the same manner.[113] Her statement legitimised armed fighting between rival factions in the name of 'defence by force'. The official support extended to the radicals in this contest further radicalised the movement and contributed to the outbreak of even more chaos in Beijing and in the provinces, reaching a new peak in July and August.

In Beijing, more than a hundred rebel and red guard organisations dispatched several thousand of their followers to Zhongnanhai. Equipped with loudspeakers, they camped outside the Party and government compound demanding, day and night during several weeks, a face-to-face confrontation with Liu Shaoqi.[114] Liu and Deng, as well as the members of the February Adverse Current continued to be vociferiously attacked.

On 7 August, Wang Li, an important member of the CCRG who had become a national hero during the Wuhan event, summoned a number of rebel representatives of the foreign ministry to a talk, where he made the explicit statement, that Mao had asked him to look into the affairs of the ministry. In his view, the rebels in the ministry lacked strength and the conservatives were too active. He pledged the CCRG's support to the rebels and encouraged them to go beyond the supervisory role, Zhou Enlai had assigned to them.[115]

Wang Li's talk greatly stimulated the morale of the rebels who renewed their attacks against the conservatives and took over the ministry's political department. On 18 August, red guards from the Beijing foreign languages institutes forced their way into the ministry claiming to offer the rebels their help to seize more power. They left after sealing the office of the ministerial Party committee and kidnapped two vice ministers, Ji Pengfei and Qiao Guanhua, who were ordered to sell red guard newspapers in the western part of the city.[116]

Wang Li's 7 August speech had strong repercussions on other ministries, where rebels, following the example of the foreign ministry, increased their attacks on the conservatives and took over political departments. The revolutionary atmosphere in Beijing became overheated and finally culminated in the attack on the British mission on 22 August.[117]

On 1 August, *Red Flag*, in a major editorial, issued a call to overthrow 'a handful of persons in power in the army who travelled the capitalist road'.[118] This legitimised previous attacks on the army establishment and signalled an official change of target of the CR from the Party to the army. During the months of August, attacks on the army multiplied. Lin Biao wrote to Mao, who was in Shanghai at that time, that in several provinces, mass organisations had stormed army store houses and looted weapons.[119]

Armed factional fighting became increasingly rampant. In Shanghai, the workers' general headquarters, in early August, launched a large-scale attack on the bastion of the conservatives, the 'Shanghai diesel engine plant revolutionary rebels' united command'. The 'united command' was eliminated, and more than six hundred people were wounded or captured by the rebel 'headquarters'.[120]

On 28 August, an armed conflict took place between the military and mass organisations in the Ningxia Autonomous Region during which 101 civilians were killed and 133 wounded.[121]

Changsha, the provincial capital of Hunan, was controlled by radical mass organisations while the suburbs were dominated by the conservatives. The two rival factions, who were fully armed, fought several battles during which both sides suffered heavy casualties. Some major cities in the province, Xiangtan, Zhuzhou, Hengyang and Changde were under the control of the conservatives who made plans to attack the provincial capital in order to liberate it from the radicals.[122]

With the aim of countering the radical mass movements, conservative organisations in Jiangxi, Sichuan, Hubei, Hunan and Henan established a 'five provinces united army liaison station' with Nanchang, the provincial capital of Jiangxi, as its base. In Chongqing, conservatives under rebel attack, retreated to the suburban areas – where they occupied a number of important industrial plants – and to the countryside.[123] In Guangzhou, a large amount of weapons were looted from the army and the Public Security Bureau. In Changchun, north China, students of the military schools engaged in armed fighting inflicting heavy casualties upon each other.

The role of the military

Initially the CR was meant to focus primarily on cultural, educational, governmental and Party institutions. The army was not to be involved in the movement.[124] But the situation developed differently, for in the course of events, the PLA became increasingly implicated in the process. In early 1967, the army was requested to give support to the left in their attempts to seize power. Two months later, the PLA was ordered to intervene to establish order, to assure the normal functioning of industry and agriculture and to exercise military control over such key departments as radio broadcasting, banks and storage facilities.

The PLA became even more embroiled at the time of the establishment of revolutionary committees at provincial and municipal levels, a procedure which took 20 months. After the establishment of such committees in the 29 provinces and municipalities in September 1968, and after the escalation of the CR into the stage of 'struggle-criticism-transformation', the military further enhanced its position through an important and highly visible presence in revolutionary committees or in military control commissions. During all these stages, the PLA moved into politics and gained power not so much through premeditated tactics, as through a gravitational pull stemming from outside its ranks.[125]

The behaviour of the PLA can, to a large extent, be explained by the organisational form into which it was moulded. In this connection, Mao had clearly defined the relationship between the PLA and the CCP as one where the Party commands the gun and the gun must never be allowed to command the Party. This principle was sustained by an organisational structure of command which secured the political superiority of the Party over the army.

The military commission of the Central Committee, headed by the chairman of the Party, was the highest organ of command of the army. From 1943 until his death in 1976, Mao had occupied the posts of the chairman of the Party and of the MC. Hua Guofeng also held the two posts until his removal from power in 1980. Thereafter, the two positions were temporarily separated, with Hu Yaobang and Zhao Ziyang serving as general secretaries of the Party, and Deng Xiaoping holding the chairmanship of the MC.[126] The two posts were again occupied by one person – Jiang Zemin – after Deng Xiaoping retired as chairman of the MC in 1989. The combination of the two positions in the hands of one person was designed to ensure the efficient control over the PLA at central level. The MC was responsible to the Standing Committee of the Politburo. Without its approval, no military order could be issued. Since Mao was in control of the Standing Committee, all final decisions on military matters were, therefore, in his hands. Even Lin Biao, in his capacity as minister of defence, was unable to order any sizeable movement of troops, aircraft or naval vessels. As we shall see later, on the eve of his flight from China, (12 September 1971) he had to request five aeroplanes from the centre.[127]

The overwhelming power of the Party centre over the army became quite evident from the way in which the latter was structured. The armed forces were geographically divided into 13 military regions and 23 provincial military districts.[128] The commanders of these regions and districts were mere administrators of the armed forces in their areas of jurisdiction. They were not autonomous military commanders, and could not, therefore, move troops without the approval of the Party centre. Although orders from Beijing were normally channelled through them, the Party centre also maintained its own direct lines of communication with regional, provincial and even local army units.[129] Moreover, regional and provincial military organisations were controlled by the Party committees and, in most cases, senior Party secretaries served concurrently as political commissars of the military regions. This organisational system continued to function during the CR, since, unlike the civilian sector, the Party structure within the army remained intact.

The CR in the PLA

Its powerful position notwithstanding, the army went through a series of agonising experiences during the CR. It was, particularly, faced with two major problems. The first was that the army had to deal with its own form of Cultural Revolution which was no less vehement than the one that was taking place in non-military circles. The second was its entanglement in the factional rivalries of the mass organisations. Although the army as such was not to take part in the CR, military training schools, artistic troupes, sports teams, literary groups and other units attached to the three armed forces were exempt from this rule.

On 25 May 1966, the general political department of the PLA issued a circular about the implementation of the May 16 circular, under the direction of the Party committees, in different academic, educational, journalistic, literary, artistic and publishing units of the PLA.[130] Having established its own 'All Army Cultural Revolution Group' (AACRG) the deputy director of the PLA's general political department, Liu Zhijian, who was heading the group, also participated in the CCRG on the same level as Jiang Qing, Wang Renzhong and Zhang Chunqiao.

In several respects, the AACRG differed from the Central CRG. It was subordinated to the MC, not to the Standing Committee. Its members were officers of the political and cultural departments of the PLA and did not belong to Mao's chosen coterie. Besides, none of its members were radicals, and the group's political prestige and authority was hardly comparable to that of the CCRG. Lin Biao did not attempt to enhance the status of the group.

As in the case of civilian schools, work teams had been sent to military schools in the early stages of the CR and had persecuted a number of students. After Mao's order to withdraw the work teams, the PLA political department, on 7 August, did the same, but, contrary to civilian units, it confirmed that the CR would again be directed by Party committees.[131] Moreover, the PLA issued a series of rules and regulations restraining CR activities in accordance with its disciplinary traditions. The students of the military schools soon began to resent those restraints and began to envy the freedom enjoyed by their fellow students in other local schools. One of the student leaders from the PLA Second Medical University, who was invited to attend National Day celebrations on 1 October at Tiananmen Square, seized the opportunity to report to Mao and Lin Biao about the restrictions in revolutionary activities imposed upon the military schools. Lin Biao, as the deputy leader of the CR, expressed his sympathy and support to the student leader. With Mao's approval, he instructed Liu Zhijian to draft a circular announcing that the CR in military schools should be carried out on the same lines as in other schools and universities. Liu's draft was submitted to the CCRG which made significant amendments before it was made public on 5 October in the form of a 'Notice Concerning the Great Proletarian Cultural Revolution of the Armed Forces'.[132]

The Notice stipulated clearly:

1 that rules and regulations restricting the mass movement in military schools were to be abolished and the CR was to be carried out in the same manner as elsewhere;
2 that all persons who had been labelled counter-revolutionaries, anti-party elements, rightists, and the like by Party committees or work teams should be rehabilitated;
3 that the confessions they had been forced to sign should be returned to them, and any dossier which had been compiled about such persons should be reviewed in consultation with the masses and eventually burnt in the presence of the persons concerned;
4 that anti-Party and anti-socialist elements among the leading members and teaching staff of the military schools must be exposed and criticised;
5 that Party committees should no longer play a leading role in the CR; and
6 that military schools should confine their activities to their own premises and abstain from interfering in the CR in the areas where they were located.[133]

The Party centre ordered the distribution of this document to all schools including non-military ones. To propagate the Notice, two mass rallies with 100,000 participants each, were held at Tiananmen Square. At the first meeting, attended by teachers, students and staff from military schools, Ye Jianying, in his capacity as vice chairman and general secretary of the MC, read the Notice to the audience. To emphasise the importance of this document, Zhou Enlai, Tao Zhu, Chen Boda, Kang Sheng, Jiang Qing and other CCRG members were present at the second meeting which was organised for non-military schools and where the Notice was again read to the public. Its basic message was to 'kick out the Party committee and leave the Revolution to the masses' (*tikai dangwei nao geming*).[134]

The Notice, and Lin Biao's National Day speech calling for a thorough criticism and repudiation of the bourgeois reactionary line,[135] had repercussions well beyond the military sector. They caused great confusion about rehabilitation and the handling of the personnel files. Party committees generally tended to restrict rehabilitation to a small number of people, especially to those who had been officially labelled, while students demanded that the authorities should apologise to those who had been subjected to different kinds of injustice. These different interpretations of the stipulation about rehabilitation gave rise to serious conflicts between the students who had been suppressed during the initial weeks of the CR and the authorities.

The issue of the dossiers was even more explosive since it had a direct effect on everybody's life. Every person in China had a dossier which was compiled and kept by the personnel department of his unit and whose exact content was unknown to the person concerned. Such dossiers contained detailed information about a person's political status, his ideological orientations, personal inclinations, professional performance, his family's political background and problems. During political campaigns the dossier could be used against the person concerned. The information it contained was equally vital for a person's career, promotion or transfer of work.[136]

The system applied to students, too. Each political campaign added material to their files. This was particularly the case during the initial stage of the CR when work teams and school authorities compiled large amounts of diverse material. It could contain large character posters written by students, accusations against them which were sent directly to Party committees or work teams, minutes of meetings containing statements or accusations, notebooks of work-team members, etc. The notice, though it ordered the return of discriminating material to the persons concerned, did not, however, specify what should be considered as 'black material' (*hei cailiao*). School authorities or work teams tended to return as little as possible material from their files to the student, while the students, on the contrary, demanded that any unfavourable information should be regarded as 'black material' and be burnt.[137]

The issue of the recovery of 'black material' by the persons concerned inevitably led to clashes between students and school authorities. Students stormed the offices of the personnel department in search of concealed 'black material'. Demands for the return of work team members whom students wanted to interrogate became increasingly vociferous. These questions became a major issue in military schools too. Students stormed the headquarters of regional or provincial military authorities with the aim of abducting work team leaders who usually were relatively high-ranking military officers and were guarded by soldiers who refused to turn them over to the assailants. As a result, clashes between soldiers and students occurred in ever greater numbers. During the fall of 1966 when the movement to criticise the bourgeois reactionary line was at its height, between one and two hundred thousand military school students came to Beijing to participate in the 'great exchange of revolutionary experiences'. Some arrived with the specific purpose of seizing work-team leaders. The students of the Harbin Military Engineering Institute, for example, arrived in Beijing in late October in search of Lu Yang, deputy director of the Commission of Science and Technology for National Defence and former work-team leader at the Harbin Institute. With the aim of abducting Lu Yang, the students broke into the Commission's building, but their attempt failed due to the resolute resistance of the soldiers guarding the building.[138]

Another illustration of the controversies between students and authorities, as well as of the dilemma which surfaced between the army CRG and the CCRG, was the siege of the ministry of defence in early November, when several hundred students from military institutes from Hebei Province attacked the ministry and finally broke through the cordon of PLA soldiers who had strict orders not to use weapons against them. The students demanded that Li Tianyu, the PLA deputy chief of staff be surrendered to them. During the incident, a number of soldiers were wounded.

After the failure of all attempts by officials of the ministry, as well as members of the army CRG, to calm down the students and to persuade them to leave, Liu Zhijian telephoned Lin Biao's office suggesting that the students should be ordered to leave the premises and, if they refused, they should be held responsible for violation of military order and their leaders should be arrested. The state of siege lasted throughout the night. It was only the next morning, that Lin Biao, whom nobody dared to disturb during the night, was informed about Liu's suggestions. The case demonstrates Lin Biao's ambivalent position in the CR. As Mao's deputy commander of the Proletarian Headquarters, he could not issue orders to suppress the students at a time when criticism of the Liu-Deng line was at its height and Mao and the CCRG strongly encouraged the student revolt. But as minister of defence, it was his duty to protect his subordinates and the ministry. In his dilemma, Lin Biao adopted an equivocal attitude informing his secretary, that he had nothing to say to Liu Zhijian's inquiry, thus leaving the decision to Liu. But his wife, Ye Qun, reminded him that if he remained silent, he would bear the responsibility if students were arrested. Lin Biao finally decided to maintain the status quo and to instruct Liu Zhijian not to arrest any students but to persevere in his efforts to persuade them to leave. The students persisted in their refusal to leave.[139]

The stalemate was finally broken only after Zhou Enlai's intervention. He persuaded Chen Boda to send Zhang Chunqiao and Qi Benyu to the ministry to present a note to the students. While the note praised the revolutionary spirit of the students, it also emphasised that the ministry of defence was under the jurisdiction of Lin Biao who was the deputy commander of the CR and should therefore be no longer molested. The influence of the CCRG was such that the students applauded Zhang Chunqiao's and Qi Benyu's presence and left the premises after having listened to the reading of Chen Boda's note.[140]

Confronted with the increasingly undisciplined behaviour of military school students and the presence of more than a hundred thousand of them in Beijing, the general political department of the MC sponsored two mass meetings of military students on 13 and 29 November. Four of the vice chairmen of the MC, the marshals Chen Yi, Nie Rongzhen, Xu Xiangqian, and Ye Jianying, addressed the gathering. In their speeches, all four attempted to persuade the students to refrain from adopting excessive slogans and from resorting to violence. They emphasised discipline and the necessity to follow official policies. Chen Yi was particularly outspoken in his criticism of the students' unruly conduct. As military students, they should distance themselves from the radical activities of others, Chen pointed out. He sharply condemned those who had forced their way into the Ministry of Defence accusing them of no longer being satisfied with attacking school presidents and members of Party committees and of attempting to escalate their struggle to involve ministers and perhaps vice premiers. This, according to Chen Yi, was not the right method of carrying out the CR.[141]

While the conservative wing of the students applauded the marshals, the radical factions declared their opposition, claiming that they were following the official policy line, and expressed their intention of holding meetings to denounce the marshals and their speeches. Zhou Enlai felt again compelled to intervene. He received representatives of the radical faction on 4 January 1967, and dissuaded them from pursuing such a course.[142]

This event illustrated the disagreements which existed between the leadership of the army and the policies advocated by the CCRG. Their conflict sharpened with the CCRG's attack on Liu Zhijian, who clashed with the CCRC on several issues. Firstly, Liu disagreed with Zhang Chunqiao and other members of the CCRG, during a discussion on 5 October 1966, over the implementation of the Notice in military schools and, in particular, about the role of Party committees in these schools. Secondly, Liu was opposed to the presence of students from outside Beijing in the capital and their intention to establish a liaison station there. He drafted a telegram to the military regions ordering them to prevent students from military schools from travelling to the capital. Chen Boda rejected the draft and denounced Liu's refusal to authorise the establishment of a liaison station. Thirdly, Liu attempted to prohibit the harassment of the regional military leaders by the students, on the ground that military operations and war readiness should not be jeopardised. Also, he suggested that any violations of this rule should be punished according to military discipline. His proposals were supported by the members of the army CRG, but rejected by the CCRG, who accused Liu of obstructing the CR on the pretext of war readiness.

Another conflict between the two groups surfaced on the issue of the siege of the ministry of defence, where soldiers, with strict orders not to strike back at students, had been badly injured. When Liu informed the CCRG that soldiers had complained about the prohibition against defending themselves, and had declared that they would prefer to be red guards than PLA soldiers, Qi Benyu was reported to have banged the table and to have exclaimed: 'Liu Zhijian, you are talking nonsense!'[143]

The disputes between the CCRG and Liu Zhijian finally led to Liu's removal not only from the army CRG, but also from all his other posts. On 4 January, Kang Sheng declared that Liu represented the bourgeois reactionary line of Liu Shaoqi and Deng Xiaoping in the army. Liu Zhijian was put into custody where he remained for more than seven years. On 11 January, the army CRG was reorganised with Xu Xiangqian as the head of the group and Jiang Qing as its advisor.[144]

The degree of confusion which reigned during this period of the CR and, in particular, the dissensions between factions and the arbitrariness with which they were defined as revolutionary or conservative, was amply illustrated by the so-called 'May 13 Event' of 1967. This event was another seemingly banal episode, but it had considerable influence on the further course of the CR. A performance by the conservative faction of an air force art troupe, staged to commemorate the 25th anniversary of Mao's 'Talk at the Yanan Forum on Literature and Art', instigated the trouble. The sponsors of this performance were a group of female dancers who had been Mao's dancing partners at the regular parties Mao used to hold at Zhongnanhai before the CR. Since these women had chosen to defend Wu Faxian, the commander of the air force, against attacks from the radicals, they were ipso facto considered to be conservatives. Their performance was attacked by the radical faction. The conflict between the two hostile factions spread to other PLA literary and artistic units and led to injuries on both sides. The dancers used their personal acquaintance with Mao to seek his support for their performance. Mao referred the question to Ye Qun, who, in agreement with Lin Biao, decided to support the dancers.[145] There were two major reasons for Lin's decision to support the conservative faction. Firstly, the young women appeared to have Mao's support. Secondly, they sided not only with Wu Faxian, but also with Li Zuopeng, the first political commissar of the navy and with Qiu Huizuo, the director of the general logistics department, who were all Lin Biao's trusted followers. Lin Biao, the chieftain of the radicals, condemned the radical faction within the army and severely criticised their attempt to jeopardise the performance of the conservatives.

Lin Biao's condemnation of the radical faction of the artistic units had repercussions on the further formation of factions within military units. With Lin Biao's support, the conservatives reorganised themselves as the 'Proletarian Revolutionaries of the Three Armed Forces'. Since the same title was used by the more numerous radicals, making it necessary to differentiate between the two groups, the conservatives were called the 'Old Three Forces' (*lao san jun*), whereas the radicals were referred to as the 'New Three Forces' (*xin san jun*) or as the 'assaulting faction' (*chong pai*), since they had disturbed the performance of 13 May.[146]

After the 'May 13 Event', the two factions decided to stage separate performances on 1 July, the birth date of the CCP. Both invited members of the proletarian headquarters to attend. Lin Biao again demonstrated his support for the conservatives by accepting their invitation. The *chong pai*, whose members had besieged the ministry of defence and harassed several regional military institutions with the support of the CCRG, had however lost the CCRG's favour after the May 13 Event, and none of its members attended their performance. Without the support of the proletarian headquarters, the faction disintegrated.[147]

Related to the May 13 Event was the removal of Xiao Hua, the director of the PLA general political department. This department was more deeply involved in the CR than any other department of the army. When Liu Zhijian, Xiao Hua's deputy, was overthrown, Xiao came under attack by the radicals as having backed Liu's activities. Jiang Qing who resented Xiao's political stance as being too close to the veteran marshals was determined to overthrow him and planned to organise a meeting of ten thousand people on 19 January, to repudiate

Xiao. It was only due to Mao's protective intervention that Xiao Hua was able to escape this fate at that time.[148]

However, Xiao Hua also failed to gain Lin Biao's support, in spite of the fact that he had worked for many years under him. During the Liberation War (1946-9), Xiao was the political commissar of the 13th Army Group of the 4th Field Army under Lin Biao's command.[149] In the 1960s, Lin Biao had nominated him to his post of director of the general political department. No details are available which explain why Xiao, after his narrow escape in January, continued to be attacked not only by Jiang Qing but also by Ye Qun who ordered the setting up of big character posters in Beijing's streets accusing him of being the 'black boss behind the screen' (*hei hou tai*) of the May 13 Event. In July, after Lin Biao refused to invite Xiao to the army's artistic performance on the first of that month, Xiao disappeared from the public scene.[150]

With the disintegration of the *chong pai*, the CR within the army had passed its peak. The conservatives or 'old proletarian revolutionaries', although they had been a minority, had won the day.

Military intervention

At the beginning of the CR, the authorities clearly had no intention of promoting military intervention in the CR. A number of directives were issued at that time which reflected the Party centre's desire to isolate the PLA from the mass movement. The first, which was addressed by the PLA general staff and political departments to the military regions and provincial military districts on 21 August 1966, prohibited military involvement in the CR. The circular emphasised that although students had demonstrated in such cities as Guilin, Lanzhou and Baotou, and, in the course of these demonstrations, had threatened local Party and government organs, under no circumstances should the armed forces suppress the revolutionary student movement.[151] The 'Urgent Notice' mentioned earlier, stipulated in fact that military schools should abstain from involving themselves in the activities of the CR in their localities.[152]

When, after August 1966, the problem of 'black material' became increasingly rampant, the army CRG sent a telegram to the military regions informing them that the provincial authorities could, if necessary, send their archives and documents to the army for safe keeping. Provincial cadres who suffered from the assaults of red guards could be admitted to military hospitals for treatment and protection.[153] Since many provincial leaders took refuge with the PLA, red guards – searching for their dossiers and for local leaders who, in their view, had formerly mistreated them – began to assault military organs. Confrontations between the red guards and the military became increasingly serious during the last months of 1966. On 14 January 1967, the Party centre issued a circular entitled 'Prohibition of Directing the Spearhead of Struggle against the Armed Forces', which portrayed the PLA as 'the most important instrument of the proletarian dictatorship' and therefore 'no person or organisation should attack the organs of the PLA'. The same circular gave permission to the local Party committees to 'temporarily transfer their important archives, documents, and confidential personnel and persons involved in radio transmissions to the military organs'.

At the same time, the circular insisted that the transfer of documents should not be used 'as a pretext to move documents for the purge of the revolutionary masses into the military organs'. If this happened, the documents 'must be returned at once and dealt with in public according to the relevant provisions of the Central Committee'. The circular also announced that 'it is necessary to make the army responsible for guarding the local radio stations, prisons, warehouses, roads and bridges', and for preventing anybody from 'encircling, attacking, occupying and sabotaging these places'.[154] Though it was not the entire army which was involved in the implementation of these measures, the number of soldiers and officers who did participate in their implementation, was nonetheless quite considerable and amounted to 2.8 million.[155]

The purpose of this circular was to solve the problems related to the transfer of personal dossiers. But, in fact, it was impossible to determine the amount of material transferred to the military organs and how much had been dealt with in public, as the circular demanded. Soon after its distribution, two other documents were issued which contradicted the previous ones and led to the army's deep involvement in the disputes of the CR. Both documents considerably complicated the tasks the army was expected to fulfil.

The first document was the 23 January order issued by the Central Committee, the military commission and the CCRG. It was the result of a request submitted by the Anhui provincial military district who demanded instructions from the central authorities as to whether it could dispatch troops to guard the site of a meeting convened by the mass organisations to criticise Li Baohua, the first secretary of the provincial Party committee. Mao responded with a short note indicating that 'the PLA should be sent to support the broad masses of the revolutionary left'.[156] The order of 23 January reiterated Mao's instructions to the Anhui military district. 'From now on', the document stated, 'the demands of all true revolutionaries for support and assistance from the army should be satisfied. The so-called "non-involvement" is false, for the army was already involved long ago.' The decision declared all past directives concerning the non-involvement of the army in the CR in local areas as void, and stipulated that 'active support must be rendered to the broad masses of the revolutionary left in their struggle to seize power. When the genuine proletarian left ask the army for help, the army should send troops to support them politically'.[157]

Mao's decision to support the revolutionary left through military means was largely inspired by the weakness of leftist forces which, in many areas, were a minority and unable to seize power on their own. But the document was ambiguous about the identification of the revolutionary left, whose characteristics were never clearly defined. Among the numerous mass organisations which had sprung up, there was not one which did not swear its loyalty to the great leader Chairman Mao and which did not claim their willingness to overthrow the bourgeois reactionary line of Liu Shaoqi. In the absence of instructions from the centre as to which organisation to support, the military were constantly confronted with the essential question of who were the left they were expected to assist in their efforts to seize power. In most cases, the local military leaders had no sympathy with the radical red guards and revolutionary rebels who had assaulted Party committees, maltreated leading cadres and attacked army installations. In view of their closeness to provincial Party committees, they were inclined to support the more disciplined conservative factions who had in their ranks numerous Party members with 'good' family backgrounds who, in many cases, represented a majority, and who tended to protect the Party committees.[158]

The second document, issued on 28 January, was an eight-point order by the MC which aimed at preventing mass organisations from assaulting military organs. During the month of January, such assaults had occurred with increasing frequency. Students of military schools attacked the Nanjing military region and humiliated eight of its leaders in struggle meetings. General Xu Shiyou, the commander of the region, vouched that, if the students attacked him, he would not hesitate to open fire. Red guards and rebels of the Shenyang military region abducted its deputy commander, General Tan Zian, who was forced to participate in struggle sessions, paraded in the street and almost tortured to death. General Han Xianchu, commander of the Fuxhou military region reported that red guards of Beijing's 'third headquarters' were creating disturbances in the region. He swore to go to the mountains to fight a guerilla war if these disruptions were allowed to continue.[159] Similar urgent reports from other localities were reaching Beijing. It appeared that the stability of the entire army was at stake.

Alarmed by the situation, Lin Biao transmitted these and similar reports to Mao. Moreover, he invited marshals Ye Jianying, Xu Xiangqian, Nie Rongzhen and the acting chief of staff, general Yang Chengwu, to discuss the situation. The meeting drafted the eight-point order which was revised by the CCRG, approved by Mao and issued on 28 January by the MC. The order stipulated that:

> the question of assaults on military leading organs which had already taken place should be dealt with on a case-by-case basis. If assaults were made by counter-revolutionaries, they should be suppressed, but no action was needed if leftists were responsible for the attacks. Henceforth no assaults or exchange of revolutionary experience shall be permitted in units of the armed forces dealing with war preparation systems and security. All material concerning the CR will be kept under seal for the time being, to be dealt with later.[160]

The order also announced that 'armies, divisions, regiments, battalions, companies and special units designated by the MC' should not carry out the CR.[161]

In order to prevent overall and generalised revolutionary activities in the military regions, the MC, on the same day issued another directive announcing that 'the CR in the military regions should be carried out stage by stage and group by group' which implied that, in order to allow for the continuation of daily work, not everyone should become involved in the CR at the same time. In some such areas as Jinan, Nanjing, Fuzhou, Guangzhou, Kunming, Xinjiang and Wuhan, which were considered to be 'on the first line of defence', revolutionary activities should be postponed.[162]

During the first half of February, Mao drafted another directive indicating to the military how to respond in the case of assault. Right-wing mass organisations, he pointed out, should not be allowed to attack the army. But if such attack took place, it should be dealt with properly. First, the PLA should try to talk to the leaders of the mass organisation to dissuade them from violent actions. If this failed, the military should retreat and allow the aggressors to break in. If they occupied the first floor, the soldiers should retreat to the second floor. If the second floor was taken over, the army should retreat to the third floor. Only if the aggressors attempted to take over the third floor, should the army open fire in self-defence.[163]

The interpretation the provincial and local military leadership gave to these documents instilled them with a sense of freedom to respond to radical assaults. They proceeded with a series of repressions of radical red guards and rebels which were later referred to as the 'February Crackdown'. On 26 January, the independent regiment in the city of Shihezi in Xinjiang joined forces with the conservative faction in an armed repression of the radicals which caused several hundred casualties.[164] The Xinjiang military region's report on this event was diametrically opposed to the CCRG's views about it. Whereas the military reported that they had suppressed hooligans after having been driven beyond the limits of forbearance, the CCRG believed the military had acted as counter-revolutionaries suppressing the revolutionary masses.[165] This controversial view about the activities of the military was characteristic for most other events related to the February Crackdown.

In Sichuan, the Chengdu military region, supportive of the conservative 'industrial army', was attacked by two radical organisations, the 'Chengdu workers' revolutionary rebel corps' and the 'August 26 militant corps' of Sichuan university. Although the MC wrote an open letter to the Sichuan radicals pointing out that their attack on the military region violated the decision of the Party centre, the radicals insisted that they were following Mao's line, and escalated their assaults. The PLA, in accordance with their interpretation of the eight-point order, reacted by arresting a large number of radicals.

Even more serious clashes, known as the 'Zhao Yongfu event' occurred in Qinghai, where the radical organisation 'August 18', after a dispute over an editorial published by the local newspaper of Qinghai's provincial capital Xining, encircled and finally seized the offices of the paper. The radicals reportedly beat to death a number of staff members of the newspaper. In retaliation, the army encircled the radicals holding the *Qinghai Daily*'s offices. Since the radicals refused to withdraw, the deputy commander of the military region, Zhao Yongfu, gave the order to open fire on the assailants. More than three hundred people were killed and wounded in the incident.[166] When Zhao reported the event to marshal Ye Jianying, he approved Zhao's action and encouraged the suppression of the rebels.[167]

Another conflict between the PLA and radical rebel organisations occurred in Wuhan where several such organisations, the 'revolutionary rebels headquarters of Wuhan steelworkers', 'the second headquarters of the steelworkers', 'the September 13 corps of steelworkers', the 'new China engineering college', the 'new Hebei university' and others, confronted the conservatives whose most representative organisation was the 'Wuhan revolutionary workers and employees association' totalling about one million members. The radicals, though their organisations were more numerous, could claim about four hundred thousand members.[168]

In early February, the radicals, justifying their action by Mao's call to wage an overall class struggle, had seized the local official newspaper, *Changjiang Daily*. On the 8th of that month, they published an editorial stating that 'great disorder is needed in Wuhan and Hubei. The disorder should be total and thorough'.[169] The next day, another editorial appeared claiming that the seizure of *Changjiang Daily* had been supported by the military region.[170] The Wuhan military region, after obtaining the approval of the army CRG, protested against the editorial and published a 'solemn statement' on 18 February denying that they had ever supported the take over.[171] In the small hours of 17 March, the Wuhan military authorities rounded up about one thousand core members of the radicals of whom some were imprisoned and others released after signing confessions. The Wuhan 'workers' general headquarters' and its associated radical organisations were condemned as reactionary and banned.[172]

In other areas, such as Guangdong, Anhui, Henan, Hunan, Fujian, Inner Mongolia and Tibet, similar incidents of suppression of radicals by the regional military authorities also occurred. Radical red guards and revolutionary rebels who had attempted to seize power during the January Storm suffered serious setbacks in the 'February crack down'. The conservatives, like the 'one million heroes' in Wuhan, the 'industrial army' in Chengdu, the 'general headquarters' in Guangzhou, the 'eight big commands' in Henan, the 'red flames of wrath' in Hunan etc., were very satisfied with these developments, since they had been ridiculed by the rebels during the campaign to criticise Liu Shaoqi as 'lao bao', a contemptuous term for conservatives or royalists. They seized the opportunity to retaliate against their adversaries and assisted the military authorities in unmasking the core members of the radical organisations. They also felt themselves the only true supporters of the present revolutionary cause.

The February Adverse Current and the February Crackdown epitomised the resistance which veteran leaders in Beijing and military leaders in the provinces had developed against the CR. Although they all professed their loyalty to the Chairman and their support for the CR, they vented their anger on the unruly radicals. And as the veteran leaders had intractable conflicts with the CCRG at Politburo meetings, the provincial and local military leaders too had similar conflicts regarding the 'truly revolutionary' nature of the mass organisations within the areas of their jurisdiction.

As with the veteran leaders involved in the February Adverse Current, the military leaders' resistance against the radicalisation of the CR was equally short lived. After Mao's severe criticism of the veteran leaders, he also gave the green light for the re-examination of the turmoil in the military regions, beginning with the events in Qinghai. After being requested by five members of the CCRG, Zhang Chunqiao, Wang Li, Guan Feng, Qi Benyu and Yao Wenyuan, to reopen the investigation of the Qinghai incident, Mao answered on 11 March: 'You may investigate. If the students opened fire first, there is no big problem. But if this was not the case, the question needs to be re-examined.'[173]

The CCRG, who met with red guard but not with military representatives from Qinghai, concluded that the students had been unarmed, that soldiers 'used force on the barehanded masses', and that Zhao Yongfu was responsible for the serious case of armed suppression of the revolutionary masses. With Mao's approval, the CC, the State Council, the MC and the CCRG jointly issued a 'decision concerning the Qinghai problem' on 24 March which stipulated the arrest and trial of Zhao Yongfu, Zhang Xiaochuan, an officer of a PLA unit in Qinghai, and of Wang Zhao, the secretary of the provincial Party committee. The 'August 18' organisation of red guards was rehabilitated as a revolutionary mass organisation. Similar decisions reversed the previous rulings on the incidents in Anhui, Inner Mongolia and Sichuan, where the military authorities were accused of having suppressed the radical organisations in these areas which were, at present, rehabilitated.[174]

On 1 April, the CC issued a document which attempted to further restrain the activities of the military against the rebel organisations. The document condemned the 'arbitrary stigmatising of mass organisations' and the 'heedless arresting of persons as counter-revolutionaries'.[175] An editorial in the *People's Daily*, published the next day, followed this up and warned against the 'counter-revolutionary adverse current' that had emerged in society and which was responsible for labelling 'young revolutionary fighters' as counter-revolutionaries. The editorial asserted that opposition against the young revolutionary fighters was equivalent to the negation of the CR.[176]

This political tide had turned again in favour of the radicals.

After the rehabilitation of the previously suppressed radical organisations, the assaults by radicals on the regional military authorities intensified. Drawing parallels with the February Adverse Current, the radicals began to accuse some of the regional military commanders as 'chieftains' of the February Crackdown. In Guangzhou, the radical organisation 'Three Red Banners' claimed that the commander of the military region, General Huang Yongsheng was Guang Lao Tan, the Tan Zhenlin of Guangzhou. Radicals in Wuhan promised to unmask the commander of the Wuhan military region, Chen Zaidao, as Wu Lao Tan, the Tan Zhenlin of Wuhan.[177]

Lin Biao realised that the decisions on the cases of Qinghai and Anhui as well as the CC directive of 1 April had effectively annulled the eight-point order. If military leaders continued to operate under this order they were liable to make the same kind of mistakes in interpreting the order as General Zhao had done in Qinghai. On 6 April, Lin Biao therefore issued a 'ten-point order', supported by the CCRG and approved by Mao, reversing the previous eight-point order and Mao's February directive.

The ten-point order prohibited the use of weapons by the military in their dealings with mass organisations, no matter whether they were 'revolutionary or controlled by reactionary elements, or whether their position is clear or not'. 'Arbitrary arrests' were forbidden and it was also prohibited to 'arbitrarily declare a mass organisation a reactionary organisation and to repress it'. The order stipulated further that 'no action shall be taken against the masses who intruded into or assaulted military organs in the past'; and that before taking any important action on current events, 'a report should be made to the CCRG and the All Army CRG and their advice sought'. The order emphasised particularly that 'counter-revolutionary elements of the Zhao Yongfu type or persons with ultra-right thought should be prevented from taking charge of support-the-left work'.[178]

The issuing, within less than two months, of two contradictory military orders demonstrated the dilemma the CR had created for both Mao and Lin. After having underlined the necessity of creating disorder, they had decided to re-establish some form of stability when the situation had become increasingly troublesome. Since in the process of stabilisation, many of their radical supporters had been sacrificed, they changed course again and took measures to endorse the radicals' actions.

These twists and turns by the political leaders made the army's task of supporting the left a very problematical undertaking. Not only did it continue to encounter difficulties in localising the faction that represented the 'true' left, but it also found itself remaining distant from the revolutionary rebels and close to the Party committees. Moreover, the military authorities who had been satisfied with the eight-point order, were now told that they had made mistakes of orientation and line and were forced to apologise to the radicals. The ten-point order exposed them again to massive assaults against which they were not allowed to defend themselves. Under these circumstances, the military in many areas relied increasingly on the conservative factions whom they provided with arms and ammunition, to maintain order and to fend off the attacks of radicals. As a result, relations between radicals and conservatives, and between the CCRG and some military regions turned from bad to worse. From late April to June, violence between the hostile factions increased considerably. The situation was particularly stormy in China's most populated province of Sichuan. In Chengdu, the powerful 'Industrial Army' supported by the military, attacked the red guards at Sichuan university. In Yibing, largescale fighting broke out between different factions in which more than ten thousand people from Chengdu took part. In Chongqing, an atmosphere of civil war prevailed in which the hostile factions fought with all kinds of weapons including anti-aircraft guns which were used to bombard the docks. Similar incidents occurred throughout the country.[179]

All these twists and turns increased the confusion. In Wuhan, the situation reached a particularly violent level. The local complexities were further compounded by the arrival on the scene of high-ranking national Party leaders, including Mao, and the kidnapping of an emissary of the CCRG.[180]

The provincial authorities of Wuhan had failed to rehabilitate the radicals who had become the victims of the February Crackdown.[181] After the publication of the ten-point order, the radicals[181] began to challenge the officials of the military region and declared their determination to abolish the 'February Black Wind' within the Wuhan area. They demanded that Chen Zaidao, the commander of the military region, be publicly criticised for his actions during the February Crackdown.[182]

The conservatives, on their part, had the sympathy of the military authorities, and, with their amalgamated organisation ('One Million Heroes', established on 16 May) challenged the authority of the radicals. Several armed confrontations between conservative and radical organisations occurred, the most serious of which, in June, left 108 dead and 2,774 wounded.[183]

In July, Mao made an inspection tour of the provinces adjacent to the Yangtze River to assess the progress of the CR in these areas. His first stop was in Wuhan where he arrived on the evening of 14 July accompanied by Wang Dongxing, the head of the general office of the CC and Yang Chengwu, the acting general chief of staff. Zhou Enlai, whose main concern was Mao's safety in the chaotic situation reigning in Wuhan, had already arrived earlier that day together with Li Zuopeng, the political commissar of the navy and a few navy and air force officers. Three other persons, Xie Fuzhi, vice premier and minister of public security, Yu Lijin, political commissar of the air force, and Wang Li, member of the CCRG also arrived in Wuhan after having sojourned in Sichuan where they had attempted to calm the turbulence. They were requested to come to Wuhan to report to Mao about their findings and the results of their intervention.[184]

On 15 and 16 July, Mao summoned Zhou Enlai, Wang Dongxing, Yang Chengwu, Li Zuopeng, Yu Lijin, Xie Fuzhi and Wang Li to discuss the situation in the area. After a thorough review of the Wuhan problem, Mao concluded that the radical organisation, the 'workers' general headquarters', should be rehabilitated and its leaders who had been arrested should be freed. He recognised the 'One Million Heroes' as a mass organisation, but one which needed conversion. Mao emphasised that the military region should support both factions. If Chen Zaidao supported the rebels, Mao said, then the rebels would also support him. He asked Zhou Enlai to stay a few more days in Wuhan and help the military to settle this problem.[185]

Between 16 and 18 July, Zhou Enlai met with representatives of the Wuhan military region and a number of high-ranking PLA officers whose mission was to support the left. He conveyed to them Mao's view that the military region had made mistakes of 'orientation and line' and should support the rebel organisations. However, Chen Zaidao refused to accept this verdict. Finally, Mao persuaded Chen to admit his mistakes and, according to Chen, promised in exchange that he would retain his position as commander of the Wuhan military region, and would act as mediator between the two factions with the aim of reconciling them. Subsequent developments, however, evolved differently.

On the evening of 18 July, Xie Fuzhi and Wang Li met with red guards from the Wuhan institute of water conservancy and hydro-electric power. On that occasion, Wang explained Mao's views on the Wuhan problem. Wang's speech was summarised in four points and broadcast by loudspeakers all over Wuhan: one, the Wuhan military region had made mistakes of line and orientation; two, the 'workers' general headquarters' should be rehabilitated; three, its members represented the revolutionary left; four, the 'One Million Heroes' were a conservative organisation.

The 'One Million Heroes', infuriated for being considered conservatives, retaliated by distributing thousands of posters attacking Wang Li. The Wuhan independent division and the 29th division, though assigned the task of supporting the left, joined up with the conservatives on 19 July. In more than one hundred army trucks they appeared at the headquarters of the military region and demanded that Wang Li answer three questions: (1), on what grounds were the 'One Million Heroes' condemned as a conservative organisation? (2) why was the 'workers' general headquarters' considered to represent the revolutionary left? (3) if the military region had demonstrated the correct orientation in supporting the left, why then were Chen Zaidao and Zhong Hanhua, the political commissar, capitulating and admitting that they had previously been mistaken?[186]

In the early morning of 20 July, members of the 'One Million Heroes' and soldiers of the independent division and the 29th division broke into the East Lake guest house to search for Wang Li. They were unaware of the fact that Mao, whose presence in Wuhan had been kept secret, was staying in a nearby building. Wang Li was captured by soldiers from the 29th division who transported him to the headquarters of the military region. The same afternoon, leaders of the military region removed Wang Li to the headquarters of the 29th division. From there, the political commissar of the division transferred Wang Li to an unknown place.

Mao, who had been aware of Wang Li's kidnapping, ordered Chen Zaidao to find Wang Li and to liberate him. Liu Feng, political commissar of the regional air force, succeeded in locating the place where Wang Li was held and, in the early morning of 22 July, obtained his release from the custody of the political commissar of the 29th division. The same afternoon, Wang Li and Xie Fuzhi flew back to Beijing.[187]

For four consecutive days, (20-3 July), the 'One Million Heroes', and fully armed soldiers supporting them, demonstrated in hundreds of thousands in the streets of Wuhan after mobilising two thousand army trucks to transport people to the city centre. Throughout the city, work and traffic came to a halt. The demonstrators carried placards and shouted slogans through loudspeakers exorting people to 'drag out Xie Fuzhi', and to 'overthrow Wang Li'. The slogans also claimed that Mao had been 'hoodwinked', and demanded that Zhang Chunqiao be overthrown and Jiang Qing 'get out of the way'.[188]

This was the largest demonstration which had ever taken place against the CCRG. It was the first time that emissaries from the centre were defied, humiliated, and one of them, kidnapped and beaten. Moreover, it was also the first time that the military, in defiance of the authorities, openly cooperated with an organisation considered conservative and rejected decisions of the Party centre. The incident was a major challenge to the central authorities.

The proletarian headquarters in Beijing reacted strongly and swiftly. Lin Biao, who was in charge during Mao's absence, believed that a mutiny had taken place among the soldiers of Wuhan. For Mao's safety, he mobilised the 8191 airborne division and the 15th army stationed in Xiaogan in Hubei province, and dispatched five gunboats of the east sea fleet to

Wuhan.[189] Zhou Enlai flew to Wuhan for the second time on 20 July to persuade Mao to leave the area. Mao flew to Shanghai in the small hours of 21 July.

In Beijing, a large-scale welcome was organised for Xie Fuzhi and Wang Li upon their arrival at the airport on 22 July. All major leaders, with the exception of Lin Biao, were present at the airport to receive Xie and Wang. The occasion was meant to demonstrate strong disagreement with the Wuhan military region and the 'One Million Heroes'.

In the evening of the same day, Lin Biao called a meeting of all CCRG members to discuss the Wuhan incident. The meeting decided:

1 to call Chen Zaidao, Zhong Hanhua and the commanders and political commissars of the independent division and the 29th division to Beijing for interrogation.
2 to send an open letter relating the position of the central authorities on the events to the people of Wuhan.
3 to hold a mass meeting of one million people in Beijing to welcome the return of Xie Fuzhi and Wang Li and to condemn the one million heroes and the Wuhan military region.
4 to instruct all localities to hold demonstrations, with the participation of the three armed forces, in support of the central authorities.[190]

On 23 July, these instructions were sent to localities throughout the country in the form of an 'emergency notice', which instigated demonstrations to condemn the counter-revolutionary riots in Wuhan. On 25 July, the mass rally which had been decided upon, took place in Tiananmen Square with full participation of the leadership. The next day, a 'public notice' condemned the Wuhan military region and its leading members who, as requested, had arrived in Beijing on 24 July. The notice, which had been sanctioned by Mao before its publication, accused Chen Zaidao of having opposed Chairman Mao, the Party centre, the MC and the CCRG.

Conforming to the 22 July decision of the Party centre, the open letter to the 'revolutionary masses and the commanders and fighters of the PLA in Wuhan' was published on 27 July. It denounced the 20 July event as a 'wild attack by a handful of capitalist roaders within the Party and the army', and claimed that 'individual leaders of the Wuhan military region had made mistakes of orientation and line'.[191]

Under the massive political offensive launched by the proletarian headquarters, the 'One Million Heroes' began to disintegrate. Many of its members deserted the organisation. Many fled to other parts of the country to avoid persecution by the workers' general headquarters. The core members of the 'One Million Heroes' were chased, and if captured, often tortured by the victorious opposing faction. Violence was not only confined to Wuhan but spread throughout the province. 184,000 people were wounded, maimed or died. In the city itself, the death toll amounted to some 600 people, and about 66,000 were wounded.[192]

The leaders of the Wuhan military region, who had been ordered to Beijing, were not only condemned by the central authorities but also assaulted by the radicals. The Jinxi guest house where they were living, was encircled by thousands of radicals, mainly members of military art troupes and military school students, who intended to capture Chen Zaidao. In spite of the resistance of the PLA soldiers who guarded the house, the demonstrators succeeded in breaking into the building. As the assault was in process, the commander of the Beijing garrison, General Fu Chongbi, ordered Chen Zaidao and his retinue to stay in an elevator which was suspended between two floors after its power had been cut.[193]

The Wuhan military leaders were saved from the mob, but not from disgrace. During a meeting on 26 July, attended by Zhou Enlai, members of the CCRG, of the MC and of the army CRG, Chen Zaidao and Zhong Hanhua were dismissed from their posts and were replaced by Zhen Siyu and Liu Feng respectively. But two major military leaders at the centre, Marshal Xu Xiangqian, General Peng Shaohui, the deputy chief of staff, and Wang Renzhong, first political commissar of the Wuhan military region were also relieved from their responsibilities after being accused of having supported Chen Zaidao.[194]

The purge was, however, not as extensive as Lin Biao and Jiang Qing would have desired. Although Chen Zaidao was accused of having staged a counter-revolutionary mutiny, he was not treated as a counter-revolutionary. Mao, to some extent, had given him protection and had said after his arrival in Shanghai from Wuhan that, if Chen had intended to stage a mutiny, he would not have been able to leave the city. Moreover, in a telegram to the Wuhan military region, Mao had referred to Chen as 'comrade' which indicated that he did not take him for a counter-revolutionary.[195]

The Wuhan event, nonetheless, gave the CCRG increased leverage for the further radicalisation of the CR. It provided it with the opportunity to deal with those military regions and provincial military districts which still sided with the conservatives or gave only nominal support to the radicals. In a *Red Flag* editorial entitled 'The Proletariat Must Take Hold of the Gun', published on the occasion of the 40th anniversary of the founding of the PLA, the CCRG called on the revolutionary rebels and red guards to 'drag out the handful of people in authority taking the capitalist road in the army'.[196]

This article marked the most critical moment for the military since the beginning of the CR. Although the PLA had been confronted with numerous problems related to the CR within its ranks and to the policy of supporting the left, the army, unlike the Party, had not been a target of the movement. The *Red Flag* article signalled a dramatic change in the situation, since it positioned the army on the same footing as the Party, where the movement was also carried out under the slogan to 'drag out a handful of persons in authority taking the capitalist road'.

Since the army was about to become a target of the CR, many provincial and local military leaders, who had failed to give active support to the radicals or had suppressed them, were facing the danger of the radicals' revenge. In Wuhan, where the radicals were riding the high tide of victory, the bewilderment of the military and the conservatives was particularly conspicuous. With Wuhan as an example, radicals everywhere were ready to direct the spearhead of the struggle against the military. The CR appeared to develop into a new stage.

Mao, however, would not allow this to happen. He considered the army as 'the great wall' in the defence of the country. By the summer of 1967, the process of seizing power had reduced the Party to shambles and badly damaged the administrative system, and the PLA remained the only relatively viable instrument of power. If the call to label military leaders as 'army persons in power travelling the capitalist road' was followed, the only remaining power structure was in danger of being destroyed. Mao understood this better than the civilian CCRG. He reversed his priorities and decided to preserve the army as a viable institution. The author of the *Red Flag* article, Guan Feng, became the scapegoat for this mistake and was purged. A number of public meetings condemned the call to attack the military, and by September, the crisis of the army was over. The CR entered a new stage during which the military establishment dominated the Chinese political scene for a number of years through revolutionary committees and through its leading role in the campaign to purify class ranks.

After September 1967, the military played a dominant role in China's civil affairs. Such involvement not only corresponded to a certain historical tradition of the PLA, but also to Mao's concepts of a socialist society where every citizen had to be involved in multi-faceted activities covering politics, agriculture, industry and education. On the eve of the collapse of the Guomindang, Mao had issued a directive to the commanders of the four field armies detailing the role of the military under communist rule. 'The army is not only a fighting force,' Mao wrote, 'it is mainly a working force. All army cadres should learn how to take over and to administer the cities.' They should learn to 'be good at managing industry and commerce, running schools, newspapers, news agencies and broadcasting stations'.[197]

In every city which was taken over by the PLA, the army established a military control commission and dispatched military control groups and army representatives to all government agencies, factories, schools and other areas of public interest. The takeover was quick and orderly. Within a few years, the army representatives in all non-military agencies cast off their uniform and became civilian leaders of the units in their charge. A similar process occurred during the CR, when during the phase of power seizure in January 1967, military control was introduced in areas such as national and local broadcasting stations, prisons, warehouses, roads and bridges.[198] Until the end of February, a few municipal and provincial revolutionary committees had been established. In March, Mao declared that revolutionary committees should become the provincial administrative organs and be established with the participation of the military, mass organisations, and veteran cadres, the so-called 'three-in-one combination'.[199]

The military represented the most powerful element in this alliance, since veteran cadres were at that time most vulnerable and mass organisations divided and inexperienced in administration. The disputes among them and the divisions between them and the army, brought the establishment of revolutionary committees practically to a halt from March 1967 onward. The incorporation of veteran cadres also posed numerous problems as different factions supported different persons. Since the administration was unable to function under such circumstances, military control was implemented. In March, a military control commission under the direction of General Huang Yongsheng, commander of the Guangzhou military region was established in Guangdong, another one in Qinghai under the leadership of the provincial military commander, General Lin Xianquan, a third one in Anhui, under the direction of General Qian Jun.[200]

At central government level, military control groups were introduced in those ministries where factional fighting was particularly rampant. In schools and colleges, workers' Mao Zedong propaganda teams under military leadership exercised control from July 1968 onwards. In enterprises and factories the military took over the administration.

When the process of establishing revolutionary committees in provinces and municipalities began to accelerate in 1968, it became evident that the military played the dominant role in these committees. Of the 479 standing committee members of revolutionary committees established until September 1968, 235 or 49 per cent were military men, 109 or 22 per cent were veteran cadres, and 132 or 27.6 per cent were representatives of mass organisations. The predominance of the PLA was even clearer at the level of directorship of these committees. Of the 29 directors, 20 or 70 per cent were PLA men.[201]

The composition of the leading organs of the Party after the 9th Party Congress demonstrated the same trend. Among the full members of the CC elected at that congress, 51.2 per cent were military representatives, 31.5 per cent were veteran cadres and 17.2 per cent representatives of mass organisations.[202]

5

FLUCTUATIONS BETWEEN ORDER AND DISORDER

From great alliances to revolutionary committees

During his talks with provincial leaders in the summer of 1967, Mao made a number of remarks which were published as his latest instructions. In comparison with his call, at the beginning of the year, to wage an 'all-round class struggle', there clearly was a change of tone. Mao now pointed out that 'there is no fundamental clash of interests within the working class. Under the dictatorship of the proletariat, there is no reason whatsoever for the working class to split into two big irreconcilable organisations'.[1] He urged the students to unite in great alliances. In view of the large number of conservatives, he played down the importance of the differences between them and the radicals. If some people had joined the conservative organisations, this was a matter of perception, he said. Even if it was a question of standpoint, as some people held, so what? The standpoint could be changed.[2]

Referring to the radicals who projected themselves as the left and demanded to be at the centre of great alliances, Mao declared that no faction or organisation should 'consider itself at the centre'. He warned 'the leaders of revolutionary rebels and the young fighters of the red guards, that now is the time that they may make mistakes'. This was a tactful way of telling the radicals that they had already made mistakes, in particular, they had failed to realise great alliances. Now he wanted them 'to combat self-interest and criticise and repudiate revisionism'.[3]

He remarked that Lin Biao had defined the CR in December 1966 as a movement to criticise, examine and educate Party cadres.⁴ Many cadres had been criticised, struggled against and even overthrown. Now it was time to rehabilitate them. Mao pointed out that 'correct treatment of cadres is the key to creating revolutionary "three-in-one combination", consolidating the revolutionary great alliance and making a success of struggle-criticism-transformation in each unit'.⁵

Mao adopted a series of measures. He condemned both the *Red Flag* editorial dealing with capitalist roaders in the army and Wang Li's speech to the foreign ministry rebels as 'poisonous weed' and ordered the arrest of Wang Li and Guan Feng, the author of the editorial.⁶ A third member of the CCRG, Qi Benyu, who had been deeply involved with the red guards, was arrested later. All three were accused of being responsible for inflaming anarchism and of instigating the radicals to attack the PLA. An order was issued on 5 September to prohibit the looting of weapons from the army.

The change of direction of the CR became public knowledge in early September. On 1 and 5 September, Jiang Qing made speeches attributing all excesses of the CR to ultra-leftism in the mass organisations and to the sinister activities of a mysterious underground organisation, the 'May 16 group'. She condemned 'the wrong slogan of dragging out a handful of capitalist roaders in the army', for the formulation of which she was at least partly responsible. With Wang Li and Guan Feng as scapegoats, she, Chen Boda, Kang Sheng and other CRG members posed as the heroic opponents to ultra-leftism.⁷

The establishment of great alliances

Mao's immediate concern was to terminate armed factional fighting. To achieve this, it was necessary to abolish the factions and to establish an alliance between the two hostile groups. This was considered crucial for the normalisation of the situation. All propaganda organs were set into motion urging the mass organisations to negotiate their merger and to set up great alliance committees.

On 16 and 17 September, Zhou Enlai, Chen Boda, Kang Sheng, Jiang Qing, Xie Fuzhi and other leaders received representatives of the two major factions of Beijing red guards urging them to cease fighting and warning them against further mistakes.⁸ Under the concerted efforts of the leadership, Shanghai was able to report that workers of the Chapei District had dissolved their separate organisations on 13 September and had established a unified organisation. Other workers followed suit, and in several districts of the city and major industrial plants, great alliances were established. Between 19 and the 21 September, 14 colleges and 273 secondary schools also set up unified organisations.[9]

In Beijing, representatives of more than a hundred factories met to encourage workers to follow Mao's instructions regarding great alliances. During the following days, over 1,800 units in industry, communication, finance and trade, and in the cultural and educational sectors reported to the Beijing municipal revolutionary committee that they had realised great alliances. By 21 September, 80 per cent of the units in Beijing's machine building, instruments and meters, and chemical industries, in municipal construction departments, as well as 20 colleges and 266 secondary schools also formed great alliances.[10]

Following the examples of Beijing and Shanghai, great alliances were established in many units in other cities. But in others, negotiations between different factions or organisations for the establishment of alliances broke down or never started.

On 10 October, the CC, the State Council and the CCRG issued a circular ordering the resumption of normal curricular activities in all primary and secondary schools and in all colleges and universities. The aim was to reassemble all students who continued to roam around the country. Another joint circular, issued on 17 October, ordered the establishment of great alliances in all factories, schools, departments and undertakings. In each case, all mass organisations were required to merge and form an alliance committee composed of representatives of the mass organisations with the proportion of representation to be established through negotiations. It was planned that the committee select representatives to the future revolutionary committee which was to be based on the principle of three-in-one combination.[11]

Rival factions in the provinces were asked to send representatives to Beijing to participate in 'Mao Zedong Thought study classes' in which they were ordered to 'combat self-interest and to criticise and combat revisionism'. In effect, this meant that opposing factions were sitting together to map out their differences. Military representatives and veteran cadres also participated in these meetings during which each faction, according to Mao's instructions, was permitted to talk only about its own shortcomings and not about those of the other factions. 'They should make self-criticism and seek common ground on major questions while reserving differences on minor ones.'[12] The 'study classes' were to continue until the factions had reached agreement on great alliances and on the establishment of a committee which would serve as the basis for the future revolutionary committees. Hard bargaining took place among the participants about the composition of the alliance committees and the future provincial revolutionary committees. The talks lasted well into 1968 when revolutionary committees were finally established in all provinces.

While these negotiations took place in Beijing, armed fighting continued in some areas. It was particularly severe in the Guangxi autonomous region and in Shanxi province, where, in July 1968, troops had to disarm the fighting factions.[13] When order was finally established, Mao, in the fall of 1968, launched the campaign to purify class ranks. The campaign, though it did not create any turmoil, ushered in one of the darkest periods of the CR.

The revolutionary committee was conceived as a provincial administrative organ to replace the authorities who had been overthrown during the seizure of power. This 'new organisational form of power for the state apparatus of the proletarian dictatorship'[14] was to be composed of mass organisations, revolutionary cadres and PLA representatives (three-in-one combination) In fact, it turned out to be a heterogeneous grouping with no clear direction.

The example of Shanghai, which Mao had cultivated as a model of power seizure, demonstrated the complexity involved in the process of overthrowing the old apparatus and replacing it by new structures. The process was complicated in spite of the fact that the Shanghai rebels not only received Mao's explicit support but also the direct assistance of Zhang Chunqiao and Yao Wenyuan, and of the local military establishment. Due to a series of controversies among the mass organisations, power seizures took place four times, before a revolutionary committee could be established.

The Shanghai workers' general headquarters had three rebel corps under its command, of which the 2nd corps, under the leadership of Geng Jinzhang, was the strongest and the most independent. After the mass rally of 6 January announcing the seizure of power from the Shanghai Party committee, the Party committee actually continued to remain in place, so that 'power seizure' had occurred on a purely declaratory level. Nonetheless, the date of 6 January was officially declared the day of power seizure.

After this day, several attempts to seize power from the municipal Party committee and government took place. On 15 January, Geng Jinzhang and the 2nd corps, together with other mass organisations, effectively took over the municipal Party committee and government. Their action was, however, not approved by Zhang Chunqiao who, after applying heavy pressure on Geng Jinzhang, forced him to withdraw. The next attempt was made by the Shanghai red guards' revolutionary rebel headquarters, also known as Shanghai third headquarters, who, albeit a rebel organisation, had strained relations with both Wang Hongwen and Zhang Chunqiao. Their power seizure on 22 January, was soon opposed by the workers' general headquarters who succeeded in overthrowing them.[15] The third attempt to seize power was made by the Revolutionary Committee of University and College Red Guards in cooperation with the Shanghai peasants' revolutionary rebel general headquarters on 25 January. This attempt also failed, since the two organisations did not succeed in gaining the cooperation of the workers' general headquarters. Finally, the workers' general headquarters, supported by Zhang Chunqiao and 38 mass organisations, established the Shanghai People's Commune. But their activities did not go unchallenged. The 'Shanghai Revolutionary Rebels' Committee of Great Alliance', which grouped 32 mass organisations headed by the 2nd corps confronted it and also claimed power. The dispute over the seizure of power came to a crucial point in early February, threatening to end in a head-on clash, when Zhang Chunqiao, with Mao's backing, invited Geng Jinzheng, the head of the Committee of Great Alliance to the negotiating table. Zhang told Geng that he and Yao Wenyuan had joined the Shanghai People's Commune and showed him Mao's instruction according to which 'Zhang Chunqiao and Yao Wenyuan should participate in the provisional organ of power in Shanghai'. Geng had to abandon his resistance and agreed to cooperate with the Shanghai People's Commune which was officially inaugurated on 5 February.[16]

The name 'People's Commune' gave rise to much discussion in Beijing. If the new organ of power was called a 'People's Commune', then all provinces and municipalities would follow this example and also adopt this name. In that case the name of the country might have to be changed to 'Chinese People's Commune'. Mao asked the question what the position of a Chinese People's Commune in the international system would be. In his view, such a denomination might induce other countries to refuse China recognition as a state. But there was a more substantial reason for the inacceptability of the term. The Paris Commune was a model of general elections incompatible with the three-in-one combination of revolutionary committees which was to be realised through negotiations and not through elections. As Qi Benyu was later to comment: 'if it does depend on balloting, our communist party would not have won the victory. From the start, revolutionaries are always in the minority.'[17] This was also the case of the revolutionary rebels at the time when the concept of revolutionary committees took form. Later, however, as the revolutionary committees became an organisational form for the restoration of order, revolutionary rebels who had fallen into disgrace, were hardly represented in their midst. It was thus decided to call the leading body in Shanghai a revolutionary committee, which was inaugurated on 24 February with Zhang Chunqiao as its director and Yao Wenyuan, Xu Jianxian and Wang Hongwen as deputy directors.[18]

In January and February, power was seized throughout the country, but only four provinces[19] and one municipality[20] succeeded in establishing revolutionary committees. The process of creating revolutionary committees appeared to be much more strenuous than expected. The main reason for this was the persistent conflict between radicals and conservatives over the question of who were the 'revolutionary cadres' to be incorporated into the three-in-one combination of great alliances. The controversy had been fuelled by official statements emphasising that power should be seized by the 'revolutionary left'.

This requirement made the realisation of great alliances extremely difficult. The radical wing of the red guards and rebels naturally claimed to be the true revolutionary left and rejected alliances with the conservatives. The numerically superior conservatives refused to yield and declared themselves proletarian revolutionaries. If they had made any mistakes, it had been that they began later than the rebels to criticise the bourgeois reactionary line. But that was a question of the past, they argued, and the rebels had no right to monopolise the title of 'revolutionary left'. The situation was further complicated by the military suppression of radical mass organisations in certain areas, which allowed the conservative wing to seize power, only to be denied recognition by the CCRG who had to approve or disprove the validity of power seizure.

In many cases, as exemplified in the split between the Shanghai workers' general headquarters and its 2nd corps, the radicals failed to unite among themselves. Other examples of disunity could be discerned in Beijing, where the radicals split into two factions, the 'Heavenly Faction' represented by the 'Red Flag' of the Beijing Aeronautical Engineering Institute and the 'Earthly Faction' represented by 'East is Red' of the Beijing Geological Institute.[21]

Mao appeared to have become increasingly aware that the emphasis on the difference between the revolutionary left and the right was harmful to the establishment of great alliances. In order to promote unity, Mao's proletarian headquarters began to refrain from labelling organisations as conservative. The Anhui events were an example of this effort. In Anhui, power was seized in January 1967 by the rebel faction who declared that their action was 'very good', *hao de hen* which led them to be called *hao pai*. The opposing faction condemned the power seizure as *hao ge pi* (as good as a fart) and were subsequently called *pi pai*. Since both factions were equally strong in numbers, the Beijing authorities who invited them to negotiate in the capital, referred to them as *hao pai* and *pi pai*, thus avoiding to characterise them as radicals and conservatives.[22] The negotiation between them lasted for 14 months before the Anhui Revolutionary Committee could be established in March 1968.

The incorporation of cadres into the three-in-one combination created even greater difficulties. Leading cadres at provincial and municipal levels, who had been either overthrown as capitalist roaders or made to 'stand aside' (*kao bian zhan*), had to 'show their face' (*liang xiang*) in order to be incorporated. To show their face meant to publicly declare their solidarity with the revolutionary left. But with such a declaration of solidarity with one faction, the cadre was bound to provoke the hostility of the other faction. As a result, different factions supported different cadres, and were unable to agree who was a revolutionary cadre.

Mao, who had expected that the establishment of revolutionary committees would take three to four months, began to realise that without the intervention of the centre, the process would be extremely slow, and in some cases impossible. The provinces, one after the other, received orders to send representatives of cadres, the military and mass organisations, usually varying between two and three hundred in number, to Beijing to negotiate and to resolve their differences under the direct supervision and the mediation of the central authorities. Most of the negotiations took place between the representatives of the two factions. If they failed to reach an agreement, the centre would make the final decision. Under this procedure, 20 provinces established their revolutionary committees. When the last two committees were set up in September 1968 in Tibet and Xinjiang, the centre announced the victory of the power seizure and declared that 'the entire country is red'.[23] A mass rally with the participation of 100,000 people was organised in Beijing on 7 September to celebrate the occasion. In his speech to the rally, Zhou Enlai declared that 'through repeated struggles during the past 20 months, we have finally smashed the plot of the handful of Party persons in power taking the capitalist road' whose aim was 'to restore capitalism'.[24] The revolutionary committees were largely dominated by the army, and, due to the continuing controversies between rival factions and the weakness of the revolutionary cadres, often resembled military control commissions rather than a unified tripartite structure. It could hardly be viewed, as Mao believed, as the ideal apparatus of political power of the proletariat.

The establishment of revolutionary committees in schools

and universities also proved to be a slow and difficult process. Mao, on 4 October, had urged the students to abandon their separate organisations and to 'build great revolutionary alliances' by establishing only one organisation in each class and school.[25]

But in the summer of 1968, there were still schools which had not succeeded in establishing them. Qinghua university was a case in point. The university's Jinggangshan red guards corps under the leadership of Kuai Daifu was unwilling to set up a revolutionary committee in cooperation with the rival faction, the Qinghua red guard 414. Kuai Daifu, in order to eliminate the antagonistic organisation, initiated a '100-day fight' between the factions. During the clashes, ten students were killed, hundreds were wounded and a large amount of teaching installations were destroyed.[26]

On 28 July at three o'clock in the morning, Mao summoned the five leaders of Beijing red guards – Nie Yuanzi, Kuai Dafu, Wang Dabing, Han Aijing and Tan Houlan – to Zhongnanhai for a talk where, for five hours, he lectured the students about the severity of their actions and the undesirability of armed fighting. He emphasised that workers, peasants, soldiers, neighbourhood residents and other students were repulsed by the red guards' activities. He said there were four options to choose from: one, to impose military control on the schools; two, to divide the schools into two parts corresponding to the factions so that they could study separately; three, to dissolve the schools; four, to continue to fight. Mentioning a CC notice prohibiting factional fighting in Guanxi and Shanxi, he said that some people claimed that the notice was not applicable in other areas. Mao declared angrily:

> If so, we issue another one for the entire country. If anybody violates it, if they attack the PLA, sabotage the communications system, kill people, commit arson, these are crimes. If a few people refuse to listen and continue to commit such crimes, they are bandits, they are Guomindang. They shall be caught. If they resist, they shall be eliminated.[27]

At the same time Mao sent 30,000 workers and soldiers under the name of 'capital workers Mao Zedong Thought propaganda team' to Qinghua. The Jinggangshan red guards entrenched in buildings which they had transformed into armed fortresses, resisted, killing five and wounding more than 700 workers before they were finally disarmed.[28]

In the wake of Mao's harsh warnings to the Beijing student leaders, the CC, State Council, the military commission and the CCRG, on 25 August, issued a joint circular announcing that workers' propaganda teams would be sent to all universities and schools. They would act in cooperation with the PLA.[29] The following day, the *People's Daily* carried an article by Yao Wenyuan which announced Mao's latest instruction on this issue:

> In carrying out the proletarian revolution in education, it is essential to have working-class leadership; it is essential for the masses of workers to take part and, in cooperation with the Liberation Army, bring about a revolutionary 'three-in-one' combination. . . . The workers' propaganda teams should stay permanently in the schools. . . . In the countryside, the schools should be managed by the poor and lower-middle peasants – the most reliable ally of the working class.[30]

On 2 September, the Military Commission and the CCRG issued a similar circular applicable to military schools, introducing workers' propaganda teams in the schools and imposing military control where the students failed to realise a great alliance.

At the beginning of the CR, Liu Shaoqi had sent work teams to the schools who had the task of controlling them. Mao subsequently accused him of having suppressed the students' movement. Two years later Mao had to resort to the same method in order to bring the chaotic situation under control. He wanted the workers' propaganda teams to stay permanently at the schools to break 'the domination of bourgeois intellectuals'. The workers, in cooperation with the PLA succeeded in establishing order and discipline in the schools, but they were unable to fulfil the tasks they were expected to carry out in the administration of the schools. In most cases, their capabilities were limited to low-level political work, and, if anything, they became a liability to the educational process.[31]

As soon as order and discipline was re-established in the schools, another problem emerged. More than 10 million students who had finished their schooling in 1966, 1967 and 1968 had not learned anything during the last three years besides 'making revolution'.[32] Due to the decline of the economy during those years, it was impossible to absorb any significant amount of new workers. Mao's solution to the problem was to send this surplus labour to the countryside and to thinly populated border areas, where these 'educated young people . . . should be re-educated by the poor and lower-middle peasants'. According to Mao's instructions, 'Cadres and other city dwellers should be persuaded to send their sons and daughters who have finished junior or senior middle school, college or university, to the countryside. Let's mobilise!'[33]

All instruments of propaganda were again set in motion and considerable political pressure was applied to enforce Mao's directive. The leadership proclaimed that going to the countryside was an act of loyalty to Mao's revolutionary line. The reaction of the youth towards this issue became a test of public opinion on his revolutionary or counter-revolutionary attitude. Many went with enthusiasm in the belief that they were serving Chairman Mao, to remote and improvised labour camps where they sometimes stayed for eight to ten years. In the first two years following Mao's instruction, more than 4 million young people left the cities. From 1968 to 1978, 16.2 million were sent to the countryside.[34]

Twists and turns from right to left

The measures Mao had taken to protect the army from open attacks, the arrests of two members of the CCRG, Wang Li and Guan Feng, and the denunciation of ultra-leftism demonstrated his determination to reinstate order within the country. On his return to Beijing on 26 September 1967, from a tour to several regions, he had expressed confidence in the termination of the CR in the spring of 1968 and in the convening of the 9th Party Congress that would formally bring to an end the process of turmoil China had been facing. It was therefore urgent, in his view, to conclude the examination of veteran cadres – many of whom he wanted to rehabilitate – in order to allow them to participate in the 9th Congress.[35]

But during the early part of 1968, the CR produced yet another campaign, thus increasing the confusion in the political arena. As the result of the criticism of ultra-leftism and the rebel movement, some conservatives and veteran cadres tried to re-evaluate policies adopted during the earlier phase of the CR and to renew their attacks on the CCRG. This was soon castigated as the 'right deviationist trend of trying to reverse correct decisions', and a campaign was started to counteract this trend. The campaign culminated in the 'Yang-Yu-Fu Event', which castigated the three military leaders, Yang Chengwu, Yu Lijin and Fu Chongbi as the major representatives of right deviationism.

The first major manifestation of the 'rightist trend' appeared in the foreign ministry. On 13 February 1968, a big character poster signed by 91 ambassadors, department directors, deputy directors and division chiefs, demanded the 'thorough repudiation of the reactionary slogan "Down with Chen Yi". The poster condmened the denunication of the leaders belonging to the February Adverse Current as a 'sinister plot designed by Wang Li and his gang'. It considered the conflict between those who had attempted to overthrow Chen Yi and those who had supported him as a 'soul-stirring class struggle in the Foreign Ministry', and enumerated Chen Yi's historical contributions to the Chinese revolution. The poster also stated that the CR in the foreign ministry had been led astray by a handful of class enemies and ultra-leftists.[36]

In March, the red guard organisation 'Daqing Commune' of the Beijing Petroleum Institute followed suit, also expressing their opposition to the criticism of the February Adverse Current.[37]

Members of Mao's proletarian headquarters came increasingly under attack. In Beijing, Xie Fuzhi (head of the Beijing municipal revolutionary committee) was questioned,[38] in Shanghai, opposition began to emerge against Zhang Chunqiao, Jiang Qing and the CCRG. At the same time, members of the conservative scarlet guards demanded the restoration of their organisation.[39]

Similar trends began to surface in other provinces. In Sichuan, the leaders of the preparatory committee for the revolutionary committee, Lin Jieting and Zhang Xiting who were backed by the CCRG, were openly attacked. The opposition also questioned the decision of the central authorities which, a year earlier, had condemned the Sichuan military authorities for their support of conservative organisations, and asked for the rehabilitation of those who had been labelled counter-revolutionaries at that time.[40]

But this reverse process did not last long. It was rapidly contained by the radicals who decided to hit back. On 21 March, Jiang Qing stated at a meeting with representatives from Jiangsu province that the purge of Wang Li, Guan Feng and Qi Benyu had fomented the rise of rightist conservatism. Kang Sheng pointed to the 'current danger of right opportunism and right splittism', and also emphasised that 'there are a handful of people who try to reverse the verdict on the February Adverse Current and of its chieftain Tan Zhenlin.'[41]

The Maoist leadership launched a campaign against this 'right deviationist trend'. Its first victims were the writers of the poster which had appeared in the foreign ministry in February. Zhou Enlai personally declared the poster 'an interference from the right', and Chen Yi was compelled to disavow it as 'rightist and conservative in spirit' which 'may encourage antagonism between its authors and the masses'.[42]

The Yang-Yu-Fu-affair

The new anti-rightist campaign, master-minded by the Maoist leadership, spilled over to the army where serious charges were made against military leaders. The so-called Yang-Yu-Fu affair had all the hallmarks of a high-level power struggle. On 22 March 1968, the CC, the State Council, the MC and CCRG issued a document announcing that Yang Chengwu, the acting chief of general staff, Yu Lijin, political commissar of the air force, and Fu Chongbi, the commander of the Beijing garrison, had 'committed serious mistakes'. The nature of these mistakes was not specified but all three were removed from their posts. The exact circumstances and the details surrounding their exclusion can be reconstituted from the different source material that are now available.

Yang Chengwu was awakened in the early morning of 23 March and asked to attend a meeting at the Great Hall of the People. Upon his arrival, he was received by Lin Biao, Zhou Enlai, Wu Faxian, Ye Qun, Chen Boda, Kang Sheng, Jiang Qing and other CCRG members. After Lin Biao announced Yang's dismissal, Yang was sent by plane to Wuhan where he was kept in custody.⁴³ Fu Chongbi, who was attending a meeting at the Beijing municipal revolutionary committee after midnight on 22 March, was also asked to go to the Great Hall of the People, where he was received by the same group. Lin Biao read out the order to dismiss Fu from his post as the commander of the Beijing garrison and to appoint him as deputy commander of the Shenyang military region. He was ordered to fly to Shenyang in the early hours of the morning, but allowed to write a note to his family informing them of his departure. He was arrested upon his arrival in Shenyang. Yu Lijin was simply arrested in his home in the small hours of 23 March.⁴⁴

In the evening of 24 March, Lin Biao, in the presence of Zhou Enlai and the CCRG, read the order about the dismissal of the three generals to a high-level meeting of military leaders. In a major speech which Lin Biao made to condemn the three, he mentioned Yu and Fu only briefly, but concentrated mainly on Yang Chengwu and his 'three serious mistakes' which were 'his mountain stronghold mentality, his double dealing and his distortion of Marxism'.⁴⁵

According to Lin Biao, Yang, with his 'mountain stronghold mentality', refused to employ cadres unless they had worked with him in the Shanxi-Rehol-Hezbei military region during the liberation war (1946–9). Lin affirmed that Yang, together with Yu Lijin, had plotted the overthrow of Wu Faxian, the commander of the air force, in order to obtain this post for one of his men. Lin also accused him of having conspired with Fu Chongbi to remove Xie Fuzhi, the head of the Beijing revolutionary committee and political commissar of the Beijing garrison. Yang was denounced for having conspired to topple a number of other generals, such as Xu Shiyou, Huang Yongsheng, Chen Xilian, and Yang Dezhi, respectively commanders of the Nanjing, Guangzhou, Shenyang and Jinan military regions.

As for Yang's 'double dealing', Lin said, that Yang had given the appearance of opposing Luo Ruiqing, He Long and Peng Zhen, but, had, in fact, sided with them. On the surface, Yang had also pretended to support Jiang Qing, but, according to Lin, he had collected material about her which he intended to use for her persecution.⁴⁶

The article Yang had written in the *People's Daily* on 24

August 1967, entitled 'To establish the absolute authority of Great Mao Zedong Thought' was also used against him. Mao had criticised Yang's term 'absolute authority'. 'It is not logical', Mao had said, 'to create the term "absolute authority", since all authority is relative.' This was now construed as a deviation of Marxism.[47]

Lin Biao also accused Fu Chongbi of having led two trucks full of armed soldiers to the compound of the CCRG with the intention of arresting people. No special reference was made to Yu Lijin.[48]

On 26 March, big character posters appeared in Beijing's streets against Yang, Yu and Fu claiming that they represented the February Adverse Current. The following day, a mass rally took place in Beijing where, with Zhou Enlai attending, Chen Boda, Kang Sheng and Jiang Qing condemned the new counter-attack of the February Adverse Current.[49] In typical Chinese fashion, all major cities followed suit and held mass rallies to celebrate the victory over Yang, Yu, and Fu and to disavow the right deviationist trend they allegedly represented.[50] The attack of ultra-leftism which had started in the fall of the previous year, was temporarily halted.

Unlike in other cases where documentation was invariably presented to justify denunciations, the accusations against Yang, Yu and Fu were not substantiated. The authorities did not provide any evidence about how Yang Chengwu had planned to proceed with his multi-faceted plot against military leaders of the air force, the Beijing garrison and several military regions, and in what way he represented the February Adverse Current. Neither Lin Biao, nor Zhou Enlai, nor the CCRG threw any light on these questions.[51]

The purge of Yang, Yu and Fu, clearly, was staged by Lin Biao with the support of Jiang Qing. By 1968, a trilateral power structure had surfaced at the upper level of the leadership. It was dominated by the group around Jiang Qing who controlled the CCRG, and the Lin Biao group which was formed by a few generals he had hand picked for their personnel loyalty to him. The third group were veteran revolutionaries, who, in spite of their large numbers, were relatively weak. Mao's proletarian headquarters was composed principally of Lin Biao's and Jiang Qing's group. No one really could maintain himself in any position of authority without aligning himself to one of these two groups. Tao Zhu, Xiao Hua and Liu Zhijian fell from power because they had alienated these power centres. Yang, Yu and Fu who, on the face of it, held positions which seemed sufficiently powerful in themselves, repeated the same mistake. Though their general attitude provided the basis for their fall, the following specific events provided the appropriate impulse.

Yang Chengwu had a long-standing history of cooperation with Lin Biao. In the early 1930s, he was under Lin's command in the red base areas in Jiangxi where he acted as commander and political commissar of a division belonging to Lin's 1st army corps. After 1946, when Lin Biao commanded the army in north-east China, Yang was stationed in the Shanxi – Rehol – Hebei area where he first commanded the 20th army corps and then the north China field army. After fighting in the Korean war, he was appointed commander of the Beijing military region. In 1959, he was nominated deputy general chief of staff, and after the purge of Luo Ruiqing, as acting general chief of staff.[52]

Yang was thus Lin's man. His career was made possible principally with Lin's backing. But this long cooperation between Lin and Yang seemed to have faded with the start of the CR. Yang Chengwu made no noticeable effort to show his loyalty to Lin Biao. Instead, he maintained good relations with Zhou Enlai and other veteran revolutionaries. In July 1967, Yang accompanied Mao on an inspection tour in July 1967, from where he reported to Zhou Enlai, but not always to Lin Biao, about the progress of the tour. During the tour, Mao made a number of favourable remarks about some of the marshals who had been harassed by red guards. Zhu De, Mao said, was a red commander in chief; Ye Jianying, in critical moments, had made a great contribution; Chen Yi was a good comrade; Nie Rongzhen was an honest man; Xu Xiangqian should not be persecuted; He Long was the banner of the second front army. They all should be invited to participate in the celebrations of the Army Day on 1 August.[53] Yang, on orders from Mao, reported these remarks to Zhou Enlai, but not to Lin Biao, who began to suspect that Yang was not as loyal to him as he had expected.[54]

A similar incident occurred after the arrival of the tour in Shanghai. Mao noticed a newspaper which carried the widely used epithet: "Long live Chairman Mao, our great teacher, great leader, great commander, great helmsman!" in Lin's calligraphy on its front page. Mao, who had begun to show signs of irritation with the exaggerated cult of his personality, remarked sarcastically, 'Who conferred these four offices on me? Was it the "forever healthy" '? The 'forever healthy' referred to Lin Biao who was well known for his all too frequent health problems.

Yang Chengwu, who was present when Mao made this statement, kept these words from Lin Biao. But since Lin heard about Mao's remarks from other sources, he resented the fact that Yang had not reported them to him.[55]

Lin Biao was even more offended by Yang's non-cooperative behaviour regarding Ye Qun's Party membership. A mass organisation had accused Ye Qun of being a 'sham Party member', alleging that she had failed to go through the procedures which were imperative to join the Party. Lin asked Yang to write a testimony in Ye Qun's favour, a service Yang refused to render on the ground that he had not known Ye Qun at that time.[56]

Another occurrence, which had all the characteristics of a palace intrigue escalated into a conflict between Yang Chengwu and Yu Lijin on the one hand, and Wu Faxian on the other. Yang Chengwu received two anonymous letters from the air force headquarters accusing four officials of the air force Party committee of having had sexual relations with unmarried women who had become pregnant. The four were Wu Faxian's subordinates and close friends of Lin Liguo, Lin Biao's son.[57] Yang Chengwu submitted the annoymous letters to Lin Biao and suggested an inquiry. Ye Qun, Wu Faxian and the accused read the letters, and, after some discussion about the handwriting, concluded that they had been written by Yu Lijin's secretary.[58]

The scandal took even larger proportions when Wu Faxian was informed that Yu Lijin's secretary, a married man, had an affair with Yang Chengwu's unmarried daughter Yang Yi, and suggested an investigation of Yu's secretary's behaviour. Wu hesitated, since he believed that there was no evidence to support the accusation. But since Ye Qun insisted that Yu's secretary should be arrested, Wu finally complied.

Yu Lijin was offended by his secretary's arrest of which he

was given no prior notice. Yang Chengwu was even more disturbed about the defamation of his daughter. His wife and Yu Lijin went to Liu Biao's residence at Maojiawan to protest, a gesture which was later construed as a collusion between Yang and Yu.[59]

Yu also had accompanied Mao on his inspection tour of July 1967. Like Yang, he failed to report to Lin about the events and especially about the various views Mao had expressed during the tour. Lin clearly considered this as a sign of disloyalty towards himself. He accused Yu of being a renegade, claiming that he had been arrested by the Guomindang during the South Anhui incident in 1941, and under pressure, had betrayed the Communist Party. Evidence for this allegation had been obtained by coercion from a former Guomindang army officer.[60]

Fu Chongbi, as deputy commander of the Beijing military region and commander of the Beijing garrison, was responsible for the security of Party and state leaders. This placed him in an awkward position with respect to the CCRG and the red guards, since high-ranking cadres, who had been put into custody, were in his charge, and since he provided them with daily necessities and medical care, and protected them against assaults by red guards. During the chaotic months of 1967, Zhou Enlai instructed Fu Chongbi to protect more than 30 high-ranking cadres, mostly provincial Party leaders who had taken refuge in Beijing and who were searched for by the local red guards with the aim of abducting them. Fu moved them into well-protected barracks in the outskirts of Beijing. But, as soon as they were safely hidden, leaders of the CCRG began to make inquiries about their whereabouts, cross-examining Fu for two consecutive days. Fu complained to Mao about this treatment, and Mao sided with him and Zhou Enlai on the case.[61]

But Fu was unable to escape the vengeance of the CCRG. The affair which finally contributed to his downfall, was the disappearance of about one thousand pages of Lu Xun's letters from the Lu Xun museum. Zhou Enlai and Yang Chengwu ordered Fu Chongbi to trace these letters. After some investigation, Fu found that the letters had been transferred from the museum, first to the ministry of culture, and then to the CCRG offices. On 8 March, Fu went with two jeeps and a number of army officers to the CCRG headquarters at Diaoyutai to retrieve the letters. As they entered the compound, Jiang Qing appeared and shouted, 'Who let you in? Have you come to arrest somebody?' During his purge, Fu Chongbi was accused of attempting to storm the CCRG headquarters and of trying to arrest somebody.[62]

Mao had no reason to purge Yang, Yu and Fu, but he approved Lin Biao's and Jiang Qing's initiative since he needed scapegoats for what he considered a dangerous right deviationist trend, just as he had earlier used Wang Li, Guan Feng and Qi Benyu as examples for ultra-leftism. Labelling the three generals as representatives of the right deviationists allowed him to reinforce the campaign against this trend.[63]

The immediate consequence of this affair was the strengthening of Lin Biao's position. It allowed him to exercise total control over the MC's top organ. The post of Yang Chengwu were taken over by the commander of the Guangzhou military region, Huang Yongsheng, who was nominated general chief of staff. Wen Yucheng replaced Fu Chongbi as commander of the Beijing garrison. Both appointees were Lin Biao's trusted followers, which enabled Lin Biao to control these sensitive posts. Huang Yongsheng also took over as the head of the MC administrative group which was in charge of the daily work of the MC. As a result, the MC Standing Committee stopped functioning as of 24 March, thus relieving the marshals and other military leaders of their responsibilities.[64]

The 9th Party Congress

After the purge of Yang, Yu and Fu, the campaign against right deviation gradually subsided, and, for a few months, no more campaigning occurred. In the fall of 1968, revolutionary committees were set up at provincial level and in major municipalities. In those units and localities where revolutionary committees were effectively functioning, they began to revive Party organisations. In this situation of relative calm, Mao decided to call the 12th Plenum before the end of 1968, so that the 9th Party Congress, delayed by 13 years, could be held in 1969.

To prepare the 9th Congress, the 12th Plenum of the 8th Party Congress met from 13 to 31 October 1968. Of 97 original central committee members, only 40 attended the meeting. Ten of the CC members had died since the last Plenum, while the others had been either labelled renegades, special agents, anti-Party elements or accused of having 'illicit relations with a foreign country' or were otherwise under suspicion. Among the 98 CC alternate members, only 19 attended the Plenum. The others were absent for different political reasons. In order to reach a quorum, ten alternate members were promoted to full membership, and the committee was enlarged by members of the CCRG, the MC administrative group, leading members of provincial and municipal revolutionary committees, the military regions and several CC organs. The Plenum was thus attended by 133 persons of whom 50 had the right to vote.[65]

On the first day of the meeting, Zhou Enlai announced the agenda which contained four items: guiding principles and methods for the election of representatives to the 9th Party Congress; the draft of a new constitution of the CCP; the internal and external situation; examination of special cases, in particular the case of Liu Shaoqi.[66]

Mao who made the major speech on that day, called on all participants to debate the merits of the CR. The issues to be discussed were whether or not there was a need for the CR and whether or not its achievements were greater than its defects. But Mao not only asked the questions; he also provided the answers. In his view, 'the current Great Proletarian Cultural Revolution was absolutely necessary and most timely for the consolidation of the dictatorship of the proletariat, the prevention of capitalist restoration and the building of socialism.' Referring to the factional fighting the CR had caused, which, he admitted, was particularly intense in Sichuan where several hundred thousand people collided in violent crashes, 'there was no need for alarm, because the heaven will not collapse'.[67] He further pointed out that: 'in the past, we fought north and south; it was easy to fight such wars, for it was obvious who the enemy was. The present Great Proletarian Cultural Revolution is much more complicated than any war. The problem is that those who commit ideological errors are mixed up with those whose contradictions are between ourselves and the enemy, and for the time being, it is difficult to sort them out.' In his view, the situation in Shanghai was better than in Beijing because in Shanghai, the 1.2 million workers of the workers' general headquarters had the situation under control. In his speech he did not spare the intellectuals whom he compared to a 'very adhesive soil' which the air could not penetrate and on which no plant could grow. Wherever intellectuals gathered, many problems arose. He concluded with a reference to the end of the CR which perhaps might last three years in all and might end in the summer of 1969. But it must be carried to the end which, in Mao's view, meant that 'mass criticism and repudiation, purifying class ranks, simplifying the administration and eliminating irrational rules and regulations' should be completed.[68]

For Mao, the 9th Party Congress would be an occasion for the entire Party to demonstrate its support for the CR. For the CCRG and the Lin Biao group, however, it was a crucial time for the redistribution of power. Both groups strove for a maximum number of important positions to be held by themselves and their followers. This could only be done at the expense of the veteran cadres who, albeit persecuted, were still popular and received the support of conservative factions who continued to be strong among Party members. Jiang Qing and Lin Biao agreed that the main issue at the 12th Plenum should be criticism of the February Adverse Current whose representatives were mainly Politburo members. Their aim was to remove as many veterans as possible from the Politburo.[69]

During the plenum, Jiang Qing's and Lin Biao's followers, therefore, began to attack those who had been involved in the February Adverse Current at group meetings convened to discuss the questions Mao had put forward about the CR. One after the other, they denounced a number of veteran cadres. Kang Sheng condemned the Febraury Adverse Current as 'an opposition to Chairman Mao, a negation of the Yanan rectification campaign and an attempt to reverse the verdict on the Wang Ming line'. Jiang Qing declared that Chen Yi, Ye Jianying and Xu Xiangqian had created disturbances in the army. Yao Wenyuan expressed the view that the February Adverse Current demonstrated an effort to reverse the verdict on Liu Shaoqi, Deng Xiaoping and Tao Zhu. Xie Fuzhi held that Chen Yun had opposed Mao, the Great Leap Forward and the General Line to build socialism. Huang Yongsheng declared that Zhu De was 'an old right-wing opportunist', that Nie Rongzhen had 'always indulged in mountain-stronghold mentality, had set up an independent kingdom and spread the theory of multi nuclea', and that Ye Jianying was the leader of the February Adverse Current. Wu Faxian challenged Zhu De to tell him how he had opposed Chairman Mao at Jinggangshan in the late 1920s.⁷⁰

Before speaking to the Plenum on 20 October, Lin Biao asked Mao's instructions as to the content of his speech in which he proposed to focus on the February Adverse Current. Mao agreed to this, but told Lin not to mention any names, since his policy towards senior cadres was 'criticism and protection' (*yi pi er bao*). Senior cadres, he said, should be elected to the 9th Congress, 'but they should not wag their tails' (*qiao weiba*).⁷¹

In his speech, Lin emphasised the achievements of the CR. He considered the political gains of the CR to be 'maximal' which he repeated three times: '*zui da, zui da, zui da*', whereas its shortcomings were 'minimal', also repeated three times '*zui xiao, zui xiao, zui xiao*'. In his view, the February Adverse Currrent was 'the most serious anti-Party event after the 11th Plenum of the CC' and represented 'a rehearsal of capitalist restoration'.⁷²

In his second speech on 26 October, Lin Biao talked at length about the historical significance of the CR. He said that cultural revolutions had occurred three times in human history. 'The first was represented by the classical Greek and Roman cultures with their lasting impact over 2,000 years. The second was embodied in the Italian bourgeois culture which reached its peak during the Renaissance period. The third was Marxism.' But 'all three cultural revolutions were not comparable to the current one led by Chairman Mao. The present CR is the greatest in the world.'⁷³

The Plenum took decisions about the representation to the 9th Party Congress and the draft of the Party constitution. It also approved a report submitted by the central special case examination group in charge of Liu Shaoqi and passed a resolution to expel the 'renegade, traitor, and scab', as Liu Shaoqi was now referred to, from the Party 'forever', to dismiss him from all his posts, and to continue to settle accounts with him and his accomplices for their counter-revolutionary crimes of betraying the Party and the country.⁷⁴

It was customary to pass resolutions unanimously. But this time, one of the participants with voting rights did not raise up her hand in approval. She was Chen Shaomin, vice president of the All China Trade Union Confederation and a veteran revolutionary who had joined the Party in 1928. Because of her old age and poor health, she was not persecuted, but she lost her posts in the Party and the National People's Congress.[75]

Mao made the closing speech on the final day of the plenum. Referring to the February Adverse Current, he said that although it was a grave affair, it should not be overrated. According to Mao, there were always right wingers, left wingers and some in the middle of the road in this world. The 'comrades of the February Adverse Current' should therefore be allowed to participate in the 9th Congress. Focusing his eyes on Chen Yi, Mao said: 'Comrade Chen Yi, you will participate as the representative of the Right.' He reiterated his policy that senior cadres should be 'criticised, protected, and watched' (*yi pi er bao san kan*). It had been suggested that Deng Xiaoping should also be expelled from the Party, but Mao rejected the proposal on the ground that 'Deng was different from Liu'.[76]

The 9th Party Congress

When the 9th Party Congress opened on 1 April 1969, it was attended by 1,512 delegates. Since Party committees had not yet been re-established in most provinces and municipalities, the representatives to the Congress were not elected by Party members, but were designated from a long list of names established under the supervision of the central authorities. The Congress's agenda proposed the discussion of the Political Report to be presented by Lin Biao, the amendments to the Party constitution, and the election of the CC.

Lin Biao's six-hour Political Report was a high-sounding eulogy of Mao and the CR. It elaborated at great length on the country's need for the CR, on its evolution, on the tasks yet to be fulfilled, and the strategy for its successful completion. Among the official documents dealing with the CR, this report was the most systematic and representative one. It reviewed the background and the evolution of the CR and insisted on the need for its continuation for two reasons: (1) 'the socialist revolution in the realm of superstructure' has not yet been carried out 'through to the end' and class struggle has by 'no means ceased in the ideological and political spheres'; (2) the revolution still had to accomplish 'a thousand and one tasks', such as 'carrying out mass criticism and repudiation, purifying class ranks, consolidating the party organisation, simplifying the administrative structure, changing irrational rules and regulations, and sending office workers to the workshops'.[77]

In spite of Mao's previous statements that the 9th Congress should terminate the CR, the most important result of Congress was to prolong it. On 28 April, Mao returned to this topic emphasising that many problems still existed at grassroot level, and especially in factories. Mao also stressed the need to establish unity among leading cadres who should solve their differences through discussion, and posed the rebuilding of the Party as an immediate imperative.[78] In a mild and conciliatory mood, he expressed the belief that the remaining tasks of the CR would be fulfilled within a year, and that he would be able to declare an end to the CR in 1970.[79] In fact, he confirmed the beginning of a new phase of political persecution which affected large numbers of people of all walks of life on a hitherto unprecedented scale.

After the usual perfunctory discussion, the Congress accepted Lin Biao's Report and adopted the new Party constitution which recorded Lin Biao as Mao's heir-apparent. This important stipulation was hailed on the same day, 14 March, by Zhou Enlai whose speech, in addition to paying tribute to Mao, included long passages in praise of Lin Biao. Zhou made a systematic review of Lin's contribution to the propagation of Mao Zedong Thought since the founding of the People's Republic, and praised Lin as Mao's best student and worthy successor. He pointed out that Lin was 'the glorious representative of the Nanchang uprising' which, in fact, Zhou himself had directed. He also emphasised that, ever since he had joined Mao at the red base area at Jinggangshan, Lin had led the Chinese revolution on the correct path which was to 'use the countryside to encircle the cities'.[80]

In response to Zhou's speech, Lin made an extempore statement expressing his uneasiness about the high attributes he had just heard. He proceeded to say that every victory of the Chinese revolution was won by the people thanks to Chairman Mao's wise leadership. Without Chairman Mao, he said, there would be no Chinese revolution. Without Chairman Mao, there would be no Lin Biao. He argued that if he had been working under He Long, he would have been eliminated long ago. He thus owed his very existence to Mao.[81]

It took ten days of preliminary discussions, deliberations and voting to elect the CC. The CC was indeed a major reshuffle. Of the 170 CC members and 109 alternate members only 53 were retained.[82] The Standing Committee of the Politburo was also elected with Mao as chairman and Lin Biao as vice chairman. The other members were Zhou Enlai, Chen Boda, and Kang Sheng.[83]

The new Politburo had 21 full and 4 alternate members. Its basic structure was its division into three groups with Mao at the apex and above them. There was the Lin Biao group with Lin Biao himself, his wife Ye Qun, the generals Huang Yongsheng, Wu Faxian, Li Zuopeng, Qiu Huizuo and Chen Boda, who after his conflict with the CCRG, had changed his allegiance to Lin Biao. Secondly, there was the Jiang Qing group led by Jiang Qing and composed of Kang Sheng, Zhang Chunqiao, Yao Wenyuan, Xie Fuzhi, Chen Xilian, commander of the Shenyang military Region and Ji Dengkui (alternate member). The third group was led by Zhou Enlai and was composed of such veteran revolutionaries as Ye Jianying, Liu Bocheng, Zhu De, Xu Shiyou, Li Xiannian, Dong Biwu, and Li Desheng and Wang Dongxing as alternate members. Although the last group was the largest in number, it was a loose association and the weakest politically, since many of its members continued to be periodically attacked. Except for Zhou Enlai, none of them was able to display vigorous political activity.[84]

On 28 April, the Politburo approved the compostion of the MC whose chairman and first vice chairman and first vice chairman were Mao and Lin Biao. Other vice chairmen were Liu Bocheng, Chen Yi, Xu Xiangqian, Nie Rongzhen and Ye Jianying. Huang Yongsheng and Wu Faxian were re-appointed as director and deputy director of the administrative group responsible for the MC's day-to-day work which enabled Lin Biao to maintain his control over the Commission.[85]

Though the Congress did not explicitly abolish the CCRG, it stopped functioning. Since the new CC and Politburo comprised the most important members of the CCRG, the group was considered superfluous. Jiang Qing and her group dominated all ideological, cultural and educational departments, Lin Biao controlled the military, whereas Zhou Enlai retained the administration as his power base. A formal balance had thus been established between the three groups. But this was only theoretical, since it laid the basis for the internecine political struggle between the groups which became a salient feature of the poltical climate in the years to come.

The campaign to purify class ranks

After the establishment of revolutionary committees in the 29 provinces and municipalities in September 1968 until the death of Lin Biao in September 1971, the campaign to purify class ranks dominated the scene of the CR. It was another type of 'red terror'. But unlike the relatively short period of 'red terror' initiated by the young and feverish red guards in the beginning of the CR, the new campaign, which was proudly referred to as the 'red typhoon', lasted much longer and involved millions of people. The campaign, however, received much less attention in the outside world. In fact, it was ignored by most writers dealing with this period many of whom consider the CR as terminated after the 9th Congress. This can perhaps be explained by the fact that, this time, the witch hunt for class enemies took place behind closed doors, and no mass meetings or demonstrations, no big character posters could be observed in the streets.[86]

On 26 August 1968, newspapers carried Mao's 'latest instructions' which stated that with the establishment of revolutionary committees, the phase of power seizure had come to an end, and the CR had entered a new phase – the phase of 'struggle – criticism – transformation'. This campaign should go through a number of steps which were: 'mass criticism and repudiation, purifying class ranks, rectifying the Party organisation, simplifying organisational structures, changing unreasonable rules and regulations, and sending people working in offices to lower levels.'[87]

When these instructions were made public, the purification campaign had already begun in a few selected units in Beijing. Mao's objective was to terminate the whole process by 1969. In fact, the campaign to purify class ranks began in late 1968 and early 1969, but gathered momentum only after the 9th Congress, where Mao had reiterated his instructions of August 1969. The movement began to ebb after Lin Biao's death, but was fully terminated only in the mid 1970s.

Mao's intention in launching the campaign was to uncover undesirable persons inside and outside the Party, among the leading cadres at various levels, and among the rank and file. This widened the dimension of the CR which, at the beginning, had been designed to purge the Party. Nobody, not even Mao, had the foresight to predict that it would develop into a purge of the entire society. But if one takes into consideration Mao's views on class struggle, the evolution of the CR appears to be a logical consequence. Mao believed that 'class struggle is an objective reality', that 'class enemies will invariably seek opportunities to assert themselves', and 'only when ghosts and monsters (Mao's synonym for class enemies) are allowed to come into the open, can they be wiped out; only when poisonous weeds (his synonym for anti-socialist writings and statements) are allowed to sprout from the soil can they be uprooted.'[88]

But there was a second motive for the widening scope of the CR. During the process of power seizure, mass organisations of red guards and revolutionary rebels were the motive force behind the CR. But they failed to achieve the great alliances which Mao wanted to promote, and thus gradually outlived their usefulness to him. Mao's attempt to unify the mass organisations in the movement to repudiate Liu Shaoqi, also failed. Instead of responding to his call for unity, factional fighting escalated to armed battles. During his inspection tour in the summer of 1967, Mao announced that the failure to establish great alliances was due to the fact that 'bad people had sneaked into the mass organisations';[89] and, from September 1967, a change of orientation of the attacks could be discerned. Initially directed mainly towards Party and government officials, they moved increasingly against the rank and file.

The campaign to purify class ranks was directed in each unit by leading bodies under different names. In some, it was the revolutionary committee or the preparatory organ for the revolutionary committee. In others it was led by the military control team or workers propaganda teams, or by a nucleus group composed of the military, 'revolutionary' cadres and a mass organisation. In most cases, these groups were dominated by the military who acted in cooperation with conservative mass organisations.

The targets were classified into three main categories: One, renegades, secret agents and die-hard capitalists; two, unreformed landlords, rich peasants, counter-revolutionaries, bad elements and rightists; three, newly emerged counter-revolutionaries.[90]

The first category concerned persons within the Party. Since the beginning of the CR, a great many cadres had been labelled 'Party persons in power taking the capitalist road'. At first they were considered enemies of the people, but due to their sheer number, the term soon lost its significance, and it was generally understood that 'capitalist roaders' should no longer be considered enemies of the people. The term 'die-hard capitalist' was then used to refer to a few persons like Liu Shaoqi, Peng Zhen, etc. The labels of renegade and secret agent also replaced the term of 'capitalist roader'. By definition, a renegade was a Party member who had been arrested during the years of the civil and anti-Japanese wars and who had allegedly betrayed the Party and surrendered to the enemy. After the condemnation of 61 high-ranking Party and government officials, the search for renegades was conducted on a nationwide scale.[91]

A secret agent was one who not only surrendered to the enemy but had agreed to work for him by infiltrating the Party. Such people turned out to be relatively few compared to the large number of Party members at all levels who were accused of being renegades from 1968 onwards.

The second category concerned people who had been labelled landlords and rich peasants based on their class status in the early years of the People's Republic and who had been considered as rightists during the 1957 campaign. The counter-revolutionaries in the category were mainly former Guomindang officials. Such persons had 'a history of counter-revolutionary activities'. Others who had been found guilty of counter-revolutionary activities after the founding of the PRC also fell into this category. But they were called 'active counter-revolutionaries'. They were usually sentenced to jail before they were put 'under the supervision of the masses'.

The bad elements in this category referred to a certain type of criminals who had been convicted of murder, arson, rape or robbery. During each political campaign, their behaviour was thoroughly scrutinised by the authorities. If anything reprehensible was discovered, they were to be condemned as 'unreformed' and subjected to further punishment. During the CR, 'bad elements' had to stay in place. They were considered hostile to the socialist system and suspected troublemakers, thus they were not allowed to join mass organisations, and even less, to establish their own.[92]

On 13 January, 1967, the CC and the State Council issued a six-point regulation about public security during the CR. Point two reads: 'Sending anonymous counter-revolutionary letters, distributing counter-revolutionary leaflets secretly or openly, writing reactionary posters, shouting reactionary slogans to attack and vilify our great leader Chairman Mao and his close comrade-in-arms Lin Biao, are all counter-revolutionary activities. The offenders are to be punished according to law.'[93] In fact, the scope of the decision was not limited to attacks against Mao and Lin but was extended to all leaders of the proletarian headquarters such as Zhou Enlai, Chen Boda, Kang Sheng, and Jiang Qing. In the initial stages of the campaign to purify class ranks, offenders of this regulation were the major 'newly emerged counter-revolutionaries'. Later investigations of this kind focused on the 'May 16 group', and turned into the largest witch hunt of the CR.

Experimental stage of purifying class ranks

At the time of planning the new campaign, Mao believed in experimenting with it first on a small scale. In his view, it was necessary 'to make a breakthrough at some single point, gain experience and use this experience as a guidance for other units.'[94] At the beginning of the campaign, he selected six factories and two universities in Beijing as subjects of experimentation.[95] As Mao's focal points, these units received the attention of the entire country.

The six factories and two universities began the campaign in early 1968 under the guidance of the military, and rapidly reported about their experience. Mao redistributed those reports he considered most useful, as examples to be emulated.

'The experiences of the six factories and two universities', as it was officially called, served as guidelines for the campaign at national level.

The Xinhua Printing House, in its report of May 1968, entitled 'Experiences of the military control team to mobilise the masses to wage struggle against the enemy', set the tone for the campaign. It stated that:

> the military control team is very resolute in mobilising the masses to struggle against the enemy. It led the masses to expose and repudiate secret agents, renegades, and a handful of capitalist roaders relentlessly. Relentless and merciless blows will be dealt especially on those counter-revolutionaries discovered to have malevolently vilified the great leader Chairman Mao and vice chairman Lin, viciously attacked the CCRG and opposed the proletarian headquarters.[96]

This report, in effect, extended the scope of condemnations from those who had made negative remarks abut Mao and Lin to people who had criticised the CCRG and other members of the proletarian headquarters. Mao sanctioned this extension. In his written comment on the report, he said that among similar reports he had seen, 'this one is the best'.

The report contained a number of examples which were meant to show the resoluteness of the military control team 'to uncover the class enemy'. It gave a detailed description of the case of a man who was suspected of having written 'a vicious reactionary slogan'. At first, the report declared, he denied it. His handwriting was thereupon examined by experts from the police, who concluded that the man had not written the slogan. But the military control team decided that the writer of the slogan had to be discovered by any means. During a meeting with the workers of the printing house, convened to discuss the problem, the participants provided the military leadership with evidence that the man had recently been showing signs of nervousness. This nervousness was interpreted as a sign of guilt, and the meeting decided that, notwithstanding the expertise on his handwriting, he was the one who had written the slogan. After repeated cross-examination, the man finally confessed, but he could not explain the difference in his handwriting. It was only through much 'education', the report said, that the man was able to confess that he had changed his handwriting with purpose to 'cheat the masses'. He also confessed that he had listened to 'enemy broadcasting' with other counter-revolutionaries and had exchanged 'counter-revolutionary words' with them. The next step was then that he was forced to denounce others. The moral of this example was that it was not enough to trust the conclusions of the police, but it was necessary to rely on the masses to expose counter-revolutionaries.[97]

The report also cited the example of a counter-revolutionary woman who was condemned to manual labour. In a moment of inattention by her guards, she rushed to the top of a building, jumped down and killed herself. The experience provided by this event was that it was difficult to prevent counter-revolutionaries killing themselves. But what was more important, the report stated, was that the woman had constituted 'a negative example' and that, due to her death, lessons could no longer be drawn from her.[98]

Another 'good experience' of the campaign at the Xinhua Printing House was the establishment of a new category of people who 'neither belonged to the People nor were class enemies'. According to the report, 'those were the persons who, at one push, would fall down, but at one pull, they would stand up.'

Four kinds of people belonged to this category. One, those who had 'serious political problems in their personal history' but could nonetheless not be considered renegades, special agents or old-line counter-revolutionaries. Two, those who had a family background of the exploiting class, and whose family members had been imprisoned or executed, or were sent to the countryside because of this background. Persons belonged to this group if they had demonstrated a 'backward political attitude' by failing to renounce their ties with their family, even if otherwise they did not 'adhere to a reactionary political stand'. Three, there were people who had not committed political errors but had made other serious mistakes which had 'provoked the fury of the masses'. Finally, there were those who had committed serious mistakes and excesses during the CR, such as beating cadres and the like. The leaders of the campaign at the Xinhua Printing House had realised the 'experience' of having successfully educated and remoulded those people who were on the brink of falling into the hands of the class enemy and to rescue them from such grave danger.[99]

These experiences received high ratings from the authorities and were widely imitated. Many people who were considered to have 'problems' were suspected to belong to this category. They were coerced into confessing their 'crimes' so that they could be 'pulled to the side of the people' instead of 'falling into the camp of the class enemy'.

The Beijing University 'Report of Investigation and of Remoulding Class Enemies' drafted in March 1970 indicated the scope of the campaign. Within two months, from July to September 1968, the campaign uncovered: 3 renegades; 55 special agents – among them 17 underground Guomindang agents; 21 persons with a history of counter-revolutionary activities; 9 active counter-revolutionaries; 14 landlords, rich peasants and bad elements. In all, this totalled 102 persons from a staff of 4,711. In order to identify these 102 persons, a much larger number of people, perhaps ten times as large, had to suffer through the process of investigation.[100]

At Qinghua University, a PLA Mao Zedong propaganda team implemented Mao's policy of 're-education' of intellectuals to 'give them a chance to turn over a new leaf'. In its report of January 1969, it claimed that intellectuals at this university fell into two categories: those who had received a capitalist education before 1949, and those who had been educated under the revisionist line after liberation. The former were bourgeois intellectuals and the latter had a bourgeois world outlook. Among the teaching staff, more than one hundred persons were labelled 'bourgeois academic authorities'. They were repeatedly submitted to criticism sessions before they were allowed to 'examine themselves'. Only when the self-examination was accepted by 'the masses', were they given the chance 'to turn over a new leaf' which implied that they could keep their teaching position. Of the 6,000 teaching and administratiron staff, 1,228 had been under investigation, 178 were labelled class enemies. In the first two months of the campaign, 10 people died of persecution.[101]

On 17 March 1969 the *Beijing Daily* published an editorial about the experiences gained by the six factories and one university in purifying class ranks, which emphasised that class struggle had to continue, and the masses had to be extensively mobilised in order to purge class enemies. The 9th Party Congress, held in April 1969, instead of ending the CR as Mao had previously intended, announced that it had to continue to implement the task of 'struggle-criticism-transformation'. With this pronouncement and the publication of the 'experiences' on a nationwide sale, the campaign to purify class ranks was in full swing.

The renegades

The campaign to uncover renegades was a horrifying ordeal to those Party and government officials who had joined the Party in the early years. In the 1930s about 130 underground Party members had been arrested by the Guomindang authorities. In most cases, they were released from prison after signing a statement denouncing the Communist Party. This was a procedure to which the Party centre at Yanan, and Mao himself had given their consent. According to organisational principles of the Party, the cases of the former prisoners had nonetheless been thoroughly examined before they were allowed to work for the Party again. In fact, all of them had resumed their clandestine or open Party activities. At the beginning of the CR, many of them had reached high-level positions. Bo Yibo, for example, was vice premier, An Ziwen was the head of the CC organisational department, Liu Lantao was first secretary of the North-west China Bureau, Yang Xianzhen was president of the Central Party School.

On 16 September, 1966, Kang Sheng wrote a letter to Mao in which he expressed his suspicion about 61 high-level cadres. He had consulted Beijing newspapers of August and September 1936, where their anti-communist statements had been published, and he concluded, in the midst of the campaign against Liu Shaoqi who had proposed the plan to free the prisoners, that the method to obtain their release was 'entirely wrong. It was an anti-communist decision.'[102] Mao, at that time, disagreed with Kang Sheng's interpretation. But in November 1966, the North-west China Bureau reported that the red guards had accused Liu Lantao of having published an anti-communist statement in the 1930s. In all likelihood, they had obtained this information from the CCRG. Zhou Enlai reminded Mao that Liu Shaoqi's decision at that time was 'indeed a decision taken by comrade Shaoqi on behalf of the Party centre. It was examined at both the Seventh and the Eighth Party Congress. Therefore, the centre must admit its knowledge about this matter.'[103] Zhou suggested that it should be made clear to the red guards that the issue was known to the Party centre. Mao agreed with Zhou's report.

But in February 1967, at the peak of the campaign against Liu Shaoqi, Mao reversed his opinion and approved the views of his evil genius Kang Sheng. In his talk with the Albanian Defence Minister, Begir Balluka, he said:

> some people had been communist Party members in the past but later became traitors and announced their opposition to the communist Party in the newspapers. At that time, we did not know they had opposed the communist Party. They referred to 'going through specific formalities', but we did not know what it was about. Now, investigations brought the real situation to light. It was to support the Guomindang, to oppose the communist Party.[104]

On 17 March 1967, the centre issued a document to the entire Party providing 'Material about the betrayal of Bo Yibo, Liu Lantao, An Ziwen, Yang Xianzhen, and others' and condemning them as the '61 renegade clique'. The document stated that 'the release after confession and surrender by Bo Yibo and others was approved behind Chairman Mao's back.'[105]

The so-called 61 renegade clique immediately became a national phenomenon, and a precedent for red guards to search for more renegades. The red guard operation was supported by the leadership. On 5 February 1968 it issued a 'Report about digging out renegades' among members of the Heilongjiang provincial revolutionary committee, one of the first to have been established. According to this report, 'Liu, Deng, Tao and their accomplices Peng, Luo, Lu, Yang, An (Ziwen) Xiao (Hua) and others, all renegades or counter-revolutionary revisionists, have hidden within the Party, usurped important posts in Party and government organs and formed a renegade clique.' It instructed the entire Party:

> to adhere to the mass line to make a thorough investigation and study of the archives of the enemy and puppet

governments, so as to uncover the renegades, secret agents, persons having illicit relations with a foreign country and all kinds of counter-revolutionaries hidden in every locality, every unit and every corner.

With such encouragement, the campaign uncovered renegades and secret agents individually and 'in cliques'.[106]

In Mao's view, the campaign against the renegades contributed to the cleansing of the Party. But Kang Sheng and Jiang Qing used it as a means to eliminate their political enemies.

In the course of the campaign, several local underground organisations, which had been established against the Guomindang or during the war with Japan, were re-examined. During the anti-Japanese war, an underground Party organisation operated in Guangdong under the leadership of Zhou Enlai and Ye Jianying. In late 1967, a special case group directed by Jiang Qing was established to investigate the activities of this organisation. Everyone, who had been involved in it, was questioned and coerced into confessing that their party branches had turned into a 'renegade branch', a 'secret agent branch' or a 'Guomindang branch'. The investigation involved 7,200 people of which 85, including Lin Qiangyun, the vice governor of the province, were tortured to death.[107]

A similar situation existed in Shanghai where, from the early 1920s, underground Party activities were flourishing. On the eve of the establishment of the PRC, more than 500 underground Party branches with about 8,000 Party members were active in this city. From 1967 onwards, more than 6,000 people who had belonged to the clandestine Shanghai Party branches before 1949 were investigated, many of them labelled renegades or secret agents. Four of them died during this procedure.[108]

In 1925 the CCP, in agreement with the Comintern, established the People's Revolutionary Party (IMPRP) in Inner Mongolia whose core members were communists. The IMPRP ceased functioning after the failure of the 1927 uprisings. In February 1968, Kang Sheng and Jiang Qing claimed that the IMPRP still existed and operated underground. The discovery of their activities should be one of the main targets of the campaign to purify class ranks in Inner Mongolia. From 1968 to the early 1970s, the CCRG engaged in a large-scale search for IMPRP members, which involved 346,000 people and physically eliminated 16,222.[109]

The Xian incident of 1936, during which Chiang Kai-shek had been captured by the generals Zhang Xueliang and Yang Hucheng and detained in Xian, also had repercussions on the CR. The issue was to persuade Chiang Kai-shek to cease hostilities against the CCP and to establish an alliance with them against the Japanese. After lengthy and difficult negotiations with Zhou Enlai, Chiang agreed to compromise, but detained the two generals who had kidnapped him. In 1946, Zhou Enlai, then the CCP representative in Chongqing, asked Chiang Kai-shek to release Yang Hucheng and Zhang Xueliang. His request was supported by a telegram signed by Lu Zhengcao, Wan Yi, Zhang Xuesi and other 39 former north-east China army generals, among them many underground Party members. Their initiative had been formerly approved by the north-east China Bureau of the CCP.[110]

In early 1968, a new and tortuous interpretation of this event surfaced. It was claimed that, since General Zhang Xueliang had established an important military base in north-east China where Lin Biao's forces also operated, the telegram asking for Zhang's release was, in fact, a plot to assassinate Lin Biao. Those who had signed the cable, it was alleged, needed Zhang to organise this plot whose ultimate aim was to surrender to Chiang Kai-shek.

At the end of 1968 the CCRG with Lin Biao's approval, established a special case group to investigate all those who had signed the telegram. Most of them were, at that time, high-ranking officials in Beijing or in the provinces. They were detained and confessions were extorted. In January 1969 a list of 90 people was established which accused 12 PLA officers above army commander level, 36 provincial army and government officials and others as 'remnant elements of the war-lord Zhang Xueling'. All of them were condemned as secret agents, renegades, or were suspected as such. They were named 'the north-east gang'.[111]

A similar case was construed regarding the release of Guomindang prisoners during the negotiations between the Guomindang and the CCP in early 1946. In 1942, the Xinjiang governor and war-lord, Sheng Shicai had imprisoned more than a hundred CCP cadres. Mao's brother Mao Zemin was among them. Some of them died in prison. After their release, the CCP members returned to Yanan. In 1967, another special case group began to investigate those who were still alive. More than twenty of them were persecuted to death, all of them labelled renegades.[112]

The surviving members of the first CCP organisation in Hebei which was established by Li Dazhao in the 1920s and which had become renowned for its dynamism during the Anti-Japanese war and the civil war, also came under attack. In late 1967, Chen Boda, in a speech delivered in the east Hebei city of Tangshan, claimed that 'the Hebei Party organisation might have been cooperating with the Guomindang. It is possible that the Guomindang played the major role in this area' which implied that Hebei was infested with renegades. Another special case group investigated 1,604 persons of which 737 were labelled renegades, secret agents, hidden Guomindang elements and capitalist roaders.[113]

Whenever Mao started a new campaign, soon afterwards he felt compelled to curb it, since, in most cases, revolutionary fervour went overboard and led to excesses. The campaign to purify class ranks was no exception. After having personally endorsed the validity of the 'experiences' of the six factories and the two universities for the entire country, he issued instructions demanding restraint. On 31 October 1968, during the closing session of the 12th Plenum of the CC, he said that 'in purifying class ranks, attention should be given to the word "accuracy". Do not try to obtain confessions by coercion and give them credence. As for the academic authorities,[114] care should be taken not to exaggerate with them.'[115] Similarly, on 26 December, Mao wrote a comment on a CC document stating: 'Among those who have made the mistake of taking the capitalist road, only very few are unrepentant die-hards. The majority of them can be educated and can correct their mistakes. Do not think that all capitalist roaders are bad.'[116] This was an important policy statement which upgraded the political status of a large number of Party and government officials who had been labelled 'capitalist roaders', thus enemies of the people. Mao's expression 'those who have made the mistake of travelling the capitalist road', reduced the number of enemies of the people to a small number of 'die-hards'.

In January 1969, Mao reiterated his determination to encourage more moderation in the campaign:

> We must pay attention to policy in dealing with counter-revolutionaries and those who have made mistakes. The scope of attack must be narrow and more people must be helped through education. The stress must be on the weight of evidence and on investigation and study. It is strictly forbidden to extort confessions and accept such confessions. As for good people who have made mistakes, we must give them more help through education. When they are awakened, we must liberate them without delay.[117]

On 11 April, in a talk with other Party leaders, he again warned against the tendency to broaden the scope of the campaign. Citing the case of a university in Beijing where 900 out of 9,000 people had been arrested, he said that with the exception of those who had committed murder and arson, or spread poison, most people should not be arrested and class enemies should stay under the surveillance of the 'masses'.

Mao's attempts to moderate the campaign were not particularly successful. If anything, it was even broadened to an absurd extent. Two other campaigns against 'one smash and three antis' and against the 'May 16 group', became part of the overall movement to purify class ranks.

A new campaign within the campaign

In January 1970, the Party CC started a campaign 'to smash the destructive activities of counter-revolutionaries'. In the following months, still another movement was launched, this time directed against corruption and theft, speculation and profiteering, and ostentation and waste. This was shortened to 'one smash, three antis' with emphasis on the destructive activities of counter-revolutionaries. The campaign was inspired by Mao's perception of national security. He feared that:

> the Soviet revisionists are conniving with the US imperialists in an attempt to launch a war of aggression against our country. The counter-revolutionaries in our country

are aware of this and are therefore on the move. This is a new trend of class struggle at the present time which deserves attention.[118]

It was therefore considered imperative to eliminate counter-revolutionaries before a war with the Soviet Union broke out. The masses were officially instructed 'to create an upsurge to inform against offenders.'[119]

The massive onslaught that was, thereafter, unleashed resulted in the citing of 1,840,000 persons as renegades, secret agents and counter-revolutionaries between February and November 1970. Of them, 284,000 people were arrested.[120] It is not known how many were executed. During the CR, executions took place every year. But under the new campaign, they reached a peak in 1970 covering most of China's 3,000 municipalities and counties. If one estimates that an average of ten people were executed in each of them, there might have been as many as 30,000 killed.

Among the arrests and executions, the proportion of 'active counter-revolutionaries' who had been found guilty of attacking Mao, Lin Biao, members of the proletarian headquarters, or the CR, was particularly high. A typical example was the case of Zhang Zhixin, a Party member who belonged to the staff of the Liaoning provincial Party committee. She openly attacked the CR, and was arrested in September 1969. Even after her arrest, she questioned Mao's decision to launch the CR in her 'Manifesto of a Communist' and another paper entitled 'Question, Denounce and Condemn . . .', both written in prison. She wrote that she did not trust Lin Biao, Mao's chosen heir, and that Lin's claim that Mao Zedong Thought was the 'summit of Marxism-Leninism' had no foundation. She also accused Jiang Qing, who falsely attacked many people as renegades, of being one herself. During the campaign 'one smash, three antis', she was sentenced to life imprisonment. Since she persisted in her criticism of Mao, Lin, Jiang Qing and others, she was sentenced to death, and finally executed in August 1975, long after the end of the campaign. To prevent her from making a speech critical of the leadership, she was brought to the execution ground with her windpipe severed. She was rehabilitated in the late 1970s and was posthumously awarded the title of 'excellent daughter of the Party'.[121]

The 'May 16 group'

During the entire process of uncovering renegades, secret agents, capitalist roaders, unreconstructed landlords, rich peasants, old-line counter-revolutionaries, active counter-revolutionaries, bad elements and rightists, no campaign was so large in scale and so absurd in practice than the one against the May 16 group (*qingcha wu yao liu*).

The group, whose full name was 'The capital red guard May 16 corps' (*Shoudu hongweibing wu yao liu bingtuan*), was presented by the authorities as a mysterious and vicious underground organisation, a 'counter-revolutionary conspiratorial clique', which was capable of infiltrating other organisations, of 'doubting everyone and overthrowing everyone'. It was charged with having directed its sinister spearhead against the PLA and with having vilely attacked Zhou Enlai, 'the best premier of the people'.[122] It was accused of having instigated and manipulated such criminal activities as setting fire to the British mission and destroying part of the buildings of the Indian, Indonesian, and Burmese missions in Beijing, thus compromising the reputation of the PRC on the international scene. Also it was considered responsible for a counter-revolutionary seizure of power in the Chinese foreign ministry in August 1967.[123]

Mao wrote in September, 1967, 'we have as yet not fully identified most of its (*the wu yao liu*'s) members and leaders, but 'things will shortly be made clear'.[124] Sure enough, the proletarian headquarters soon discovered that the leaders of the May 16 group were Wang Li and Guan Feng, two important members of the CCRG. During their purge in September, 1967, they were accused of promoting ultra-leftism and of manipulating the May 16 group. In January 1968, Qi Benyu, another member of the CCRG, was arrested as the third manipulator of the group. The authorities denounced all three as responsible for ultra-leftist trends rampant during the early stage of the CR. An editor of *Red Flag* was, at some point, incriminated as the leader of the group, but due to his junior status, soon faded from the picture. When Yang Chengwu, Yu Lijin and Fu Chongbi were purged in March 1968, as representative of the right deviationist trend, they were added to the list of manipulators of the May 16 group. The list was gradually extended to include Xiao Hua, the director of the PLA general political department, Chen Boda, and finally even Lin Biao.

Western observers, usually critical of official Chinese statements, accepted the official version of the Chinese authorities in their assessment of the May 16 group.[125] When it became obvious in the early 1970s, that the group was mainly an official fabrication, the leadership avoided to further mention it. In the late 1970s, it was officially admitted that the group was an invention.

At the origin of these developments was a group of radical red guards, which emerged at the height of the criticism against the February Adverse Current and which launched an attack against Zhou Enlai. When the May 16 circular of 1966 was published in May 1967, they spread the view that the publication of the circular had ushered in a new phase of the CR, and that after the downfall of Liu Shaoqi and Deng Xiaoping, a campaign against another important leader was about to start. Having been informed by the CCRG, that Zhou was, in fact, behind the February Adverse Current, they established, on 14 June 1967, the 'Capital Red Guard May 16 Corps' for the purpose of collecting material against Zhou. The leaders of the group were Zhang Jianqi of the Beijing Iron and Steel Institute, Liu Lingkai of the Beijing Foreign Languages Institute, and Su Haidong of the Normal University.[126] In view of the fact that Chen Boda and Kang Sheng, under instructions from Mao, had made public statements against any attack on Zhou Enlai, they chose to operate underground. They also realised that, given his wide popularity, open harassment of Zhou would provoke strong opposition from moderate red guards. In a period when open criticism against the Party leadership was rampant, they clandestinely put up a number of posters which carried the titles: 'What is Premier Zhou up to?'; 'Premier Zhou is the back-stage boss of the February Adverse Current'; 'Zhou Enlai's crime is his betrayal of the May 16 circular'. They claimed that at the present stage of the CR, 'the main contradiction is the one between the new CCRG and the old government'.[127] As a result, they attacked many vice premiers and the administration in general, which was Zhou's domain.

Since the organisation did not operate openly and was very small, its influence on other radicals was minimal. Many people in Beijing did not even know of its existence. In the chaos which reigned during the month of August, the May 16 group became more active, distributing mimeographed letters at Beijing Normal University denouncing Zhou Enlai. Posters signed *'wu yao liu'* (5.16 for May 16) appeared in Beijing's streets claiming that Zhou was 'the traitor of Mao Zedongism' and reiterating that he was 'the back-stage boss of the February Adverse Current'.[128]

The May 16 group became active at a time, when Mao wanted to restore order in the country and terminate the CR within a year. He was concerned with the establishment of 'great alliances' which should precede the creation of revolutionary committees. Also he wanted to avoid the destabilisation of the PLA which was the only remaining bastion of order. Besides, he needed Zhou Enlai who was tireless in his efforts to administer the country. Mao therefore decided to destroy the May 16 group.

On 11 August, Jiang Qing, Chen Boda, and Kang Sheng called a meeting of representatives of Beijing red guards to inform them about the existence of the counter-revolutionary May 16 group who attacked the Premier and the Party centre.[129]

Under instructions from the proletarian headquarters, more than one thousand red guard organisations held a mass rally to condemn the 'reactionary organisation "The capital May 16 group" ' and the 'Capital May 16 black bandit corps' at the Beijing Iron and Steel Institute. Zhang Jianqi and other leaders of the group were strongly criticised, and one small group at the Beijing Foreign Languages Institute, named 'June 16' and closely associated with the May 16 group, was destroyed.[130]

In her speeches on 1 and 5 September, Jiang Qing again denounced the May 16 group as a counter-revolutionary organisation which was responsible for a great deal of disturbances during the CR.[131] The group became an important issue, when Mao himself condemned it as a conspiratorial organisation, after it had, in fact, already been destroyed by other red guard organisations in response to Jiang Qing's call.

On 8 September, the *People's Daily* published an article by Yao Wenyuan against Tao Zhu. It ended with a paragrah which people in Beijing soon understood as having been added by Mao himself. It read:

> Comrades, please note that there are now a handful of counter-revolutionaries who are . . . using slogans sounding extremely 'Left', but in essence are extremely 'Right'. They have stirred up evil gusts of 'doubting everyone', bombarding the proletarian heaquarters, creating dissension and exploiting confusion. To achieve their sinister ulterior aim, they have vainly attempted to shake and split the proletarian headquarters headed by Chairman Mao. The organisers and manipulators of the so-called May 16 group are just such a scheming counter-revolutionary gang. It must be thoroughly exposed. . . . This counter-revolutionary organisation has two aims: one is to undermine and split the leadership of the Party's CC headed by our great leader Chairman Mao, and the other is to undermine and split the main pillar of the dictatorship of the proletariat, the great Chinese People's Liberation Army. It has hidden itself underground in Peking for the last few months. We have as yet not fully identified most of its members and leaders. For they sent their people out to paste up broadsheets and paint slogans only in the silence of the night. The broad masses are making investigations in relation to these people, and things will shortly be made clear.[132]

Immediately after the publication of this article, the May 16 group, or what was left of it, was exposed to severe criticism, its members identified, its leaders imprisoned. But this was only the beginning of a ruthless large-scale campaign against them. In 1968, the centre established a special May 16 case group headed by Chen Boda.[133] Its members included Xue Fuzhi and Wu Faxian. The May 16 group became a national issue. In 1969, many units in Beijing began the campaign to purify class ranks with that group as one of the major targets of investigation, since the chances of unearthing more renegades, secret agents, die-hard capitalist roaders and the like had been basically exhausted.

On 27 March 1970, the proletarian headquarters issued a circular about 'cleaning up the May 16 counter-revolutionary conspiratorial clique' which was read at meetings in every unit and which asserted that 'the May 16 counter-revolutionary conspiratorial clique, manipulated by the counter-revolutionary double dealers Xiao Hua, Yang Chengwu, Yu Lijin, Fu Chongbi, Wang Li, Guan Feng and Qi Benyu, had committed heinous crimes with its ferocious attacks on the Great Proletarian Cultural Revolution. Some people made the mistake of completely denying the existence of this counter-revolutionary clique, which obstructed the process of cleaning it up, and even attempted to reverse the verdict on it. Now, the struggle against it is in full swing.' But the circular warned against the tendency to exaggerate its importance by attacking mass organisations which existed publicly, and pointed out that 'in some units, one seventh of its members were labelled "May 16 elements" '. The circular pointed out that only 'core members of the clique and its back-stage manipulators' should be exposed. It stipulated that 'more people should be helped by educating them, so that the scope of attack could be narrowed'. It further stated that 'the struggle against internal and external class enemies is very complicated. The group is definitely not the only counter-revolutionary organisation. There are others. All counter-revolutionary organisations should be uncovered.'[134]

The circular was another example of many absurd documents issued during the CR. It did not attempt to explain what the May 16 counter-revolutionary conspiratorial clique really amounted to. Was it the 'Capital Red Guard May 16 Corps' which had already been attacked and largely eliminated by the authorities in August and September of 1967 as a clandestine red guard organisation? Since no red guard organisation was allowed to exist outside schools and universities, why did the search for further members of the group not stop at this point? On the contrary, the 27 March circular declared that the organisation was manipulated by a number of high-ranking leaders. But no explanation was given as to how they manipulated it. The generals Xiao Hua, Yang Chengwu, Yu Lijin and Fu Chongbi were purged by the proletarian headquarters as rightists in 1967 and early 1968. Wang Li, Guan Feng, and Qui Benyu were members of the CCRG and condemned as ultra-leftist. No signs of cooperation between them during the CR can be detected. There was, however, evidence of political conflicts between Fu Chongbi and Yang Chengwu on the one hand, and the CCRG on the other.

The publication of the circular radicalised rather than moderated the campaign to uncover May 16 elements in different work units, most of which were considered to have been infiltrated by members or supporters of the clandestine group which had thus become omnipresent. The campaign developed into a competition between different units who were vying with each other to discover the greatest possible amount of members of the group. The number of the accused became so large that the CC, on 8 February 1971, felt compelled to establish a 'joint special case group' to coordinate the investigations between the centre and the provinces.[135]

In the meantime, the list of prominent supporters of the group had expanded. During the 2nd Plenum of the 9th CC held in Lushan in August 1970, Jiang Qing and her followers accused Chen Boda, who was then the head of the 'leading special case group on Wu Yao Liu' of the Party centre, as its 'black back-stage boss'. After his death in September 1971, Lin Biao was also accused of having supported the group. Thus, two among the five top leaders, Mao, Zhou, Lin, Chen and Kang, were allegedly guilty of involvement with the counterrevolutionary clique. No proof for these arbitrary accusations was ever provided. The mysterious death of the leading investigator of the May 16 group, the Minister of Public Security Li Zhen, who, according to official statements had committed suicide, also added to the strangeness of the entire affair.[136] After Lin Biao's death, when the leadership was entirely preoccupied by the purge of Lin Biao's followers in the PLA, the campaign against Wu Yao Liu terminated quietly in 1972 without an official conclusion. But it took years before people accused as Wu Yao Liu elements were rehabilitated.[137]

No statistics are available about the number of members of the organisation who had been unearthed within the country. According to Wang Nianyi, professor at the University of National Defence, their number amounted to several millions.[138] Professor Jin Chunming of the CCP Central Party School, corroborates this estimate. Wang Li, who had been condemned as the back-stage boss of the May 16 group, said in an interview in 1988, that the number of people accused amounted to 10 million.[139] Selected examples confirm these estimates. In Nanjing, a city of more than one million inhabitants, 270,000 persons were suspected of belonging to the organisation. In one of its factories which employed 6,000 workers and office personnel, 2,000 were accused of being May 16 elements.[140]

The Chinese Ministry of Foreign Affairs, where Wang Li's famous 7 August speech had fuelled the CR, became an outstanding example of the purge against the group. A rumour, that Yao Dengshan, a diplomat at department director level, had taken over the Foreign Ministry during the month of August, was contrived and widely spread. According to the different versions promulgated, Yao was said to have become a self-styled foreign minister for four days, or half a month. Yao was investigated at length and finally condemned to prison. He was incarcerated for ten years and finally released and rehabilitated in 1980 when the accusation of his taking over the foreign ministry was withdrawn.[141]

In the ministry, the campaign to 'uncover' members or sympathisers of the group began in January 1969 and reached its height in 1970. In the spring of 1970, Ma Wenbo, the military representative directing the campaign to purify class ranks in the foreign ministry, reported to Zhou Enlai, that more than 1,000 May 16 elements were discovered among the roughly 2,000 staff members of the ministry.[142] In many departments of the ministry, 50 to 70 per cent of their personnel was accused of belonging to the clandestine counter-revolutionary group.

The campaign was another manifestation of factional fighting where, this time, radical red guards and rebels became the targets of the conservative faction. They formed the contingents to carry out the operation of 'uncovering' May 16 elements under the leadership of the military. The tactics they employed, assured them of a snowball effect. By means of coercion, they forced confessions and denunciations of others. Radical red guards and rebels, and many moderates thus were implicated in this process which provided the leadership with scapegoats for the chaos and disorder which the CR had created during its first phase. For the conservatives, the campaign was an opportunity to settle accounts with their former adversaries where personal vendetta played a major role.

6
THE LIN BIAO AFFAIR

The way to Lushan

The rise and fall of Lin Biao was one of the most dramatic developments of the CR. After Peng Dehuai's fall, Mao entrusted Lin Biao with the army where he promoted its political indoctrination through intensified study of Mao Zedong Thought. Lin's activities had two major results. First, they increased the role of the PLA in the ideological and political sphere, and second, they transformed the army into a revolutionary instrument which in turn allowed Mao to attack his political enemies without hesitation.

Lin was capable of grasping Mao's changing objectives and of playing the role of the major spokesman for the CR. With the exception of Mao himself, Lin delivered the most important speeches elucidating the necessity, the purpose and the achievements of the CR. With varying success he performed the ungrateful and contradictory task of supporting the troublesome left wingers and of maintaining order and stability within the army during the chaotic phase of the CR. But at the same time, he worked for his own prestige and was able to establish his own power centre within the Party. He reached the summit of his career at the 9th Party Congress in April 1969 when his status as Mao's successor was officially proclaimed and consecrated in the new Party constitution which declared that 'Comrade Lin Biao has consistently held high the great banner of Mao Zedong Thought and has most loyally and resolutely carried out and defended Comrade Mao Zedong's proletarian revolutionary line. Comrade Lin Biao is Comrade Mao Zedong's close comrade-in-arms and successor.'[1]

But little more than a year later, the relationship between Mao and Lin ended with a severe confrontation at the Lushan conference in August 1970. And in the aftermath of the conference, the conflict between them became so acute that it ended in a struggle from which Mao emerged as the stronger of the two, and in which Lin perished. What were the factors which led to such a dramatic conclusion? How did it happen that Lin Biao – a formal successor of Mao – locked horns with Mao and finally disappeared from the political scene?

In order to answer this question, it is necessary to examine Lin Biao's status within the Chinese power structure at that time. This is particularly important, since different interpretations regarding the cause of the controversies between the two leaders have been brought forward. It has been argued that Lin Biao and the PLA dominated the 9th Party Congress at a time when Mao wanted to restore the supremacy of the Party over the army in order to ensure that the CCP did not 'take the same road as the KMT'.[2] Also, it has been suggested that 'the Lin Biao affair has been in essence a struggle for control of the political apparatus between Mao and his designated successor';[3] or that the confrontation between the two erupted due to the unexpected surprise attack that Lin had launched at the Lushan conference challenging Mao's authority.[4] Most of these interpretations were based on the argument that Lin and the army had become so powerful and so influential that they represented a serious threat to Mao's position.

Lin had indeed become a powerful leader during the early years of the CR. As the only vice chairman of the CCP and Mao's successor he commanded, since May 1967, the loyalty of generals Wu Faxian, Li Zuopeng, Qiu Huizuo and Huang Yongsheng, all of whom held key positions in the headquarters of the General Staff, the General Logistics Department, the air force and the navy. Lin had also reinforced his position in the administrative group of the MC which directed the day-to-day work of the Commission. The administrative group, consisting of ten members, was headed by Huang Yongsheng with Wu Faxian as his deputy and with Ye Qun, Li Zuopeng and Qiu Huizuo as its key members. On the other hand, the traditional military leadership structure composed of the ten marshals nominated in 1955, had largely disintegrated. Peng

Dehuai had been purged in 1959. He Long spent the last years of his life in custody, where he died in 1969. Zhu De was removed from the military commission during its reorganisation in 1969. Liu Bocheng retained his position at the MC, but was blind and politically inactive. And finally, Chen Yi, Xu Xiangqian, Nie Rongzhen, and Ye Jianying, re-elected vice chairmen of the MC in 1969, all of them were politically weakened by the criticism directed against them during the early phase of the CR. Lin Biao, thus, was the only person among the vice chairmen of the MC who was politically blameless.

After 1968, the military as a whole, had reached a peak of power and prestige. The times when military leaders at different levels had been harassed by the radicals and accused by the CCRG of supporting the wrong factions belonged to the past. Through their appointments as military representatives to work units throughout the country, their control over the economy, the administration, as well as the political leverage over the 'campaign to purify class ranks', the essence of power lay in their hands.[5]

The PLA, furthermore, was strongly represented in the leading political organs of the country. In the CC, the percentage of army delegates had increased from 19 to 45. Lin Biao's four trusted generals and his wife Ye Qun were members of the Politburo. Equally, the PLA dominated provincial revolutionary and Party committees. Twenty-one of the 29 provincial revolutionary committees and 22 of the provinces' Party committees were headed by military men.[6]

However, despite all this, Lin Biao was nonetheless unable to realise the historical tradition of a general who had become strong enough to reduce the emperor to a figure head and to rule in his place. Mao was too formidable an emperor, and Lin Biao's ascendancy to his powerful position at the centre, like anybody else's, had been made possible by Mao's willingness to permit him to reach such a position. Lin Biao's dependency on Mao was his greatest weakness. That Lin Biao was fully aware of this, can be gauged from the emotional extempore statement he pronounced at the 9th Party Congress in response to a panegyric speech Zhou Enlai had made about him. Lin said:

To speak frankly, I have been supporting Chairman Mao for decades. Unlike what the Premier said, my own ideological level has been extremely low. It was only under the wise guidance of Chairman Mao that I obtained some achievements in my work. Without the leadership of Chairman Mao, the Party would not have achieved the victories it can account for today. Without Chairman Mao, there would be no Lin Biao. . . . Chairman Mao played a great role. The role I played was very small, very small, very small.[7]

Lin Biao assiduously tried to avoid any suggestion of equality between Mao and himself. It can be safely assumed, that this attitude was influenced by Mao's treatment of Liu Shaoqi who had been publicly viewed as 'another sun in the sky'. When a red guard organisation published 'Quotations from Comrade Lin Biao', he ordered the confiscation of all copies in circulation because this amounted to his assuming equal status with Mao and to the *Quotations from Chairman Mao* which he had sponsored himself. In a letter to Zhou Enlai and the CCRG in June 1967, he said that the slogan wishing 'eternal health to vice chairman Lin Biao was inappropriate'. When Lin discovered a document which referred to him as the 'deputy commander in chief', he ordered its destruction. In the summer of 1968, when big character posters appeared in Beijing's street 'in memory of vice chairman Lin Biao's August 9 speech', Lin had them torn down. Even Lin Biao's son, who was officially accused of having plotted Mao's assassination, realised that his father was no match for Mao in a contest of power. He said, 'The Chairman commands such high prestige that he need only utter one sentence to remove anybody he chooses.'[8]

Although Lin Biao dominated important sections of the PLA headquarters, the extent of his control over the army as a whole is open to debate. The structure of the PLA with its divided loyalties was too complex to refer to it as a homogeneous entity; it was not.[9] This was recognised by Lin's own men. In the words of 'project 571', the secret document drafted by his supporters in preparation of a coup against Mao, 'B–52s (i.e. Mao) divide and rule policy' has fostered 'fairly complex internal contradictions within the army, which makes it difficult to form a united force which we can control'.[10]

Mao's 'divide and rule policy' may have played a certain role in accentuating the complexities of the PLA, but the major cause for the lack of homogeneity was the traditionally deep-rooted sectarianism within the army which the Chinese call 'mountain-stronghold mentality' (*shan tou zhu yi*).

This phenomenon can be traced back to the early days of the PLA. In the early 1930s, before the Long March, three front armies were formed in the three different base areas of Jiangxi province, north-west Hunan and south-west Hubei, and in the Sichuan-Shanxi border area. In the fourth base area, the Shanxi-Gansu area, two army units, the 26th and the 27th army, were established. All these armies were located far apart from each other and with little intra-army communication. There was really no organisational structure to assure united command.[11]

Although efforts to unite the armed forces were made during the anti-Japanese and the civil war when the four field armies and four army groups were placed under the direct command of the army headquarters, the PLA continued to be divided into military regions after the founding of the PRC.[12] In 1969, there were 11 military regions, 25 provincial military districts, three military districts at army level, and six garrisons.[13]

The PLA was, and still is, a complex organ, to which not only soldiers but also storage houses, schools and universities, research institutions, hospitals, and art groups have been attached. According to 1972 statistics, the PLA employed a total number of 5,953,000 persons of which 3,060,000 were combat troops, 1,620,000 were supporting troops of various kinds, and the rest were engaged in other activities mentioned above.[14]

Sectarianism based on old allegiances played an important role in the life of the military. Former subordinates tended to maintain their loyalties towards their previous superiors who, in turn, tended to use their services and to promote them. The relationship between Lin Biao and Luo Ruiqing before the latter fell from power, was based on this tradition. After Luo's downfall, Lin replaced him with Yang Chengwu, also a former subordinate whose relationship with Lin began in the 1930s. When Lin Biao began to doubt Yang's loyalty, Lin removed him in 1968. The third general chief of staff chosen by Lin was Huang Yongsheng, again one of Lin's subordinates from the late 1920's who had served with him at the Jinggangshan base area in 1927. During the liberation war, Huang was the deputy commander of the 14th army group in Lin Biao's 4th field army.

The ten marshals who founded and developed the red army, and who had been appointed in 1955 to the rank of top leadership in the PLA, also maintained strong historical bounds with the generals who had been under their jurisdiction during the revolutionary years. None of them could claim to possess the loyalty of the entire red army and their generals. The relationship between military leaders forged by historical ties could not be erased despite the fact that Lin Biao had obtained a position which had raised him above the marshalls. The only exception to this principle was Mao who was able to control everyone – the marshals and the PLA.

Had Lin Biao been able to maintain a major stronghold in the PLA, the purge of the army after his death, when its headquarters and military regions were combed with the aim of unearthing Lin's followers, would have yielded numerically greater results than it actually did. During the investigations between September 1971 and October 1975, only General Liang Xingchu of the Chengdu military region and four political commissars disappeared from the scene. In fact, the major supporters of Lin Biao were found to be the four generals at the PLA headquarters in Beijing.[15]

Lin Biao's inability to efficiently control the PLA can also be gauged from the difficulties his son encountered when he planned to assassinate Mao. The simple fact that he contemplated Mao's assassination rather than a military coup d'état indicates that Lin did not dominate the army. During the last days of his life, Lin Biao was not even able to control his own body guards. As part of the PLA 8341 unit in charge of the major leaders' security, they obeyed the directives of the Party centre.

Lin Biao's situation as a leader of the CR also had become increasingly paradoxical. On the one hand, as the second in command of the army, he had the obligation to protect lower-level military leaders against pressures and assaults from the revolutionary left which on the other, he was also expected to support it. In this contradictory position, he often chose to ignore even the most urgent appeals of his subordinates. When Han Xianchu, the commander of the Fuzhou military region, who had been under Lin's command in the 4th field army, repeatedly asked to report to Lin personally about the problems created by the CR in the Fuzhou military region, he disregarded Han's request. Instead, Lin ordered his secretary to receive Han who complained to him about the harassments and abuses the military were suffering in the area under his jurisdiction. Han implored Lin's secretary to arrange a meeting with the minister of defence so that he could obtain his instructions. Lin gave his secretary ten minutes to sum up Han's long report and discarded it without response.[16] Xiao Hua, head of the PLA general political department, was another example. Violently attacked by students of the military schools during the summer of 1967, he requested a meeting with Lin Biao to present his case. But Lin refused to see him.[17] As a consequence of Lin's attitude in these and other similar cases his relations with a number of senior military leaders at provincial level had been seriously affected.

Lin's personality and work style also contributed to his alienation from other major army leaders. He lived in self-imposed seclusion which created an aura of mystery around him. Very little was known about his personal life until Zhang Yunsheng, one of his secretaries who had worked with him from 1966 to 1970, threw some light on it. According to Zhang's account, Lin Biao lived a simple life, ate simple food and neither smoked nor drank. Unlike Mao and Zhou who both worked throughout the night and slept in the morning, Lin Biao had a very regular time schedule. He rose every morning at six, took a nap after lunch until two o'clock and went to sleep at eleven with the help of sleeping pills. Lin's sleep, like Mao's, was sacred, and was not to be interrupted under any circumstances.[18] Lin was unsociable, aloof and to some extent eccentric. He seldom invited any guests to his home and would not accept any invitation. He had no hobby, and, unlike Mao and other major leaders, showed no interest in theatre or music.

Lin lived and worked at his residence at Maojiawan, a small lane in the western part of Beijing. 'Maojiawan' symbolised the nerve-centre of the Lin Biao group. During the CR, Lin employed six secretaries. One of them was in charge of the

Party branch which, like in any other work unit, also existed at Lin's office. Two secretaries were involved with incoming and outgoing documents and mail. The fourth secretary had the sole obligation of reading books for Lin Biao and to note anything which might be useful to Lin's work. One of the most important aspects of this reading exercise was to trace the source of Mao's numerous historical quotations and references. The fifth secretary was in charge of Lin's security, and the sixth of various tasks related to Lin's household.[19]

Aside from the PLA 8341 unit who guarded his residence, Lin employed two body guards, two soldiers as servants and two medical doctors. His wife had three room servants. All together, there were over twenty persons serving Lin and his wife as messengers, cooks and other personal household.[20]

Lin Biao, who never read documents himself, relied completely on his secretaries and personnel to brief him on important events. During the CR, the two secretaries in charge of incoming papers, regularly read between one and three hundred thousand characters (roughly 250–750 pages) of material per day. Twice a day, they briefed Lin for 20 to 30 minutes about the material they had read. This method, which gave little time for information about the most important events, may have been Lin Biao's way of avoiding bureaucratism which was much criticised at that time.[21]

Another 16 persons, who were not on the list of Lin Biao's official personnel, worked at Maojiawan. They were mostly experts on Chinese and foreign philosophy and literature, on foreign history, international relations, or ghost writers who were 'borrowed' by Lin's wife Ye Qun from different institutions. Their task was to read books, to collect material and to brief Lin Biao and Ye Qun on different aspects of political life.[22]

Their reading of books and collection of material, served three major purposes: first was to assist in the tracing of the sources of Mao's frequent references to history, literature and philosophy.[23] The second was to enhance Lin Biao's own ability to use quotes and references from the classics and from foreign history in his speeches. The experts provided Lin with material for some of his major speeches. His theory about the threat of a revisionist coup d'état in China, which he developed in his famous 18 May speech to the Politburo, was based on the material that was provided to him and that mentioned the '61 coups d'état in the capitalist countries of Asia, Africa and Latin America since the 1960s', and the number of coups d'état that had taken place in China within the last two thousand years.[24] Lin's speech about the four cultural revolutions which had taken place in world history, was also based on material provided by this group of experts.[25] The third task of the experts was to brief Ye Qun about major events in world history.[26]

Lin Biao rarely received his subordinates and seldom called a meeting in his office. He spent most of the time pacing or sitting in his room, whose temperature was constantly kept at 21 degrees and where window curtains were always drawn since he loathed the brightness of Beijing light. He also disliked wind, a frequently occurring phenomenon in Beijing's climate, and therefore never went out other than for short drives in his car through the capital.[27]

Lin Biao, although refusing to read documents, insisted on writing most of his speeches himself, with the exception of those he had to deliver on ceremonial occasions. Even though he asked his staff to prepare drafts for his speeches, he usually discarded them. While preparing for a major speech, he would spend days in his office pacing and thinking, and suddenly scribble down a few sentences on a sheet of paper. He would throw the paper to the floor and continue to pace, think and scribble until the floor was full of paper. He then asked one of his secretaries to pick up the papers. He put them in order, used them as an outline for his speech and elaborated upon it orally as he proceeded with the speech. This way, during the first years of the CR, he delivered a number of such major thematic speeches as the one at the May 1966 Politburo meeting which marked the beginning of the CR, the three speeches in August 1966 which explained the purpose of the CR, and the talk about the two-line struggle at the working conference in October 1966. These speeches carried a weight that equalled Mao's statements. Their language was original and avoided the official jargon found in the newspapers.[28]

Lin's rather eccentric working methods may be explained by his poor health. He was thin and pale and suffered from a malfunctioning of his hidrosis system that provoked heavy sweating on all occasions and that made him ill-at-ease. When he had to receive foreign visitors, usually military men from allied nations, simply shaking hands with them would lead to an outbreak of sweat. Lin thus tried to avoid any such contacts. Withdrawn as he was, he allowed his wife to run his office for him. As Marshall Nie Rongzhen remarked in 1980, 'Lin was a fatuous and self-indulgent ruler (*hunjun*). It was his wife Ye Qun who was the real master of his affairs.'[29]

Ye Qun, who was born in Fujian province in 1919, was 12 years younger than Lin Biao. Although her father was a Guomindang general, Ye Qun, at an early age, became involved in anti-Japanese and anti-Guomindang activities of the communist Party, and, like many other students, joined the communist retreat in Yanan with the resolution to oppose the Japanese invasion. There, she married Lin Biao who was then in his mid-thirties.[30]

Ye Qun, an energetic, active and ambitious woman, headed Lin Biao's office at the outbreak of the CR with the rank of a division commander of the PLA. Lin Biao gradually began to dislike her for her long-winded speeches and her activities which he was unable to control. Nonetheless, he relied on her in many respects. She represented Lin on many occasions when he, due to his seclusion, preferred not to attend. She became his link to the outside world, and particularly to Jiang Qing's group, the other CR power centre. As a result, she was in total control of anybody's access to Lin Biao.[31]

Lin Biao could hardly be considered a threat to Mao. Neither was the PLA a threat to the Party although Mao himself invoked this danger and criticised the PLA on several occasions. Mao stated that decisions of a Party committee should not be further discussed by the army, that the military should adopt a more prudent attitude and that the army should learn from the people.[32]

Since Mao, in November 1938, had made his famous statement, that 'the Party commands the gun, and the gun must never command the Party',[33] a political and organisational system was established which guaranteed the implementation of this principle. The army as a whole was controlled by the MC headed by the Chairman of the Party. At all levels within the army, Party committees controlled military affairs. In any military region, field army, PLA division or regiment, the Party committee was the highest organ of command. At company level, there was a Party branch in charge of political and military matters. While during the CR, the Party system in the civilian sector was paralysed for several years, it remained intact in the military sector. During this period, the military controlled administrative and government affairs as well. But once the Party system was re-established, all military personnel in the civilian sector returned to the army following a Party instruction in August 1972.[34]

The relations between Lin Biao and Jiang Qing had changed considerably. At the beginning of the CR, it was with Lin Biao's help that Jiang Qing rose to prominence. In early 1966, Lin invited Jiang to direct a forum on literature and art in the armed forces. He wrote a summary of the forum which was published as a Pary document, and in which Lin praised Jiang Qing's competence on matters of literature and art. He gave instructions that 'from now on, the army's documents concerning literature and art should be sent to her. . . . Keep her well posted on the situation on literature and art work in the army. Ask her for her views, which will help to improve this work.'[35] Lin was instrumental in establishing Jiang Qing's image as the 'standard bearer' of the revolution in the fields of literature and art.

With Mao's approval, Lin and Jiang forged an alliance against such veteran leaders as Peng Zhen, Luo Ruiqing, Lu Dingyi and Yang Shangkun. They cooperated closely in the purge of Liu Shaoqi, He Long, and the three generals of the Yang-Yu-Fu affair. Their cooperation extended even to personnel matters. Jiang Qing, who lived in constant fear of possible revelations about her past, in the late 1950s had given a letter to Zheng Junli, a Shanghai film director and personal friend since the 1930s, to be forwarded to her former husband Tang Na, who lived abroad. Afraid that the letter might compromise her, she asked Ye Qun's help to retrieve it. In October, 1966, Ye Qun asked Jiang Tengjiao, the political commissar of the air force of the Nanjing military region to search Zheng's house for the letter which was assumed not to have been sent. The commissar instructed a number of soldiers disguised as red guards to carry out the search. The letter was never found. Zheng, however, was incarcerated and died in prison.[36]

In November 1966, Lin Biao nominated Jiang Qing as advisor on PLA cultural activities. As a reward, Ye Qun was allowed to participate in CCRG meetings as Lin Biao's liaison officer.

When the army CRG was reorganised in the beginning of 1967, Jiang Qing became its advisor and Ye Qun a member of the group. When Lin Biao established the administrative group of the MC in August 1967 with Wu Faxian as its head and Ye Qun as one of its members, he did so with the explicit support of Jiang Qing who viewed the decreased influence of the veteran military leaders in the commission with a favourable eye.[37]

In November, 1967, Mao instructed Zhang Chunqiao, Jiang Qing's close collaborator, to begin work on the revision of the Party constitution. Both Zhang and Jiang agreed to demand that Lin Biao's status as Mao's successor should be formally included in the new constitution. According to Zhang, 'the Party members and the revolutionary masses in Shanghai strongly demanded that vice chairman Lin's status as Chairman Mao's successor be written down in the Party constitution to ensure that our Party will never turn revisionist, and our country will never change colours.'[38] As a reward Lin recommended Zhang's appointment as political commissar of the Nanjing military region.

At the end of 1967, at Jiang Qing's suggestion, Ye Qun became a regular participant at the meetings of the CCRG.[39] Fully understanding the special role played by Mao's wife, Ye Qun stated that 'the chief [i.e. Lin Biao] follows the Chairman, I follow Jiang Qing.'[40]

When Lin Biao announced the purge of Yang, Yu, and Fu at the meeting of PLA officers at the Great Hall of the People, he used the occasion to pay public tribute to Jiang Qing's capacities. He said:

> Comrade Jiang Qing is one of the outstanding women comrades in our Party and also a most outstanding cadre in our Party. Her thinking is very revolutionised. . . . She has faithfully carried out Chairman Mao's directives; she has shown her creative talent by recognising problems and finding solutions. She has achieved a great deal during the CR. . . . She has her own unique function, and is standing at the frontline of the struggle in this movement.[41]

Close cooperation and mutual tributes in public, however, did not necessarily prevent Lin and Jiang from falling out in private. One instance of violent quarrel between them occurred as early as in January 1967 at Lin's residence at Maojiawan. The reasons for this dispute are not known, but witnesses overheard that Lin threatened to throw Jiang out of his house.⁴² After Lin and Jiang Qing had gradually consolidated their own power centres, rivalries and differences of interest became increasingly manifest and inevitably led to conflicts between them. Both were arrogant, highly ambitious and unscrupulous in their attempts to strengthen their own position.

Actually, it would seem that Lin Biao did not hold Jiang Qing in high esteem. His views about Zhang Chunqiao and Yao Wenyuan, whom he also considered as upstarts, were equally unflattering.⁴³ Even Chen Boda was nothing but a 'bookish scholar' in Lin's eyes.⁴⁴

Lin Biao's political position was ambiguous. As vice chairman of the Party, he ranked above the CCRG. But since the CCRG was the leading organ of the CR and had taken over the role of the Politburo, it dominated the political scene at that time. Even in the military sector, it had the leading role on all matters relating to CR policies. Lin Biao knew its weight. Any major decision he made in the name of the military commission had to be discussed with and approved by the CCRG. The eight-point decision and the ten-point decision⁴⁵ regarding the CR in the army had gone through this procedure. Lin Biao was instinctively opposed to disorder, and his disdain for the leftist intelligentsia and the awareness of their powerful influence had probably led him to distance himself from them, a factor which might have contributed to his self-imposed seclusion. He began to disapprove of Ye Qun's frequent visits to Diaoyutai, the CCRG's headquarters.⁴⁶

The January order to support the left became a major cause of controversy between the CCRG and the army. As we have seen, opposition to CR policies was widespread among the provincial military leadership. Although Lin Biao, in March 1967, pronounced a major speech to expound the significance of the CR, to warn against right deviation and to emphasise the necessity of supporting the left, the PLA tended to extend its assistance to the conservatives and, as a result, was accused of suppressing the revolutionary masses. Military leaders of Qinghai, Anhui, Inner Mongolia, Shangdong, Jinan, Fujian, Sichuan, Gansu, Guangdong, Hunan, Jiangxi, Henan and Jilin were found guilty of having made 'mistakes of orientation and line' and forced to make self-criticism. In all these cases, it was not Lin Biao but the CCRG that took the initiative of exposing the military's anti-leftist conduct.[47]

As Jiang Qing's power status grew, she became increasingly unscrupulous in her interference in military affairs. She began to develop an aversion against Huang Yongsheng, who was appointed to the post of general chief of staff in March 1968, and who, instead of fawning to the first lady of China, kept a respectful distance from her. First, Jiang Qing complained that Huang was not a good choice for this post.[48] Then she accused him of not having reported the transfer of some troops to the CCRG. When Huang retorted that he had followed Mao's orders, which did not contain instructions about informing the CCRG about the troop movements, Jiang Qing flew into a rage and announced that Huang – scheduled to lead a delegation to Albania – would not be allowed to leave. Mao himself had to intervene so that Huang could proceed with his travel plans.[49]

A similar case occurred on the occasion of Wang Hongkun's nomination as director of the PLA general political department. Jiang Qing remarked that Wang was too conservative and asked for his removal from this post. This simple remark caused the administrative group of the CMC to reconsider Wang's appointment. Since the group failed to agree on another candidate, and Jiang Qing did not anymore insist, Wang was finally kept on in his post.[50]

The appointment of Wen Yucheng as deputy general chief of staff, head of the operational department of the general chief of staff, and, in March 1968, as successor to Fu Chongbi as commander of the Beijing garrison, was another example of the rivalry which existed between the two groups. Although Wen had been known as a follower of Lin Biao, Huang Yongsheng and Ye Qun suspected him of having close connections with Jiang Qing and of having switched allegiances to her. Wen was accused of having planted a spy in Huang's office whose task was to report to Jiang Qing about Huang's activities. They convinced Lin Biao to demote Wen to the post of a deputy commander of the Chengdu military region.[51]

Chen Boda's case represented an even more pertinent illustration of the competition that increasingly dominated the relations between Jiang Qing and Lin Biao. Chen Boda, though he occupied the fourth position within the hierarchy of the Party and was the appointed leader of the CCRG, was unable to maintain a power status equivalent to his official position. Jiang Qing, whose political activism had increased considerably since the formation of the group, had effectively taken charge of it. His lack of interest in administrative problems, his bookish style, his clumsy behaviour and his unintelligible Fukian speech made him an easy victim of Jiang Qing's arrogance and domineering ways, who referred to him condescendingly as the 'old scholar' (*lao fuzhi*). Already in February 1967, he complained to Wang Li about Jiang Qing's attitude towards him and even threatened to kill himself. When Jiang Qing learned of his remarks, she shouted at him that he would not have the courage to do such a thing.[52]

On another occasion Jiang Qing humiliated Chen Boda openly when he had dared to make some critical remarks about her frequent violent outbursts.[53] Other members of the CCRG, such as Kang Sheng, Zhang Chunqiao and Yao Wenyuan, also failed to support him, and his isolation within the group became increasingly noticeable. When Chen Boda was charged with the preparations of the political report for the 9th Party Congress, Jiang Qing and other members of the CCRG criticised his draft as 'revisionist'. Mao thereupon removed Chen from the drafting group and asked Kang Sheng to supervise the preparations of the report.[54]

As the relations between Jiang Qing and Chen Boda deteriorated, Chen's contacts with Ye Qun increased remarkably, and by the time the 9th Party Congress was convened, Chen Boda had switched allegiance to Lin Biao.[55] This congress marked the end of the cooperation between Lin Biao and Jiang Qing.

Prelude to the conflict at Lushan

The causes of controversies between Mao and Lin Biao during and after the Lushan conference were complex, and, up to this day, are difficult to evaluate. According to the evidence available, one of the major factors leading to the conflict between the two leaders, was a power struggle which erupted between the Lin Biao and the Jiang Qing groups. At the conference, the question as to whether Mao was a genius and whether he should serve as head of state, became a matter of furious disputes between the two groups. But the real issue was Lin Biao's attempt to weaken the Jiang Qing group.

Mao had decided to convene the 2nd Plenum of the CC at Lushan to discuss three issues: (1) the revision of the constitution of the state; (2) the national economic planning; (3) war readiness. After the Plenum, Mao planned to hold the long-delayed 4th National People's Congress with which he intended to rehabilitate a large number of cadres and to phase out the CR.[56]

Mao considered the question of war readiness a major issue of debate for the Plenum. By the latter part of 1969, he had become convinced that the international situation was deteriorating and that the threat of a Soviet attack on China might suddenly become a reality. Although Soviet and Chinese deputy foreign ministers were holding talks on the border dispute at that time, the Chinese leadership suspected that the Soviets had agreed to hold these talks with the aim of lulling them into false security while their true intention was to launch a surprise attack on Chinese territory.[57] On 31 January, Mao instructed the entire nation to be prepared for war and decided to accelerate the production of war material within the framework of the secret 'third-line construction'.[58] On the basis of these instructions, the State Council developed the 1970 economic plan and the fourth five-year plan which contained a series of important provisions based on the principle of 'taking war preparedness as the key link'.[59]

Lin Biao apparently saw the meeting of the Plenum as an occasion to curb Jiang Qing's growing influence and continuous interferences in military matters. Because of Jiang Qing's special status, it was of course prudent not to attack her directly. But it was possible 'to revile the locust while pointing to the mulberry' (*zhi sang mahuai*) by compromising some of her entourage. Lin's malevolence was directed against Kang Sheng and especially Zhang Chunqiao who, on several occasions, had been a cause of irritation to Lin. During the early stages of the CR, Zhang had supported the 'red rebel brigade', a radical organisation at the PLA medical college in Shanghai which had launched a severe attack against Qiu Huizuo. In retaliation, Lin had supported the campaign to 'bombard' Zhang Chunqiao which Lin's followers had initiated in Shanghai.⁶⁰ Lin became particularly concerned when Mao remarked that Zhang may be a good candidate to succeed Lin.⁶¹

During the preparations for the Lushan conference, a controversy erupted among the members of the group working on the revision of the state constitution. Three questions had become the subject of differences. Firstly, should the words referring to Mao's defence and development of Marxism-Leninism 'with genius, creatively and comprehensively'⁶² be written into the constitution? Secondly, should 'Mao Zedong Thought as the guiding principle' be introduced? And thirdly, should the constitution stipulate that the post of the chairman of the state be retained?⁶³

Zhang Chunqiao, who had produced a draft without the three items, argued that the Chairman himself had deleted the first two items from the draft of the Party constitution before the 9th Congress, and he had also stated that there should be no head of state. Wu Faxian, for his part, insisted that the three points should be retained, since Mao's actions could only be explained by his great modesty. Zhang Chunqiao conceded to retain the sentence that 'Mao Zedong Thought is the guiding principle of all work'. But unpleasant exchanges took place with respect to the genius question.⁶⁴

Regarding the chairmanship of the state, the question had been discussed with Mao on several occasions. In the course of the preparations for the forthcoming National People's Congress, Mao, on 8 March 1970 had suggested abolishing the position.⁶⁵ But on 11 April, Ye Qun called Mao's secretary to inform him about Lin's suggestion that Mao should himself occupy this post 'otherwise it would not be in accord with the psychology of the people'.⁶⁶ According to the telephone records, Mao's secretary called Ye Qun back, telling her that the Chairman had smiled at the suggestion and said: 'to keep the chairmanship of the state? Who will be the chairman? I cannot take up this position again. Perhaps Dong Lao (Dong Biwu) could be the chairman.'⁶⁷ On the following day, Mao wrote a comment on the minutes of a Politburo meeting repeating that Lin's suggestion 'is inappropriate. I cannot occupy this post again.'⁶⁸ However, Lin's view on this question appeared to have been echoed by some other members of the Politburo which produced two versions of the revised draft constitution, one with and one without the articles pertaining to the chairmanship of the state.[69]

In late April, Mao again rejected explicitly the suggestion that he could occupy the post. He explained the reasons for his refusal by a historical analogy from the period of the three kingdoms. At that time, Sun Quan, king of Wu, A.D. 220–166 suggested to Cao Cao, king of Wei, the most powerful of the three kingdoms, to serve as emperor. Cao Cao refused, saying to become the emperor was equivalent to being cooked on the stove. Mao reminded the Politburo of Cao Cao and told them not to play the role of Sun Quan.[70] For Mao, the state chairmanship was only a formal position which should not be created for the sake of a person, a view which he stressed in mid July, during a session of the Politburo group in charge of the revision of the constitution.[71]

It has been frequently suggested in official Chinese statements issued after Lin Biao's death that Lin Biao himself coveted the post of chairman of the state. The suggestion was taken up in the Western academic writings.[72] But there is no evidence that Lin, although he appeared to have been in favour of retaining the post, wanted to occupy it. The suggestion that he did, was based on a statement Wu Faxian made during his confession after Lin Biao's and Ye Qun's death, according to which Ye Qun had asked Wu Faxian in private: 'If there were no state chairman, what would Lin Biao do? What would become of him?'[73] It is doubtful that Wu Faxian's confession which was obtained under duress, could be taken at face value. But it suited both him and the authorities to implicate Lin Biao in that manner. After his arrest Wu Faxian was accused of having appointed Lin Liguo, Lin Biao's son, as deputy head of the operational department of the air force headquarters which he confessed of having done. During his trial in 1980, his sister Lin Liheng testified that this was not the case. Wu Faxian later admitted that he had made not only this but also other false statements.[74] But even if it is assumed that Ye Qun did, indeed, make such a statement, it can also be construed that she made it without Lin Biao's knowledge, since she was well known for her independent activities. Lin Biao himself complained about Ye Qun's initiatives and once ordered his secretary to give her a couplet which reads: 'Do not be garrulous when you speak; do not do anything without a mandate!'[75] Lin was also fully aware of the fact that the chairmanship of the state was a mainly ceremonial post involving a great deal of official representation, which he abhorred.

The Lushan conference never discussed the question whether Lin Biao should become the head of state. There are, however, indications that Lin Biao may have used the issue of state chairmanship, and especially the one about the genius formula at the Lushan conference, to manipulate the meeting with the aim of inflicting damage to his political enemies. The conference thus developed into another manifestation of a power struggle between factions. On the eve of the 2nd Plenum, which began on 23 August, Mao called a Politburo meeting during which Lin Biao and Chen Boda again suggested in most flattering terms that Mao should be the head of state. Mao, irritated by these repetitions, remarked that whoever wanted to be the head of state, may add the necessary clauses to the constitution.[76]

The next day, Lin Biao made the opening speech, which contained long panegyric passages about Mao. According to Lin, the constitution's main feature should be to emphasise 'the status of Chairman Mao as a great leader, head of state and supreme commander . . . it is very important to take Mao Zedong Thought as the guiding thought for all the people.' Lin also emphasised that, in his view, 'Mao is a genius', and hinted that a group of people had a 'different centre'.[77]

The same evening, Wu Faxian proposed to the Politburo which met in the absence of Mao and Lin, to deviate for a time from the agenda of the meeting, and to discuss Lin's tape recorded speech in the different group meetings of the Plenum. His proposal was accepted.[78] The next day, Chen Boda, Wu Faxian, Ye Qun, Li Zuopeng and Qiu Huizuo all made speeches at group meetings which focused on the issue of Mao's genius.[79] The question of state chairmanship became a secondary issue.

Chen Boda's speech was the most elaborate among the five. With the help of a series of Marxist-Leninist quotations, he proceeded to provide the rationale for the existence of genius from a Marxist point of view which allowed him to conclude that it was ideologically justified to call Mao a genius. Based on this theoretical overview, he began to attack 'certain persons' who refused to admit that Mao was a genius and objected to Mao's nomination as head of state. His speech stirred up strong indignation among some participants against those who had dared to oppose the Chairman. Some requested Chen Yi, who was present and was considered to have opposed Mao during the CR, to express his opinion on this issue. Chen Yi made an extempore speech eulogising the Chairman and quoting historical facts, to prove that Mao was indeed a genius.[80]

The generals' speeches were strong and emotional. According to Wu Faxian, someone in the group working on the revision of the constitution had said that the statement 'Chairman Mao has inherited, defended and developed Marxism-Leninism with genius, creatively and comprehensively' was incorrect. 'On hearing that,' Wu said, 'I was so angry that I trembled.' He called on the participants to guard against such people who tried to denigrate Mao Zedong Thought by taking advantage of Mao's modesty.

Ye Qun also affirmed that Mao was a genius, in fact the greatest, since his knowledge was greater than that of Marx and Lenin. 'Should the three of them be revoked?' she asked, and added emotionally: 'No, they will not be revoked, even if there is a knife at my throat!' Lin Zuopeng and Qiu Huizuo spoke on the same lines.[81]

Lin Biao's second echelon, such as Wang Weiguo, political commissar of the 4th army air force in Nanjing, Chen Liyun, political commissar of the 5th army, Wang Bingzhang, minister of the commission of science and technology for national defence, and others followed suit in support of the generals' speeches. But even CC members, who were normally not under Lin Biao's influence, vied with each other to swear their loyalty to Mao and expressed their indignation against those who dared to offend him. Even Wang Dongxing, Mao's trusted aid in charge of his security, leader of the 8,341 troops and director of the CC general office, expressed his and his staff's support for Lin Biao's and Chen Boda's speeches and the hope that 'Chairman Mao will be the chairman of the state.'[82]

A brief report published on 24 August is illustrative of the atmosphere prevailing at the conference:

> All participants warmly support the speech vice chairman
> Lin delivered yesterday. It is a very important, good and

significant speech. We all believe that vice chairman Lin's speech is highly significant in guiding the 2nd Plenum of the 9th CC. Having listened to the speeches made by comrade Chen Boda and another comrade [Chen Yi] at the group meeting, all of us feel that we developed a deeper understanding of vice chairman Lin's speech. We learned in particular, that there are people in our Party who dare to reject the concept that our great leader chairman Mao is the greatest genius of our era. We all express the strongest, greatest indignation at them. We consider this a very serious issue since it is evident that, after four years of the CR, there still are persons in the Party with such reactionary thinking. They are careerists, conspirators and reactionaries, in and out counter-revolutionary revisionists . . . they should be exposed to the public, expelled from the Party and struggled against. . . . We all give wholehearted support to the addition of a chapter about the state chairmanship into the constitution . . . with Chairman Mao as the head of state and vice chairman Lin Biao as the deputy head of state.[83]

At Lushan, the word soon spread that it was Zhang Chunqiao who denied that Mao was a genius, and a large number of participants demanded his exposure and repudiation. Yang Dezhi, then commander of the Jinan military region, later recalled that Zhang was nervous and pale when he was being attacked in meetings of the east China group as an opponent of Mao.[84]

Jiang Qing who saw one of the core members of her group in great danger of being overthrown, appealed to Mao. Mao received Zhang Chunqiao and Yao Wenyuan who informed him about the unexpected deviation from the agenda of the conference and the attacks launched by Chen Boda and the generals at the group meetings. Mao did not tolerate the disruption of the plans he had made for the Lushan meeting and decided to bring the conference back on the course he had planned for it. He was again in full command. At a meeting with the Standing Committee and the heads of the area groups which he called the next day, he ordered that the discussions on Lin Biao's speech should be interrupted immediately, revoked the Plenum's report and condemned Chen Boda's speech as a violation of the 9th Congress's policies.⁸⁵ He emphasised that he had no intention of becoming head of state and that Lin Biao also should not aspire to this post.⁸⁶

Once Mao had taken such a clear stand, the situation immediately changed. The atmosphere at the meeting, which had been very tense, began to relax, but it now was the turn of Lin Biao's group to become disheartened. Wu Faxian, ten years later, recalled the moment when he learned about Mao's decision: 'My heart sank to the bottom,' he said, 'and I was very nervous. But the mistake had been made. It is too late to mend it.'⁸⁷

The next day, on 26 August, the Plenum returned to its original agenda. The Lin Biao group went into retreat. Ye Qun tried to destroy the minutes of her declaration. Qiu Huizuo, in vain, attempted to revoke his speech. Wu Faxian was ordered to make self-criticism during the Plenum, and Zhou Enlai and Kang Sheng received instruction that they should have serious talks with Wu Faxian, Li Zuopeng and Qiu Huizuo.⁸⁸

However, the major retaliation against the Lin Biao group was not directed against Lin Biao himself, but against Chen Boda. On 31 August, Mao wrote a text he called 'Some of My Views' in a style similar to the one he had used for his big character poster of August 1966 in which he condemned Liu Shaoqi for having 'imposed a bourgeois dictatorship' and a 'white terror'. He accused Chen Boda of harbouring 'wild ambitions' and of resorting to a 'surprise attack' in an attempt 'to raze Lushan to the ground or stop the earth from revolving'. Mao also said that he had worked with 'Chen Boda, the genius theoretician, for more than thirty years. There has never been any cooperation from him on major issues.'⁸⁹ Mao also told the participants that he had consulted Lin Biao on the question of genius and that they both agreed that 'the traditional Marxist-Leninist position should be maintained, and we should not get involved in Chen Boda's rumour-mongering and sophistry'.⁹⁰

Mao's statement was the political death sentence for Chen Boda who had been his political secretary for decades, and whom he had appointed to head the CCRG. Mao's status gave any of his over-statements the full force of law. The Plenum followed him without hesitation in the repudiation of Chen Boda whom it had supported only a few days earlier.

In his speech at the closing session on 6 September, Mao again made a number of sarcastic comments about Chen Boda and the Marxist quotations he had used to prove his theory about the existence of genius in a socialist society. He emphasised that high-ranking officials should read Marx and Lenin, and books about Chinese and Western philosophy, so that 'they would not be taken in by black scholars' such as Chen Boda.

The political offensive which Lin Biao had initiated thus proved to be a failure. But since Mao had taken a rather conciliatory stand towards Lin, his only reaction was to send Ye Qun and the generals to Jiang Qing and offer his and their apologies. In their meeting with Jiang Qing, Ye Qun laid the entire blame on Chen Boda claiming that he had deceived them all. Jiang Qing, apparently magnanimous, agreed.[291]

Lin, although defeated, may have hoped that, in view of the fact that Chen Boda had been selected as the scapegoat, the events at Lushan would have no further consequences. Moreover, the controversies at Lushan did not pertain to real political issues. None of the two questions under debate had been classified as a 'matter of ideological and political line'. At the conference, Lin had not attacked Mao, he had merely used his hitherto successful tactics of eulogising him to enhance his own position. Even if his expectation had been more pessimistic, he could not have been aware of the fate that lay ahead of him. However, he was later accused of having 'started a counter-revolutionary coup d'etat which was aborted at the second session of the 9th Party Congress in August 1970'.[92]

Some Western academic studies accepted the official Chinese interpretation that Lin had confronted Mao at Lushan and 'in league with Chen Boda and all of China's top military leaders' – Huang, Ye, Li and Qiu could hardly be considered as such – 'openly challenged Mao's authority on such fundamental questions as to what the structure of power and the correct ideological and political line in China should be.'[93] In fact, the problem was far less dramatic. In the power struggle which confronted Lin and Jiang Qing at Lushan, Mao arbitrated in favour of Jiang Qing, and it took him one day to bring the conference back onto the course he had designed for it.

The fall of Lin Biao

In Mao's view, the controversies at Lushan were a problem of political line and principle. 'When it comes to questions of line and of principle,' he said, 'I take a firm hold and do not relax my grip.'[94] Indeed, after the end of the Lushan conference, Mao proceeded step by step towards the elimination of Lin Biao. One month after Lushan, Ye Qun, Wu Faxian, Li Zuopeng and Qiu Huizuo submitted their written self-criticism to Mao, in which they expressed regret for their statements at the Lushan conference. They admitted that they had interfered with the agenda of the Plenum and that, due to their low level of understanding of Marxism-Leninism, they had made mistakes of political line. They claimed to have been misled by Chen Boda on the question of genius. They promised to reform themselves through the intensified study of Marxism-Leninism and of Mao Zedong Thought which would enable them to raise their 'level of consciousness of line struggle'.[95]

This perfunctory and standard type of confession failed to satisfy Mao who expected a thorough explanation of the reasons and circumstances that had inspired their actions at Lushan. Mao scribbled a few acerbic comments on the texts, criticising Wu Faxian for his 'lack of frankness and uprightness', and Ye Qun for her 'swaggering and holding her nose high after becoming a member of the CC' and for 'casting the line of the 9th Party Congress into the winds'. Mao also accused her of 'refusing to do as I say, but dancing immediately when Chen Boda blew the trumpet'.[96]

In his criticism of the members of the Lin Biao group, Mao referred repeatedly to their violation of the line established by the 9th Party Congress and of the Party constitution adopted by the Congress. The line, symbolised by the formula 'to unite and to win victory',[97] represented Mao's strategic design to phase out the CR and to restore stability.[98] The violation of the Party constitution referred to Chen Boda's, Ye Qun's and others' insistence on reinserting the words 'with genius, creatively and comprehensively' into the paragraph dealing with Mao's development of Marxism-Leninism, which Mao himself had deleted.[99] Since Chen Boda had suddenly allied himself with the military, and since he was the first to rock the boat at Lushan, Mao believed that, under the cover of panegyrics, there was a hidden scheme which he intended to discover by escalating the campaign against Chen. On 16 November, 1970, the centre issued a directive together with Mao's 'some of my views' calling for Chen's repudiation as a sham Marxist, careerist and conspirator.[100]

Within the framework of the campaign, the Party committee of the 38th army (a part of the 4th field army which Lin Biao commanded during the liberation war) stationed in Hebei province, transmitted a report on 10 December to the Party centre, exposing Chen Boda's 'anti-Party crimes'. Besides accusing Chen of having 'opposed the great leader Chairman Mao and his close comrade-in-arms Lin Biao', the report claimed that he had engaged in 'sectarian activities in an attempt to disrupt the army' and that he had 'incited army fighting, suppressed the masses and sabotaged the great alliance and the three-in-one combination' in Hebei province. In fact, during the factional strife of the early period of the CR, Chen Boda and the CCRG had sided with the radical faction which had been suppressed by the 38th army, but supported by the Hebei military district headquarters.[101]

The report was a typical example of the kind of 'information' produced during campaigns, distorted and grossly exaggerated, but with a grain of truth in it. It perfectly suited Mao's plans to vilify Chen Boda. He issued instructions to organise a conference of the Beijing military region whose purpose, in his words would be, to establish 'the reason why Chen Boda had become the overlord of the Beijing military region and the North China area'.[102]

The conference, though it lasted more than one month, did not provide any additional information about Chen Boda's subversive activities. But it reorganised the Beijing military region; Li Xuefeng, first secretary of the Party committee and political commissar of the Beijing military region was replaced by Xie Fuzhi, and Li Desheng took over the post of commander of the region from Zheng Weishan.[103]

The campaign against Chen Boda, nonetheless, escalated. On 26 January the centre distributed 'Material about the crimes of the anti-Party element Chen Boda', according to which Chen had been an anti-communist reactionary since his youth. After his arrest by the Guomindang, he had become a renegade. He had followed Wang Ming and Liu Shaoqi in opposing Mao's revolutionary line in the 1930s. Before the CR, he had been a 'black scholar' of Liu Shaoqi's headquarters. During the CR, he became the 'back-stage boss' of Xiao Hua, of Yang, Yu, Fu, of Wang Li, Guan Feng and Qi Benyu, and finally of the 'May 16 counter-revolutionary conspiratorial clique'. At the Lushan conference, he had plotted to split the party.[104] All this were standard accusations which indicated that nothing new had been discovered in Chen Boda's case.

The MC, too, was instructed to hold a meeting from 9 January onwards to criticise Chen and to rectify its working style. On 19 February Mao denounced the meeting for having lasted more than a month without yielding any results. In fact, he said the meeting had failed to repudiate Chen Boda. To comply with Mao's complaints, Huang Yongsheng produced a report to confess the MC administrative group's 'poor understanding of the significance of repudiating Chen', on which Mao commented that 'they always have had a poor understanding' and urged them to 'change from a passive to an active state' of criticism.[105]

At the end of February, the Party centre informed all Party members and the general public about the campaign to criticise Chen Boda. The campaigning whose official title was to 'criticise revisionism and rectify the style', did not mention Chen Boda's name but referred to him as a 'sham Marxist swindler'.

In April, the campaign began to focus increasingly on the rectification of style, which Mao qualified as one of 'arrogance and self-complacency' of leading cadres at various levels, but with special emphasis on the military leadership.[106] Mao, since he had received another written self-criticism by Ye Qun and the four generals in March, that again did not satisfy him, began to intensify his criticism.[107] On 29 April, Zhou Enlai delivered a speech dealing with the campaign where he concluded that Ye Qun and the four generals had made errors of political line and practised sectarianism.[108]

Mao also took a number of administrative measures against the Lin Biao group. Describing his reaction to the Lushan meeting, Mao stated later that, after the conference, he had taken three measures: 'One was to throw stones. The second was to mix sand with clay, The third was to dig out the cornerstones from below the walls.'[109] The stones he threw, were the disparaging remarks he made on the general's self-criticism.

'Mixing the sand' meant to introduce his own followers, Ji Dengkui and Zhang Caiqian, into the military commission, and especially into its administrative group, in order to end Liu Biao's domination of the Commission. Finally, 'digging out the corner-stone' implied the reorganisation of the Beijing military region.[110]

He also ordered the establishment of a central organisation and propaganda group under the Politburo, the purpose of which was to administer the CC organisational department, the central broadcasting bureau, the all China trade union confederation, and the youth league. It was headed by Kang Sheng with Jiang Qing, Zhang Chunqia, Yao Wenyuan, Ji Dengkui and Li Dengshen as its members.[111] The newly created group was a powerful organ controlling ideological, cultural, and propaganda activities, as well as, through the CC organisational department, the party's personnel policies. By consolidating the position of the members of the former CCRG at the power centre, it provided a balance to Lin Biao's forces in the Politburo. But it also gave new impetus to Jiang Qing's political stance. As Kang Sheng, due to his illness, became increasingly secluded, and Li Desheng took command of the Shenyang military region, the group was entirely controlled by Jiang Qing.[112]

Parallel to the campaign against Chen Boda, a movement 'to strengthen ideological and political education' was also started among the Party's leading officials. At the closing session of the Lushan conference and on other occasions, Mao had complained that, for years, nobody had seriously studied Marxism-Leninism, mainly because Lin Biao had advocated the exclusive study of Mao's works.[113] A list of books to be studied by cadres and intellectuals was publicised, reading material was distributed and study sessions to discuss their contents were organised. Among these books were, first of all, Marx's *Communist Manifesto*, followed by *Anti-Düring* and *The French Civil War*, Lenin's works *On Materialism*, *On Imperialism* and *On the State* also had become required reading. For lack of books on Chinese philosophy, which Mao had included in the list of suggested studies, a book on Chinese history was substituted. It was a work by the well-known Chinese historian Fan Wenlan and covered the period from the Yellow Emperor to the Song Dynasty. A history of European philosophy and a history of the world written by a group of scholars from the Soviet Academy of Sciences were also to be studied. The ideological education through reading and study sessions began to spread in 1972 and continued for several years.

That Mao continued to be seriously preoccupied by the events at the Lushan conference can be gauged from the fact that he showed more interest in reports about the course of the campaign than about Henry Kissinger's first visit to China. When Zhou Enlai and Xiong Xianghui, an official from the headquarters of the general chief of staff[114] came to Mao's study on 9 July 1971 to report about their first contacts with Kissinger during his secret mission to China, Mao considered it more important to first inquire about the campaign to criticise Chen Boda at the headquarters of the general chief of staff. Xiong told Mao that at the meeting to criticise Chen Boda, Huang Yongsheng and Wu Faxian both had claimed that the general chief of staff had nothing to do with Chen Boda, that they had not talked about their own activities at the Lushan conference and had not shown their self-criticism to anyone. Mao, after some deliberation, declared: 'they engaged in a sinister plot at Lushan. Their self-criticism was a fake. The Lushan affair is not finished, the problem is not at all solved. There is a sinister scheme. They have a back-stage boss.'[115] Until then, Mao had avoided implicating Lin Biao, and this was the first time that he brought him into the picture, short of mentioning his name.

Mao's changing relations with Lin Biao

At the outset of the CR, Lin occupied a privileged position in Mao's entourage. But Mao's appreciation of Lin Biao appeared to have gradually declined over the next few years. The first manifestation of Mao's discontent was contained in his letter to Jiang Qing where he expressed reservations about Lin's statement with respect to the danger of a coup d'etat. But it was the cult of his personality promoted by Lin Biao which became a source of irritation to him. He felt 'quite uneasy' about this matter, he wrote to his wife: 'I have never believed that the several booklets I wrote would have so much supernatural power. Now, after he [Lin] exaggerated them the whole nation has exaggerated them.'[116] This was the first time, Mao made a critical statement about Lin Biao's panegyrics. In the course of the next few years, he made a number of similar remarks.

Mao seemed to have been of two minds regarding the question of personality cult. On several occasions, he had made appreciative remarks about the cult of his personality, which he considered a vitally necessary political instrument and which, he thought, was due to him, for he was undoubtedly convinced that he himself was the most capable and supreme leader in the country. Edgar Snow reported that Mao 'thought . . . we needed some personal worship'.[117] For years, and especially during the first phase of the Cultural Revolution, he had been a willing object of popular admiration and adulation.

At the same time, Mao showed certain signs of displeasure with some forms of the cult of his personality. In the summer of 1967 he frowned upon the 'four greats' published in Lin Biao's calligraphy in a Shanghai newspaper.[118] In 1969, he insisted on deleting references to his genius that promoted correct Marxist theories 'creatively and comprehensively', from the Party constitution. But it was after the Lushan conference, that his irritation with Lin Biao's panegyrics became even clearer. Stating that 'someone had said, to oppose genius means opposing me. But I am not a genius. Genius does not depend on a single person. It depends on the Party, which is the vanguard of the proletariat. Genius depends on the line of the masses and is the result of collective wisdom.'[119]

In his talk with Edgar Snow in December 1970, he complained that the cult had been 'overdone' and 'a lot of formalism' had been allowed to develop. As far as the 'four greats' were concerned, in his view they were nothing but 'a nuisance'.[120]

If, in the early stages of the CR, Lin Biao had obtained Mao's support in the purges of a number of military leaders, such as Luo Ruiqing, He Long, Yang Chengwu, Yu Lijin and Fu Chongbi, Mao later refused to endorse Lin's plans to remove Xu Xiangqian, Chen Yi, Nie Rongzhen and Ye Jianying whom Lin Biao attempted to topple during the 12th Plenum of the

CC in October 1968. Although he had earlier criticised the marshals, Mao, on that occasion, protected them, emphasising that they should be allowed to air their views.[121] His protection of the veteran military leaders was clearly inspired by considerations of balance of power. If he had allowed them to be purged, Lin's control over the army would have considerably increased.

At the Lushan conference, Lin Biao had launched another power struggle, this time directed against the CR faction. He neither had consulted Mao beforehand, nor had he apologised for his conduct afterwards. The Lushan events occurred when Mao had been particularly preoccupied with Soviet threats to China's external security. As a result of his perception, war readiness had become one of the major items on the agenda of the Lushan conference. Under these circumstances, Lin's disruption of the conference procedures could only lead to Mao's disenchantment with his designated successor.

It should be noted here that Lin's views on Sino-Soviet and Sino-American relations did not constitute an issue in this context. According to some interpretations, Lin had interfered with Mao's foreign policy line and criticised his decision to improve Sino-American relations as an abandonment of 'proletarian internationalism'.[122] During the ensuing campaign against him, Lin was accused of having conducted 'illicit relations with foreign countries'. This however, was a standard accusation which during the Cultural Revolution was also made against such other leading cadres as Peng Dehuai and Liu Shaoqi. Contrary to many assumptions – which demonstrate a lack of real understanding of the decision-making process in Chinese foreign policy at that time – Lin's involvement in foreign policy was nil. Foreign policy was a highly centralised issue whose conceptions were, in Mao's own words, solely developed by himself and executed by Zhou Enlai.[123] Foreign-policy statements or references to foreign-policy issues in speeches or publications were without exception cleared by Zhou Enlai himself. If, as claimed by some writers, Lin Biao or General Huang Yongsheng continued to refer to the US as a declining and dangerous capitalist state in 1970 and 1971, this did not reflect a pro-Soviet position, but the official wording at the time, which changed only after the normalisation between the US and China had taken more concrete shape.

The events at the Lushan conference might have brought back to Mao's mind a number of misgivings he had nurtured against Lin for some time. Mao's ambivalent attitude towards the issue of personality cult has already been mentioned. Other misgivings were based on Lin's allegations about a possible coup d'état in early 1966 and again in 1968 when he accused the acting Chief of Staff, Yang Chengwu, of having plotted to overthrow the Party centre.

Lin's increasing inactivity also irritated Mao. While Lin had made the army a pioneer of cultural revolutionary policies in the early stages and had delivered a number of important speeches at major turning points in the Cultural Revolution, in the late 1960s, on the grounds of poor health, he retired more and more into the isolation of his residential offices. Mao once sarcastically referred to Lin as the 'forever healthy'.[124] Ye Qun's functions in Lin Biao's office also irritated him. In his talks with provincial leaders in August 1971, he declared: 'I have always objected to having one's wife serve as the director of one's office. The four persons – by which he meant the four generals – must first see her in order to ask instructions from Lin.'[125]

Nonetheless, Lin Biao refused to read documents and relied increasingly on his wife for his daily work. He rarely attended Politburo meetings, unless they were convened by Mao himself, and usually sent his wife to replace him. All this contributed to Mao's disillusionment with his designated successor. This disillusionment turned into anger when it became obvious that Lin was not ready to utter a word of apology for his behaviour at Lushan and even less volunteered to make self-criticism.

In August 1971, Mao left Beijing for an inspection tour of Central China. In Wuhan, Changsha and Nanchang, he held long meetings with local Party, government and military leaders. His talks were later summarised and distributed to the entire Party as a CC document.[126] According to the document, Mao described the events at Lushan as the last of ten 'struggles of line' which had taken place during the 50 years of Party history. Like the eighth struggle of line with Peng Dehuai, and the ninth struggle of line with Liu Shaoqi, the struggle with Lin Biao was also one 'between two headquarters'. Mao accused Lin and his followers of having launched 'a surprise attack' and of having engaged in 'underground activities'. . . . 'Their programme was to appoint a state chairman, and to extol "genius" '. In other words, they 'opposed the line of the 9th Congress' and planned to abolish the 'three-point agenda of the 2nd Plenum of the 9th CC'. Mao also emphasised that 'a certain person was anxious to become state chairman, to split the Party and to seize power'.[127] Mentioning Lin Biao by name, he complained that 'Comrade Lin Biao did not discuss his speech [at Lushan] with me, nor did he show it to me. . . . I mentioned to Comrade Lin Biao that some of the things he said were not appropriate.'[128] Mao further pointed out that 'on the previous nine occasions [of line struggle], we drew some conclusions, while this time we have shielded vice chairman Lin and have not drawn conclusions concerning an individual. He must, of course, assume some responsibility.' But, he added, 'we still want to protect Lin.'[129]

Referring to Lin and his followers, Mao asked, 'what are we to do about these people?' . . . 'We should still operate a policy of educating them.' He declared that upon his return to Beijing, he would talk to them. If they failed to come to see him on their own, Mao said, 'I will go to see them.'[130] He added, 'it is difficult for someone who has taken the lead in committing major errors of principle, errors of line or direction, to reform.' Naming the leaders of the previous nine struggles of line, he concluded, 'they did not reform'.[131]

Although Mao stated that he still planned to protect Lin, his remarks about the tenth line struggle implied that Lin Biao's position as the second in command of the Party and the army, and of heir apparent was seriously jeopardised. But it was not clear whether he considered Lin Biao or Chen Boda as the chieftain of the tenth line struggle, since he attributed only 'some responsibility' to Lin Biao.[132]

It is not known to what extent Mao was aware of Lin Biao's projects. But during his inspection tour, he changed his travel plans several times. While in Wuhan, Changsa and Nanchang, Mao held numerous talks with local leaders from 15 provinces, municipalities and five military regions. After his arrival in Hangzhou on 3 September, however, Mao's working style suddenly changed and he held only two brief meetings with four local leaders.[133]

In Hangzhou, Mao became particularly concerned about his personal safety. The man in charge of security during Mao's stay in Hangzhou was Chen Liyun, commander of the local garrison, political commissar of the 5th army of the air force and a follower of Lin Biao. Since his arrival in Hangzhou, Mao's travel plans, their timing and their destination were surrounded by meticulous precautions and by a cloud of secrecy. He ordered his train to be moved from its special track, located close to the airport, to Shaoxing, a safer location more than one hour's drive from Hangzhou.[134]

Without prior notice, he suddenly departed for Shanghai on 10 September where he stayed for a much shorter period than expected. The next morning, Mao, who had not left his train, received Xu Shiyou, the commander of the Nanjing military region and Wang Hongwen. After their departure, Mao ordered the train to return to Beijing.[135]

Although the reasons for Mao's sudden change of schedule and the increased secrecy of his travel plans have never been revealed, it is known that, after his arrival in Nanchang, Cheng Shiqing, head of the Jianxi revolutionary committee and political commissar of the provincial military district, informed Mao about the abnormal activities of one of Lin Biao's followers in Nanchang, Zhou Yuchi. Zhou was deputy director of the general office of the Air Force and member of Lin Liguo's Joint Fleet. Cheng also reported to Mao, that Lin's daughter Lin Liheng, had warned Cheng's wife to abstain from friendly contacts with the Lin family. According to Lin Liheng, members of her family were involved in dangerous activities.[136]

Lin Biao's plot

The campaign against Chen Boda, Mao's critical remarks about the five generals and their inadequate self-criticism and the reorganisation of the MC administrative group and of the Beijing military region all exemplified the increasing threat to Lin Biao's political position. But Lin was ready to defend himself. Unlike Liu Shaoqi and most other senior Party leaders, who, even after their arrest did not voice any opposition against Mao, but instead continued to blame themselves for having misunderstood the political line imposed by the Chairman, Lin was much too arrogant not to think of his own protection. What were the possibilities of self-defence which were at Lin's disposition? His inferiority to Mao had already been amply demonstrated at the Lushan confrence where, in view of Mao's defiance, his carefully planned tactics had met with complete failure. In an open conflict with Mao, Lin could count neither on the CC where the military held a 51 per cent majority, nor on the army as a whole or on important sections of it. It was inconceivable that troops would follow Lin's orders unless they were corroborated by Mao himself.[137]

It is, however, conceivable that Lin planned to stage a coup d'etat against Mao. Such a strategy would have been compatible with Lin's perception of the world and of history and with his concept of political power. In his remarkable speech to the Politburo on 18 May 1966, he described Chinese history as characterised by a sequence of revolts:

> Throughout the history of our country, there have been changes of government every 10, 20, 30 or 50 years. In the spring and autumn periods, the small states kept on fighting one another. People killed one another. The son of a king told his father to kill himself; the father obeyed. The ministers of the State of Qin fought and killed one another in a struggle for power. People seized power not only by murder but also by ruses and intrigues. The son of the first emperor killed his brothers and sisters. After the 12-year rule of the founder of the Han dynasty, Empress Lu seized power; then two ministers overthrew the Lu family. Emperor Wen of the Sui dynasty killed his two brothers. After the death of the First Emperor of the Ming dynasty, who had ruled for 31 years, his fourth son revolted against the old emperor's grandson; the two parties kept up their mutual slaughter for three years, and the palace at Nanjing was burnt down. Emperor Kang Xi wanted his 14th son to inherit the throne, but he was cheated by Prince Yong, the fourth son, who killed many of his brothers. When the Republic was established, Sun Yat Sen became President, but three months later Yuan Shih Kai seized power. Four months later he made himself emperor. He was overthrown.

Years of internal struggle followed. Chiang Kai-shek seized power and killed many of his enemies.[138]

Lin applied his paranoic perception of history to the present world where 'change of political power results from either people's revolution, which starts from below ... or counter-revolutionary coups d'etat, which include coups d'etat, internal coups d'etat, collusion of the high and the low, collusion with the subversive activities of foreign enemies or with armed invasion, in combination with natural calamities. This has been so historically, and it is true in the present.' It would be hardly surprising that, with such a world outlook, Lin would be capable of contemplating violent action which he might have seen as the only option left to him to assure his political survival. But since Lin Biao had become increasingly inactive, he entrusted his son, Lin Liguo, with the operational planning of the action. Lin Liguo who was very close to his father, had also become increasingly concerned about Lin Biao's safety. In May 1970, Lin Liguo had established an 'investigation and research group' composed mostly of officers of the air force headquarters. This group which was later known as the 'joint fleet', had 93 members who were mainly officers in the air force.[139]

Affiliated to the joint fleet was a 'Shanghai group' of about 30 carefully selected people from the air force 4th army and a special training brigade under the leadership of Wang Weiguo and Jiang Guozhang. In Guangzhou, a 'fighting detachment' with about 90 people was established by Lin Biao's follower, Mi Jialong, the political commissar of the Chinese civil aviation which was under the jurisdiction of the PLA Air Force.[140]

On 21 March 1971, Lin Liguo, Zhou Yuchi, Yu Xinye, and Li Weixin met in Shanghai to assess Lin Biao's situation. While they believed that Lin's power was still very strong, they also feared that his opponents, the 'literati' were on the rise. In their view, Lin's chances to succeed Mao had considerably diminished, and the possibility that Zhang Chunqiao might take over Lin's position, could not be excluded. They saw three scenarios for Lin's future. He would either be able to peacefully take over from Mao, or he would be by passed by someone else, or he had to forcefully take over from Mao. The group decided to be prepared for the latter possibility. One of the participants in the discussion, Yu Xinye, drafted a plan for a forceful take over which later became known by the code name '517 project'.[141] The handwritten 24-page plan was a rough draft of the '517 project' which was anything but a well-calculated plan for an armed uprising and which was never finalised. It was later found in a notebook left behind in the helicopter which Yu Xingye used when he fled on 12 September 1971.[142] Among the nine items listed, two are particularly interesting because they demonstrate the inefficiency of the preparations. The ensuing discussions which took place between the members of the joint fleet, also showed that the tight control which the centre exercised over the army made it impossible to realise a military coup.

The first item of the project dealt with the possibilities of a coup d'etat, the second assessed the forces Lin Biao could rely upon.[143] The removal of 'B-52' (the code name for Mao) was considered inevitable. For this purpose, the joint fleet considered the use of 'special means, such as poison, gas, biological weapons, bombs "543" (a new type of weapon), car accident, assassination, kidnapping, small urban guerilla bands'.

The next step would be to create a fait accompli for the rest of the leadership. 'When B-52 is in our hands and all of the enemy's main battleships [other leaders] are in the palm of our hand; utilise high-level meetings and get them all in the net at once. Force B-52 to surrender.'[144]

The forces which were considered to be at Lin Biao's disposal were the joint fleet and its associated organs in Shanghai and Guangzhou; the 5th air force corps controlled by Chen Liyun; the AF 9th and 18th air force divisions stationed in Yunnan and Guangxi; the 21st tank regiment (probably stationed in Hebei); civil aviation; the 34th division (probably also in Hebei).[145]

Lin Biao's basic strength lay with the air force. Of China's 170–80 army divisions,[146] only one division and one tank regiment were mentioned as potentially useful for Lin's purpose. This fully revealed Lin's inability to control the armed forces and his weakness in any confrontation with Mao.

It is not known whether Lin Biao ever read the 571 project. Given his seclusion, it is possible that he did not have any detailed knowledge of it and that the implementation of the project was left to his son and his associates.

In the summer of 1971, Lin's situation had become more

and more precarious. Ye Qun, Wu Faxian, Li Zuopeng and Qui Huizuo feared that Mao might use the occasion of the forthcoming 3rd Plenum of the Central Committee or of the soon-to-be-held 4th People's Congress to publicise Lin's case.

But it was during Mao's visit to the southern provinces in August and September that the threat with which Lin Biao was faced became evident. Mao left Beijing on 14 August. Although Lin and Ye Qun tried to follow closely Mao's activities during his trip, it was only on 6 September that they received the first information. Gu Tongzhou, chief of staff of the air force of the Guangzhou military region reported to Lin about Mao's talks with the Party, government and military leadership in Wuhan. On the same day, Li Zuopeng, who was accompanying a foreign delegation to Wuhan was informed by Liu Feng, political commissar of the Wuhan military region, about the views Mao had expressed about Lin Biao and the Lushan conference. Li Zuopeng immediately relayed this information to Lin Biao and Huang Yongsheng.[147]

After 6 September, the atmosphere in Lin Biao's headquarters in Beidaihe became very tense. Mao clearly was planning to confront Lin Biao at the forthcoming 3rd Plenum of the CC. In that case, Lin would lose his posts and be subjected to investigations similar to those inflicted upon Chen Boda. There was also little doubt that the activities of Lin Liguo's joint fleet would be discovered.

After two days of confusion and of intense discussions between Lin, his wife, his son, and Zhou Yuchi, Lin Biao issued a handwritten order instructing the joint fleet 'to follow Lin Liguo's and Zhou Yuchi's instructions'. The order was signed 'Lin Biao, September 8'.[148] The order was carried to Beijing by Lin Liguo the following day. From September 9 to 11, Lin Liguo convened a meeting of core members of the joint fleet to discuss plans to assassinate Mao while he was travelling on his inspection tour and to occupy Jiang Qing's headquarters at Diaoyutai at the same time. They expected Mao to remain in Hangzhou and Shanghai until 25 September.

During the following days, several plans were discussed for carrying out the assassination. Different means were considered such as using flame throwers, bombs, or rockets against Mao's special train in Hangzhou or in Shanghai; to kill

Mao by pistol in Shanghai. Wang Weiguo, in charge of the Shanghai garrison, was chosen to execute this part of the plan; to blow up a railway bridge at Shoufang near Suzhou which Mao's train had to pass; to storm Diaoyutai with an air force training battalion.[149] But some unsolvable problems seemed to be inherent in all those proposals. Chen Liyun was against the bombing of Mao's train in Hangzhou. Jiang Tengjiao considered it impracticable to move anti-aircraft guns to the parking track of Mao's train without being discovered. He pointed out that Mao's train was bullet proof and heavily guarded. Jiang argued that if Mao's guards resisted for only half an hour, it would be long enough for other troops to come to Mao's rescue. He also argued that the Shanghai air force training brigade which was to be used to attack the train, could not be relied upon since they were trained to be loyal to Mao. The proposals to use flame throwers against Mao's train and to blow up the Shuofang bridge were also rejected on the grounds that nobody in the air force knew how to efficiently use flame throwers or dynamite. It was also believed that Wang Weiguo would be unable to perform a face-to-face execution of Mao. As for occupying Diaoyutai, Wang Fei, who was to be in charge of this action, explained that he had only one air force training battalion at his disposal. Moreover, troops were not allowed to enter Beijing. Even if he succeeded in reaching Diaoyutai, the troops stationed there would retaliate and soon obtain the assistance of the Beijing garrison. In the end, no definite decision was made on how to proceed.[150]

Lin Liguo and Zhou Yuchi realised that without ground troops at their disposal, they would not be able to realise their objective. They called Guan Guanglie, the political commissar of the army division unit 0190 to Beijing to discuss with him the possibility of transferring a company of flame throwers from Wuhan to Shanghai and of two battalions from Guan's division to Beijing to assist Wang Fei in occupying Diaoyutai.[151] Guan Guanglie argued that no troops could be moved without the approval of the division's Party committee. Even if such an approval could be obtained, the transport of the troops had to be authorised by the headquarters of the military region which, in turn, would have to seek approval from the Party centre in Beijing. It was, therefore, impossible to move two battalions for Lin Liguo's purpose. The possibility of secretly moving a company of flame throwers was also ruled out by Guan Guanglie.[152]

On the evening of 11 September, Lin Liguo summoned Lu Min to a discussion of the possibility of blasting the railroad bridge at Shuofang. Lin Liguo suggested that Lu Min, an air force officer, lead a group of men which would be supported by an army battalion, to blow up the bridge. But Lu Min replied that, since he was a pilot and had never served in the army, he was unable to direct such an operation.[153]

Mao's unexpected return to Beijing terminated the fruitless discussions. Mao's train, after a short halt in Nanjing, travelled directly to the Beijing area. Before entering the capital, Mao took a last precaution. He ordered the train to stop in Fengtai, a country town in the vicinity of Beijing, where Mao received Li Desheng and Ji Dengkui who must have assured him that there was no danger in entering the city. Lin Liguo was informed during the night of 11 September by a telephone call by Wang Weiguo that Mao's train had already left Shanghai. The scheme to assassinate Mao was aborted before it went beyond its planning stage.[154]

Li Weixin, in his confession, described the atmosphere of a midnight meeting of leaders of the joint fleet on 11 September, after Mao's return to Beijing had become known. For a while, he said, nobody was able to utter a word. Then Lin Liguo burst into tears saying that the did not know how to face Lin Biao. Zhou Yuchi became hysterical and proposed that, on National Day, on 1 October, he would fly a helicopter over the tower gate of the Imperial Palace and crash onto Mao. This was rejected as unrealistic by the other participants of the meeting.[155]

The eve of Lin Biao's disappearance

Mao's unexpected return to Beijing in the afternoon of 12 September precipitated events at Lin Biao's headquarters and elsewhere. According to the 'project 571', an alternative plan had been devised in case the attempt to assassinate Mao failed. It proposed that Lin Biao establish another political centre in Guangzhou from which he would be able to confront Mao. At about 6.30 pm on 12 September, Lin Liguo and Zhou Yuchi met with other core members of the joint fleet in an isolated building of the air force institute in a Beijing suburb. Zhou informed the participants about Lin Biao's decision to fly to Guangzhou in the early morning of the following day. He claimed that five planes were available to move members of the joint fleet to Guangzhou and ordered Wang Fei to make detailed preparations for their flight from Beijing in the early morning of the next day.[156]

An important issue of the meeting dealt with the four generals, Huang, Wu, Li and Qiu, who had been kept in the dark about the joint fleet's activities.[157] Lin Biao had apparently decided that, as Politburo members and high-ranking military leaders, the four generals were too much in the public eye to involve them in a secret plot. But more important was perhaps their uncertain political situation. Since the Lushan conference, they had been under Mao's close scrutiny, and any unusual activity on their part would have increased Mao's suspicion even more. The generals might be reluctant to follow Lin Liguo's instructions to flee to Guangzhou. If this was indeed the case, it was decided that they should be forced to go.[158]

The choice of Guangzhou as a possible alternative, if it had ever been seriously considered, appears to be highly unrealistic. The subsequent investigation showed that both Ding Sheng, the commander of the Guangzhou military region, and Liu Xingyuan, the political commissar of the region, were not Lin Biao's followers. After Lin Biao's death, they were still at their posts.[159] In Guangzhou, Lin Biao could only rely on Gu Tongzhou, the regional air force chief of staff, and on less than one hundred personnel of the Guangzhou fighting detachment associated with the joint fleet. It was later alleged that Lin Biao wanted to use Guangzhou as a springboard to flee to Hong Kong. But the plan to go south was never carried out. Around midnight of 12 September, Zhou Yuchi informed Wang Fei by telephone that the plan had been 'exposed', and that Lin Biao had decided to fly north instead.[160]

In the late 1980s, a number of eye-witness accounts were published about the events in Lin Biao's residence in Beidaihe on the eve of his departure.[161] All these accounts, although they permit the reconstruction of certain events, at Lin Biao's Beidaihe residence on the eve of his departure, have a major shortcoming. None of the eye-witnesses, including Lin Liheng, had access to Lin Biao's private rooms, where Lin, Ye Qun and Lin Liguo were holding intense discussions and making preparations for their departure. They, nonetheless, convey an impression of the hectic and confusing atmosphere that reigned in Lin Biao's house.

The account of Lin Biao's daughter and Lin Liguo's fiancee Zhang Ning are perhaps the most important ones. According to Lin Liheng's writings, her brother, on 7 September, informed her that Huang Yongsheng had related to him and Ye Qun, Mao's critical remarks about Lin Biao. In Lin Liguo's view her father had three ways to react. Either they were to assassinate Mao, or fly to Guangzhou where he could establish a Central Committee to confront the central authorities in Beijing, or he could escape to the Soviet Union. Lin Liheng did not agree with any of these options. She suggested that her father step down from his posts and give up all responsibilities as Zhu De had done before him. But Lin Liguo refused to believe that this was a possible option. In his view his father would be put into custody which, with his fragile health, he would not survive.[162]

After this conversation, Lin Liheng firmly believed that her mother and brother were trying to abduct Lin Biao to an unknown place. For several days, she tried to persuade some trustworthy leaders of the 8341 military unit, responsible for Lin's security, that Lin was in urgent need of additional protection.

Zhang Ning, describes the confusion that reigned in Lin Biao's house during the last hours of 12 September and the circumstances under which Lin Biao left. In the late afternoon of 12 September, Lin Biao told his secretary in charge of security, Li Wenpu, that he was planning to fly to Dalian early next morning. At about 8 p.m., a Hong Kong film was shown to celebrate the engagement of Lin Liheng with Zhang Qinglin, a young PLA medical doctor. At about 9 o'clock, Lin Liguo returned from Beijing and immediately went to see his father together with Ye Qun. At 10 o'clock, another film was projected. It was watched by all members of Lin Biao's household and staff except Lin Biao himself, Ye Qun and Lin Liguo. At about 10.30, Ye Qun realised that Lin Liheng was also no longer watching the film. According to Li Wenpu, she had left the building and had gone to the office of the troop unit 8341 from where she reported to the general office of the Central

Committee that Lin Liguo and Ye Qun had planned to abduct Lin Biao the next morning. Upon her return to the main building, Ye Qun instructed her to make preparations to leave with them for Dalian the following morning. Her fiancé Zhang Qinglin and Lin Liguo's fiancée Zhang Ning were also to go with them.[163]

Some time after 11 o'clock, when the second film was about to end, Ye Qun rushed into the hall and announced that their departure for Dalian had been advanced and would take place very soon. Lin Liheng immediately returned to the office of the 8341 unit to report Lin's and Ye Qun's intentions to depart.[164]

At about a quarter to midnight, Lin Biao, Ye Qun, Lin Liguo, Liu Peifeng, a member of the Joint Fleet, and Li Wenpu got into Lin Biao's car and drove to Shanhaiguan airport. Alerted by Lin Liheng, the garrison leader decided to pursue Lin Biao's car.[165] After the car reached the airport at 12.32 a.m., its occupants rushed on to the plane which took off without waiting for the co-pilot and the navigator, and flew towards the northwest in the direction of the nearest Chinese borderline. It crossed the border at 1.55 a.m. and crashed at about 2.30 a.m. on Mongolian territory.

Zhou Enlai, on the evening of 12 September, presided over a Politburo meeting to discuss the draft report on government activities to be presented to the forthcoming 4th National People's Congress. At 11 p.m., a report from Lin Liheng about unusual activities at Lin Biao's residence in Beidaihe was transmitted to him. Lin Liheng was convinced that her mother and brother intended to pressure Lin Biao into making a dangerous move, and if necessary, would not hesitate to abduct him. She also informed Zhou about the presence of a Trident aircraft at Shanghaihuan airport near Beidaihe. Zhou Enlai interrupted the meeting and called Wu Faxian by phone instructing him to investigate, without delay, whether there was a plane at Shanhaiguan and, if so, to find out the reasons for the aircraft's presence at that airport. Wu Faxian called back shortly thereafter confirming that a Trident was indeed at Shanhaiguan. He added that the plane had gone there on a test flight. When Zhou ordered its immediate return to Beijing, Wu said that the plane could not take off since it had some mechanical problems. Zhou Enlai's suspicion grew. He ordered Wu Faxian to see to it that the plane would be repaired and that it returned to Beijing without delay.¹⁶⁶

The Trident had been put at Lin Liguo's disposal by the deputy chief of staff of the air force, Hu Ping. When Hu Ping was contacted by Wu Faxian in the course of his inquiries about the plane, he realised that Zhou Enlai had learned about the matter. Hu Ping immediately informed Lin Liguo that Zhou Enlai had discovered the Trident's whereabouts.¹⁶⁷

At 11.22 p.m., Zhou Enlai received a telephone call from Ye Qun who informed him that Lin Biao intended to leave for Dalian early next morning and needed a few aeroplanes for himself and his staff. When Zhou asked her whether she had already ordered planes she denied it, which increased Zhou's suspicion even further.¹⁶⁸ He immediately took a number of measures. He dispatched Yang Dezhong, one of his senior staff, to Wu Faxian's offices to supervise his activities. He sent Li Desheng to the headquarters of the air force to take over command, and instructed Ji Dengkui to supervise the activities of the Beijing Military Region headquarters. He gave orders to the Shanhaiguan airport to prevent the take off of the Trident specifying that the plane could leave the premises only by an order jointly signed by Huang Yongsheng, Wu Faxian, Li Zuopeng and himself.¹⁶⁹

To avoid contact between Lin Biao and Huang Yongsheng who was at the meeting with Zhou Enlai, Zhou ordered Huang to stay with him and to handle the Trident situation. He instructed Wu Faxian to prepare two planes for his own immediate use. His intention was to fly to Beidaihe as soon as possible and try to dissuade Lin Biao from any rash action.¹⁷⁰

At midnight, after Zhou Enlai was informed about Lin Biao's departure to the airport, he issued two orders. One, no plane was allowed to fly to Beijing, and two, all planes throughout China were to stay grounded unless they received an order signed by Mao, Zhou, Huang Yongsheng, Wu Faxian, and Li Zuopeng.¹⁷¹

Afterwards, Zhou and Ji Dengkui left for Zhongnanhai to report to Mao about the latest developments. While they were in Mao's study, Wu Faxian who monitored the movements of Lin's plane, reported that it was flying towards the Mongolian border and asked whether the plane should be shot down while it was still within shooting range. Ji Dengkui, in an interview in the late 1980s recalled Mao's response in the form of a Chinese proverb: ' "rain has to fall, a (widowed) mother wants to marry". These things are immutable, let him go'.[172]

After Lin Biao's flight had been reported to Zhou Enlai, he informed the Foreign Ministry about Lin's disappearance in the morning of 13 September. He instructed the ministry to record and examine carefully all reports of foreign news agencies concerning Lin Biao's fate, and to develop contingency plans, in case Lin reappeared publicly in a foreign country.

On the morning of 14 September, the Chinese embassy in Ulaan Baatar was informed by the Mongolian authorities that a Chinese military aircraft had violated Mongolian airspace and crashed at Ondorhaan. The Chinese Ambassador decided that this was a case of emergency and he should reopen the telephone line between Ulaan Baatar and Beijing which had been unused for a number of years due to the deterioration of relations between the two countries, in order to inform the Chinese foreign ministry as quickly as possible about these events. The telephone call reached the foreign minister Ji Pengfei, at noon that day. Ji Pengfei instructed one of the vice ministers, Wang Hairong, to inform both Mao Zedong and Zhou Enlai about the telephone message from their embassy in Mongolia. Both Mao and Zhou were awakened from their sleep and instructed the foreign ministry to make a written report on this matter. The report was delivered in the evening to Zhou Enlai who informed the Politburo about the state of affairs.[173]

The Chinese ambassador was instructed to accept the Mongolian invitation to visit the site of the plane accident in order to confirm the Mongolian investigation. The nine people who died were later identified as Lin Biao, Ye Qun, Lin Liguo, Lui Peifeng, member of the joint fleet, Pan Jingyin, the pilot, Yang Zhengang, Lin Biao's driver, Shao Qiliang, Zhang Tingkui and Li Ping, mechanics.[174] Xu Wenyi, the Chinese ambassador, was instructed to have a report of his investigations hand delivered to Beijing. It arrived on 19 September, and corroborated that it had indeed been Lin Biao's aircraft which had crashed and that those killed in the accident were Lin and his entourage.[175]

The aftermath of the Lin Biao affair

The first result of Lin's disappearance was a purge of his supporters. On 24 September, the Party centre issued an order stipulating the removal of Huang Yongsheng, Wu Faxian, Li Zuopeng and Qiu Huizuo from their posts. This was followed by the abolition of the MC administrative group on 3 October. The direction of the Military Commission was taken over by Ye Jianying. On the same day, a special investigation group on the Lin Biao affair was established under Zhou Enlai's direction. A campaign against Lin Biao and a purge to eliminate his followers in the army began and was drawn out until May 1973.[176]

The victims of this purge were classified into four categories. First there were the 'die-hard gangsters', (*sidang*) to which the 93 members of the joint fleet, the four generals Huang, Wu, Li and Qiu, as well as Chen Boda, belonged. In the second category were these 'who took the bandits boat' (*shang liao zai chuande*). The most prominent among them were Liu Feng, political commissar of the Wuhan military region, who had sent reports to Lin about Mao's movements and talks during his travels in the area in the summer of 1971, and Cheng Shiqing, the Director of the Jianxi Revolutionary Committee, who had reported to Mao about Lin's activities. Cheng, having displayed his knowledge about Lin's conspiracy, was suspected of having been in the same boat with him. Others were Gu Tongzhou, chief of staff of the Guangzhou air force, Li Xuefeng, political commissar and Zheng Weishan, commander of the Beijing military region.[177] In the third category were those who had committed 'serious mistakes'. They were considered to have belonged to Lin Biao's faction without being aware of Lin's activities. The fourth category of persons had merely 'committed mistakes'.[178] Throughout this campaign, the purge focused strongly on the air force, tha navy, the headquarters of the general chief of staff and the general logistics department.[179]

The process of investigation and extracting confessions lasted for about two years before it was determined to which category the suspected person belonged. Lin Liheng, Zhang Ning and all of Lin Biao's office personnel had to go through the investigation. In 1972, they were sent to a labour camp from which they were finally released in 1975.[80] Lin Liheng remained in the provinces until 1988, when Zhao Zhiyang granted her request to settle down in Beijing.[181]

The Lin Biao affair still remains full of mysteries and unanswered questions. First, how could Lin Biao have assumed that an attempt to assassinate Mao might succeed, when many of the young and inexperienced planners of such a coup were reluctant to really pursue such a plan at a time when Mao still remained a sacred figure; besides, to harm him was not only inconceivable, but also extremely dangerous. Furthermore, the practical difficulties involved in such a plan, which required the utilisation of military equipment without official approval, were at that time almost impossible to solve. Secondly, how could Lin Biao have considered the establishment of a second 'centre' in Guangzhou which would be able to challenge the central government in Beijing and of splitting up the country? Even if he had the support of the Guangdong Military Region commanders, he could not have been sure that they would endorse a plan of secession. And if they had, how long would they have been able to challenge the central government without risking a civil war which Guangzhou would have undoubtedly lost? The most plausible assumption still remains that Guangzhou might have been used as a stepping stone to Hong Kong.

Why did Lin Biao finally decide to fly to the Soviet Union? There are controversial views on this question. The most simple explanation suggests that, under the circumstances of his hasty departure, he needed to fly to the nearest border. Some writers have assumed that Lin Biao disapproved of China's rapprochement with the United States, with China's hostile attitude towards the Soviet Union, and that, in fact, he had maintained regular contacts with Soviet officials with whom he had plotted to overthrow Mao Zedong. It can be safely assumed that if such a cooperation between Lin and the Soviets had existed, the official investigation report on Lin Biao's case would not have failed to mention it.

Although Lin Biao had obviously disappeared from the public, no explanations were given by the Chinese authorities as to his whereabouts. Instead, there was a lot of warning about the dangers of an impending war. Slowly, more and more information about Lin's disappearance percolated through to the public. After much delay, the 'September 13 Event' was made known to the Chinese public in late 1971.[182] At first, when the CC documents about Lin Biao's flight and death were read to them, most people were shocked – that the deputy commander of the Proletarian Headquarters and the 'brilliant example' to the Chinese people, had turned out to be a conspirator and careerist, who did not even hesitate to plot an attempt on Mao's life. How could such a person have been chosen as a successor by Mao who was said to be the wisest and greatest leader not only of China but of all revolutionary peoples in the world? Liu Shaoqi had already been accused of being a renegade, hidden traitor and scab. Now Lin Biao was a 'bourgeois careerist, conspirator, doubler-dealer, renegade and traitor'.

The Lin Biao affair had profound repercussions on Chinese political life. It undoubtedly created a great disarray among the Chinese authorities. First, it was a serious shock to Mao's charismatic leadership and to the Cultural Revolution, of which Lin Biao had been such a stout supporter. Mao's designated successor, the deputy chief leader of the Cultural Revolution, the architect of a personality cult in favour of the Chairman, had in fact, neglected the campaign to purify class rank, which Mao had conceived for the purpose of establishing a pure socialist system, and had obviously been more interested in the enhancement of his own personal power and in the elimination of his major rivals represented by Jiang Qing than in Mao's designs for a socialist society.

Secondly, the Lin Biao affair was a serious blow to Mao himself, both mentally and physically. The man he had chosen as his successor, whom he had cultivated and trusted, had ended up as his fatal enemy. It is not possible to assess the extent of his personal disappointment, but it must have been deep.

According to the reminiscences of Zhang Yufeng, who was his closet private secretary at that time, the Chairman's health suddenly deteriorated. He was no longer the beaming and buoyant leader he used to be, and he fell seriously ill at the end of 1971. Had he finally realised that he was not a god and that he was not as infallible as he had thought himself to be, or as his adulators had propagated? In January 1972, the 77-year-old chairman suffered a stroke.[183] As his health deteriorated, so did his revolutionary fervour. He was now an ailing man who no longer talked about his great strategy of 'struggle – criticism – transformation' which was to be achieved by the Cultural Revolution. Yet he continued to be deeply involved in his concept of the Cultural Revolution. He never failed to justify it at all costs and he was unable to tolerate any doubts about the movement he had launched. The defence of the Cultural Revolution had become his major concern.

7
FINAL POWER STRUGGLES

The criticism of Lin Biao and Confucius
Deceitful calm

The period between Lin Biao's disappearance in September 1971, and the inauguration of a nationwide campaign 'to criticise Lin Biao and Confucius' (*pi Lin pi Kong*) in January 1974, was marked by an unusual calm in terms of mass campaigns. In 1971, the movement to purify class ranks was still in full swing, but it lost much of its momentum during the following year, partly because an overwhelming number of 'class enemies' had already been unmasked, and partly because the Lin Biao affair had diverted the attention of the leadership to more pressing matters.

Ever since Khrushchev's ascent to power in the Soviet Union, Mao had been obsessed with the necessity of grooming his own successor, in order to prevent the occurrence of a 'Khrushchev-type revisionism' in China and to establish 'successors of the revolutionary cause'.[1] A year after the death of his second successor, Mao was again preoccupied with this question. In the 21 member Politburo, 7 were no longer in office.[2] The remaining members ranked as follows in order of importance: Mao, Zhou Enlai, Kang Sheng, Jiang Qing, Zhang Chunqiao.[3] Zhou and Kang, because of their age, uncertain health and other reasons could not be considered as possible heirs of Mao. Neither could Jiang Qing. Mao had become increasingly dissatisfied with her activities which, in his view, were inspired by wild ambitions and general incompetence. The only likely candidate was Zhang Chunqiao. Mao and Lin

Biao had once talked about the possibility of making Zhang their successor, since Mao was elderly and Lin in poor health.[4]

In 1972, Zhang Chunqiao was 55 years old. He had played an important role during the CR and had been able to survive the ordeals of the chaotic years. The attack which Lin Biao's group had waged on him during the Lushan conference only enhanced his prestige. However, Mao did not choose him. Surprising everyone from Politburo members to the man in the street, he announced that the 37-year-old Wang Hongwen would be his successor.[5]

Wang Hongwen was one of six deputy directors of the Shanghai municipal revolutionary committee.[6] Born in 1935 in Changchun, north-east China under Japanese occupation, he spent his childhood in a poor family in the countryside. At the age of 16, Wang joined the liberation army and was sent to the Korean front where he first served as a messenger soldier and later as a body guard to a leading officer. During his service in the army, he joined the Party. After his demobilisation, he was assigned to the Shanghai no. 17 cotton mill as a maintenance worker. In 1964, he was promoted from worker to cadre and moved to the security section of the mill. At the same time, he became commander of the militia unit of the mill.[7]

With the CR, his life greatly changed. On 12 June 1966, he put up his first big character poster which attacked the mill's Party committee. After the 11th Plenum, Wang became increasingly involved in radical policies.[8] On 9 November 1966, the Shanghai workers revolutionary rebels general headquarters elected Wang as their leader which allowed him to play a major role in the overthrow of the Shanghai municipal Party committee and government. In February 1967, he became deputy director of the Shanghai municipal revolutionary committee, and in April 1969, the 9th Party Congress elected him to the CC.[9]

On Mao's orders, Wang was transferred to Beijing on 7 September 1972. Wang was not aware of the reasons for his transfer and the tasks that lay ahead of him. To his surprise, Mao received him personally in his study, asked him many questions and concluded with satisfaction, that Wang Hongwen had 'combined in himself worker, peasant, and soldier', since, during his life, he had exercised all these functions.

Mao told Wang that his duty in Beijing was 'to study Marxist – Leninist books, and to attend certain meetings to learn different things'.[10]

Thus began Wang's apprenticeship as Mao's successor. The heavy volumes of complete works of Marx, Engels and Lenin were provided for his study, but given his poor educational background, he found these books difficult to read. He was sent to attend meetings dealing with the 7th machinery ministry, with Hunan, Hebei and over provinces, which were a strain to him. Many of the meetings he had to attend, were scheduled according to Mao's and Zhou's work habits. Both got up at noon and worked throughout the afternoon and the night until about six o'clock in the morning.

Frustrated with his new assignment, Wang made long telephone calls to his friends in Shanghai, complaining about the boredom of his life in Beijing and expressing the desire to return to Shanghai.[11] But Mao appeared to be satisfied with Wang's apprenticeship. The news of his appointment as Mao's successor was announced on 28 December 1972, on the last day of a conference of the Beijing military region Party committee. According to the custom, leaders of the centre, in this instance Zhou Enlai, Ye Jianying, Li Xiannian, Jiang Qing, Zhang Chunqiao, Yao Wenyuan, and Wang Hongwen, met with the participants of the meeting on its last day. Ye Jianying declared that 'the Chairman had talked about the problem of a successor since 1964'. He introduced Wang Hongwen as having grown up in a poor peasant family, having taken part in the Korean war and having been a worker afterwards. 'The Chairman has noticed him,' Ye said, 'he has to be cultivated.'[12] Zhou Enlai followed suit and told the participants of the conference that it was Mao's intention 'to choose young men' between the ages of 30 and 40, and who had been peasants or workers, 'to be vice chairman of the Party and of the MC'.[13]

In line with his policy to choose young men, Mao, in March 1973, invited Wang Hongwen, Hua Guofeng, and Wu De to participate in Politburo meetings. They thus became part of the national leadership and participated in the decision-making process on major policy issues.[14]

During the preparations for the 10th Party Congress, Wang's position was again strengthened when Mao appointed him to head the Election Preparatory Committee which wielded great influence in the process of nominating CC members. While Wang headed the committee, such old timers as Zhou Enlai, Ye Jianying, Kang Sheng, Li Desheng and even Jiang Qing served as his deputies.[15] Wang Hongwen was also in charge of the Party constitution amendment group whose task it was to prepare the new constitution.[16]

The 10th Party Congress was convened in Beijing from 24 to 28 August 1973 under Mao's chairmanship. Zhou Enlai presented the Political Report which had been drafted by Yao Wenyuan and Zhang Chunqiao[17] and which stressed 'the shattering of the Lin Biao anti-Party clique' as the 'greatest victory since the 9th Congress'. It also affirmed the continuity of the political line established by the 9th Congress.[18] Wang Hongwen delivered the report on the revision of the Party constitution, in which he announced that the paragraph concerning Lin Biao would be deleted. The revised Party constitution confirmed the CR as a 'great political revolution carried out by the proletariat against the bourgeoisie and all other exploiting classes to consolidate the dictatorship of the proletariat and prevent capitalist restoration.[19]

The most important aspect of the Congress was the reorganisation of the leadership. A total of 195 and 124 alternative members were elected to the CC, which represented an increase by 40 over the number of people elected at the 9th Congress. The composition of the CC was marked by a decline of military representation, a logical consequence of Lin Biao's fall and of the termination of general military control within the country.[20] The erosion of military influence was compensated by the return of a number of such veteran revolutionaries as Deng Xiaoping, once the number two capitalist roader of the nation, Tan Zhenlin, once the notorious 'black general of the February Adverse Current', Wang Jiaxiang, who had been accused of having initiated the 'three peace and one less' foreign policy in 1962,[21] Ulanfu, the leader of the Inner Mongolia who had been condemned as the instigator of the underground Mongolian People's Party, and Li Jingquan, the former secretary of the south-west bureau, who had been considered the 'biggest capitalist roader in South West China'.[22]

The Jiang Qing group also consolidated its position in the CC through the election of an increased number of its supporters. Among them were Xu Jingxian, Ma Tianshui, and Wang Xiuzhen, all leading members of the Shanghai municipal Party committee and government. Others were Jiang Qing's confidants such as Yu Huiyong, a composer, Liu Xiangping, Xie Fuzhi's wife, and Xie Jingyi a former staff member of the CC general office.[23]

The 10th CC held on 30 August, elected Mao as the chairman and five vice chairmen who were, in hierarchical order, Zhou Enlai, Wang Hongwen, Kang Sheng, Ye Jiangying and Li Desheng.[24] The most important result of the Congress was the change in the power structure in the newly established CC. The Congress abolished the tripartite structure established at the 9th Congress and replaced it by a dual structure.

The CC and the Politburo were clearly divided into two factions, the old guard and the CR factions. In the Standing Committee, three (Wang Hongwen, Zhang Chunqiao, Kang Sheng) of its nine members belonged to the CR faction. In the 21-member CC, four (Wang Hongwen, Zhang Chunqiao, Jiang Qing and Yao Wenyuan) represented the CR faction. Ji Dengkai, a former Party secretary in Henan province, and a favourite of Mao, Chen Yonggui, leader of the Dazhai PC, Wu De, first secretary of the Beijing Party committee, and Chen Xilian, commander of the Shenyang military region, although not members of the CR faction, were considered close to it.[25]

Though the old-guard faction headed by Zhou Enlai, was numerically stronger than Jiang Qing's faction, it was politically relatively inactive. Many of its members were elderly and had hardly recuperated from the shocks the CR had inflicted upon them. They were continuously overshadowed by the smaller, but more ambitious and aggressive CR faction which controlled the mass media, and therefore was capable of exercising strong influence on public opinion.

The 80-year-old Mao towered above the two factions, trying to balance them out or to mediate between them. But the basic interests between the two groups were fundamentally different. Jiang Qing and her group had risen to power in the wake of the CR. It was therefore in their interest to perpetuate CR policies. The old guard had been attacked and humiliated during the CR, which had jeopardised their political career for a number of years, and, in many cases, had threatened their very survival. It was in their interest to restrain, not to expand CR policies. This power structure, where both groups strove

The campaign against ultra-leftism

After Lin Biao's disappearance, a campaign against him had begun to take effect. Officially, it was called 'criticise revisionism and rectify working style'.[26] But it was clearly understood that, in this particular case, revisionism and work style were a paraphrase for Lin Biao.

The campaign against Lin Biao at first focused on the '571 project', allegedly designed by Lin Liguo to assassinate Mao. In early 1972, it was extended to a reappraisal of Lin Biao's military career. Since Lin's credentials as a brilliant strategist and military leader had been firmly established,[27] it was difficult to question his achievements during these campaigns; but all this apparently did not discourage the 'revolutionaries' to take liberties with historical facts in incriminating him.

During the military campaigns of Liaoxi – Shenyang and Beijing – Tianjin in the 1940s, Lin had made a number of tactical recommendations which Mao overruled. In 1972, the telegrams containing his 'wrong' suggestions were taken as evidence of his 'crimes', and it was claimed that, if Mao had not corrected Lin's errors, these decisive battles would certainly have been lost. But the debasement of Lin's military achievements was the least convincing part of the campaign and before long, the media had exhausted its litany of propaganda against him.[28]

Zhou Enlai seized the stalemate to give the campaign a new impetus and direction. In his view, the campaign should not be confined to Lin Biao's person and deeds, but focus on the ultra-leftism Lin had incited among the people.[29] In his aversion against radicalism, Zhou believed that now was the right time to settle accounts with the radicals, and, at the same token, to rehabilitate more veteran cadres.

Zhou's campaign against ultra-leftism began with his instructions to the *People's Daily* to publish an editorial which, in April 1972, waged a sharp attack against the previous persecutions of veteran cadres by the masses.[30] In May, Zhou extended the campaign to the educational sector. The State Council convened a meeting to discuss the situation in universities and colleges, during which the participants had the opportunity, for the first time since the beginning of the CR, to vent their concern about the damages done to higher education.[31] In July, Zhou asked Professor Zhou Peiyuan, a well known physicist at Beijing University, to write an article arguing for the necessity and importance of theoretical research in science, which had been grossly neglected during the CR.[32] Zhou himself emphasised the desirability of recruiting university students among senior middle-school graduates,[33] a system which had been abolished as a 'bourgeois educational policy' and which was replaced by the 'newly emerged' practice of choosing students from workers' peasants' and soldiers' families.[34]

While in 1971 and 1972, the State Council began to reinstate work in various fields such as state planning, public security, publication, science and technology and public health, Zhou continued to make speeches rejecting the ultra-leftism and anarchism which Lin Biao's activities had allegedly promoted.[35] In the middle of 1972, Zhou enlarged the areas of his campaign to foreign affairs and the press. On 1 August, during a meeting with Chinese ambassadors accredited in foreign countries, he criticised the foreign ministry, the *People's Daily* and the Xinhua news agency for their failure to thoroughly repudiate ultra-leftism.[36]

Zhou clearly aimed at a comprehensive repudiation of radicalism and anarchism. At the time of the campaign, his political position was particularly strong, since Mao had entrusted him with the chairmanship of the Politburo. Among the five members of the Standing Committee, Lin Biao had disappeared, Chen Boda was in custody, and Kang Sheng was seriously ill. Only Mao and Zhou were left. Under the circumstances, Zhou was able to rehabilitate a number of veteran revolutionaries such as Chen Yun and Wang Zhen. In early 1973, Zhou suggested to Mao to withdraw the cases against 300 high-ranking cadres still under supervision or in custody. But due to the opposition of the CR faction, this plan was not fully carried out.[37]

On 14 October 1972, the *People's Daily* devoted an entire page to three articles focusing on the repudiation of anarchy. They were the strongest condemnation of the excesses of the CR hitherto made public, and they again protested at the persecution of veteran cadres. The criticism against ultra-leftism and anarchism touched on a number of aspects, including the creation of upheaval, the rejection of the guidance of the Party, the persecution of cadres, and of millions of rank and file, all of which had been advocated by Mao himself during the first stage of the CR. In fact, the CR itself was an ultra-leftist movement characterised by anarchism. It was therefore not surprising that the criticism initiated by Zhou met with a great deal of resistance from supporters of the CR. Zhang Chunqiao and Yao Wenyuan, whose careers were based on CR policies and which would have been compromised if Zhou was allowed to persist with his campaign, were the first to retaliate. Upon their instructions, the Shanghai *Wenhui Bao* published a report about a workers' meeting where participants had angrily denounced the *People's Daily* articles as a 'negation of the CR and a repudiation of the masses.'[38] Confused by these attacks, Wang Ruoshui, the PD editor responsible for the publication of the three articles, and who was himself convinced about the correctness of the line represented in his newspaper, wrote a letter to Mao about the open differences between the *People's Daily* and the *Wenhui Ribao* and asked for the chairman's instructions.[39]

The problem was indeed a fundamental one. If Lin Biao's policies were ultra-left, then the foremost conclusion was that Lin Biao, who had wielded widespread influence over the CR, had directed it on a wrong course. To negate the CR together with Lin Biao, was only one further step to take. Mao, who was fully aware of this danger, ruled that Wang's views were 'incorrect'. On 17 December, in a meeting with Zhang Chunqiao and Yao Wenyuan, he expressed the strange view that Lin Biao's policies had not been ultra-left but ultra-right, since he had practised 'revisionism, conspiracy, betrayal' and 'aimed at schism in the Party and the State'.[40]

On 19 December, the chief editors of PD were invited to a meeting with Jiang Qing, Zhang Chunqiao, Yao Wenyuan, Zhou Enlai and a number of other Politburo members. Formally, Zhou Enlai changed completely. In his opening statement, he reneged on his previous views on ultra-leftism and adjusted himself to those expressed by Mao. Pointing out that Wang, in his letter to Mao, had mentioned his speech to the Chinese ambassadors, Zhou declared that he had been referring to foreign policy only and not to the political line pursued by Lin Biao. Lin's betrayal of the Party and the state could not be considered ultra-left but was clearly ultra-right in nature. Linking the campaign against ultra-leftism with Lin Biao could only lead to the criticism of the masses. He concluded that Wang, by publishing the three articles on Lin Biao's ultra-leftism in the PD, had made a mistake. Jiang Qing, Zhang Chunqiao and Yao Wenyuan also reiterated Mao's views on the problem and sharply criticised Wang Ruoshui and the PD.[41]

Zhou Enlai thus suffered his first setback since Lin Biao's death. Criticism of ultra-leftism was halted and the entire nation followed Mao's new verdict that Lin Biao's policies had been ultra-rightist.

In their attempts to justify and safeguard the CR, Mao and the CR faction began to step up their criticism of Lin Biao with the aim of making him a credible scapegoat for whatever had gone wrong with the CR. This escalation established a link between Lin Biao and Confucius who, in Mao's view, both represented retrogression and the desire to turn back the wheels of history.

The linkage was established after Jiang Qing ordered a search of Lin Biao's home with the intention of finding evidence about Lin's interest in Confucianism. During the search, a number of scrolls written in Lin Biao's and Chen Boda's calligraphy were found in Lin Beijing residence. They were copies of quotations from Confucius' teachings, such as 'of all things, the most important is to restrain oneself and to return to the rites'; 'no ruler of any dynasty can surpass the Chou emperor Wen.';[42] 'want of patience in small matters confounds great plans'. A notebook containing more references to Confucius and allegedly belonging to Lin Biao was also discovered. But the notebook also contained such statements as 'boldly combat the ultra-left trend of thought' and 'resolutely combat the right deviation', both of which were interpreted as an application of the Confucian doctrine of the mean.[43]

Based on these findings, Mao, in a talk in July 1973, announced his new concept regarding Lin Biao to Wang Hongwen and Zhang Chunqiao. The Guomindang, Mao said, revered Confucianism, and so did Lin Biao. On the same occasion Mao expressed the view, that Qin Shihuang who was regarded as a despotic ruler, should not be condemned, since he had opposed Confucianism and supported the legalist school.[44]

In the following months a new poem by Mao, was widely circulated. It read:

Please, my friend, do not be too ready to condemn Qin Shihuang;

There is something to be said for his burning of books and burying scholars.

After Zu Long[45] passed away, his sons still remained.

But despite its high reputation, Confucianism blew away like chaff.

A hundred generations have gone by applying Qin's way of ruling.

The essay 'ten criticisms' is not a good thing.[46]

Study well the Tang scholars' 'dissertation on the system of principalities'.

Do not bark at King Wen while following Zihou.[47]

On 23 September, Mao talked again about Confucious and Qin Shihuang, this time to the vice president of Egypt who was visiting China. 'Qin Shihuang was the first well-known emperor of China', Mao said to the foreign visitor. 'I am also Qin Shihuang. Lin Biao condemned me as such.[48] In China there are always two different views. Some people endorsed Qin Shihuang, while others opposed him. I support Qin Shihuang, I do not support Confucius.'[49]

Mao's remarks ushered in a new campaign on a nationwide scale to repudiate Confucius. Under Jiang Qing's directive, a 'two schools' criticism group' composed of selected scholars from Beijing and Qinghua universities was established. Its publications went under the name of *liang xiao* ('two schools'). In Shanghai, a 'writing group of the Shanghai municipal party committee' – publishing under the name of Luo Siding – was set up under the control of Zhang Chunqiao and Yao Wenyuan. The central Party school created a writing group under Kang Sheng's direction which took the name of Tang Xiaowen. Jiang Qing set up still another group within the ministry of culture.⁵⁰ These groups began to publish articles elaborating on Mao's thinking on Confucius and Lin Biao. The basic message of these publications can be summarised as follows:

1 Confucius was a representative of retrogression, restoration and reactionary thinking. In his lifetime during the late spring and autumn period (722–481 BC), according to Mao, he advocated and worked for the restoration of the slave ownership system of the Zhou Dynasty.
2 The Legalist school, represented by Shang Yang (who died in 338 BC), Xun Kuang (around 312–238 BC) and Han Fei (around 380–232 BC) propagated the view that 'man's will can conquer heaven'. Unlike Confucianism which required that 'man should abide by the will of heaven', the Legalists advocated political reform and opposed retrogression.
3 The emperor Qin Shihuang was the representative of a rising landlord class who, as a Legalist, adopted revolutionary measures to defeat the attempted restoration of the slave-owning aristocracy and succeeded in consolidating the rule of the new landlord class against the established aristocracy. His first measure was to eliminate his prime minister Lu Buwei (?–325) and his supporters, which was followed by burning books and burying Confucian scholars.
4 The history of China is characterised by a succession of struggles between the Legalist school and Confucianism, between progress and retrogression, and between restoration and revolution.
5 Political swindlers like Liu Shaoqi and Lin Biao revered Confucianism because it stands for the reactionary ruling class, whereas the proletarian revolutionaries support Legalism because it defends the interests of the rising class.⁵¹

The 1974 New Year's editorial stressed the fundamental purpose of the new campaign which was to develop a 'correct' attitude towards the CR, the masses and oneself (*san ge zhengque duidai*). Leading cadres, especially, were requested to look after the interests of the Party with the same concern they had for their own life, and to subordinate their personal interests to those of the Party. They should support the CR, despite any sufferings and humiliations which might have been imposed on them during its course, since the CR represented the interests of the Party and the advancement of society along the path of socialism. Leading cadres should not position themselves above the masses, as they had often done before the CR, nor should they antagonise the masses because they had suffered injustice from them. Instead, they should identify themselves with the masses and be aware of their own shortcomings and mistakes. The mass movement was meant to temper them, not to punish them.

Pi Lin, pi Kong, and the 'back door' issue

At the beginning of 1974, the campaign against Lin Biao and Confucius began to be implemented on a massive scale. On 12 January, Jiang Qing and Wang Hongwen proposed to Mao that they distribute publicly a collection of material entitled 'Lin Biao and the Doctrines of Confucius and Mencius' which the Beida and Qinghua criticism group had prepared.[52] It contained a series of Lin Biao's writings, some in his calligraphy, which were construed as an expression of Lin's veneration for Confucius. With Mao's approval, this material was circulated as the no. 1 CC document of the year 1974.[53] It constituted the basis for the campaign of criticising Lin Biao and Confucius.

Jiang Qing started the campaign with a meeting of ten thousand people from the Beijing area military units on 24 January. The meeting was followed the next day by a second one, gathering another ten thousand people from CC and State Council units. At these meetings, in addition to denouncing Lin Biao and Confucius, Chi Qun, Party secretary of Qinghua university, who was one of the main speakers, condemned the practice of using personal relations in order to obtain results, through the 'back door', as 'a total betrayal of Marxism–Leninism and of Mao Zedong Thought'.[54]

This was a new aspect of the campaign which attracted a great deal more attention than the problem of Lin Biao's attitude towards Confucianism. Although writings on this subject filled the pages of newspapers, people had become tired of the successive political campaigns. The last one, filled with philosophical and historical allusions, was considered by many as an esoteric intellectual discussion which failed to motivate the masses. But the 'back door' problem touched upon everyone's daily life and had given rise to considerable indignation among the great majority of people who had no access to a 'back door' of some weight.

If the practice of obtaining results through personal connections had somewhat dampened down during the second half of the 1960s, it became rampant again in the early 1970s among high-ranking cadres. One example was the implementation of the policy to send young people to the countryside. Although Mao had decreed that all young people should go to the countryside after terminating middle school, it had become a common practice among high-ranking cadres to use their personal connections to send their children to the army instead, which was considered a rare privilege. Higher education for one's children was a similar case. Although Mao had emphasised that university students should be recruited from peasant, worker and soldier families, high-ranking cadres still succeeded in having their children admitted to universities.[55]

If Jiang Qing and her radical collegues hoped to revive revolutionary fervour among the people, the back-door issue was a real stimulant. Since they were called upon to link *pi Lin pi Kong* with the 'back door' issue, people began to participate in the campaign, and, as in the beginning of the CR, veteran cadres, much to the liking of Jiang Qing and her group, became once again targets of attack. Wang Hongwen made an announcement according to which 'the campaign to criticise Lin Bio and Confucianism was a second CR'.[56]

Mao, however, did not agree with this interpretation of the campaign against Lin Biao and Confucianism. He did not want another phase of the CR with veteran cadres as targets of attack. Therefore, he began to restrain Jiang Qing. In a written instruction dated 15 February, he called her 'metaphysical [the Chinese expression for unrealistic] and one sided'.[57] He also emphasised that to insist on the 'back door' problem would lead to the dilution of the real issue which was to criticise Lin and Confucius, and that those who went through the back door were not necessarily all bad; while those who went through the front door were not necessarily all good.[58] With these remarks, he not only failed to put an end to 'back door' practices, but, in fact, consented to them. As a result, the practice developed again into an integral part of Chinese social life.

'Set fire' in the army

Jiang Qing paid special attention to the army which she considered as the most conservative force in society. Many military leaders used the campaign to criticise Lin to eliminate his one-sided emphasis on politics to the detriment of military training. But they showed no particular enthusiasm about the campaign to criticise Lin Biao and Confucianism.

Jiang Qing, for her part, used the campaign to increase her own influence in the army. In January 1974, she sent material about Lin Biao's connection with Confucius to the PLA air force and the navy. She also wrote to the leaders of the MC, and through them, to the entire army to impress upon them the utmost importance of the campaign.[59]

But the military's response was, at best, lukewarm. Jiang Qing was particularly dissatisfied with the situation at the headquarters of the general staff and their general political and logistics departments, where, according to Jiang Qing, some 'die-hard bureaucrats' were in charge. In the air force, the campaign which had hardly begun was, in Jiang Qing's view, already 'cooling down'. Wang Hongwen and Zhang Chunqiao, in their capacity as Politburo members, called a meeting of the MC to criticise the above-mentioned military units for their passive and perfunctory attitude towards the campaign.[60] Other units, such as the PLA engineering corps, the railway corps, and the artillery were also criticised for their perfunctory approach to the campaign. Zhang Chunqiao especially singled out Chen Shiju, the commander of the engineering corps, as 'the first person to be condemned' for his inefficiency in leading the campaign in the unit under his jurisdiction.[61]

Intellectuals in the campaign

The campaign *pi Lin pi Kong* was unique in the CR, in the sense that it represented an attempt to reinterpret an important period of Chinese cultural history. Confucianists and Legalists were associated with antagonistic classes in accordance with Mao's conception that 'the history of civilisation for thousands of years' had been marked by class struggle.⁶² It was therefore not surprising, that the new interpretation of Confucianism and Legalism met with considerable reservation among the intellectuals. But it was also a source of apprehension among those who had been involved in the study of these schools of thought. Guo Moruo, on whose writings about Confucius Mao had expressed a negative judgement, was the first to feel the pressure of the new campaign. He wrote a poem 'To Chairman Mao' where he stated that, in spite of his assiduous studies for more than thirty years, he had remained ignorant, and was enlightened only by the Mao's criticism of Confucianism which 'woke him up like a spring thunder storm'.⁶³

Feng Youlan, a professor at Beida, who was considered a major authority on Chinese philosophy, had defended Confucianism in his book *History of Chinese Philosophy* which was published in the 1940s. Feng had been an early target of the CR which, in its initial stages, had condemned him as a 'big reactionary academic authority'. As the campaign to criticise Lin and Confucius began to unfold, he did not wait until he again became a target of attack, but took the initiative to criticise himself for his approval of Confucius in two articles which he published in the *Beida Journal*. Feng thus escaped another wave of attack and was recruited by Jiang Qing as a member of Liang Xiao.⁶⁴

A noteworthy exception among the scholars, who all accepted, at least outwardly, the new official interpretation of Confucianism, was Liang Shuming. He had been a distinguished young philosopher in the new democracy movement in 1919 and later became a convinced Confucianist.⁶⁵ After the establishment of the PRC, Liang became a member of the Chinese People's Political Consultative Conference (CPPCC). He was perhaps the only person in the PRC who dared to argue openly with Mao who, in 1953, devoted an entire speech to refute him.⁶⁶ But Mao protected him during the early stages of the CR. In the campaign to criticise Confucius, Liang was a natural target. At the January rally, Jiang Qing attacked him in front of ten thousand people. But Liang replied with a long article entitled 'How Should We Evaluate Confucius Today?' where he stated his disagreement with the prevailing views. He argued that Confucian values should be judged by the success or failure of Chinese culture in the world and refuted the allegation that Confucius represented a return to old times and social retrogression. He also denied any link between Lin Biao and Confucius.[67] When asked to express his views about Lin Biao and Confucius at a political study session of the CPPCC, he said:

> I speak, since you insist that I should. In my opinion Lin Biao should be criticised, Confucius should not. To be a man, and not a ghost, one should be open and above board. Lin Biao is a ghost. Liu Shaoqi held many views, but they were expressed openly. Peng Dehuai's letter to Chairman Mao was also an open one. My thinking is perhaps more complicated than Lin Biao's. But I am open and above board. I am an upright person. Lin Biao ruined himself. He has no qualification to be a man.[68]

Such outspokenness was unusual. But it echoed the views of many people who remained unconvinced about the validity of the linkage betwen Lin Biao and Confucius. Many intellectuals with historical knowlege considered the summing up of Chinese history as a struggle between Confucianism and Legalism as an over-simplification. The Lin Biao affair had greatly damaged Mao's image as an infallible ruler. And Mao's judgement about Lin Biao's ultra-rightism, his praise of Qin Shihuang who, for centuries had incarnated the image of a despot, and of the Legalist school whose historical impact was minimal in comparison to Confucianism, all contributed to the development of a great deal of scepticism.

The campaign against Zhou Enlai

The main target of the campaign, however, were the veteran cadres and Zhou Enlai who represented them. The campaign, soon developed into *pi Lin, pi Kong, pi Zhou Gong*.[69] Zhou Gong is also a respectful address for some one named Zhou. Zhou Enlai had been known as Zhou Gong during his underground work in Guomindang areas in the 1940s.

Zhou reached the height of his career after Lin Biao's death, when he became the second in rank in the hierarchical structure and took charge of the purge of the Lin Biao group in the army.[70] But he suffered a major setback when Mao, at the end of 1972, halted the campaign against ultra-leftism which

Zhou had so actively promoted. In spite of Zhou's rapid change of attitude in this matter, Mao's confidence in Zhou appeared to have been impaired. But it was Zhou's rising international prestige which became a source of irritation to Mao who could not tolerate that his subordinate enjoyed a greater reputation in foreign countries than he did himself. During the following year, Mao uttered several critical remarks concerning Zhou Enlai which were immediately used by Jiang Qing and her followers to launch a veiled campaign against the premier.

The first manifestation of Mao's discontent surfaced in July 1973, during his talk with Wang Hongwen and Zhang Chunqiao about Lin Biao and Confucius. On that occasion, Mao expressed reservations to recent developments in the Foreign Ministry which was under Zhou's direct supervision. The ministry, Mao said, had failed to discuss 'important matters' with him, while sending him reports on 'minor matters'. He warned that 'if the situation does not improve, revisionism is bound to occur'.[71] It was clear that Mao was in fact, criticising Zhou Enlai.

Other signs of dissatisfaction with Zhou appeared during a private talk, in November with Wang Hairong, Mao's grand niece and vice foreign minister, and Nancy Tang, Mao's interpreter and director of the foreign ministry's American and Oceanic department. Both reported to Mao that Zhou had made 'unauthorised statements' during his talks with Henry Kissinger. These statements pertained to a number of issues, but particularly to the Taiwan question, on which Zhou, in view of the nuclear arsenal the US had assembled in the region, appeared to have been particularly cautious. On 17 November, Mao himself had taken a rather belligerent stance on the Taiwan issue, saying that it was wrong to talk about two possibilities, namely peaceful means or war, to solve this question. 'We should fight', Mao said, 'as we have fought in the past for any small fortified village.'[72]

In December, Zhou's work at the Politburo also came under fire. Mao pointed out, that the Politburo under Zhou's chairmanship had 'frequently failed to discuss politics' and added another warning about the danger of a return of revisionism.[73] Wang Hairong, complained to Mao that Zhou's attitude towards the CR was characterised by the Confucian philosophy of the mean. Mao was reported to have said that 'the time is ripe to criticise Zhou Gong'.[74]

During the same month, Mao convened a Politburo meeting with the special purpose of criticising Zhou,[75] where Jiang Qing claimed that the present struggle was one of the '11th line'[76] and that Zhou was 'to impatient to wait to replace Chairman Mao'.[77] These were momentous accusations which attempted to place Zhou into the same category as Liu Shaoqi, Lin Biao and other serious offenders before them. But Zhou's removal was not within Mao's reckoning. This, he made clear in a talk with Zhou and Wang Hongwen on 9 December, when, on the one hand he emphasised the need to criticise Zhou, but on the other hand, he nonetheless thought that Jiang Qing's accusations were exaggerated. 'Somebody has made two wrong remarks, one about an 11th line struggle . . . and the other about the Premier's impatience to replace me. . . . In fact, it is she who is too impatient to wait.'[78]

The campaign to criticise Lin Biao and Confucius began to transform itself into a movement to criticise Lin, Kong and Zhou Gong. The writing groups began to attack Zhou by innuendo. An article in *Red Flag*[79] depicted Zhou in the role of Confucius who was prime minister of the state of Lu[80] and was critically ill. Zhou was hospitalised at that time. Another article[81] described Confucius as a sick man with a bending arm.[82] But more often, he was likened to Lu Buwei, the Confucian prime minister of the Qin dynasty, 'a slave owner' who 'vigorously promoted a reactionary political line for the purpose of restoring slavery'.[83] Luo Siding, the Shanghai writing group, described Zhou as Tian Qianqiu, a prime minister of the Western Han Dynasty (206–223 AD) who was said to be 'a very shrewd old bureaucrat' who was 'good at handling human relations', and who was 'ambiguous and who, in order not to offend anybody, never revealed his true attitude'.[84]

While the official press attacked Zhou by innuendo, Jiang Qing was more explicit. She said to a group of journalists that 'the most important Confucianist of moder times is not Chiang Kai-shek, nor Lin Biao nor Liu Shaoqi'.[85] Who, among the leading personalities could she have had in mind, if not Zhou Enlai?

Other incidents of criticism against Zhou Enlai also began to appear. Jiang Qing used several events in the cultural sphere

FINAL POWER STRUGGLES

to continue her attacks against him. In 1972, the Italian film director Antonioni produced a TV documentary on China. In the present campaign, Antonioni was accused of hostility against China and the CR, since, according to the official press, he had chosen to show the backward and dark side and not the progressive and bright side of Chinese life. It was also noted, that the film failed to show a single scene from any of Jiang Qing's model operas. The documentary was considered 'a product of the cooperation between spies and traitors'.[86] Since the foreign ministry had approved Antonioni's visit and had provided the facilities to produce his film, it was Zhou who was indirectly blamed for these comments. Another occasion was an exhibition of paintings by some of China's best-known artists which Zhou had commissioned with the intention of choosing paintings for the decoration of the Chinese embassies abroad. Jiang Qing considered this an exposition of 'black paintings' representing anti-proletarian themes. The paintings were never sent to the embassies abroad.[87]

Reactions to the campaigns

In spite of all official efforts, the campaign against Lin Biao, Confucius and Zhou Gong, whose purpose was to safeguard the CR and to combat retrogressive tendencies symbolised by Confucius' teachings, met with lukewarm response not only among military leaders but also among ordinary people who had become increasingly disenchanted and even exasperated by the CR. The disillusionment created by Mao's abortive succession policies contributed to this tendency. Moreover, people were relieved by the disappearance, after Lin Biao's death, of many of the practices introduced into their daily lifes by Lin and the PLA. The abandonment of the practice 'to ask for the Chairman's instructions' at the start of the day and, in the evening, 'to confess mistakes made during the day', for example, and the fading of a great deal of other verbal and ritual formalities greatly alleviated people's lifes. The feeling about the absurdities of campaigns and of revolutionary policies found their expression in a number of ironical remarks about the so-called achievements of the CR which were clandestinely but widely circulated. They vented discontent, sarcasm and criticism through mockery. The achievements of the

CR in the cultural field, for example, were paraphrased as *wenhua da geming shi da ge wenhua ming* ('the great CR has eliminated culture').[88]

Another example was provided by the rise to high office of 'revolutionary' artists and sportsmen. The opera singer and leading character of the model opera *Red Lantern*, Hao Liang, and the dancer in the ballet *The Red Detachment of Women*, Liu Qintang, were nominated vice ministers of culture; and the ping-pong player Zhuang Zedong was promoted to head the National Sports Commission. These appointments were greeted with the rhyme:

> *Pa xueshan guo caodi, buru chang chu hongdengji*
> *chi jin wanli changzheng ku, buru tiao ge baleiwu*
> *fushou ganwei ruzi niu, buru da ge pingpangqiu.*

(Those who once climbed the snowy mountains and tramped the grass lands are not better than the one who sings the Red Lantern. It is no use to have survived the hardships of the Long March, better dance a ballet. Head bowed like a willing ox, I serve the children; still I am inferior to the ping-pong player)[89]

While revolutionary innovations increasingly became the target of mockery, such pragmatic policies as Zhou Enlai's suggestions for policy changes within the educational sector were receiving widespread support. The educational sector had particularly suffered from revolutionary policies. Between 1966 and 1972 the school system had practically broken down. When universities began to function again in 1972, the educational level of students was so low, that universities were caricatured as 'a college in name with middle school teaching material and elementary school level students'.[90] A report to the State Council and the CC on the state of sciences, social sciences and education corroborated the situation. It pointed out, that 'great confusion' and even 'attack' on the CR were rampant in those circles. The report emphasised the widespread belief among intellectuals that Lin Biao represented ultra-leftism, and not, as the authorities claimed, ultra-rightism. The report also stated that the slogan of 'struggle-criticism-transformation' had been carried too far, and had contributed to the development of ultra-leftism. The report further pointed out that there was much criticism of the educational system which had considerably deteriorated since the introduction of the system of recruiting students among peasants, workers and soldiers. The educational reform during the CR had the reputation of being characterised by confusion (*luan*) messiness (*zao*) and low quality (*di*).[91]

'Going against the tide'

Mao was fully aware of the widespread doubts about the CR and the desire to return to normality, which he considered to be a rising tendency in society. In his view, this trend was an 'adverse tide of right deviation' which had to be resisted. He declared at the 10th Party Congress, that 'going against the tide is a Marxist-Leninist principle' which every Party member should adopt.[92] Parallel to the campaign of criticising Lin, Kong and Zhou Gong, Jiang Qing started another one to counteract the increasing trend towards normalisation. The campaign used a series of minor events as examples of 'going against the tide'.

In April 1973, the State Council reintroduced entrance exams as a supplement to political qualifications for students' admissions to universities. Jiang Qing equated this measure with the restoration of the principle of 'giving priority to intellectual qualifications'. At that time, Mao's nephew Mao Yuanxin, who was Party secretary of Liaoning and Jiang Qing's confident, discovered a young man in his province who, in September 1973, had handed in a blank paper at a university entrance examination. On the back of the paper, he had written, that examinations were a discrimination against people like himself, who, unlike privileged young men, had to work in the field and had no time to prepare for exams. The case was publicised in Liaoning and in Beijing as 'the restoration of the old examination system', 'a counter-attack of the bourgeoisie against the proletariat'. The young man, Zhang Tiesheng, was hailed as 'a hero who dared to swim against the tide'.

Entrance exams were again eliminated. Zhang Tiesheng entered an agricultural college, joined the Party, became a member of the college's leading group and was elected to the National People's Congress the following year.[93]

In July 1973, Zhang Yuqin, a 15-year-old middle-school student from Tanghe county in Henan province, wrote an improvised verse on her English examination paper: 'I am Chinese, why should I learn English. Without learning a b c d, I can still be a successor' (to the revolutionary cause). After her teacher had criticised her for this attitude, she felt humiliated and drowned herself in a river. Jiang Qing, who read about the event, brought it up during a meeting on 25 January 1974 as a case of murder committed by 'the revisionist education line'. The girl's middle school became an example of bourgeois restoration in the educational field. The teacher and the principal of the school were thrown into prison.[94]

The 12-year-old pupil of a Beijing elementary school, Huang Shuai, wrote a letter to the *Beijing Daily* on 21 October 1973 in which she complained against her teacher whom she believed had disciplined her without justification. *Beijing Daily* published the letter with a comment according to which 'the 12-year-old pupil put forward an important problem of educational revolution in the spirit of going against the tide'. The problem was defined as one of the Confucian concept of 'dignity of the teacher'. As a result, a wave of criticism of Confucian principles in education developed in schools.[95]

Mao's vacillation

As the campaign unfolded, the cleavage between the Jiang Qing faction or CR faction (*wenge pai*) and the old guard faction *lao tou pai*) became increasingly evident and finally took the form of a violent power struggle. Mao, while trying to maintain a balance between the factions, developed a more and more ambiguous stance, as he vaccilated between the desire for normalisation and the intention to assert the goals of the CR.

In 1974, factionalism became increasingly rampant, and the CR faction sought 'to seize power' for the second time. In some areas, weapons to be used in the power seizures were stolen from military depots; warehouses were robbed and armed fighting broke out among rival factions. Veteran cadres who had recently been reinstated, again became targets of attack. Disputes among the different factions paralysed large parts of the transportation system. As a result, industrial production was declining. Fearing a recurrence of the situation of the spring and summer of 1967, Mao issued instructions which specified that the campaign was to be directed by Party committees; that no mass organisations should be established; and no exchange of experiences across different professions and trades, or between different localities were allowed to take place.[96]

After Zhou's hospitalisation on 1 June 1974, the radicals launched a strong propaganda offensive against retrogression and restoration. But Mao felt the need to restrain the movement. At a Politburo meeting on 17 July he warned Jiang Qing to be more careful. 'Other people are unhappy with you', he told her, 'but they are too shy to tell you'. He also advised her not to 'set up two factories, one iron and steel factory, and one hat factory'. With this he meant to say that Jiang Qing should stop treating people harshly and that she should not charge them with unjustified accusations.[97] On the same occasion, he also declared 'Jiang Qing does not represent me, she represents herself . . . she belongs to the "Shanghai gang".' Finally, he advised her not to form 'a small faction of four people'.[98] This was the first time that Mao mentioned a 'Shanghai gang' which he later called the 'gang of four'.

In the following months, Mao's main concern seemed to have been the establishment of stability and unity in the country. Zhou Enlai was seriously ill. Mao's health had also deteriorated. He had increasing difficulty in speaking, walking and standing up. It was also found that he was suffering from cataracts, and was rapidly losing his eyesight.[99] In October 1974, he announced that the 4th National People's Congress should be held in early 1975. The promotion of the economy and the reorganisation of the government should be the meeting's major themes. But reorganisation of the government also meant redistribution of power. In view of Zhou Enlai's poor health, the post of prime minister became the focus of contention. The CR faction promoted the candidature of Zhang Chunqiao for this position, but since Deng Xioping's unexpected rehabilitation in March 1973, their main concern was to prevent Deng from ascending to this office.

At a Politburo meeting in preparation of the 4th National People's Congress, Jiang Qing used the so-called 'Feng Qing event' to launch an attack against Deng. Feng Qing was the name of the ocean-going cargo ship designed and built in

China. The ship had made its maiden voyage to Europe from where it had returned on the eve of the Chinese National day. The ship was considered a symbol of Mao's policy of independence and self-reliance, since it was the only ocean liner built in China during the CR.

To enhance the importance of the ship and its first voyage, the Ministry of Communications had appointed two of its high-level cadres, Li Guotang and Gu Wenguang, to the posts of political commissar and deputy political commissar of the ship's crew. During the voyage, political study sessions celebrated Mao's successful policy in ship building and criticised the policy of buying or renting ships from abroad as slavish comprador philosophy. However, Li Guotang and Gu Wenguang, fully aware of the fact that China could not afford to build an entire fleet on its own, defended the rationale of the ministry of communications policies. Moreover, Li made some sarcastic remark about Jiang Qing and her model operas.

Li's and Gu's remarks were reported to Jiang Qing who construed them as a 'counter-revolutionary scheme'. Wang Hongwen ordered the arrest of Li and Gu and to submit them to struggle sessions. Jiang Qing, at the Politburo meeting, declared that the ministry of communications was dominated by a 'bourgeois comprador dictatorship' and called upon the State Council to take this matter in hand. She attempted to coax Deng to state clearly his view on this matter. But Deng refused to commit himself and merely promised to investigate the case. As Jiang Qing persisted, Deng accused her of trying to impose her opinions on others, and of displaying an attitude which made cooperation in the Politburo an impossible task. He left the meeting in protest.[100]

Jiang Qing's next move was to inform Mao about the events at the Politburo meeting. On 18 October, Wang Hongwen went to Changsha to report to Mao about the dispute between Jiang Qing and Deng Xiaoping over the Feng Qing event. According to Zhang Yufeng, Mao's private secretary, Wang did not limit himself to the events at the Politburo meeting. He also said that the atmosphere in Beijing was as tense as it had been during the 1970 Lushan conference. Zhou Enlai, though critically ill, had called a number of people to his hospital bed in order to discuss the preparations for the forthcoming 4th

National People's Congress. Deng Xiaoping, Ye Jianying and Li Xiannian were among Zhou's frequent visitors.

Mao who did not seem impressed by Wang's account, failed to comment on it. Instead, he told Wang to talk with Deng Xiaoping if he had any disagreement with him. He also advised Wang to develop his contacts with Zhou Enlai and Ye Jianying and to decrease his involvement with Jiang Qing.[101] Two days later, Mao sent a message to Zhou Enlai stating his intention to maintain Zhou in his post as prime minister after the 4th National People's Congress and instructing Zhou and Wang Hongwen to jointly take care of the preparations for the Congress, including questions of personnel.[102]

Mao, though old and infirm, was in total control. He informed the Politburo of his intention to appoint Deng Xiaoping vice chairman of the Party, first vice premier, vice chairman of the MC and general chief of staff. On 6 November, Zhou wrote to Mao to report on the preparations for the 4th Congress and, at the same token, expressed his 'warm support' of the chairman's decision to promote Deng Xiaoping, a decision which could only have been to his liking although he played no role in it.[103]

Deng's promotion was a defeat for Jiang Qing. But she was also aware that she and her radical friends were playing a significant role in the preservation of the CR which was of great importance to Mao. In the contest for positions of influence, she tried to assure the promotion of a number of her own people. On 12 November, she wrote to Mao suggesting the appointment of Xie Jingyi[104] as chairperson of the National People's Congress, and of Chi Qun[105] to minister of education. She also proposed the promotion of Qiao Guanhua, the foreign minister, to vice premier. Her associates Mao Yuanxin, Chi Qun, Xie Jingyi and Jin Zumin – a CC member from Shanghai – should be regular participants in Politburo meetings so that they could prepare themselves for higher positions. But Mao who was not sympathetic to her suggestions. wrote the following comment on her letter: 'Do not make too many appearances in public, refrain from commenting on too many documents, do not organise a cabinet from behind the screen. You have provoked too much enmity'.[106]

Jiang Qing asked Wang Hairong and Nacy Tang when they met Mao in Changsha to convey a message to Mao to nominate

Wang Hongwen as vice chairman of the National People's Congress. Mao's reaction was again negative. He told Wang and Tang that 'Jiang Qing is ambitious. She wants to make Wang Hongwen the chairman of the National People's Congress so that she can take over from him the chairmanship of the Party'.[107]

On 19 November, Jiang Qing who desired more power and responsibility, wrote again to Mao to complain that she had been 'basically an idle person since the 9th Party Congress. I have not been given any work. This has been even more the case recently.' But Mao wrote back to her: 'Your work consists in following the internal and the external situation. This is indeed an important responsibility. I told you so many times, do not say that you have no work to do.'[108]

Zhou Enlai directed the preparations for the 4th National People's Congress from the hospital. One of his major tasks was the organisation of the future cabinet. He was aware of the fact that Jiang Qing and Zhang Chunqiao were fighting for the control of a number of ministries, including those of culture, education and sports. After discussing the problem with Deng Xiaoping, Zhou decided to leave the ministry of culture, and ministry of public helath and the sports commission to the CR faction, but to keep the ministry of education under his own jurisdiction.[109]

On 23 December, Zhou left his sick bed, and, together with Wang Hongwen, flew to Changsha to report to Mao about the state of affairs. Mao agreed to Zhou's proposals about the government's organisation. He also praised Deng Xiaoping as capable of taking charge of the activities of the State Council, while Zhou should concentrate on his medical treatment.[110]

This visit marked Mao's further disillusionment with his latest chosen successor, when Wang passed on a message from Jiang Qing which emphasised the need to consider a candidate for the premiership due to Zhou's deteriorating health. Mao, greatly displeased, told Wang that he, Jiang Qing, Zhang Chunqiao and Yao Wenyuan had been functioning as a 'gang of four', and demanded that Wang should do self-examination of this problem.[111] Wang's status as Mao's successor seemed to have become endangered.

FINAL POWER STRUGGLES

The last succession crisis

The rise and fall of Deng Xiaoping

Many Chinese leaders were victims of the twists and turns of the CR, but none of them had the same dramatic experience as Deng of falling from the highest level of leadership twice and rising again to this level.

After his condemnation in 1966 as the second leading 'Party person in power taking the capitalist road', Deng remained in custody at Zhongnanhai, where he was forced to endure struggle meetings for several years. In October 1969, he was evacuated to Nanchang in Jiangxi province for more than three years.[112] He and his wife lived in a secluded building in the Nanchang army school and worked at a nearby tractor repair shop. They were deprived of any other contact with the outside world.[113]

After his first rehabilitation in 1973, Deng took full responsibility of Party and state affairs in place of the ailing Zhou Enlai. But in the spring of 1976, he was again stripped of all his posts and condemned, this time as a 'die-hard capitalist roader'. He rose to power for the third time in 1977, a year after Mao's death and the fall of the 'gang of four', and eventually became the most powerful man in China.[114] Deng's fall in the 1970s was a reflection of Mao's ambiguous state of mind. It was also the result of a fierce power struggle between the CR faction and the veteran cadres which had been brewing since the fall of Lin Biao.

After his return to Beijing, Deng's rise to power was meteoric. His Party membership was restored by a CC decision of 10 March, 1973, which also reappointed him as vice premier.[115] In August of the same year, the 10th Party Congress elected him to the CC.[116] In December, Mao acknowledged the quality of Deng's work in front of the Politburo and proposed his nomination to the Politburo and the MC.[117] During a talk with Zhou Enlai about Deng, Mao scribbled four characters on a piece of paper: *ren cai nan de* ('a person of rare talent').[118]

Zhou Enlai's health deteriorated considerably during 1974. After his hospitalisation on 1 June, Wang Hongwen took charge of the day-to-day activities of the Party, while Deng was given the responsibility of government and administrative affairs.[119] In January 1975, the CC appointed him as vice chairman of the MC and general chief of staff, vice chairman of the

Party and member of the Standing Committee. During the same month, the 4th National People's Congress nominated him as the first among 12 vice premiers. With this position, he ranked third in the Party hierarchy, next only to Mao and Zhou Enlai, both of whom were ill.[120]

What were the reasons which prompted Mao to call back Deng Xiaoping from his exile and to reinstate him in even more elevated positions than he had occupied before he was purged in 1966? After Lin Biao's death, Mao's health deteriorated rapidly. He preferred to remain in seclusion, and he seemed to have developed a certain nostalgia for his old comrades. On 6 January 1972, Chen Yi, who had worked with him since the days of Jinggangshan, died of cancer. The outspoken Chen Yi had angered Mao on several occasions with his sarcastic remarks about the CR, and Mao had said publicly that Chen was qualified to participate in the 9th Congress only as representative of the right. But after Chen's death, Mao, who had hardly recovered from a stroke, decided to attend his memorial service, stubbornly refusing to accept the advice to the contrary of his medical personnel. Wearing a heavy coat over his pyjamas, he was driven to Babaoshan[121] where he stood beside Chen's wife. He held her hand and said tearfully: 'Chen Yi was a good comrade.[122] He was a good man. He made a great contribution to the Chinese revolution and to the world revolution.' Mao's physical condition was so poor, that, after the funeral, he had to be carried into his car.[123]

Mao's presence at Chen Yi's funeral and his remarks came as a surprise to everybody. But, at the time, Mao appeared to be in the mood to make amends to some of the military leaders whom Lin Biao had earlier purged. Luo Ruiqing was rehabilitated in the spring of 1973. Zhu De, whom Mao had called a 'black commander opposing Chairman Mao', at a meeting of the MC in December 1972, was turned into a 'red commander' and also rehabilitated.[124] Mao also told the MC that Marshal He Long had been wrongly accused by Lin Biao.[125] Mao further stated that he had believed in Lin Biao's accusations against Yang Chengwu, Yu Lijin, and Fu Chongbi but was now ready to bear the responsibility for the false accusations. He announced the reversal of the verdict against these men.[126]

If these rehabilitations surprised many people, his reaction to Deng Xiaoping was even more unexpected. After he had

FINAL POWER STRUGGLES

been informed about the Lin Biao affair, Deng wrote a letter to Mao (3 August 1972) disclosing everything he knew about Lin Biao and repudiating him. On 14 August, Mao made a lengthy comment on Deng's letter:

> The errors committed by Comrade Deng Xiaoping were serious. But a distinction must be made between him and Liu Shaoqi. (1) Deng has been rectified in the Central Soviet Areas. He was one of the four offenders [the other three were Mao Zetan, Xie Weijun and Gu Bo]. He was the head of the Mao faction [as opposed to the international faction who accused Mao of being a right-wing opportunist]. Documentation about Deng's rectification can be found in two books: *Two Lines* and *Since the 6th Congress*. The man who rectified him [Deng] was Zhang Wentian. (2) He has no historical problems. That is, he never capitulated to the enemy. (3) He was very helpful to comrade Liu Bocheng during the war and has war merit. It was not true that he did not do anything good after entering the city. For example, he never capitulated to Soviet revisionism when he led a delegation to Moscow. I have talked about all this many times in the past. Now I repeat it.[127]

While Mao's comments paved the way for Deng's rehabilitation,[128] he became increasingly critical towards Jiang Qing. At a Politburo meeting on 3 May 1975, Mao accused her of functioning as a 'gang of four' with Zhang Chunqiao, Wang Hongwen and Yao Wenyuan. All four were instructed to make self-criticism about their tendency to gang up.[129] After the meeting, which was the first since Mao's return to Beijing after an absence of ten months, Wang Hongwen was relieved from his responsibility of directing day-to-day work at the Party centre, a task which was taken over by Deng Xiaoping.[130] Deng thus reached a new height in his career.

Mao was obviously disappointed with his third chosen successor Wang Hongwen. The young rebel leader failed to display the necessary competence in administering the Party apparatus. In his meeting with Zhou and Wang in Changsha on 3 December 1974, Mao had pointed his finger at Wang saying that Deng 'is better than him in politics and ideology'.[131] Mao, on several occasions, also warned Wang to refrain from forming a small faction with Jiang Qing and from engaging in sectarianism.[132]

The negative effects of the campaign against Lin Biao and Confucius, and against the resurrection of right deviation also became increasingly obvious. Factional conflicts flared up in the revolutionary committees. Some recently rehabilitated cadres were again attacked. Former rebels who had been suppressed, attempted a come back under the favourable conditions of the campaign against right deviation. The former conservatives were divided in their attitude towards Zhou Enlai who was under attack in the *pi Lin, pi Kong, pi Zhou Gong* campaign. Factional difference also survived in the newly restored Party committees. In several provinces, PLA weapon depots were plundered, and armed fighting reminiscent of the early period of the CR erupted again.[133]

Academic and scientific research again came to a standstill. Literary and artistic activities, with the exception of the eight model operas, were paralysed. Even Mao complained about the lack of creative work. 'There are not enough model operas, and no more hundred flowers,' he said. 'Some changes have to be made in the Party's literary and artistic policies. Literary and artistic programmes should be expanded step by step during the next one, two, three years. There are not enough poems, novels, prose and literary reviews.'[134]

The renewed political instability affected the economy. Disputes among different factions paralysed large parts of the transportation system. In many harbours, ships waited for months before they were loaded or unloaded. Only about 50 per cent of the trains were running on schedule, and the entire railway system was plagued by an unusual amount of accidents which seriously affected the distribution network throughout the country. As a result, coal was piling up in major production areas while in other parts of the country, there were shortages of fuel for steam engines and industrial production.[135]

Industrial production, which had began to improve in 1972 and 1973, fell again in 1974. During the first half of that year, when the campaign against Lin Biao and Confucius reached its peak, the output of coal, steel and fertilisers fell by 6.2 per cent, 9.4 per cent and 3.7 per cent respectively in comparison to the same period of the previous year.[136] Government and foreign trade deficits were rising. Rice, wheat, meat, sugar, cigarettes, spirits, edible oil, etc., had been rationed for years. In spite of the rationing some products such as meat, cigarettes, and spirits were in short supply, and others, such as paper and kitchen utensils practically disappeared from the market.[137]

Another severe problem had been created by the forced emigration of millions of young people to the countryside. Disillusioned and frustrated, they returned to the cities in increasingly large numbers. The majority of them found no other outlet than to join the already large ranks of the unemployed. Intellectuals and government employees also returned to the cities from the May 7 cadre schools, often to find their positions occupied by others. There were hundreds of cadres in each ministry in Beijing, who stayed at home with full pay, waiting for reassignment of work.

Mao was increasingly preoccupied with the economic situation, and seemed to realise that the crisis had its origins in the CR. In August 1974, he stated that 'the CR has already lasted eight years. It is now time to establish stability. The entire Party and the Army should unite.'[138] In November, in a discussion about the economic situation with Li Xiannian and other Party officials, he emphasised the necessity of focusing on economic problems in the coming year.

All these problems needed urgent attention. Since Zhou Enlai was ill, some other leader had be found to take over the daily routine work from him. Wang Hongwen had been already eliminated. Zhang Chunqiao who was competent and politically experienced, was another candidate. But Mao did not consider him, perhaps because he was too closely identified with Jiang Qing and her faction and had considerably alienated the veteran revolutionaries who still represented a majority in the Party. Hua Guofeng, whom Mao had promoted from Hunan province to the Politburo in 1973, and to vice premier in January 1975, lacked political experience at national level. In fact, none of them had the experience, the talent and the prestige of Deng Xiaoping whose rehabilitation was welcomed by most of the people and, in particular by the veteran cadres, who, exhausted by the incessant campaigns in the last nine years, longed for some order and peace.

On 13 January 1975, Zhou Enlai left his hospital bed to make his last public appearance at the opening session of the 4th National Congress where he presented the report on government activities. The report was long and contained a considerable amount of déjà vu references to the achievements of the CR, but it also put forward the goal for the 'four modernisations' of industry, agriculture, national defence, and science and technology.[139] After years of chaos, there seemed to be a glimpse of hope for improvement of people's livelihood.

With Mao's support, the 71-year-old Deng began to work with tremendous vigour. In his view, industry, agriculture, commerce, trade, finance, education, literature, art, science and technology and the army, were all in need of improvement.[140] To achieve progress in all these areas, the Party organisation, considerably weakened during the years before, had to be strengthened at all levels.[141] Factionalism had to be eliminated. Rules and regulations, abolished in the early stages of the CR, had to be re-established in all trades and professions, and general discipline in all areas had to be improved.

Deng began by concentrating his efforts on those industrial sectors which had been most severely affected by the recent factional disputes. In February 1975, a meeting with Party secretaries in charge of industrial affairs in provinces, municipalities and autonomous regions was convened where Deng called for the reorganisation of the railway system.[142] A series of measures were adopted, a number of people engaged in factional fighting or sabotage or the railway system were arrested with the result that normal railway traffic resumed in April.[143]

The iron and steel industry was in a particularly sorry state. Persistent factionalism dividing workers into rebels and conservatives, and 'weak, lazy and lax' management were the main causes for sluggish production.[144] After the reorganisation of management and the introduction of clear regulation, Deng was able to reverse the sluggish trend, and, by the summer, these sectors showed signs of improvement.[145]

In June and July, Deng, in cooperation with Marshal Ye Jianying, began to tackle the problems in the army. The number of soldiers and officers had increased considerably during the CR reaching the figure of 6.1 million, of which 1.5 million were officers – about 600,000 more than necessary.[146] At a meeting of the MC in July, Deng characterised the state of the army in five words: 'bloating, laxity, conceit, extravagance and inertia.'[147] The meeting decided to cut the total number of military down to 4.5 million within three years. In 1976, the total number of military men was reduced by 13.6 per cent.[148]

The agricultural sector, too, was in need of reform. In many rural areas, the Party structure continued to be weak and was unable to provide consistent direction for agricultural policies. Deng, as he pointed out at a conference on agriculture held in September and October, considered the consolidation of the Party in rural areas as 'the central task'. The conference decided to send a million cadres from various local governments to the rural areas to help in the overhauling of People's Communes and production brigades and to increase the efficiency of agricultural production. Family sideline production which had been considered capitalist and abolished, was again encouraged.[149]

Deng took action in other areas, too. He appointed Hu Yaobang to the Academy of Sciences to save it from paralysis.[150] He adopted resolute measures to terminate factional disputes in the seventh ministry of machine building which was reponsible for research and development of strategic missiles and nuclear weapons.[151] The newly appointed minister of education, Zhou Rongxin criticised the leftist educational policies and made proposals for reforming the system. Deng gave instructions to reduce the time spent on political studies and to increase the time spent by teachers, scientists, academicians, writers and researchers on their work to five-sixths.[152]

The atmosphere in society became more relaxed. Some of the films which had previously been banned, reappeared in the cinemas. Books on subjects, other than Marxism-Leninism and Mao Zedong Thought, became more easily available. To counteract the ideological and theoretical monopoly of the CR faction, Deng established his own Political Research Office at the State Council which was staffed by such scholars and Party ideologues as Deng Liqun, Hu Qiaomu, Wu Lengxi, Hu Sheng, Yu Guanyuan who began to work by writing a long article entitled 'The general programme of work of the Party and the

State' which provided the theoretical basis for Deng's policies.[153] The document was based on three of Mao's repeated directives, namely to study the theories of proletarian dictatorship, to achieve stability and unity, and to accelerate economic progress. But it omitted the formula of 'class struggle as the basis for all political activities' and explicitly refuted a series of ultra-leftist views. The document focused on the strengthening of the Party apparatus as the key element for the restoration of order. The Party was called upon to develop 'ideological positions' and to take back 'the lead in power which had been usurped by political swindlers and sham Marxists like Lin Biao'.[154]

For the first time since the beginning of the CR, the veteran cadres had gained a certain leverage over the CR faction. But Deng Xiaoping was aware that he was taking risks with his attempts to normalise the economic and political situation. In October 1975, he remarked that 'some people will say that the "home going legions" have returned and that a restoration has occurred.'[155] He insisted that the veteran cadres should be more conscious of the potential threat inherent in their activities. They 'must firmly make up their minds and even dare to risk their lives. They must be courageous and cast away all fear. The worst that can happen is to be overthrown a second time.'[156]

Counter-attack

The parlous state of the economy was, however, not Mao's sole preoccupation. At the age of 81 he continued to be persecuted by nightmarish visions of revisionism and capitalism. In his talk with Zhou Enlai and Wang Hongwen in Changsha on 26 December 1974, Mao asked: 'Why did Lenin speak of exercising dictatorship over the bourgeoisie? Tell (Zhang) Chunqiao to write an article about it. Lack of clarity on this question will lead to revisionism. This should be made known to the entire nation'.[157] Expressing his concern with egalitarianism, he added:

> At present our country practises a commodity system. The wage system with its eight-grade scale is also unequal. Under dictatorship of the proletariat, such

things can only be restricted. Therefore, if people like Lin Biao come to power, it will be easy for them to re-establish a capitalist system. This is the reason why we should read more Marxist-Leninist works. Lenin said that 'small production engenders capitalism and the bourgeoisie daily, hourly, spontaneously and on a large scale'. Capitalism and bourgeoisie are also engendered among part of our working-class and Party members.[158]

Mao had cherished the ideal of egalitarian utopianism for many years. The intiation of the GLF in 1958 had already been an attempt to establish such a society and, with the same purpose, he had launched the CR. Notwithstanding the disastrous consequences of these policies, Mao had not abandoned his idea. The Politburo, after being informed by Zhou Enlai and Wang Hongwen about Mao's remarks, issued an edition of quotations by Marx, Engels and Lenin which had been prepared by Zhang Chunqiao and Yao Wenyuan. On 22 February, the *People's Daily*, the *PLA Daily* and *Red Flag* published editorials stressing the importance of studying the theory of proletarian dictatorship thus inaugurating a new campaign to study Marxism-Leninism which began to overshadow the campaign to criticise Lin Biao and Confucius.[159]

Within the framework of the new campaign, two major articles, published in March and April by Yao Wenyuan and Zhang Chunqiao respectively elaborated on the need for a continuing revolution with a proletarian dictatorship.[160] Both articles had been discussed by the Politburo and approved by Mao prior to their publication.[161] The crux of these writings was to justify the continuation of the CR and to criticise veteran cadres. Zhang emphasised that 'new bourgeois elements are engendered in the wake of the development of capitalist factors in town and country'. He declared that 'there were still many "fortified villages" held by the bourgeoisie.'[162] With this, he implied that there were work units dominated by cadres who actually represented the bourgeoisie. At the same time, Jiang Qing, Zhang Chunqiao and Yao Wenyuan emphasised in speeches and articles that the major threat at present was empiricism.[163] This implied that practical problems were given priority over politics and ideology. During the Yanan rectification campaign Zhou Enlai and Peng Dehuai had been criticised as empiricists.[164] Now it was Deng Xiaoping, who according to the CR faction, was 'finding fault with the CR' and acting as an 'empiricist'.[165] With these publications, the confrontation between moderates and radicals began again to sharpen.

Mao, however, did not approve of the radicals' focus on empiricism. In his view, empiricism should not be singled out as a criterion for criticism and that 'revisionism, including both empiricism and dogmatism' was the fundamental problem. He emphasised that:

> there were not many people in our Party who have a real understanding of Marxism-Leninism. Some people believe that they understand it, but actually they do not. They indulge in self approbation and are ready to reproach others which is a manifestation of their poor understanding of Marxism-Leninism.[166]

This statement by Mao changed the tone of the new campaign. Its major consequence was to dampen the attacks on empiricism and its representative, Deng Xiaoping.

The CR faction met with another setback during the meeting of the Politburo which Mao called on 3 May 1975, after his return from Wuhan and Changsha where he had stayed for ten months. At the meeting, Mao, though he spoke with considerable difficulty, did most of the talking, rambling about a number of subjects. He said that he had not been allowed to eat eggs for two years because someone in the Soviet Union has written an article according to which eggs were too rich in cholesterol. He talked about a poem he had recently written[167] and about intellectuals who were needed although they belonged to the 'stinking 9th category'. But his principal message was that revisionism, including empiricism and dogmatism, continued to be the main threat to society. Ignoring his statement that 'the philosophy of the Communist Party is a philosophy of struggle', he emphasised 'stability and unity'[168] which implied that he did not wish to see confrontation between different factions. He also reiterated his principle of the 'three things to do and three things not to do'[169] which he had announced during the 1970 Lushan conference. Addressing Jiang Qing and her associates he warned them not to establish a 'gang of four'. 'Why are you still doing it?' he asked. 'Why do you not unite with the 200 or more members of the CC?' He continued, 'Those who criticise empiricism are themselves empiricists.' And 'Jiang Qing is an empiricist herself, since she does not have much experience.'[170] Mao continued to criticise Jiang Qing and other radicals for their views on the 'back-door' practises, which, he said, involved 'millions of people, including myself', since he had sent his daughter to Beijing university through a 'back-door'.[171] He also referred to Jiang Qing's distribution of material concerning the campaign against Confucius to the air force and the navy, warning her not to 'do things as you like. Abide by discipline and be careful. Do not make independent decisions without discussion with the Politburo.'[172] He also suggested that Jiang Qing, Zhang Chunqiao, Yao Wenyuan and Wang Hongwen should make self-criticism in front of the Politburo about their 'ganging up' which Mao had criticised on several occasions since November 1973.[173]

The four proceeded with their self-criticism at two Politburo meetings on 27 May and 3 June apologising for the mistake of 'ganging up'. This was the first time, since the beginning of the CR, that the veteran cadres had the opportunity to criticise Jiang Qing and her acolytes and that they received Mao's clear encouragement for the continuation of their work of normalisation.[174] Moreover, Mao expressed the intention to terminate the CR which he assessed in terms of achievements and deficiencies to be evaluated at 70 per cent and 30 per cent respectively.

During most of the year of 1975, the political tide appeared to favour the veterans. But in the second half of the year, a new wave of attack was launched, which, again, did not receive Mao's full approval. It took the form of the 'Water Margin' campaign with which the CR faction attempted to discredit Deng Xiaoping, Zhou Enlai and their followers.

In September, the PD published an editorial on the classical novel *Water Margin (Shui Hu)*. It reopened the debate about revisionism, which, in the form of 'capitulationism' had dominated the Party for more than fifty years.[175] The background of this new approach to revisionism can be traced back to an extempore comment which Mao had made in front of his secretary Zhang Yufeng and Lu Di, a teacher of classical Chinese at Beijing University whom Mao, nearly blind, had engaged in May 1975, to read classical literature to him.[176] On 24 August, Lu Di asked Mao about his views on *Water Margin*[177] Mao made a lengthy comment stating that:

> The good thing about the book is its description of capitulationism. It can be used as a negative example to enable people to recognise capitulationists. Song Jiang capitulated, practised revisionsism and changed Cao Gai's hall of justice to a hall of loyalty and righteousness to seek imperial pardon. The struggle between Song Jiang and Cao Gai was a struggle of one faction against another within the landlord class.[178]

In view of the importance attributed to Mao's every word, Lu Di recorded Mao's views. Since the People's Publishing House was preparing a new edition of *Water Margin*, Zhang Yufeng suggested that Mao's comments should be printed as a preface to the classical novel. Mao declined but approved the distribution of his comments to the Politburo.

Yao Wenyuan suggested to Mao that his comments should be widely published and writers should be invited to contribute articles about them. With Mao's approval, the *People's Daily* in its 4 September editorial 'Promote Comments on Shui Hu' emphasised that:

> to study and comprehend Chairman Mao's instructions by promoting comments and discussions on Shui Hu is of important and profound significance not only in the study of classical literature but also in upholding Marxism, opposing revisionism, and persisting in Chairman Mao's revolutionary line in the sphere of literature, philosophy, history, and education . . . the history of our Party for over fifty years has proved that all those who practised revisionism are capitulationists.

With the publication of Mao's comments and the *People's Daily* editorial, the mass media was set into motion to repudiate capitulationism – another wave of attack by innuendo which implied that Deng's and Zhou Enlai's efforts to restore order, discipline, rules and regulations was capitulation to capitalism at the expense of the CR. Deng was likened to Song Jiang who had betrayed Cao Gai and capitulated to the emperor. Jiang Qing brought the assaults to a head at the Dazhai conference on agriculture in September and October 1975, where she stated: 'The comment on Shui Hu must be linked to realities. Song Jiang made Cao Gai a figure head. Are there people making Chairman Mao a figure head? I believe there are. Someone has enlisted a number of local despots into the government.'[179] Zhou Enlai, who was in the hospital, was shocked by Jiang Qing's attack. In deep frustration, he rejected the accusation of being a capitulationist and confirmed his 'loyalty to the Party and to the people'.[180]

Jiang Qing intended to distribute her speech to the entire Party, but Mao, who had become increasingly irritated with her, stated that her remarks at the conference were 'wide off the mark' and refused his authorisation for its circulation.[181] With these remarks, Mao aborted the *Water Margin* campaign relatively quickly and, during most of 1975, the political tide was in favour of Deng Xiaoping and his policies of normalisation. Mao's repeated criticism of Jiang Qing and the 'gang of four' were purposefully leaked out by the veteran cadres and became widespread public knowledge. But not for long; for in early November, the political climate changed suddenly to Deng's disadvantage and eventually brought about his second downfall.

Deng's second fall

Deng's second fall was ignited by seemingly unrelated quarrels within the Party committee of Qinghua university. Liu Bing, deputy Party secretary of Qinghua university and three members of the Party committee reported to Mao about the objectionable conduct of Chi Qun, the Party secretary and of Xie Jingyi, his deputy secretary. Chi Qun, who had been Jiang Qing's candidate for minister of education, had made a scene when he was not nominated to the post. He was in such a rage, that Xie Jingyi, who was said to have had illicit relations with him, kneeled down in from of him and begged him to calm down. Liu Bing and three other Party committee members were so shocked by Chi's behaviour that they wrote two letters to Mao about his case. The letters were not addressed to Mao directly but to Deng Xiaoping who was asked to forward them to the chairman.[182]

Mao made a few remarks on the letters which were reported

to the Qinghua university Party committee on 3 November. He had said that: 'The motivation for these letters was not pure. They want to overthrow Chi Qun and Xiao Xie (Xie Jingyi). The spearhead is directed against me.' He accused Deng of being 'partial to Liu Bing' and of 'siding with him'.[183]

In the second half of November, Mao's remarks were read out to more than 30 leading members from Party, government and military agencies. At this meeting, organised by the Politburo, they were informed that:

> the problem of Qinghua university is by no means isolated. It is a reflection of the current struggle between two classes, two roads and two lines. It is also a reflection of the wind of Right deviation aimed at reversing the verdict of the CR . . . There are some people who are not satisfied with the CR. They want to settle accounts with it and attempt to reverse the verdict.[184]

This instigated a campaign against 'the right deviationist wind' with Deng Xiaoping as its principal target. It quickly accelerated and by the end of the year, he was deprived of all his responsibilities except for foreign affairs. Zhou Enlai died on 8 January. Deng made his last appearance in public on 15 January when he pronounced the memorial speech for Zhou.

On 21 January, the Politburo appointed Hua Guofeng as the acting prime minister. A few days later, Ye Jianging, a close ally of Zhou and Deng, was removed from his post at the military commission and replaced by Chen Xilian, the commander of the Beijing military region.[185] On 5 February, the centre issued a document with unrestricted circulation to announce the criticism of Deng, and on 25 February Hua Guofeng called for a 'deep-going exposure and criticism of Comrade Deng Xiaoping's errors of revisionist line'.[186]

Deng's fall, just as his rise, was Mao's decision. In his self-imposed seclusion, Mao, who was ageing and ailing, had an aversion of showing himself to others in such a state.[187] Only very few people knew that he had become almost completely blind since 1974. An operation in August restored the sight to one of his eyes, but, at the same time, he suffered increasingly from Parkinson's disease and pulmonary emphysema.[188] In 1975, he presided over only one Politburo meeting. All others were chaired by Deng Xiaoping. From September 1975 onward, he used his nephew Mao Yuanxin as his liaison officer with the Politburo. Deng, before his second disgrace, Wang Hairong and Nancy Tang were among the very few people who had regular access to Mao.

Mao Yuanxin, a student at the Harbin military engineering college at the beginning of the CR, had rapidly risen to the post of deputy political commissar of the Shenyang military region in the early 1970s. After his appointment to Mao's staff, he took part in all Politburo meetings, reported to Mao about the discussions and conveyed Mao's instructions to the Politburo.[189] Mao Yuanxin, who was close to Jiang Qing, seemed to have reinforced the Chairman's radical impulses by feeding him with information which subtly discredited Deng. According to Mao Yuanxin, Deng seldom mentioned the achievements of the CR, and was even less inclined to talk about Liu Shaoqi's revisionist line; Deng had neglected Mao's instruction about taking 'class struggle as the key link', instead he stressed the importance of rules and regulations and worked solely for the promotion of the economy. Mao Yuanxin compared Deng's activities with Zhou Enlai's criticism of ultra-leftism which had been a negation of the CR and suggested that Deng fostered a trend to disparage the CR which was even stronger than the one developed in 1972 by Zhou Enlai.[190]

Mao, who continued to regard the CR as one of his greatest achievements, did not tolerate its denigration. He also began to have doubts about Deng's systematic corrections of leftist CR policies. Fully aware that Deng received widespread support for his rectification, he declared: 'The thinking of some comrades, mainly senior comrades is still in the stage of bourgeois democratic revolution. They have a poor understanding of socialism. They do not like it and even oppose it.'[191] He added, 'they do not want to go forward; some have moved backward and oppose the revolution. Because they have become high officials, they want to protect the interests of high officials.'[192] Referring to Deng, Map declared that 'this man never grasped class struggle . . . sticking to his "white cat or black cat" '.[193]

Moreover, Mao insisted that 'capitalist roaders are still on the capitalist road.'[194] By reviving the issue of 'capitalist roader', which had disappeared from the daily political vocabulary for a number of years, Mao provided the radicals with a powerful weapon in their fight against the veterans. In the present campaign, the radicals developed an equation which was fatal for the old guard: veteran cadres were democratic revolutionaries who were liable to become capitalist roaders. Therefore, 'the capitalist roaders are not just a few, they form a whole stratum.'[195]

Deng Xiaoping was again exiled, this time to Guangzhou. Zhou Rongxin, the outspoken minister of education, was submitted to 'political struggle' and collapsed at an interrogation meeting in April 1976. The same evening, he died at the age of 59.[196] Wan Li, the Minister of Communications, Hu Yaobang, who served as Party secretary at the Chinese Academy of Science, Deng Liqun, head of the policy research department of the state council, were all considered representatives of the 'right deviationist wind' and investigated. In July, the campaign was carried into the State Council which, under Hua Guofeng's chairmanship, had convened an enlarged meeting to discuss questions relating to national planning. During the meeting, the radicals suggested that the 'right deviationist wind' had originated in the State Council, and expressed doubts that the 'power of government was in the hands of real Marxists'. Some of them went so far as to criticise Hua Guofeng for having authorised Deng to make the major speech at Zhou Enlai's funeral ceremonies.[197]

By 1975, people had become weary of never-ending political campaigns and discontent with the deterioration of their living standards. Many were sympathetic to the more pragmatic policies implemented by Deng and Zhou who both became increasingly popular. Zhou's death and Deng's fall were a blow to many people who saw their hope for a better life extinguished. Their pent-up wrath culminated in a popular movement which found its expression in the manifestations at Tiananmen Square in late March and early April 1976, where, in thousands of poems, people paid tribute to Zhou Enlai and vented their resentment against Jiang Qing and her acolytes and their aversion to the CR.[198]

On the evening of 4 April, after more than a million people had poured into the square, the Politburo discussed the situation. Hua Guofeng declared that 'a group of bad people has come out. Some of their writings are aiming at the Chairman, many are attacking the centre'.[199] Wu De, the mayor of Beijung called the events 'counter-revolutionary' and 'planned', and Jiang Qing demanded the removal of the wreath and the arrest of those who had made 'counter-revolutionary' speeches. The Politburo decided that 'there exists an underground Petöfi Club'[200] engaging in planned counter-revolutionary activities. The next evening, the loudspeakers at Tiananmen broadcast a speech by Wu De which linked Deng Xiaoping with the events and condemned Deng, the die-hard capitalist roader, together with 'the bad people' who were engaging in counter-revolutionary activities at Tiananmen Square.[201] The Politburo unanimously decided to suppress the movement which had spread to other cities, a decision which Mao approved.[202] On 5 and 6 April, workers militia, police and PLA battalions cleared the square. The next day, Mao issued an official declaration that Deng was dismissed from all his posts, but that he was allowed to retain his Party membership. Hua Guofeng was appointed prime minister and first vice chairman of the Party.[203]

The elimination of the gang of four

The year 1976 was perhaps the most eventful one in the history of the PR. It opened with the death of Zhou Enlai at the age of 78. It was followed by the downfall of Deng Xiaoping and the crackdown on the first spontaneous protest movement since the beginning of the PRC. Hua Guofeng, a relatively unknown moderate was chosen as Mao's fourth heir apparent. Marshal Zhu De, another outstanding leader, died at the age of 90. On 28 July a fierce earthquake destroyed the industrial city of Tangshan, situated at about 100 km north of Beijing, leaving a quarter of a million dead and more than 150,000 seriously injured.[204] And finally, on 9 September, Mao died at the age of 83. His death precipitated the power struggle between the radicals and the moderates which ended with the arrest of Jiang Qing, Zhang Chunqiao, Wang Hongwen and Yao Wenyuan.

Mao's last months

The last months in Mao's life were marked by solitary seclusion. He spent his last Chinese New Year, which, in 1976, fell on 31 January, in the company of his faithful attendant Zhang Yufeng who later described it in her memoirs:

> It was a cold winter night with a few dim stars in the sky. Chairman Mao's residence in Zhongnanhai seemed to be shrouded in darkness.
>
> There were no visitors, no family members. Chairman Mao spent his last Spring Festival with those who served him.
>
> I had to feed him his New Year's Eve dinner with a spoon, since he could not use his hands. To open his mouth and to gulp down his food also was increasingly difficult for him.
>
> I helped him from his bed to the sofa in the sitting room. For a long time, he put his head on the back of the sofa without uttering a word . . . Suddenly, from far away, we heard fire crackers. In a low and hoarse voice, Mao asked me to explode some fire crackers . . . A faint smile crept over his old and weary face when he heard the fire crackers in the courtyard[205]

Mao's wife had moved out of Zhongnanhai and lived at Diaoyutai, the guest house which had served as headquarters to the former CCRG. She and her daughters, after their marriage, were not allowed to see Mao without prior permission. Mao obviously had developed an aversion to Jiang Qing. As for his daughters, he did not want them to see him in his sorry condition. Of the two sons he had, one died during the Korean war, and the second suffered from mental disorder. Mao saw him only rarely.[206]

In spite of his aggravated health, Mao made considerable effort to meet foreign visitors. In February, he received Richard Nixon who described his meeting with Mao in the following terms: 'The onset of Parkinson's Desease had stiffened his movements. His shambling stride had become an 82-year-old man's slow shuffle. His mind was still quick and incisive, but his speech was just grunts and groans.'[207] In April, he met with Malton, the prime minister of New Zealand, although the meeting lasted only ten minutes. Lee Kuan Yew, prime minister of Singapore met with Mao for a few minutes on 12 May. The last visitor Mao met was the prime minister of Pakistan, Zulfikar Ali Bhutto, also in May 1976.[208] During these meetings, Mao could hardly speak or stand. He could see his guests only dimly with the partially recovered sight of one of his eyes. With his head resting on the back of the sofa, he would murmur some words which his grand-niece Wang Hairong would try to make intelligible for the interpreter. Sometimes, Mao scribbled a few words on a piece of paper to make himself understood. In his talks with Chinese leaders, Zhang Yufeng would translate Mao's remarks into understandable Chinese.[209]

Nobody in the Politburo or in the State Council dared to suggest that Mao should avoid receiving foreign visitors. Finally, it was Mao himself who decided after Bhutto's visit that he would not see any more foreign guests, a decision which was soon publicised in an official government statement.[210]

In June 1976 – the exact date is not known – Mao summoned Hua Guofeng, Jiang Qing, Wang Hongwen, Zhang Chunqiao, Yao Wenyuan and Wang Hairong to his sick bed where he made the following statement:

> Since ancient times it has been rare for someone to live to the age of 70. I am now over 80. In old age, one often thinks about death. There is a saying that final judgement on a man can be passed only when the lid is on the coffin (*gai guan lun ding*). Perhaps, a final judgement can be passed now. In my life I have done two things. First I have fought Chiang Kai-shek during a few decades and I have driven him to a few islands. After eight years of war against the Japanese, they were sent home. We fought our way to Beijing and, at last, to the Forbidden City. There are not many people who do not recognise these achievements. Only a few talked into my ears trying to urge me to recover those small islands. The second thing you all know. It was to initiate the CR which is now supported by few and opposed by many. But this matter is not finished yet. It is a legacy which has to be handed down to the next generation. How to hand it down? If not in peace, then in turmoil. If this is not properly handled there will be bloodshed. Only heaven knows what you are going to do.[211]

During the night of 8 September, all members of the Politburo were summoned to Mao's bedside, where Mao lay under a white sheet, breathing feebly, to say good bye to him. Five years later, Ye Jianying recalled the scene. He led the line of Politburo members who slowly passed by Mao's bed. Ye, who was about to leave the room, was suddenly called back to Mao's bedstead. Mao's eyes opened and he tried to speak, but only a hoarse sound escaped his throat.[212] A few hours later, at 12:10 a.m. on 9 September, Mao died.

The final act

During the last months of his life, Mao had destroyed the delicate balance between the veteran cadres and the CR faction by purging Deng Xiaoping. While Mao's body lay in state from 11 to 17 September, and thousands of people walked by his coffin to pay a last homage to the great leader, the power struggle between the two factions accelerated.

The power structure, which had begun to take shape after the 10th Party Congress in October 1973 and which was consolidated by the National People's Congress in January 1975, took on a tripartite form composed of radicals, moderates and veteran cadres. The three groups differed in many respects, but most significantly in their appraisal of the CR. The radicals, Mao's close allies when he launched the CR, rose to power because of it. The veteran revolutionaries, targets of attack in the name of the CR, all suffered in various degrees because of it. Mao was certainly right in his assumption that they had an aversion to the CR. The moderates, many of whom had risen to prominence during the CR, were politically tied to it, but not necessarily to the CR faction. In the confrontation which developed after Mao's death, they tended to side with the veteran cadres.

Significant changes had taken place in the Politburo since its election in 1973. The 21-member Politburo had been reduced to 16. Among them were six veteran cadres: Ye Jianying (vice chairman of the Party and the MC), Liu Bocheng (vice chairman of the MC), Li Xiannian (vice premier), Xu Shiyou (commander of the Guangzhou military region), Wei Guoqing (political commissar of the Guangzhou military region), Li Desheng (commander of the Shenyang military region).[213] In the Standing Committee, the situation was similar. Since its last election, five of its nine members had died. Li Desheng withdrew in January 1975. Only one veteran, Ye Jianying and two radicals, Wang Hongwen and Zhang Chunqiao, and Hua Guofeng who could be considered a moderate, remained in the Standing Committee.[214] The group of radicals was composed of Jiang Qing, Zhang Chunqiao, Wang Hongwen, and Yao Wenyuan.[215] The group of moderates included Hua Guofeng, Chen Xilian, Ji Dengkui, Wang Dongxing, Wu De, and Chen Yonggui.[216]

The more than 20 ministries of the State Council were largely under the control of the veterans. Only the ministries of culture, of public health and the sports commission were in the hands of the radicals.[217] But they had supporters in other ministries, such as the ministry of public security and the ministry no. 7 of machine building in charge of the defence industry.[218]

Although Zhang Chunqiao and Wang Hongen were members of the MC standing committee, their influence over the PLA was negligible. Among the 11 military regions, the radicals could count only three real supporters, Ding Sheng, the commander of the Nanjing military region, Sun Yuguo, one of the six deputy commanders of the Shenyang military region, and Mao Yuanxin, one of the two political commissars of the Shenyang military region.[219] Although at the end of August 1977, several thousand persons were found to be involved with the gang of four in one way or the other, their real followers were very few.[220]

Before and immediately after Mao's death, Jiang Qing's group dominated the political scene. They had virtual control over the mass media and used it to their advantage. Besides, Jiang Qing's status as Mao's widow also added to their credit. But the old guard were organisationally stronger both in the Party and in the government. The weakest point of the CR faction, as Wang Hongwen later admitted, was their lack of control over the army.[221]

According to official Chinese sources, Jiang Qing attempted to seize power immediately after Mao's death. Her plan was to publicise incriminating material against Hua Guofeng, Ye Jianying and other veteran cadres, which had been collected by her followers in Shanghai and Changsha. Her next step would have been to demand the removal of these persons, to become herself chairwoman of the Party and to appoint Zhang

Chunqiao, Wang Hongwen and Yao Wenyuan as vice chairmen. Then Jiang Qing would have convened the 3rd Plenum of the CC to approve her actions.[222] At their public trial in November 1980, where the gang of four was formally charged for attempting to seize the supreme power in the Party and the state, no evidence was produced to prove that they had planned to overthrow Hua Guofeng and other leaders.[223] It can indeed be safely assumed that Jiang Qing and her group had little legitimacy, and were easily overwhelmed by their adversaries.

Immediately after Mao's death, at a Politburo meeting convened to discuss Mao's funeral arrangements, Jiang Qing began her attack on the veteran cadres. She insisted that the campaign to criticise Deng Xiaoping and rightist deviation should not be neglected because of the funeral ceremonies. In her view, the campaign had hitherto not been carried out efficiently, because the Party centre was 'far from being conscientious' and 'incompetent and weak' in its work.[224]

Her group instigated a series of activities meant to undermine the authority of the veteran leaders and to enhance its own status. On 12 September, Wang Hongwen – through his secretary Mi Shiqi – issued an order to the provincial authorities to contact Mi on all matters of importance and to seek instructions from the Party centre only through him. Shortly thereafter, Hua Guofeng received a telephone call from the Party secretary of Hunan province who asked him who Mi Shiqi was and whether he had to conform to Wang's instructions, which Hua clearly answered in the negative.[225] While Mao's body was laying in state, letters from all over the country began to pour in demanding that Jiang Qing take over the chairmanship of the Party.[226]

But it was the controversy about Mao's 'last statement',[227] that dominated the struggle for power between the contending groups. It assumed absurd proportions. On 16 September, Hua, to his surprise, read in the *People's Daily* that Mao, shortly before his death, had issued the instruction that all must 'abide by set principles' (*an ji ding fangzhen ban*).[228] But Hua claimed to have received Mao's written instruction recommending to 'abide by past principles' (*zhao guo qu fangzhen ban*). A dispute about the question developed between the radicals, who attempted to obtain a measure of legitimate power after Mao's death, and Hua, who denied their claim.[229]

On 19 September, Jiang Qing asked Hua Guofeng to call a meeting of the Standing Committee where Yao Wenyuan and Mao Yuanxin, but not Ye Jianying, who was amember of the committee, should participate. At the meeting, Jiang Qing, as Mao's widow, requested the right to safeguard all of Mao's papers and books. Her claim was refused despite her vigorous protests, on the grounds that Mao's papers belonged to the Party.[230] At the same meeting, the two opposing groups also clashed on a number of other issues. Zhang Chunqiao proposed that Jiang Qing, considering her merits during the CR, should be awarded a special post besides her membership in the Politburo. This request was refused. The veteran leaders, on their part, demanded that Mao Yuanxin should return to his post in Shenyang, but Jiang Qing disagreed on the grounds that Mao was needed for the preparations of the forthcoming 3rd Plenum of the CC.[231]

Mao's death provided the veteran leaders with the opportunity to deal with the radicals, a problem which some veteran leaders such as Ye Jianying, Nie Rongzhen and Zhou Enlai's widow Deng Yinchao had already begun to discuss before Mao's death. On 12 September, Nie discussed the same question with Yang Chengwu who had been rehabilitated and resumed the post of deputy general chief of staff. In Nie's view, resolute and 'pre-emptive measures' should be taken to solve the problem of the 'gang of four'.[232] Chen Yun, vice chairman of the National People's Congress and Wang Zhen, vice premier, and two generals, Su Yu, member of the MC standing committee and Song Shilun, president of the military academy, all had secret discussions with Ye Jianying about the elimination of the gang of four.[233]

The key figure for the successful implementation of the plan to eliminate the gang was Hua Guofeng, who, as Mao's successor, not only had to be won over, but also had to be persuaded to take the lead. Ye Jianying discussed the question with him on the day after Mao's death, but Hua appeared to evade the issue. During the following days, Ye made several more attempts to persuade him of the necessity to eliminate the gang, but him continued to hesitate. It was only after the meeting on 19 September, that Hua decided to act. Two days later, he visited Li Xiannian at his house where he told him that he was convinced of the necessity to take action against the 'gang of four' and that Ye Jianying should be charged with its organisation and timing.[234]

Two events in early October caused the veteran cadres to speed up their preparations to eliminate the 'gang'. On 2 October, Ye Jianying learned that an armoured division from Shenyang, under order of Mao Yuanxin, was heading towards Beijing. Ye ordered the troops to return to their barracks.[235] But it was again the quarrel about Mao's last edict that brought the conflict between the two groups to a climax. Hua Guofeng, while reviewing the speech Qiao Guanhua was to present at the UN General Assembly, found Jiang Qing's version of Mao's last edict in the text and deleted it. Two days later, on 4 October, the *Guangming Daily* published an article by Liang Xiao under the title 'Abide by Chairman Mao's Set Principles' which asserted that 'capitalist roaders; were trying to 'distort Chairman Mao's set principles . . . Such distortions amounts to the betrayal of Marxism, of socialism and to the betrayal of the great theories of continuing revolution under proletarian dictatorship.' The article concluded that 'any revisionist chieftain who dares to act that way, will come to no good'.[236]

Hua Guofeng was alarmed and convinced that the attack was aimed at him. At the same time, he learned that the Shanghai authorities were distributing a large amount of weapons to the local militia which operated under Wang Hongwen's command. The veteran leaders decided to act quickly. Ye Jianying and Wang Dongxing, the commander of the 8341 troops reported to Hua about the final preparations. Hua gave his approval to act in the evening of 6 October.

On 6 October, Zhang Chunqiao, Wang Hongwen and Yao Wenyuan were asked to attend a meeting of the Standing Committee of the Politburo in the evening of the same day, which was to discuss the publication of Mao's selected works and problems of propaganda, both of which related to their work. Since Jiang Qing, was neither a member of the Standing Committee nor in charge of propaganda, she was not invited.[237]

The first to arrive was Wang Hongwen, who found only Hua Guofeng and Ye Jianying on the scene. Wang Dongxing and a group of soldiers were hidden behind a screen which divided the room. As soon as Wang Hongwen entered the meeting hall, he was seized by four soldiers. Hua Guofeng announced to him: 'You have entered into an anti-Party and anti-socilaist alliance with Jiang Qing, Zhang Chunqiao and Yao Wenyuan in a vain attempt to usurp the Party and to seize power. Your problem is very serious. The centre has decided to put you under custody for examination.'[238] Zhang Chinqiao and Yao Wenyuan were arrested in the same manner and the same announcement was made to them.[239] During the same hour, Jiang Qing was arrested in Mao's residence in Zhongnanhai where she had returned a few days before Mao's death.[240]

At the same time, a number of such important followers of the Jiang Qing as Mao Yuanxin, Chi Qun, the Party secretary of Qinghua university and Xie Jingyi, secretary of the Beijing municipal Party committee were also placed in custody. More arrests were to follow in the subsequent days. The gang of four was eliminated over night, less than a months after Mao's death, and without resistance.

The next day, a Politburo meeting ratified the arrest of the gang and elected Hua Guofeng as chairman of the Party and of the MC. Between 7 and 14 October, the Politburo briefed leading members of the Party, government, the PLA and provincial and municipal authorities about the elimination of the gang of four.[241] By 10 October, rumours about the arrest of the gang were already widespread among Beijing citizens.[242] In the wake of the official announcement of the event which was made on 18 October, 1.5 million people held demonstrations in Beijing in support of the elimination of the gang. Similar activities took place in other cities and in the provinces throughout the country.[243]

Jiang Qing, Zhang Chunqiao, Wang Hongwen and Yao Wenyuan were the earliest as well as the last supporters of the CR. Mao had left to them the legacy of the CR, but not the power of Party and state. With their downfall, the CR came to an end.

CONCLUSION

The Cultural Revolution ultimately did not reach any of the goals Mao had wanted to achieve. It neither established the new socialist society he had so much desired, nor did it produce the new man devoted to the cause of a revolutionary society. Its performance had been so devastating that it left behind a memory of ten years of horror for most people who lived through that period.

To this date, it continues to be difficult to completely assess the impact of the CR on the Chinese people and on the nations' social, cultural and economic life. During this period, political persecution was practised at an unprecedented scale, victimising innumerable people of all walks of life. As many as 100 million people were involved in one campaign or another during the different stages of the CR. Statistics about the death toll during the Red Storm or during armed factional fighting are hardly available.

At leadership level, too, the CR had devastating effects: 71 per cent of the members and alternate members of the 8th Central Committee were subjected to various forms of political persecution. Among the Chinese top-echelon leaders, there appears to be only one person, who was able to survive the CR without being politically destroyed, and that was Zhou Enlai. But even he did not survive out of his own strength, but because, in moments of severe crisis, Mao protected him.

The immediate after-effect of the CR was a restoration. At all levels of society, those who had opposed the destruction of the Party establishment emerged as victors. This was particularly conspicuous at leadership level where the great majority of the senior leaders returned to power.

CONCLUSION

Underneath the surface of restoration and continuity, however, society had changed profoundly. The Cultural Revolution had tempered the revolutionary fervour of the average Party member and of non-Party members as well, and the campaigns met with a great deal of passive resistance and scepticism at all Party levels. In fact, the Cultural Revolution had shaken the very foundation of the Party's structure and of its ideological outlook. Before the Cultural Revolution, an authoritarian and highly disciplined Party had exercised effective and tight control over every individual in society, and society as a whole functioned according to the rules and the discipline imposed by the Party. The Party was feared and widely respected as 'great, glorious and correct'.

This changed considerably after the Cultural Revolution. The Party was torn by factionalism, its members divided according to the factions they had belonged to during the Cultural Revolution, and according to victors and victims.

Although its membership had increased, the Party lost a great deal of its former discipline, and the sense of loyalty to the Party and its causes all but disappeared. Those who had been Party members before the Cultural Revolution, had become disillusioned by it, and those who became Party members later had joined it out of all kinds of motivations but rarely because of dedication to the socialist cause. The effectiveness of the Party as an instrument of control decreased remarkably.

The Cultural Revolution led to the liberation of people's minds. For decades, they had been trained to think and to speak according to the official line and to consider Mao as their great and infallible leader. Now the halo surrounding Mao Zedong had been destroyed. The demi-god was reduced to a human being who had committed numerous errors while ruling the country. Also gone with the image of the demi-god were the sacred remnants of Marxism-Leninism and Mao Zedong Thought. They lost their weighty power over people's minds. The Chinese people, the intellectuals in particular, experienced an emancipation of mind that would have been unimaginable on such a scale before the Cultural Revolution. Once the ideological shackle had been broken, they began to think and to discuss more freely. They refused indoctrination from above and started to use their own judgement. The Cultural Revolution had exposed the evils and drawbacks of a totalitarian society to the point of shaking its very foundations, so that the superiority of a socialist system was called into question.

NOTES

1. Origins

1 *Resolution on History of the Communist Party of China*, Beijing, People's Publishing House, 1981, p. 22.
2 Ibid., p. 23.
3 Wang Nianyi, *Dadongluan de Niandai (Years of Turmoil)*, Henan, Henan People's Publishing House, 1988, p. 601.
4 Schram, Stuart, *The Thought of Mao Tse-Tung*, London, SOAS Contemporary China Institute Publications, 1989, p. 171; Wang Nianyi, 'Mao Zedong Tongzhi fadong "wenhua dageming" shi dui xingshi de guji' ('Comrade Mao Zedong's estimate of the situation at the time when he launched the "Cultural Revolution" '), *Dangshi Yanjiu Ziliao*, no. 4, p. 772.
5 Zheng Fulin, ed., *Zhongong Dangshi Zhishi Shouce (Handbook of Party History)*, Beijing, Beijing Press, 1985, p. 172.
6 Schram, Stuart, *Mao Tse-Tung Unrehearsed – Talks and Letters: 1956–1971*, Harmondsworth, Penguin, 1974, p. 89; *Renmin Ribao*, 2 May 1957.
7 *Zhonggong Dangshi Dashi Nianbiao (Chronology of Major Events in the History of the CCP)*, Central Research Department of History, Beijing, People's Publishing House, 1986, p. 277, henceforth *Chronology*: 'contradictions between the proletariat and the bourgeoisie have been basically solved.'.
8 Ibid.,: 'the major contradiction still existing in China was between the advanced socialist system and the backward production forces in society'.
9 Ibid., p. 278.
10 Twenty-three letters by comrade Mao Zedong, from 'Selections of Mao's letters', *People's Daily*, 25 December 1983.
11 Schram, Stuart, *Mao Tse-Tung Unrehearsed* op.cit., p. 124.
12 Schram, Stuart, *Mao Zedong: a Preliminary Reassessment*, Hong Kong, the Chinese University Press, 1983, p. 46, henceforth Schram, *Mao Zedong*.
13 Mao's speech of 20 January, 1956, *Ziliao Xuanbian (A Collection of Mao's Unpublished Speeches and Writings)* Beijing, 1967, p. 162.

14 *The Cambridge History of China*, vol. 14, Cambridge, Cambridge University Press, 1987, p. 243.
15 *People's Daily*, 27 April 1957; Ladany, Laslo, *The Communist Party of China and Marxism, 1921–1985: a Self Portrait*, London, C. Hurst and Co., 1988, p. 224.
16 *Selected Works of Mao Tse-tung*, vol. 5, Beijing, Foreign Languages Press, 1977, p. 391.
17 Ibid.; *The Cambridge History of China*, vol. 14, op. cit. p. 250.
18 Ibid.
19 *The Cambridge History of China*, vol. 14, op. cit., p. 252.
20 Ibid.
21 *Selected Works of Mao Tse-tung*, vol. 5, op. cit., p. 440.
22 Ibid., p. 441.
23 Ibid., p. 442.
24 Schram, *Mao Zedong*, op. cit., p. 46.
25 *Selected Works of Mao Tse-tung*, vol. 5, op. cit., p. 409.
26 The term was coined in a *People's Daily* article of 2 February 1958.
27 Quoted by Schram, Stuart R., 'Mao Tse-tung and the Theory of the Permanent Revolution, 1958–69', *The China Quarterly*, April–June 1971, pp. 226–7.
28 *Quotations from Chairman Mao Tse-tung*, Bejing, East Is Red Press, 1967, pp. 69–70; henceforth: *Quotations*.
29 Schram, *Mao Zedong*, op. cit., p. 50.
30 Cong Jin, *Quzhe Fazhande Suiyue (Years of Developments with Changing Directions)*, Henan, Henan People's Publishing House, 1989, pp. 139–40.
31 Schram, *Mao Zedong*, p. 46.
32 *The Cambridge History of China*, op. cit., p. 305.
33 Ibid., p. 365.
34 Dittmer, Lowell, *China's Continuous Revolution: the Post-Liberation Epoch, 1949–1981*, Berkeley, University of California Press, 1987, p. 41; henceforth: *Revolution*.
35 Rodzinsky, Wiethold, *The People's Republic of China: a Concise Political History*, New York, The Free Press, a Division of Macmillan, 1988, p. 65.
36 Hao Mengbi, Duan Haoran, *Zhongguo Gongchandang Liushinian, (Sixty Years of the CCP)*, Beijing, PLA Press, 1984 pp. 326–33.
37 After 1958, village-level agricultural production brigades, (APCs) were called 'production brigades'.
38 Schram, *Mao Zedong*, op. cit., p. 50.
39 More details about the Lushan conference later in this chapter.
40 *Peking Review*, no. 34, 1967; Li Rui, *Lushan Huiyi Shilu (A Factual Record of the Lushan Conference)*, Hunan, Spring and Autumn Press, 1988, p. 366.
41 MacFarquar, Roderick, *The Origins of the Cultural Revolution, vol. 2: The Great Leap Forward, 1958–1960*, Oxford, Oxford University Press, 1983, pp. 326–31; according to Dittmer, industrial output decreased by 38.2 per cent, agricultural output by 26.3 per cent, *Revolution*, op. cit., p. 35.

NOTES

42 *The Cambridge History of China*, vol. 14, op. cit., pp. 370, 371; according to Chinese sources, the population decreased by 13 million from 1959 to 1961. With a normal net increase of population by 20 per thousand, China's population should have increased by 27 million during the same period. The final demographic consequences thus were a loss of 40 million in three years. See Cong Jin, op. cit., p. 272.
43 Figures about state procurement in Dittmer, *Revolution*, op. cit., p. 35.
44 *A Collection of Mao's Unpublished Speeches*, op. cit., p. 247.
45 Quan Yanchi, *Lingxin Lei (Tears of a Leader)*, Beijing, Qiushi Press, 1989, pp. 29, 33.
46 Hu Sheng, *Zhongguo Gongchandangde Qishinian (Seventy Years of the Chinese Communist Party)* Beijing, CCP Publishing House, 1991, p. 382.
47 Hao and Duan, op. cit., p. 530–1.
48 *The Cambridge History of China*, op. cit., p. 323.
49 Schram, *Unrehearsed*, op. cit., p. 159; Hu Sheng, op. cit., p. 393.
50 *Chronology*, op.cit., p. 310.
51 Schram, *Mao Zedong*, op. cit., p. 59.
52 Refutation of the so-called state for the whole people; refutation of the so-called party of the entire people; in *The Polemic on the General Line of the International Communist Movement*, Peking, Foreign Languages Press, 1965, pp. 444–59.
53 Schram, *Unrehearsed*, op. cit., p. 191.
54 Speech at a Central Work Conference, 9 August, 1962, in *A Collection of Mao's Unpublished Speeches and Writings*, op. cit., p. 270.
55 Schram, *Unrehearsed*, op. cit., p. 188.
56 *Chronology*, op. cit., p. 326.
57 Ibid., p. 326.
58 Cong Jing, op. cit., p. 526.
59 Hao and Duan, op. cit., p. 555.
60 Ibid., p. 556.
61 *Chronology*, op. cit., p. 337.
62 Ibid., p. 338.
63 Personal Notes.
64 Hao and Duan, op. cit., p. 540.
65 Ibid., also see *The Cambridge History of China*, vol. 14, op. cit., pp. 435, 436.
66 Cong Jing, op. cit., p. 436.
67 *The Cambridge History of China*, op. cit., p. 443.
68 Ibid.
69 Ibid., pp. 444–5.
70 Quoted in Hsü, Immanuel C. R., *The Rise of Modern China*, 3rd ed., New York, Oxford University Press, 1983, p. 701.
71 *Peking Review*, no. 22, 1966.
72 *The Cambridge History of China*, vol. 14, op. cit., p. 444.
73 Ibid.

74 Personal Notes: when these articles were condemned in 1966 by the media and in political study sessions, most people had not understood them as a criticism of Mao when they first read them in the early 1960s.
75 Schram, *Unrehearsed*, op. cit., p. 165.
76 Ibid.
77 Ibid. p. 166.
78 Ibid., p. 167.
79 *Peking Review*, 2 June, 1967, p. 11.
80 Personal Notes.
81 *The Cambridge History of China*, vol. 14, op. cit., p. 453.
82 Ibid., p. 454.
83 Qi Benyu, 'How should we look at the surrender of Li Xiucheng?' in *Guangmin Ribao* (Illumination Daily) 23 August, 1963.
84 *Selected Works of Mao Zedong*, Beijing, Foreign Languages Press, 1965, vol. 1, p. 316.
85 Ibid., vol. 4, p. 428.
86 Schram, Stuart, ed., *Chairman Mao Talks to the People. Talks and Letters: 1956–1971*, New York, Pantheon Books, a division of Random House, 1974, p. 331; henceforth: *Chairman Mao Talks to the People*.
87 *The Cambridge History of China*, vol. 14, op. cit., p. 454.
88 Schram, *Unrehearsed*, op. cit., p. 195.
89 According to large character posters at the Beijing municipal Party committee criticising Peng Zhen in 1966.
90 *Selected Works of Mao Tse-tung*, op. cit., vol. 3, p. 86.
91 Ibid., p. 86.
92 Ibid., p. 91.
93 Cong Jin, op. cit., p. 548.
94 Schram, *Unrehearsed*, op. cit., p. 204.
95 Qi Benyu and Lin Jie, 'Comrade Jian Bozan's outlook on history should be criticised', *Red Flag*, 24 March 1966, Joint Publication Research Service, 35, 137.
96 *The Cambridge History of China*, vol. 14, op. cit., p. 462.
97 Ibid., p. 463–4.
98 Ibid., p. 465.
99 Lin Qingshan, *Kang Sheng Waizhuan (An Unofficial Biography of Kang Sheng)*, Beijing, China Youth Press, 1988, p. 211; henceforth: *Kang Sheng*.
100 *Chronology* op. cit., p. 327.
101 The other members were Lu Dingyi, minister of the CC propaganda department, Zhou Yang, vice minister of the CC propaganda department, Wu Lengxi, director of the Xinhua news agency and of the *People's Daily*, and Kang Sheng as the only radical.
102 'Decision of the CCP Central Committee concerning the great proletarian Cultural Revolution', *Peking Review*, no. 33, 1966.
103 Mao's conversation with Malraux, in: *Chinese Law and Government*, vol. 9, no. 3, autumn 1976.

NOTES

104 *Red Flag*, no. 4, 1975.
105 Mao described his visions about such a society in his 7 May 1966 letter to Lin Biao (*People's Daily*, 1 August 1966). If the soldiers' main task was to fight, they should also 'learn politics, military affairs and agriculture. They should engage in agricultural production and side occupations, run some medium-sized or small factories and manufacture a number of products to meet their own needs or to exchange with the state at equal value' . . . 'While the main activities of the workers is in industry, they should also study military affairs, politics and agriculture, they should engage in agricultural production and side operations.' The same principle should also be applied to students, peasants and all other groups in society.
106 *People's Daily*, 6 November 1967.
107 This can be gauged from the role Mao played at several high-level meetings. At a Politburo meeting on 14 September 1938, presided over by Zhang Wentian, Mao presented the political report. At the 6th Plenum of the 6th Congress (29 September to 6 November), he proposed a 'new phase', a strategy for the war against Japan. At an enlarged Politburo meeting from 3 July to 25 August, 1939, he made the concluding speech about the work of the Party during the last two years. *Chronology*, op. cit., pp. 134–40.
108 *The Cambridge History*, vol. 14, op. cit., p. 60; *Issues and Studies*, November 1981, p. 92; see also 'Liu Shaoqi and Yang Shangkun criticised for breach of discipline in issuing documents in the name of the CC without authorisation, *Selected Works of Mao Tse-tung*, vol. 5, op. cit., p. 92.
109 The CCP had six consecutive leaders from 1921 to 1943. Mao was the sixth. Zheng Fulin, op. cit., p. 799.
110 *Chronology*, op. cit., p. 160.
111 Xia Honggen, ed., *Dangshi Zhishi Zhenwenlu (Knowledge of Party History)* Beijing, PLA Press, 1988, p. 36; Ladany, op. cit., p. 65.
112 Xia Honggen, op. cit., p. 37.
113 *Selected Works of Mao Tse-tung*, vol. 4, op. cit., p. 171.
114 *Chronology*, op. cit., p. 175.
115 Dittmer, Lowell, *Liu Shaoqi and the Chinese Cultural Revolution: the Politics of Mass Criticism*, Berkeley, University of California Press, 1974, p. 24; henceforth: *Liu Shaoqi*.
116 Xia Honggen, op. cit., pp. 38–9.
117 Zheng Fulin, op. cit., p. 742; *Chronology*, op. cit., p. 240.
118 *Mao Zedong Poems*, Changsha, Hunan People's Publishing House, 1980, p. 41.
119 Yao Wenyuan, 'Lun Lin Biao Fandangyituande Shehui Jichu' ('On the social basis of the Lin Biao anti-Party clique'), *People's Daily*, 1 March 1975; Starr, John Brian, *Continuing the Revolution: the Political Thought of Mao*, Princeton, Princeton University Press, 1979, p. 127.
120 Hucker, Charles, O., *China's Imperial Past: an Introduction to*

Chinese History and Culture, Stanford, Stanford University Press, 1975, pp. 43–4.
121 *A Collection of Mao's Unpublished Speeches*, op. cit., p. 218.
122 *Guangming Ribao*, 26 October 1978.
123 Xia Honggen, op. cit., p. 179.
124 *Liu Shaoqi Xuanji (Selected Works of Liu Shaoqi)*, vol. 2, Beijing, People's Publishing House, 1985, p. 271.
125 *People's Daily*, 5 April, 1956.
126 MacFarquhar, vol. 1, op. cit., p. 104
127 Ibid., p. 104.
128 Ibid., pp. 99–100.
129 Hollingsworth, Clare, *Mao*, London, Triad Paladin Grafton Books, 1985, p. 101.
130 *Jianguo Yilai Mao Zedong Wengao (Mao's Writings after the Founding of the People's Republic)*, vols. 1–4, Beijing, Central Documentation Publishing House, 1990, pp. 192, 234, 528.
131 Ibid, p. 528.
132 Xu Qingqing, op. cit., pp. 65, 66.
133 Shi Shanyu et al., eds, *Zhongguo Gongchandang Dangshi Zhishi Jicheng (A Collection of Events in the History of the Chinese Communist Party)*, Beijing, Great Wall Press, 1991, p. 97.
134 MacFarquhar, op. cit., vol. 1, p. 105.
135 Ibid.
136 Schram, Stuart, *Chairman Mao Talks to the People*, op. cit., p. 99.
137 *Chronology*, p. 307.
138 Lin Qingshan, *Lin Biao Zhuan (A Biography of Lin Biao)*, Beijing, Knowledge Press, 1988, p. 112; henceforth: *Lin Biao*.
139 Ibid., p. 113.
140 *Quotations*, op. cit., p. V.
141 Cong Jin, op. cit., p. 411.
142 *Quotations*, op. cit., p. iii.
143 Personal Notes.
144 Snow, Edgar, *The Long Revolution*, New York, Vintage Books, 1973, p. 68.
145 Ibid., p. 70.
146 Meisner, Maurice, *Marxism, Maoism and Utopianism*, Madison, Wisconsin, University of Wisconsin Press, 1982, pp. 168–9.
147 Ibid., p. 169.
148 Decision of the 6th Plenum, in Myers, James T., Domes, Jürgen and Von Groeling, Erik, *Chinese Politics, Documents and Analysis*, vol. 1, Columbia, University of South Carolina Press, 1986, p. 40; henceforth: Myers.
149 Personal Notes.
150 Dittmer, Lowell, *Revolution*, op. cit., pp. 49–50.
151 *Memoirs of a Chinese Marshal: the Autobiographical Notes of Peng Dehuai (1898–1972)*, Beijing, Foreign Languages Press, 1986, p. 517.
152 Ibid., p. 514.

153 Ibid., p. 510; Li Rui, 'Why Peng Dehuai wrote his letter'; *Encounter Monthly*, Shanghai, January 1989.
154 'Mao's talk at the Lushan conference', 23 July 1959, in Schram, Stuart, *Mao Talks to the People*, op. cit., p. 142.
155 *Memoirs of a Chinese Marshal*, op. cit., p. 494.
156 Dittmer, *Revolution*, op. cit., p. 37.
157 'Guanyu Geren Chongbaide Yanjiu' ('A study of the personality cult'), *Dan Xiao Luntan*, 1989, no. 2.
158 Ibid.
159 *World Affairs*, no. 20, 1988.
160 *Selected Works of Mao Tse-tung*, vol. 5, op. cit., p. 92; *Issues and Studies*, November 1981, p. 91.
161 Cong Jin, op. cit., p. 414.
162 Hao Mengbi and Duan Haoran, op. cit., p. 538.
163 Ibid., p. 546.
164 *A Collection of Mao's Unpublished Speeches*, op. cit., p. 269.
165 Ibid., pp. 270, 275.
166 Xi Zhongxun was vice prime minister, Jia Taofu, a member of the CC and deputy director of the State Council's economic commission. Both were veteran revolutionaries who had worked with Gao Gang in the north-east base area in the 1930s. They provided material to a writer of a novel about the revolution in this area and, as a result, were considered to have extolled Gao Gang who had been purged in 1955 for anti-Party activities. See Hao Mengbi and Duan Haoran, op. cit., pp. 543–8.
167 Ibid., p. 547.
168 Cong Jin, op. cit., p. 529.
169 This term was used during the anti-Japanese war where, in areas that were disputed by the Japanese and the communist armies, people were pro-Japanese during the day and pro-communist during the night.
170 Mao later referred critically to this view on several occasions during the purge of Liu Shaoqi. See *Collection of Mao's Unpublished Writings*, op. cit., p. 329.
171 Zheng Fulin, op. cit., p. 414; Dittmer, Liu Shaoqi, op. cit., p. 242.
172 Hei Yannan, *Shinian Dongluan (A Decade of Turbulence)* Xian, International Culture Publishing Company, 1988, p. 51.
173 Hei Yannan, op. cit., p. 51.
174 Schram, *Unrehearsed*, op. cit., p. 266.
175 Mao's criticism of the 'three evil winds' at the 10th Plenum of the Central Committee in 1962 aimed not only at Liu Shaoqi but also at Chen Yun; see Cong Jin, op. cit., p. 483.
176 Schram, *Unrehearsed*, op. cit., p. 66.
177 Zheng Fulin, op. cit., p. 745.
178 Deng Zihuai, head of the CC rural work department; Li Weihan, head of the CC united front department; Lu Dingyi, head of the CC propaganda Department; An Ziwen, head of the organisational department.
179 This was defined as follows: 'First place must be given to man

in handling the relationship between man and weapons; to political work in handling the relations between political work and other work; to ideological work in relation to routine tasks in political work; and in ideological work, to the living ideas in a person's mind as distinguished from ideas in books. That is to say, first place to ideological work and first place to living ideas.' The 'three-eight working style' was expressed in three phrases and eight additional characters meaning 'a firm, correct political orientation; a plain, hard-working style; flexibility in strategy and tactics; and unity, alertness, earnestness and liveliness'.

180 *Red Flag*, no. 12, 1 August 1967.
181 Lin Qingshan, *Kang Sheng* p. 143.
182 Ibid., p. 144.
183 Ibid.
184 Ibid., p. 149.
185 Ibid., p. 167.
186 Cong Jin, op. cit., p. 511.
187 Ibid., p. 512.
188 Lin Qingshan, *Kang Sheng*, op. cit., p. 202.
189 Ibid., p. 249.
190 Zheng Fulin, op. cit., p. 587.
191 *Chronology*, op. cit., p. 442.
192 Witke, Roxan, *Camarade Chiang Ching*, Paris, Robert Laffont, 1978, pp. 232–3, 274–5.
193 *Issues and Studies*, no. 8, May 1971, p. 220.
194 *New China Record*, p. 337.
195 *Dangdai (Current Era)*, no. 3, 1989, p. 35.
196 Zhonggong Yanjiu, *Zhonggong Wenhua Dageming Zhongyao Wenjian Huibian*, (*CCP Studies: Collection of Important Documents on the CCP Cultural Revolution*) Taipei, 1973, p. 254, henceforth: *Collection of CCP Documents*.
197 *Lianhe Bao (United Times)*, Shanghai, 23 December, 1988.
198 'Eliminate the ideology of the bourgeois right', *People's Daily*, 13 October 1958.
199 Ye Yonglie, *Zhang Chunqiao Fuchen Shi* (*The Rise and Fall of Zhang Chunqiao*), Changchun, Time Literary Press, 1988, p. 103; Schram, *Mao Zedong*, op. cit., p. 61.
200 Ye Yonglie, op. cit., p. 103.
201 Ibid.
202 Shajiabang is the name of a village.
203 The article appeared on 10 June 1957.
204 *People's Daily*, 14 June 1957.
205 *Chronology*, op. cit., p. 348.
206 Gao Gao and Yan Jiaqi, *Wenhua Da Geming Shinian Shi* (*A Ten Year History of the Cultural Revolution*), Tianjin, Tianjin People's Publishing House, 1986, p. 11.

NOTES

2 Backdrop

1 *Resolution on Party History*, op. cit., pp. 36–9.
2 Myers, op. cit., vol. 1, pp. 194–7.
3 *Peking Review*, 2 June 1967.
4 *Peking Review*, 27, May 1966.
5 Myers, op. cit., vol. 1, p. 220.
6 Hei Yannan, op. cit., p. 1.
7 *A Collection of Mao's Unpublished Speeches*, op. cit., p. 247.
8 Tan Zongji et al. *Shinian Houde Pingshou (Critical Comments after Ten Years)*, Beijing, Historical Materials Press, 1987, p. 3; Peng Cheng et al. *Zhongguo Zhengju Beiwanglu (A Memorandum about the Chinese Political Situation)*, PLA Publishing House, Beijing, 1989, p. 73.
9 Zi Ling, Zi Zhen, *Wu Han He Hai Rui Baguan (Wu Han and his 'Hai Rui Dismissed From Office')*; see Zhou Ming, ed., *Lishi Zai Zheli Chensi (Pondering about History)*, Beijing, Huaxia Press, 1986, vol. 2, p. 3.
10 Ibid., p. 5.
11 Lin Qingshan, *Jiang Qing Chen Fu Lu (The Rise and Fall of Jiang Qing)* Beijing, China News Press, 1988, p. 307; henceforth: *Jiang Qing*.
12 Ibid.
13 Lin Qingshan, *Kang Sheng*, op. cit., pp. 249–55.
14 See Jiang Qing's speech in *Issues and Studies*, May 1971.
15 *Memories of a Chinese Marshal*, op. cit., p. 522.
16 Schram, *Unrehearsed*, op. cit., p. 237.
17 *Selected Works of Mao Tse-Tung*, vol. 5, op. cit., p. 150.
18 Gao and Yan, op. cit., p. 6.
19 Lin Qingshan, *Jiang Qing*, op. cit., p. 315.
20 Gao and Yan, op. cit., p. 7.
21 Ibid.
22 *Wenhui Bao*, 10 November, 1965.
23 Shuai Dongbing, 'Peng Zhen Zai Baofengyu Qianye' ('Peng Zhen on the eve of the storm'), in *Mingren Zhuanji*, no. 11–12, 1988.
24 Ibid., no. 11–12, 1988.
25 Myers, op. cit., p. 133.
26 Shuai Dongbing, op. cit., p. 11.
27 *Chronology*, op. cit., p. 344.
28 Shuai Dongbing, op. cit., p. 11: 'Conversation with comrades Kapo and Balluku', *Chinese Law and Government*, vol. 9, no. 3, autumn 1978, pp. 140–2.
29 Shuai Dongbing, op. cit., p. 11.
30 Ibid.
31 Ibid., Zheng Derong, *Xin Zhongguo Jishi, 1949–1984 (Records of New China)*, Changchun, North East Normal University Press, 1986, p. 381.
32 Ibid., see also Gao and Yan, op. cit., p. 9.
33 Shuai Dongbing, op. cit., p. 16.

34 *People's Daily*, 30 December 1965.
35 Myers, vol. 1, op. cit., pp. 157–9;.
36 Gao and Yan, op. cit., p. 9; Dittmer, Lowell, *Liu Shaoqi*, op. cit., p. 72.
37 Tan Zongji, op. cit., p. 7.
38 Ibid.
39 Ibid., p. 9.
40 Myers, vol. 1, op. cit., p. 196
41 Ibid.
42 Qin Xiaoying, *Buxu Chuan Junzhuang De Jiangjun (A General Deprived of His Uniform)*, Beijing, Huaxia Press, 1988, p. 15.
43 Cong Jin, op. cit., p. 622.
44 *People's Daily*, 28 May, 1967.
45 *Peking Review*, 2 June, 1967.
46 *Issues and Studies*, vol. 7, no. 8, May 1971.
47 Tan Zongji, op. cit., p. 10.
48 Cong Jin, op. cit., p. 625.
49 *Chronology*, op. cit., p. 344.
50 Hu Sheng, op. cit., p. 424.
51 Ye Yonglie, *Zhang Chunqiao*, op. cit., p. 152.
52 Ibid.; Cong Jin, op. cit., p. 627.
53 Ibid.
54 Myers, op. cit., pp. 211, 213.
55 *Jiefang Ribao* (Shanghai), *Wenhui Bao*, (Shanghai) 10 May, 1966, *Peking Review*, no. 22, 27 May 1966.
56 Qi Benyu, 'On the bourgeois stand of *Frontline* and *Beijing Daily*', *Red Flag*, 11 May 1966; Lin Jie, 'Uncover Deng Tuo's anti-Party, anti-Socialist true nature', *People's Daily*, 14 March 1966.
57 Zhou Ming, op. cit., vol. 3, p. 64.
58 Ibid., vol. 2, p. 14; vol. 3, pp. 67, 127.
59 Peng refers to Peng Zhen; Luo Ruiqing was PLA chief of staff and vice premier; Lu Dingyi was an alternate member of the Politburo, minister of the CC department of propaganda and minister of culture; Yang Shangkun was the chief of the general office of the CC.
60 *The Cambridge History of China*, vol. 14, op. cit., p. 327.
61 Ye Yonglie, *Zhang Chunqiao*, op. cit., pp. 152, 153.
62 Gao and Yan, op. cit., p. 15.
63 Wang Nianyi, *Dadongluan*, op. cit., p. 9.
64 Ibid., p. 10.
65 Ibid., p. 11.
66 Ibid.
67 *Peking Review*, no. 21. 19 May, 1967.
68 Ibid.
68 Hei Yannan, op. cit., p. 9.
70 *Quotations*, op. cit., p. v.
71 Hei Yannan, op. cit., p. 12.
72 Ibid., p. 13.
73 Wang Nianyi, *Dadongluan*, op. cit., p. 18.

74 It has been argued that Luo Ruiqing and Lin Biao differed in their attitude towards the Soviet Union and the United States. See *Cambridge History of China*, op. cit., vol. 14, pp. 339, 340.
75 Hei Yannan, op. cit., p. 34.
76 Lin Qingshan, *Lin Biao*, op. cit., p. 125.
77 Cong Jin, op. cit., p. 632.
78 Tan Zongji, op. cit., p. 68; Zhou Ming, op. cit., vol. 1, p. 333.
79 *Jiefang Junbao*, 22 August, 1967.
80 Cong Jin, op. cit., p. 634; see also Gao and Yan, op. cit., p. 197.
81 Tan Zongji, op. cit., p. 66.
82 *Peking Review*, 4 August 1967.
83 Gao and Yan, op. cit., p. 200.
84 *Chronology*, op. cit., p. 341.
85 Yu Gong, *Lin Biao Shijian Zhenxiang (The True Story about the Lin Biao Affair)*, Beijing, China Broadcasting and Television Press, 1988, p. 394.
86 Ibid., p. 393.
87 Wang Nianyi, *Dadongluan*, op. cit., p. 18.
88 Hao and Duan, op. cit., p. 579.
89 *Peking Review*, no. 21, 19 May 1967.
90 Ibid.
91 Ibid.
92 Ibid.

3 The case of Liu Shaoqi

1 Lin Qingshan, *Kang Sheng*, op. cit., p. 266.
2 Yue Dayun and Wakeman, Carolyn, *To the Storm: the Odyssey of a Revolutionary Chinese Woman*, Berkeley, University of California Press, 1985, pp. 148, 160.
3 Ibid., pp. 147, 148; Dittmer, *Liu Shaoqi*, op. cit., pp. 78, 79.
4 Gao and Yan, op. cit., p. 20.
5 Jin Chunming et al., *Wenge Shiqi Guaishi Guaiyu (The Absurdities of the Cultural Revolution)*, Beijing, Qiushi Press, 1989, p. 155.
6 Ibid.
7 Ibid.
8 Ren Jian, *Gongheguo Yuanshouzhi Shi (The Death of the Head of the Republic)*, Hong Kong, Haiming Cultural Press, p. 23.
9 Ibid.
10 *Encounter Monthly*, no. 9, 1986; Dittmer, *Liu Shaoqi*, op. cit., p. 81.
11 Gao and Yan, op. cit., p. 24.
12 See Dittmer, *Liu Shaoqi*, p. 86 for a different view.
13 Liu Guokai, *A Brief Analysis of the Cultural Revolution*, New York, M. E. Sharpe, Inc. 1987, p. 18.
14 Ibid., p. 20.
15 Jin Chunming, op. cit., p. 134; see also Wang Nianyi, *Dadongluan*, op. cit., p. 42.
16 Jin Chunming, op. cit., p. 135.

17 Wang Nianyi, *Dadongluan*, op. cit., p. 42.
18 *Peking Review*, no. 21, 1967.
19 Wang Nianyi, *Dadongluan*, op. cit., p. 6; Myers, op. cit., p. 64.
20 *People's Daily*, 25 July 1967.
21 *Peking Review*, no. 31, 29 July 1966.
22 Gao and Yan, op. cit., p. 32.
23 Ibid., p. 33.
24 Ibid.; Dittmer, *Liu Shaoqi*, op. cit., pp. 89, 90.
25 Gao and Yan, op. cit., p. 35.
26 Ibid.
27 Ibid., p. 48; Dittmer, *Liu Shaoqi*, op. cit., p. 90.
28 Dittmer, *Liu Shaoqi*, op. cit., p. 95; Heinzig, Dieter, *Die Krise in der KPC in der Volksrepublik Chinas*, Hamburg, 1969.
29 Wang Nianyi, *Dadongluan*, op. cit., pp. 50, 51.
30 Ren Jian, op. cit., p. 35.
31 Ibid.
32 *People's Daily*, 5 August 1967. The poster was published one year later after the political verdict on Liu Shaoqi had become public knowledge.
33 Dittmer, *Liu Shaoqi*, op. cit., p. 93.
34 *Encounter Monthly*, no. 9, 1986.
35 Quoted in Dittmer, *Liu Shaoqi*, op. cit., p. 93.
36 Myers, op. cit., pp. 270–7; *Peking Review*, no. 33, 12 August 1966.
37 *Peking Review*, no. 33, 1966.
38 Ibid.
39 Hao and Duan, op. cit., p. 585.
40 Wang Nianyi, *Dadongluan*, op. cit., p. 88.
41 Ibid., p. 94.
42 *Peking Review*, no. 41, 7 October 1966.
43 Li Ke and Hao Shengzhang, *Wenhua Dageming Zhongde Remin Jiefangjun (The PLA in the Cultural Revolution)*, Beijing, CCP History Material Press, 1989, pp. 31, 32.
44 *Chronology*, op. cit., p. 354.
45 *A Collection of Mao's Unpublished Speeches*, op. cit., p. 331.
46 Hao and Duan, op. cit., p. 587.
47 Ibid.
48 Liu Yan, Mi Zhenbo, *Zhou Enlai Yanjiu Wenxuan (Selected Articles on Zhou Enlai)*, Tianjin, Nankai University Press, 1987, p. 552.
49 China News Agency, no. 663, June 9, 1967; Dittmer, *Liu Shaoqi*, op. cit., pp. 97–99.
50 Zhou Ming, vol. 1, op. cit., p. 7.
51 Schram, *Unrehearsed*, op. cit., pp. 265, 267; Dittmer, *Liu Shaoqi*, op. cit., pp. 99, 100.
52 Schram (*Unrehearsed*), op. cit., p. 332.
53 Dittmer, *Liu Shaoqi*, op. cit., p. 100.
54 *Red Flag*, no. 14, 1 November 1966.
55 Wang Nianyi, *Dadongluan*, op. cit., p. 108.
56 Peng Cheng, op. cit., p. 106.
57 Wang Nianyi, *Dadongluan*, op. cit., p. 145.

NOTES

58 Ibid.
59 Ibid.
60 Dittmer, *Liu Shaoqi*, op. cit., p. 149.
61 Ren Jian, op. cit., pp. 93, 94.
62 *People's Daily*, 1 January 1967.
63 Gao and Yan, op. cit., pp. 408, 411.
64 Dittmer, *Liu Shaoqi*, op. cit., p. 15.
65 Gao and Yan, op. cit., p. 406.
66 *Collection of CCP Documents*, op. cit., p. 210.
67 Ibid.
68 The article entitled 'Patriotism or national betrayal?' was published on 1 April 1967.
69 *Peking Review*, no. 15, 7 April 1967; *Red Flag*, 30 March 1967.
70 Gao and Yan, op. cit., p. 156.
71 'Betrayal of proletarian dictatorship is an essential element in the book on "Self-cultivation" ', *Red Flag* and *People's Daily*, joint editorial, 8 May 1967.
72 Jin Chunming, op. cit., pp. 362–8.
73 Zhou Ming, op. cit., p. 13.
74 Ren Jian, op. cit., pp. 128, 135.
75 Ibid.
76 Zhou Ming, op. cit., pp. 27–8; Ren Jian, op. cit., p. 165.
77 Ibid., pp. 173, 178.
78 Zhou Ming, op. cit., pp. 27, 32.
79 Huang Zheng, 'Liu Shaoqi Zai Wenhua Dagemingzhong' (Liu Shaoqi in the Cultural Revolution) *Dangde Wenxian* (Party Documentation), No. 5, 1988.
80 *Zhonggong Dangshi Yanjiu*, no. 5, 1989, p. 79.
81 Huang Zhen, op. cit., p. 97.

4 The great chaos

1 In his letter to Jiang Qing, Mao expressed this concept in the form of an ancient Chinese saying: *cong tianxia daluan dadao tianxia dazhi* ('from great disorder under heaven to great order under heaven), *Chinese Law and Government*, summer 1973, no. 2, p. 96.
2 Yu Gong, *Lin Biao Shijian Zhenxiang (The True Story About the Lin Biao Affair)*, Beijing, China Broadcasting and Television Press, 1988, p. 395.
3 Schram, *Mao Zedong*, op. cit., p. 67.
4 Lin Biao, *Report to the Ninth Congress of the CCP*, Peking, Foreign Languages Press, 1969, p. 35.
5 Su Caiqing, *Hongweibing Yundong Jiqi Lishi Jiaoxun (The Red Guard Movement and its Historical Lessons)*, Beijing, Party School Press, 1987, p. 173.
6 Ibid.
7 *A Collection of Mao's Unpublished Speeches*, op. cit., p. 29.
8 *People's Daily*, 1 August, 1966.

9 Gao and Yan, op. cit., p. 41.
10 Ibid.
11 Wang Nianyi, *Dadongluan*, op. cit., p. 52.
12 *Peking Review*, no. 33, 12 August 1966.
13 Su Caiqing, op. cit., p. 173.
14 Jin Chunming, op cit., p 203.
15 Ibid., p. 204.
16 Ibid., p. 303.
17 'The Great Proletarian Cultural Revolution Engulfs Beijing's Streets', 23 August 1966.
18 *Peking Review*, no. 36, 2 September 1966.
19 Wang Nianyi, *Dadongluan*, op. cit., pp. 69–71.
20 People with a class or political background of landlord, rich peasant, counter-revolutionary, bad element and rightist belonged to this category, whom the red guards believed to be 'ghosts and monsters'.
21 Wang Nianyi, *Dadongluan*, op. cit., p. 71.
22 Ibid., see Also Liu Guokai, op. cit., pp. 25, 26.
23 *Peking Review*, no. 36, 2 September 1966.
24 Tan Zongji, op. cit., pp. 21, 22.
25 Wang Nianyi, *Dadongluan*, op. cit., pp. 77, 78
26 Su Caiqing, op. cit., p. 179.
27 Ibid.
28 Jin Chunming, op. cit., pp. 283–4.
29 Liu Guokai, op. cit., pp. 32–3.
30 Ibid., pp. 29–30.
31 Hong Yung Lee, *The Politics of the Chinese Cultural Revolution: a Case Study*, Berkeley, University of California Press, 1978, p. 110–3.
32 Ibid., p. 113.
33 *Peking Review*, no. 35, 26 August 1977.
34 Hong Yung Lee, op. cit., p. 112.
35 Wang Nianyi, op. cit., p. 80.
36 Ibid., p. 81.
37 The full names of these organisations were: the Headquarters of Red Guards of Beijing Institutions of Higher Learning (first headquarters); the General Command of the Red Guards of Beijing Institutions of Higher Learning (second headquarters); the General Headquarters of the Red Guards for Revolution and Rebellion of Beijing's Institutions of Higher Learning (third headquarters).
38 Hong Yung Lee, op. cit., p. 114.
39 Wang Nianyi, *Dadongluan*, op. cit., p. 80; Jin Chunming, op. cit., pp. 106–9.
40 Ibid.
41 Ibid.
42 Su Caiqing, op. cit., p. 184.
43 Gao and Yan, op. cit., p. 81.
44 Ibid., p. 123, Hong Yung Lee, op. cit., pp. 125, 126.

45 Qiao Yi, 'Lian Dong Shijian' (The Committee of United Action) *Pursuit*, no,. 5, 1988.
46 Ibid.
47 Ibid.
48 Gao and Yan, op. cit., p. 117.
49 Tan Zongji, op. cit., p. 43.
50 Liu Guokai, op. cit., p. 44.
41 Ibid., p. 44.
52 Ye Yonglie, *Wang Hongwen Xingshuai Lu* (*The Vicissitudes of Wang Hongwen*), Changchun, Time Literary Press, 1989, p. 85.
53 Ibid.
54 This incident became known as the Anting event, see: Jin Chunming, op. cit., p. 117.
55 Ye Yonglie, *Wang Hongwen*, op. cit., p. 85.
56 Wang Nianyi, *Dadongluan*, op. cit., p. 136.
57 *Red Flag*, no. 3, 1967.
58 *Peking Review*, no. 21, 19 May 1966.
59 Ibid., no. 33, 12 August 1966.
60 Ye Yonglie, *Wang Hongwen*, op. cit., p. 167; White, Lynn T, III, *Politics of Chaos, the Organisational Causes of Violence in China's Cultural Revolution*, Princeton, Princeton University Press, 1989, pp. 240–1.
61 Ye Yonglie, op. cit., p. 177; Bergère, Marie-Claire, *La République populaire de Chine de 1949 à Nos Jours*. Paris, Armand Colin, 1987, pp. 126–7.
62 Ye Yonglie, *Wang Hongwen*, op. cit., p. 181.
63 Ibid.
64 Ye Yonglie, *Zhang Chunqiao*, op. cit., p. 185.
65 Wang Nianyi, *Dadongluan*, op. cit., p. 171.
66 Ibid., p. 172.
67 *Peking Review*, no. 3, 13 January 1967.
68 Ye Yonglie, *Wang Hongwen*, op. cit., p. 185.
69 Ibid., pp. 188–91.
70 *Chronology* op. cit., p. 357.
71 *Peking Review*, no. 4, 20 January 1967.
72 Hao and Duan, op. cit., p. 590.
73 *Peking Review*, no. 4, 20 January 1967.
74 Ibid.
75 Ibid.
76 Ye Yonglie, *Wang Hongwen*, op. cit., p. 199.
77 *Peking Review* no. 4, 20 January 1967.
78 Ibid.
79 Ibid., no. 5, 27 January 1967.
80 Ibid.
81 *Collection of CCP Documents*, op. cit., p. 227.
82 Wang Nianyi, *Dadongluan*, op. cit., pp. 186–8.
83 *Collection of CCP Documents* op. cit., pp. 226–8.
84 *People's Daily*, 22 January, 1967.
85 Gao and Yan, op. cit., p. 239.

86 Zhou Ming, op. cit., vol. 1, p. 156; Ladany, op. cit., p. 161.
87 Wang Nianyi, *Dadongluan*, p. 150.
88 Ibid., p. 151.
89 Ibid., p. 187.
90 *Guanyu Jianguo Yilai Dangde Ruogan Lishi Wenti De Jueyi Zhushiban (Resolution on Party History with Notes)*, Documentation and Research Department of the Central Committee. Beijing, People's Publishing House, 1986, p. 411.
91 Ibid., p. 407.
92 Wang Nianyi, 'Guanyu Eryue Niliu De Yixie Ziliao' ('Some facts about the February Adverse Current') *Dangshi Yanjui Ziliao (Material on the Study of Party History)* no. 1, 1990, p. 4. henceforth: 'Guanyu Eryue Niliu'
93 Hao and Duan, op. cit., pp. 592–3.
94 Zhou Ming, op. cit., vol. 2, pp. 66–7.
95 Ibid., vol. 2, p. 69.
96 Ibid.
97 Ibid., p. 67.
98 Wang Nianyi, *Guanyu Eryue Niliu*, op. cit., p. 4.
99 Ibid.
100 Ibid., p. 6.
101 Ibid.
102 Ibid.
103 Gao and Yan, op. cit., p. 145.
104 Ibid., p. 146.
105 Li Ke and Hao Shengzhang, *Wenhua Dageming Zhong De Renmin Jiefangjun (The PLA in the Cultural Revolution)*, Beijung, the CCP Historical Materials Press, 1989, p. 49.
106 Mao used a play on words, transforming the word ying mo (plot) into yang mo, yang meaning open, a combination of characters which had not been used before. He said: 'This was an open plot, not a secret one', quoted in Hei Yannan, op. cit., p. 175. He expressed the same view at the Central Committee meeting in October 1968. See Jin Chunming, op. cit., p. 11.
107 In his talk with Albanian visitors in September 1967, Mao said he was anxious to see great alliances establish themselves. But since it seemed impossible to do so, he would systematically promote them. See *Collection of CCP Documents* op. cit., p. 210.
108 Under the State Council, there were 37 ministries and commissions, as well as some 30 special offices and agencies. They were divided into administrative systems headed by a vice premier. For example, Chen Yi was in charge of the Foreign Affairs System which incorporated all ministries, special offices and agencies dealing with political and trade relations with foreign countries, as well as the foreign languages schools. Tan Zhenlin headed the agricultural and forestry system; Li Xiannian was in charge of the financial and trade system. Each system incorporated some schools. Kaplan, Frederic M., Sobin, Julian M.,

NOTES

Andors, Stephen, *Encyclopaedia of China Today*, New York, Eurasia Press, 1979, pp. 71–7.
109 Gao and Yan, op. cit., pp. 144, 145.
110 Ibid., 110; See also Robinson, Thomas W., *The Cultural Revolution in China*, California, California University Press, 1971, p. 222.
111 Li Ke and Hao Shengzhang, op. cit., pp. 231–5.
112 Wang Nianyi, *Dadongluan*, op. cit., p. 266.
113 Jin Chunming, op. cit., p. 84.
114 Ren Jian, op. cit., p. 165.
115 Interview with Yao Dengshan who was present at the meeting, Beijing, March 1991.
116 Ibid.
117 *Chronology*, op. cit., p. 361.
118 *Peking Review*, no. 32, 4 August 1967.
119 Zhang Yungsheng, *Maojiawan Jishi*, (*A Factual Account about Maojiawan*) Beijing, Spring and Autumn Press, 1988, p. 129.
120 Wang Nianyi, *Dadongluan*, op. cit., p. 267.
121 Ibid., p. 268.
122 Hei Yannan, op. cit., p. 227.
123 Ibid.
124 Myers, op. cit., pp. 276–7; Domes, Jürgen, 'The Role of the Military in the Formation of Revolutionary Committees, 1967–8', *The China Quarterly*, October-December 1970.
125 Li Ke and Hao Shengzhang, op. cit., pp. 226, 244; Joffe, Ellis, 'The Chinese Army after the Cultural Revolution: the Effects of Intervention', *The China Quarterly*, July-September 1973, p. 452.
126 Zheng Fulin, op. cit., p. 457.
127 *History of the Chinese Communist Party: a Chronology of Events (1919–1990)*, Beijing, Foreign Languages Press, 1991, p. 509; henceforth *History of the CCP*.
128 Military regions were named after the location of their headquarters and generally comprised military districts which were identical to the province in which they were located. See Nelson, Harvey, 'Military forces in the Cultural Revolution', *The China Quarterly*, July-September 1972, pp. 445, 446.
129 Ibid., p. 447.
130 Wang Nianyi, *Dadongluan*, op. cit., p. 24; Li Ke and Hao Shengzhang, op. cit., p. 24.
131 Ibid., p. 28.
132 Zhang Yunsheng, op. cit., p. 42.
133 Zheng Derong, op. cit., p. 411.
134 Li Ke and Hao Shengzhang, op. cit., pp. 33, 35.
135 *Red Flag*, no. 13, in *Peking Review*, no. 41, 1966.
136 Personal Notes.
137 Wang Nianyi, *Dadongluan*, op. cit., p 99.
138 Ibid., p. 119.
139 Zhang Yunsheng, op. cit., pp. 56–8.
140 Ibid., pp. 61–2.
141 Tie Zhuwei, *Chen Yi Yuanshuai Zai Wenhua Dageming Zhong* (*Mar-*

shal Chen Yi in the Cultural Revolution) Beijing, PLA Literary Press, 1986, pp. 123, 124.
142 Wang Nianyi, *Dadongluan*, op. cit., p. 151.
143 Tie Zhuwei, op. cit., pp. 109–11.
144 Wang Nianyi, *Dadongluan*, op. cit., p. 151.
145 Zhang Yunsheng, op. cit., p. 113.
146 Ibid., p. 123.
147 Ibid.
148 Ibid., p. 67.
149 Zheng Fulin, op. cit., p. 787.
150 Zhang Yungsheng, op. cit., pp. 118–9.
151 Wang Nianyi, *Dadongluan*, op. cit., p. 87.
152 Ibid., p. 97.
153 Tie Zhuwei, op. cit., p. 110.
154 Myers, op. cit., pp. 317–18.
155 Support to the revolutionary left and to industrial and agricultural production; military control and military training of students; see Jin Chunming, op. cit., p. 30.
156 Zhang Yunsheng, op. cit., pp. 83, 84.
157 Myers, op. cit., p. 319.
158 Joffe, op. cit., p. 454; Zhang Yunsheng, op. cit., p. 85.
159 Ibid., p. 76.
160 Myers, op. cit., pp. 320, 321.
161 Ibid.
162 Ibid., p. 322; Myers, op. cit., p. 323.
163 Zhang Yunsheng, op. cit., p. 87.
164 Liu Guokai, op. cit., p. 61.
165 Wang Nianyi, *Dadongluan*, op. cit., p. 202.
166 Liu Guokai, op. cit., p. 61.
167 Wang Nianyi, *Dadongluan*, op. cit., p. 204.
168 Robinson, Thomas W., 'The Wuhan incident', *The China Quarterly*, July-September 1971, p. 428.
169 Chen Zaidao, 'Wuhan 7.20 Shijian', (The Wuhan incident of July 20), in Peng Cheng, op. cit., p. 3.
170 Ibid.
171 Ibid., p. 4.
172 Ibid.
173 Zhang Yunsheng, op. cit., p. 96.
174 Ibid., p. 97; Liu Guokai, op. cit., p. 69.
175 Wang Nianyi, *Dadongluan*, op. cit., p. 218.
176 *People's Daily*, 2 April 1967.
177 Li Ke and Hao Shengzhang, op. cit., p. 49.
178 Myers, op. cit., pp. 323–4; Robinson, Thomas W., 'The Wuhan Incident', *The China Quarterly*, July-September 1971, p. 415.
179 Wang Nianyi, *Dadongluan*, op. cit., p. 259.
180 According to Western sources, the two emissaries of the central authorities, Wang Li and Xie Fuzhi, had been captured by the rebellious masses in cooperation with the military. We base most of our factual account about Wang Li's arrest and of the events

NOTES

in Wuhan on a recent publication of Chen Zaidao, then commander of the Wuhan military region, who provided a number of details about the dramatic occurrences at that time.
181 The radicals were represented by the workers' general headquarters, see footnote 168.
182 Chen Zaidao; op. cit., p. 5.
183 Robinson, *The China Quarterly*, op. cit., p. 418.
184 Gao and Yan, op. cit., p. 261.
185 Chen Zaidao, op. cit., p. 9.
186 Ibid., pp. 12, 14.
187 Ibid., pp. 15, 17, 18.
188 Wang Nianyi, *Dadongluan*, op. cit., p. 263.
189 Robinson, *The China Quarterly*, op. cit., p. 426.
190 Gao and Yan, op. cit., p. 265.
191 Ibid., p. 267; Wang Nianyi, *Dadongluan*, op. cit., p. 265.
192 Chen Zaidao, op. cit., p. 27.
193 Ibid., p. 22.
194 Wang Nianyi, *Dadongluan*, op. cit., p. 265.
195 Chen Zaidao, op. cit., p. 24.
196 *Peking Review* no. 32 1967.
197 *Mao's Selected Works* op. cit., vol. 4, p. 337.
198 Li Ke and Hao Shengzhang, op. cit., p. 237.
199 *People's Daily*, 10 March 1967.
200 Li Ke and Hao Shengzhang, op. cit., p. 237.
201 Ibid., p. 244; Joffe, op. cit., p. 456.
202 Ibid., p. 457

5 Fluctuations between order and disorder

1 *People's Daily*, 1 October 1967.
2 Liu Guokai, op. cit, p. 107.
3 *Peking Review*, no. 42, 13 October 1967.
4 Yu Gong, op. cit., p. 398.
5 *Peking Review*, no. 44, 27 October 1967.
6 Dong Baocun, *Yang Yu Fu Shijian Zhenxiang (The Truth about the Yang-Yu-Fu Event)*, Beijing, PLA Press, 1987, p. 75.
7 *Wuchan Jieji Wenhua Dageming Shengli Wansui (Long Live the Great Proletarian Cultural Revolution)*, The Chinese People's University, Beijing, Xinhua Printing House, 1969, pp. 254, 255.
8 Liu Guokai, op. cit., p. 105.
9 *Peking Review*, no. 40, 29 September 1967.
10 Ibid.
11 *People's Daily*, 19 October, 1967.
12 *People's Daily*, 22 December 1967.
13 Liu Guokai, op. cit., p. 118.
14 *Red Flag*, no. 3, 1967.
15 Ye Yonglie, *Wang Hongwen*, op. cit., pp. 210, 218.
16 Ibid., 246.

17 Harding, Harry, *Organising China: the Problem of Bureaucracy, 1949–1976*, Stanford, Stanford University Press, 1981, p. 251.
18 Gao and Yan, op. cit., p. 442.
19 Shanxi, 19 January; Heilongjiang, 31 January, Shandong, 3 February, Guizhou, 14 February, Zheng Derong, op. cit., p. 419.
20 Shanghai, 24 February, ibid.
21 Hong Yung Lee, op. cit., pp. 216, 217.
22 Wang Nianyi, *Dadongluan*, op. cit., p. 271.
23 *Chronology*, op. cit., p. 366.
24 *Peking Review*, no. 37, 13 September 1968.
25 *People's Daily*, 19 October 1967.
26 Su Caiqing, op. cit., p. 186.
27 *Collection of CCP Documents*, op. cit., p. 218.
28 *Chronology*, op. cit., p. 365.
29 Zheng Derong, op. cit., p. 450.
30 *Peking Review*, no. 35, 30 August 1968.
31 Wang Nianyi, *Dadongluan*, op. cit., p. 304.
32 Tan Zongji, op. cit., p. 146.
33 *People's Daily*, 12 December 1968.
34 Tan Zongji, op. cit., p. 149.
35 Hei Yannan, op. cit., p. 226.
36 Gurtov, Melvin, 'The foreign ministry and foreign affairs in the Chinese Cultural Revolution', *The China Quarterly*, October-December 1969, p. 94; *Collection of CCP Documents*, op. cit., pp. 414–17.
37 Wang Nianyi, *Dadongluan*, op. cit., 279.
38 Xie Fuzhi was at that time the head of the Beijing municipal revolutionary committee, Gao and Yan, op. cit., p. 269.
39 Wang Nianyi, *Dadongluan*, op. cit., p. 281.
40 Ibid., p. 279.
41 Ibid., p. 284.
42 Chen Yi exculpated himself with these declarations, but the authors of the poster had to make self-criticism in a series of meetings, see Gurtov, op. cit., p. 94.
43 Dong Baocun, *Yang Yu Fu Shijian Zhenxiang (The Truth about the Yang Yu Fu Event)* Beijing, PLA Press, p. 31.
44 Ibid., pp. 15, 24, 27.
45 Myers, op. cit., vol. 1, pp. 383–7.
46 Ibid.
47 Ibid.
48 Ibid.
49 Dong Baocun, op. cit., pp. 8, 9.
50 Ibid.
51 Years later, at a meeting of the CMC on 21 December 1973, Mao admitted that he had listened to Lin Biao's one-sided opinion on Yang, Yu and Fu, and that they had been wrongly accused. The three generals were formally rehabilitated in July 1974.
52 *Zhongguo Renmin Jiefangjun Jiangshuai Minglu (Who is Who in the PLA?)*, Beijing, PLA Press, 1986, p. 90.

NOTES

53 Dong Baocun, op. cit., p. 47; Ji Xichen, *Diaoyutaide Fengbo, (Storm at Diaoyutai)*, in Yu Gong, op. cit., pp. 27, 28.
54 Dong Baocun, op. cit., p. 47; Ji Xichen, op. cit., p. 31.
55 Ibid.
56 Ji Xichen, op. cit., pp. 32, 33.
57 The four officials were Wang Fei, Zhou Yuchi, Liu Peifeng, and Yu Xingye.
58 Ji Xichen, op. cit., pp 34, 35.
59 Zhang Yunsheng, op. cit., pp. 142–4.
60 Dong Baocun, op. cit., p. 133; during the process of Yu's rehabilitation after Lin Biao's death, it was established that Yu had never been arrested by the Guomindang, ibid,; see also Ladany, op. cit., p. 316.
61 Hei Yannan, op. cit., p. 252.
62 Dong Baocun, op. cit., pp. 98–103.
63 Yang, Yu and Fu were kept in custody until 1974. During the years of imprisonment, Yang lost three members of his family, including his daughter Yang Yi who had been accused of an illicit love affair, *Xinhua Wenzhai*, no. 12, 1985.
64 Jin Chunming, op. cit., pp. 243, 244; Wang Nianyi, *Dadongluan*, op. cit., p. 297.
65 *Chronology*, op. cit., pp. 367–8; Hao and Duan, op. cit., p. 601.
66 Ibid.
67 Wang Nianyi, *Dadongluan*, op. cit., p. 311.
68 Ibid., p. 312.
69 Zhang Yunsheng, op. cit., p. 198.
70 Wang Nianyi, *Dadongluan*, op. cit., p. 313.
71 Zhang Yunsheng, op. cit., p. 200.
72 Wang Nianyi, *Dadongluan*, op. cit., p. 313.
73 Ibid.
74 *People's Daily*, 1 November, 1968.
75 Qin Xiaoying, op. cit., p. 191.
76 Wang Nianyi, *Dadongluan*, op. cit., p. 315.
77 Myers, op. cit., pp. 68, 69.
78 Schram, *Unrehearsed*, op. cit., pp. 282, 289.
79 Wang Nianyi, *Dadongluan*, op. cit., p. 323.
80 Copy of Zhou Enlai's Speech, Fairbank Centre, Harvard University.
81 Copy of Lin Biao's Speech, Fairbank Centre, Harvard University.
82 *History of the CCP*, op. cit., p. 346.
83 Ibid., p. 347.
84 Ibid.
85 Hao and Duan, op. cit., p. 606.
86 See Hong Yung Lee, op. cit., pp. 288–95, who offers a rather detailed description of the campaign which is based primarily on official proclamations and red guard material.
87 *People's Daily*, 26 August 1968.
88 *Mao's Selected Works*, op. cit., vol. 5, p. 454.
89 Wang Nianyi, op. cit., p. 299.

90 *People's Daily*, 1 January, 1968.
91 Jin Chunming, op. cit., p. 242.
92 Wang Nianyi, op. cit., p. 193.
93 *Records of New China*, op. cit., p. 420.
94 *Mao's Selected Works*, vol. 3, op. cit., p. 117.
95 They were the general knitwear mill; the Xinhua printing house; the no. 3 chemical works; the February 2nd rolling mill; the northern suburb timber mill; the Nankou rolling mill, Qinghua and Beijing University, Jin Chunming, op. cit., p. 79.
96 *Xinhua News Agency*, no. 1,220, 1968.
97 Gao and Yan, op. cit., pp. 298–301.
98 Ibid., p. 299.
99 Ibid., p. 301.
100 Wang Nianyi, *Dadongluan*, op. cit., p. 331.
101 Jin Chunming, op. cit., p. 79.
102 Gao and Yan, op. cit., pp. 163, 164.
103 Wang Nianyi, *Dadongluan*, op. cit., p. 225.
104 *Chinese Law and Government*, op. cit., vol. 9, no. 3, 1976, p. 143.
105 Jin Chunming, op. cit., p. 78.
106 Hao and Duan, op. cit., p. 595.
107 Jin Chunming, op. cit., pp. 25, 26.
108 Ibid., p. 61.
109 Ibid., pp. 120, 121.
110 Ibid., p. 152.
111 Ibid., p. 153.
112 Ibid., p. 373.
113 Ibid., p. 386.
114 The term does not only refer to academic circles but also to those in any work unit who were competent but not 'red'.
115 Wang Nianyi, *Dadongluan*, op. cit., p. 315.
116 Ibid., p. 318.
117 *People's Daily*, 1 January, 1969.
118 Jin Chunming, op. cit., p. 4.
119 Ibid.
120 Wang Nianyi, *Dadongluan*, op. cit., p. 337.
121 Gao and Yan, op. cit., p. 315.
122 Yao Wenyuan's article on Tao Zhu's book, *People's Daily*, 8 September 1967.
123 Gurtov, op. cit., p. 86.
124 *People's Daily*, 8 September 1967.
125 See for example Jack Chen, *Inside the CR*, London, Sheldon Press, 1976, pp. 268–9; 330–41; 291–2; Ladany, op. cit., pp. 307–10; Hong Yung Lee, op. cit., p. 202; Burton, Barry, 'The Cultural Revolution's Ultraleft Conspiracy: The May 16 Group', *Asian Survey* no. 11, November 1971; *The Cambridge History of China*, vol. 15, p. 185.
126 Jin Chunming, op. cit., p. 101.
127 Ibid., p. 102.
128 Hei Yannan, op. cit., p. 195.
129 Wang Nianyi, op. cit., p. 271.

130 Gao and Yan, op. cit., p. 290.
131 Ibid.
132 *Peking Review* no. 38, 15 September, 1967.
133 Jin Chunming, op. cit., p. 313.
134 Wang Nianyi, *Dadongluan*, op. cit., p. 338; Hao and Duan, op. cit., p. 609.
135 Personal Notes.
136 Jin Chunming, op. cit., p. 314.
137 Personal Notes.
138 Wang Nianyi, *Dadongluan*, op. cit., p. 273.
139 *United Times*, 23 December, 1988.
140 Hei Yannan, op. cit., p. 198.
141 See Western accounts of Yao Dengshan's seizure of power in the foreign ministry in Gurtov, op. cit.; *The Cambridge History of China* vol. 15, p. 185. Interviewing Yao Dengshan in Beijing in March 1989, the authors were shown a copy of the foreign ministry document in which the widepsread accusations against Yao were refuted.
142 Interview with Zhang Dianqing, former rebel leader of the foreign ministry, Beijing, March 1989.

6 The Lin Biao affair

1 *Peking Review*, no. 18, 30 April 1969.
2 MacFarqhuar, in *The Cambridge History of China*, vol. 15, op. cit., p. 313.
3 Bridgham, Philip, 'The fall of Lin Biao', *The China Quarterly*, no. 55, 1973, p. 428.
4 Kau, M. Y. M., *The Lin Biao Affair*, New York, The International Sciences Press, 1975, p. xxii.
5 See Chapter 5.
6 Kau, op. cit., p. xxxii; Li and Hao, op. cit., p. 244.
7 Lin Biao's speech on 14 September, 1969, Fairbank Center Library Collection.
8 Myers, op. cit., p. 154.
9 Kau, op. cit., Introduction.
10 Myers, op. cit., p. 149.
11 Zheng Fulin, op. cit., pp. 772–5.
12 Ibid., pp. 783–90.
13 Li and Hao, op. cit., p. 355.
14 Ibid., p. 364.
15 Ibid., p. 356.
16 Zhang Yunsheng, op. cit., p. 305.
17 Ibid., p. 119.
18 Lin Qungshan, *Lin Biao Zhuan*, op. cit., p. 337; Yu Gong, op. cit., p. 262.
19 Zhang Yunsheng, op. cit., p. 5.
20 Ibid., p. 21.

21 Yu Gong, op. cit., p. 249.
22 Zhang Yunsheng, op. cit., p. 370.
23 Ibid.
24 Kau, op. cit., pp. 328–31; Zhang Yunsheng, op. cit., p. 45.
25 See Chapter 5.
26 Zhang Yunsheng, op. cit., p. 374.
27 Ibid., p. 13.
28 Ibid., p. 46.
29 *Shidai Baogao (Report about an Era)*, no. 4, 1980.
30 Lin Qingshan, *Lin Biao*, op. cit., pp. 433, 447.
31 Myers, op. cit., vol. 2, p. 162.
32 Ibid., p. 161; Wang Nianyi, *Dadongluan*, op. cit., p. 441.
33 *Selected Works of Mao*, op. cit., vol. 2, p. 224.
34 Li and Hao, op. cit., p. 242.
35 *Peking Review*, no. 23, 1967.
36 Hei Yannan, op. cit., pp. 104–6; Lin Qingshan, *Jiang Qing*, op. cit., pp. 376, 377.
37 Zhang Yunsheng, op. cit., p. 177.
38 Ye Yonglie, *Zhang Chunqiao*, op. cit., p. 233.
39 Wang Nianyi, *Dadongluan*, op. cit., p. 383.
40 Ibid.; Yu Gong, op. cit., p. 337.
41 Myers, vol. 1, op. cit., pp. 386–7.
42 Yu Gong, op. cit., pp. 311, 312.
43 Zhang Yunsheng, op. cit., p. 157.
44 Wang Nianyi, 'Guanyu Eryue Niliu,' op. cit., p. 77.
45 Zhang Yunsheng, op. cit., p. 299.
46 Yu Gong, op. cit., p. 299.
47 Li and Hao, op. cit., pp. 235, 236.
48 Zhang Yunsheng, op. cit., p. 202.
49 Hei Yannan, op. cit., pp. 287–8; Zhang Yunsheng, op. cit., p. 205.
50 Zhang Yunsheng, op. cit., p. 209.
51 Ibid., p. 219.
52 Wang Nianyi, 'Some facts about the February Adverse Current', op. cit.
53 Hei Yannan, op. cit., p. 145.
54 Lin Qingshan, *Lin Biao*, op. cit., p. 613, 617.
55 Ibid.
56 Hu Sheng, op. cit., pp. 447, 448; Wang Nianyi, *Dadongluan*, op. cit., p. 323.
57 *Chronology*, op. cit., p. 372; Zhang Yunsheng, op. cit., p. 316.
58 *Chronology*, op. cit., p. 373, Wang Nianyi, *Dadongluan*, op. cit., p. 363.
59 Ibid.
60 Zhang Yunsheng, op. cit., p. 189.
61 Jia Sinan, *Mao Zedong Renji Jiaowang Shilu*, (*Mao's Relations with Other people*) Jiangsu, Jiangsu Literary and Art Press, 1989, p. 273; Myers, op. cit., vol. 2, p. 154.
62 *Quotations*, op. cit., Introduction.

63 Yu Nan, 'Lin Biao Jituan Xingwang Chutan' (A study of the rise and fall of the Lin Biao group), in *Critical Comments after Ten Years*, op. cit., p. 87.
64 Wang Nianyi, op. cit., p. 398.
65 Lin Qingshan, *Lin Biao*, op. cit., p. 686.
66 Ibid., p. 687.
67 Zhang Yunsheng, op. cit., p. 384.
68 Ibid.
69 Ibid.
70 Lin Qingshan, *Lin Biao*, op. cit., p. 688.
71 Wang Nianyi, op. cit., p. 394.
72 MacFarquhar, in *The Cambridge History of China*, op. cit., vol. 15, pp. 314, 315; Bridgham, op. cit., p. 433.
73 Lin Qingshan, *Lin Biao*, op. cit., p. 688.
74 Interview with Lin Liheng in *The Mirror*, (Hong Kong), no. 6, 1988.
75 Yu Gong, op. cit., p. 293.
76 *The Cambridge History of China*, vol. 15, op. cit., p. 317; Wang Nianyi, op. cit., p. 396.
77 Hao and Duan, op. cit., p. 614; Zhu Zhongli, *Nuhuangmeng: Jiang Qing Waizhuan (The Dream of an Empress: an Unofficial Biography of Jiang Qing)*, Beijing, The Oriental Press, 1988, p. 405.
78 Shao Yihai, *Lianhe Jiandui De Fumie, (The Collapse of the Joint Fleet)*, Henan, Spring and Autumn Press, 1988, p. 82.
79 Hao and Duan, op. cit., pp. 614, 615.
80 Tie Zhuwei, op. cit., p. 256.
81 Lin Qinshan, *Lin Biao*, op. cit., p. 696.
82 Wang Nianyi, *Dadongluan*, op. cit., p. 399.
83 A summary of the discussions was published by the secretariat of the Plenum in *Brief Report*, no. 6 of the North China Group, quoted in Wang Nianyi, *Dadongluan*, op. cit., pp. 400–1.
84 Both Yang Dezhi and Zhang Chunqiao belonged to the East China Group. Interview with Yang Dezhi in 1983, when he was General Chief of Staff; quoted by Tie Zhuwei, op. cit., p. 257.
85 Ye Yonglie, op. cit., p. 257.
86 Yu Nan, op. cit., p. 91.
87 Shao Yihai, op. cit., p. 90.
88 Yu Nan, op. cit., p. 90.
89 Lin Qingshan, *Lin Biao*, op. cit., p. 708.
90 Wang Nianyi, op. cit., p. 403.
91 Yu Gong, op. cit., p. 88.
92 Zhou Enlai, *Report on the Work of the Government*, Beijing, Foreign Languages Publishing House, 1975, p. 6.
93 Bridgham, op. cit., p. 434.
94 Schram, *Mao Talks to the People*, op. cit., p. 295.
95 Hao and Duan, op. cit., p. 619.
96 Lin Qingshan, *Lin Biao*, op. cit., p. 716.
97 Lin Biao, *Political Report*, op. cit., p. 105.
98 Wang Nianyi, *Dadongluan*, op. cit., p. 323.

99 Ibid, p. 400.
100 'Directive concerning the transmission of Chen Boda's anti-Party problem', quoted in Hao and Duan, op. cit., p. 617.
101 Zhang Yunsheng, op. cit., p. 182.
102 Hao and Duan, op. cit., p.618.
103 Li and Hao, op. cit., p. 120.
104 Wang Nianyi, *Dadongluan*, op. cit., pp. 408–9.
105 Ibid., p. 414.
106 Harding, op. cit., pp. 302–3.
107 Wang Nianyi, *Dadongluan*, op. cit., p. 415.
108 Kau, op. cit., p. 65; Li and Hao, op. cit., p. 122.
109 Schram, *Mao Talks to the People*, op. cit., p. 295.
110 Ibid., p. 295; Ladany, op. cit., p. 335.
111 Hao and Duan, op. cit., p. 618.
112 Ibid., p. 618.
113 Wang Nianyi, *Dadongluan*, op. cit., p. 404.
114 Xiong Xianghui was a high-ranking official at the headquarters of the general chief of staff in charge of international relations who acted as Zhou's assistant during the talks with Henry Kissinger.
115 *Xin Guancha*, (*New Observer*), Beijing, no. 10, 1986.
116 *Chinese Law and Government*, vol. 6, no. 2, 1973.
117 Snow, Edgar, *The Long Revolution*, New York, Vintage Books, 1973, p. 169.
118 Dong Baocun, *Zai Lishi Xuanwozhong (In the Whirlpools of History)* Beijing, Foreign Culture Publishing Company, 1990 p. 44.
119 Shram, *Mao talks to the People*, op. cit., p. 293.
120 Snow, op. cit., p. 169.
121 Wang Nianyi, op. cit., p. 315.
122 Ross, Robert, 'From Lin Biao to Deng Xiaoping: Elite Instability and China's US policy,' *The China Quarterly*, June 1989, p. 268; Dittmer, *Revolution*, op. cit., pp. 112–4.
123 *Chinese Communist Affairs: Facts and Features*, vol. 1, no. 3, 29 November 1967, pp. 24–5.
124 Dong Baocun, *Zai Linhi*, op. cit., p. 45.
125 Myers, op. cit., vol. 2, p. 162.
126 Ibid., pp. 157–63; Schram, *Mao Talks to the People*, op. cit., pp. 290–9.
127 Schram, *Mao Talks to the People*, op. cit., p. 293.
128 Ibid., p. 294.
129 Ibid.
130 Ibid.
131 Ibid.
132 Ibid.
133 Gardner, John, *Chinese Politics and the Succession to Mao*, London, Macmillan Press, 1982, p. 53; Yu Gong, op. cit., p. 130.
134 Ibid.
135 Gardner, op. cit., p. 56, Yu Gong, op. cit., p. 131.

136 Lin Qingshan, *Lin Biao*, op. cit., p. 821; Zhang Yunsheng, op. cit., p. 256.
137 Gardner, op. cit., pp. 41, 42.
138 Kau, op. cit., pp. 326–8.
139 Interview with Ji Dengkui who was in charge of arresting the members of the joint fleet after Lin Biao's death; in Guo Simin, ed. *Wo Yanzhong De Mao Zedong (Mao As I Saw Him)*, Hebei, Hebei People's Press, 1990, p. 256. The core members were: Lin Liguo, Lin Biao's son and deputy director of the PLA air force general office and operations department, commander of the joint fleet; Zhou Yuchi, deputy director of the air force general office; Wang Fei, deputy chief of staff of the air force, Chen Liyun, alternate member of the CC, political commissar of the air force 5th army in Zhejiang Province; Wang Weiguo, alternate member of the CC, political commissar of the air force 4th army in Shanghai; Zhou Jianping, deputy commander of the Nanjing military region air force; Gu Tongzhou, chief of staff of the Guangzhou military region air force.
140 Gao and Yan, p. 361; Yu Gong, op. cit., pp. 57–8.
141 The letters *wu qi yi* are a homonym for armed uprising (*wuzhuang qi yi*).
142 Another, less plausible version claims that Yu Xinye forgot his note book in a building of the air force institute in Beijing which the joint fleet used for their meetings. Shao Yihai, op. cit., p. 105.
143 Myers, vol. 2., op. cit., pp. 147–8.
144 Ibid.
145 Ibid., p. 150.
146 Li and Hao, op. cit., p. 365.
147 Lin Qingshan, *Lin Biao*, op. cit., p. 779.
148 Ibid., p. 797.
149 Ibid., p. 799.
150 Ibid., pp. 800, 801.
151 Ibid., p. 815.
152 Ibid., p. 816.
153 Ibid., pp. 820–1.
154 Yu Gong, op. cit., pp. 130–1.
155 Ibid.
156 Ibid., p. 132.
157 The investigation after Lin Biao's death revealed that they had not been informed of Lin Biao's plans.
158 Lin Qingshan, *Lin Biao*, op. cit., p. 836.
159 In 1975, Ding Sheng was appointed commander of the Nanjing military region, and Lui Xiangyuang became commander of the Chengdu military region, see: Li and Hao, op. cit., p. 356.
160 Yu Gong, op. cit., p. 149.
161 Lin Liheng, Lin Biao's daughter; Zhang Ning, Lin Liguo's fiancée; Liu Jichun, deputy section chief of the 8341 unit; Li Wenpu, Lin Biao's secretary in charge of security; Jiang Zuoshou, leader of the 8341 unit in Beidaihe; Yu Rentang, deputy leader of the 8341

unit in Beidaihe, Xiao Zhang, Xiao Chen, both Lin Biao's private attendants. The accounts were collected by Shao Yihai, op. cit., and by Yu Gong, op. cit.
162 Yu Gong, op. cit., pp. 111–12; Lin Qingshan, *Lin Biao*, op. cit., pp. 784–6.
163 Yu Gong, op. cit., pp. 232–5.
164 Lin Qingshan, *Lin Biao*, op. cit., p. 846.
165 Ibid., p. 848, Gardner, op. cit., p. 57.
166 Li Desheng, 'Huainian Zhou Zongli' ('In memory of comrade Zhou Enlai'), *People's Daily*, 17 March 1988; Lin Qing, *Zhou Enlai, Zaixiang Shengya (Zhou Enlai's Premiership)*, Beijing, Great Wall Cultural Press, 1991, pp. 202–4.
167 Yu Gong, op. cit., p. 141.
168 Li Desheng, op. cit., Lin Qing, op. cit., p. 205.
169 Li Desheng, op. cit., p. 207; Lin Qing, op. cit., p. 207.
170 Ibid., p. 208.
171 Ibid., p. 218.
172 Guo Simin, op. cit., p. 255.
173 Fu Hao, 'Guanyu Jiuyaosan Shijian' ('About the September 13th event); *Zhonggong Dangshi Fengyunlu (Major Events in the History of the Chinese Communist Party)* Beijing, People's Publishing House, 1990, p. 385. The author was then vice minister in the foreign ministry.
174 Ibid., pp. 386, 387.
175 Xu Wenyi, 'Lin Biao Jihui Renwang Xiangchang Ji', ('On the spot investigation of the crash of Lin Biao's plane), in Yu Gong, op. cit., pp. 155, 161, 162, 170.
176 Wang Nianyi, *Dadongluan*, op. cit., pp. 435, 463.
177 The latter two were later rehabilitated, interview with a former PLA officer, Beijing, March 1989.
178 These two categories involved a large number of persons.
179 Li and Hao, op. cit., p. 140.
180 Lin Qingshan, *Lin Biao*, op. cit., pp. 881–3.
181 Lin Liheng's relevations in: *Mirror*, no. 6, 1988.
182 Wang Nianyi, *Dadongluan*, op. cit., p. 437.
183 Zhang Yufeng, 'Mao Zedong Zhou Enlai Wannian Ersan Shi' ('A few things about Mao Zedong's and Zhou Enlai's last years'), *Yanhuang Zisun, (Offspring of Emperors Yan and Huang)* Beijing, no. 1, 1989.

7 Final power struggles

1 *People's Daily*, 14 July 1964.
2 They were Lin Biao, Ye Qun, Chen Boda, Huang Yongsheng, Wu Faxian, Li Zuopeng, Qiu Huizuo.
3 Zheng Fulin, op. cit., p. 748.
4 Zhang was the only person other than Mao, who was mentioned

NOTES

in Lin Liguo's 'project 571' as a target of elimination; Myers, op. cit., vol. 2, p. 152.
5   Ye Yonglie, *Wang Hongwen* op. cit., p. 382.
6   Zhang Chunqiao headed the committee. Deputy directors were in order of importance: Yao Wenyuan, Xu Jingxian, Liao Zhengguo, Wang Shaoyong, Ma Tianshui, Wang Hongwen. Ibid.
7   Ibid., pp. 22–6.
8   Ibid.
9   Ibid., p. 85.
10 Ibid., p. 265.
11 Ibid., p. 266.
12 Wang Ruoshui, *Cong Pizuo Daoxiang Fangyou, (From Criticism of the Left to the Opposition of the Right)*, Hong Kong, *Mingbao*, no. 3, 1989.
13 Ibid.
14 Hua was transferred from Hunan to Beijing; Wu De was director of the Beijing municipal revolutionary committee.
15 Ye Yonglie, *Zhang Chunqiao*, op. cit., p. 267.
16 Ye Yonglie, *Wang Hongwen*, op. cit., p. 389.
17 Hu Sheng, op. cit., p. 458.
18 *The 10th National Congress of the CCP*, Peking, Foreign Languages Press, 1973, p. 6.
19 Ibid., p. 62.
20 Wich, Richard, 'The Tenth Party Congress: the power structure and the succession question', *The China Quarterly*, no. 58, 1974, p. 12; *Chronology*, op. cit., p. 385.
21 Cong Jin, op. cit., p. 500.
22 *Chronology* op. cit., p. 385.
23 Zheng Fulin, op. cit., pp. 749–52.
24 *Chronology* op. cit., p. 386.
25 Ibid.
26 *People's Daily*, 1 January 1972.
27 Lin Qingshan, *Lin Biao*, op. cit., p. 62; Jian Sinan, op. cit., p. 269.
28 Wang Ruoshui, op. cit.
29 Lu Xingdou, ed., *Zhou Enlai He Tade Shiye, (Zhou Enlai and His Cause)*, Beijing, CCp History Publishing House, 1990, p. 597.
30 *People's Daily*, 24 April, 1972.
31 Zheng Derong, op. cit., p. 513.
32 Lu Xingdou, op. cit., p. 600.
33 Ibid.
34 *People's Daily*, 22 July, 1968.
35 Lu Xingdou, op. cit., p. 597.
36 Gao and Yan, op. cit., p. 471.
37 *People's Daily*, 17.3.1988.
38 *Mingbao*, no. 3, 1989.
39 Ibid., p. 7.
40 *Chronology*, op. cit., p. 383.
41 *Mingbao*, no. 3, 1989.

42 King Wen appears in early Chinese historical writings as a paragon of benevolence and wisdom, Hucker, op. cit., p. 31.
43 Wang Nianyi, op. cit., pp. 474, 475.
44 Peng Cheng, op. cit., p. 37.
45 Refers to Qin Shihuang.
46 Refers to a book by Guo Moruo.
47 Zihou refers to Liu Zhongyuan, 773–819, an official and scholar of the Tang dynasty who wrote a 'dissertation on the system of principalities' to praise Qin Shihuang. King Wen of the Western Zhou dynasty practised this system'.
48 The 571 project equates Mao to Qin Shihuang as the greatest feudal despot in Chinese history, Mryes, op. cit., vol. 2, p. 148.
49 Peng Cheng, op. cit., p. 39.
50 Gao and Yan, op. cit., p. 489.
51 'Confucianism and Confucious; reactionary thought', *Beijing Daily*, 4 September 1973; 'On revering Confucianism and opposing legality', *Beijing Daily*, 15 September 1973; 'The progressive role played by Qin Shihuang', *Beijing Daily*, 7 September 1973; 'The struggle between restoration and counter-revolution in the course of founding the Qin Dynasty', *Red Flag* 12 October 1973.
52 Wang Hongwen and Zhang Chunqiao were members of the Standing Committee of the Politburo, Jiang Qing and Yao Wenyuan were members of the Politburo, thus politically less important. Yet, Jiang Qing dominated the group of four.
53 Hao and Duan, op. cit., p. 633.
54 Ibid., p. 634.
55 Gao and Yan, op. cit., p. 496.
56 Ibid., p. 497.
57 Jin Chunming, op. cit., p. 41.
58 Gao and Yan, op. cit., p. 498.
59 Li and Hao, op. cit., p. 168.
60 Ibid., p. 170.
61 Ibid., p. 171.
62 *Mao's Selected Works* op. cit., vol. 4, p. 428.
63 Gao and Yan, op. cit., p. 506.
64 Later Feng described the motivation which had led him on that course, in a self-critical book. see: Gao and Yan, op. cit., pp. 506, 507.
65 *The Cambridge History of China*, op. cit., vol. 12, pp. 354, 372.
66 *Mao's Selected Works*, vol. 5, pp. 121–9.
67 Wang Nianyi, *Dadongluan*, op. cit., p. 498.
68 Ibid.
69 Zhou Gong, duke of Zhou, was a statesman of the Western Zhou dynasty – 11th century to 770 BC – who had formulated a large number of the rules and regulations established during that dynasty.
70 Zhou was the head of the central investigation group of the Lin Biao affairs set up in October 1971. see: Wang Nianyi, *Dadongluan*, op. cit., p. 435.

71 *Chronology* op. cit., p. 385.
72 Peng Cheng, op. cit., p. 38.
73 Hao and Duan, op. cit., p. 632.
74 Lin Qingshan, 'Sirenbang Zuguo Meng De Pomie', ('The failure of the gang of four to seize power'), *Mao Zedong Sixiang Yanjui, (Study of Mao Zedong, Thought)*, Sichuan Academy of Social Sciences, no. 3, 1988.
75 Peng Cheng, op. cit., p. 38.
76 According to Mao, ten 'struggles of line' had so far occurred in the history of the party,. The struggle with Liu Shaoqi was the 9th, the one with Lin Biao was the 10th struggle of line.
77 Wang Nianyi, op. cit., p. 471.
78 Ibid.
79 'Confucius, what kind of man was he?', *Red Flag*, 1 April 1974.
80 Confucius never held such a post.
81 *Beijing Daily*, 17 May 1974.
82 Zhou could not straighten his right arm which had been injured in Yannan in the 1940s, thus he usually held it in front of his waist.
83 Zhu Zhongli, op. cit., p. 463.
84 *Xuexi Yu Pipan (Study and Criticism)*, Shanghai, no. 4, 1973.
85 Zhu Zhongli, op. cit., p. 463.
86 Wang Nianyi, *Dadongluan*, op. cit., p. 484.
87 Gao and Yan, op. cit., p. 503.
88 Schram, *Mao Zedong*, op. cit., p. 71.
89 Dittmer, Lowell and Chen Ruoxi, *Ethics and Rhetoric of the Chinese Cultural Revolution*, Berkeley, University of California Press, 1981, p. 50.
90 Jin Chunming, op. cit., p. 43.
91 Zheng Derong, op. cit., p. 527.
92 The 10th Party Congress, op. cit., p. 19.
93 Gao and Yan, op. cit., pp. 481–2; Jin Chunming, op. cit., p. 170.
94 Ibid., pp 70–1.
95 Zheng Derong, op. cit., pp. 537–8.
96 Hao and Duan, pp. 636–7.
97 To put a hat on someone's head means to attribute a negative political label to him. See Peng Cheng, op. cit., p. 42.
98 Ibid., p 43.
99 Zhang Yufeng, op. cit., p. 6.
100 *People's Daily*, 22 July, 1978.
101 Ye Yonglie, *Wang Hongwen*, op. cit., p. 408.
102 Ibid., p. 409.
103 Wang Nianyi, op. cit., p. 510; Peng Cheng, op. cit., p. 45; Zhou Ming, op. cit., vol. 1, p. 75.
104 Former secretary of the CC general office and then one of Jiang Qing's principal assistants.
105 Former chief of the propaganda section of the 8341 troops and then Party secretary of Qinghua University.
106 Hao and Duan, op. cit., p. 638.

107 Ibid.
108 Lin Qingshan, *Jiang Qing*, op. cit., p. 704.
109 Zhou Ming, vol. 1, p. 75.
110 Ibid., vol. I. p. 76.
111 Ye Yonglie, *Wang Hongwen*, op. cit., pp. 413–15.
112 Uli Franz, *Deng Xiaoping, Biographie*, Paris, Ciel 12 Fixot, 1989, p. 221.
113 Lin Qingshan, *Fengyun Shinianyu Deng Xiaoping, (Deng Xiaoping in the Storm of Ten Years)* Beijing, PLA Press, 1989, p. 216.
114 *History of the CCP*, op. cit., p. 382.
115 Hao and Duan, op. cit., p. 624.
116 Ibid., p. 629.
117 Ibid., pp. 632–3.
118 Peng Cheng, op. cit., p. 47.
119 Ye Yonglie, *Wang Hongwen*, op. cit., p. 406.
120 Sabatier, op. cit., p. 190.
121 The cemetery for prominent persons outside Bejing.
122 See a different version in Harding, *The Cambridge History of China*, vol. 15, p. 178.
123 Zhang Yufeng, op. cit., p. 4.
124 Li and Hao, op. cit., p. 214.
125 Ibid. He Long died in custody in June 1969.
126 Dong Baocun, op. cit., p. 135.
127 Jia Sinan, op. cit., p. 319.
128 Deng's letter and Mao's comment were distributed to the central leadership. See: Lin Qingshan, *Deng Xiaoping*, op. cit., p. 268.
129 Ye Yonglie, *Wang Hongwen* op. cit., p. 420.
130 Ibid., 422.
131 Peng Cheng, op. cit., p. 46.
132 Ibid., p. 43.
133 Tan Zongji, op. cit., p. 104.
134 Wang Nianyi, op. cit., p. 519.
135 Liu Suinian and Wu Qungan, *Wenhua Dageming Shiqide Guomin Jinji (The National Economy During the Cultural Revolution)*, Harbin, Helongjiang People's Publishing House, 1986, p. 76.
136 Ibid.
137 Ibid., p. 78.
138 Hao and Duan, op. cit., p. 637.
139 *Report On The Work of the Government*, Beijing, The Commercial Press, 1975, p. 16.
140 *Deng Xiaoping Wenxuan, 1975–1982 (Selected Works of Deng Xiaoping)*, Beijing, People's Publishing House, 1983, pp. 1–43.
141 Ibid., p. 32.
142 Deng Xiaoping, op. cit., p. 4.
143 Liu Suinan and Wu Qungan, *China's Socialist Economy: an Outline History (1949–1984)* Beijing, Beijing Review, 1986, p. 396.
144 Deng Xiaoping, op. cit., pp. 8–11.
145 Liu and Wu, *China's Socialist Economy*, op. cit., p. 397.

146 Li and Hao, op. cit., p. 152.
147 Deng Xiaoping, op. cit., p. 15.
148 Li and Hao, op. cit., pp. 150, 158.
149 Tan Zongji, op. cit., p. 192; Liu and Wu, op. cit., pp. 398–9.
150 Sabatier, op. cit., p. 194; Liu and Wu, *China's Socialist Economy* op. cit., p. 399.
151 Tan Zongji, op. cit., p. 118.
152 Wang Nianyi, *Dadongluan*, op. cit., pp. 521, 522; Dittmer, *Revolution*, op. cit., pp. 200–1.
153 Rodzinsky, op. cit., p. 193, Tan Zongji, op. cit., p. 123.
154 *Chronology*, op. cit., p. 158.
155 'Home going legions' were armed contingents organised by landlords in rural areas to reclaim their land after it had been confiscated by peasant uprisings.
156 Lin Qingshan, *Deng Xiaoping*, op. cit., pp. 363, 364; Sabatier, op. cit., p. 199.
157 Peng Cheng, op. cit., p. 48.
158 *History of the CCP*, op. cit., p. 365.
159 Ibid. p. 367.
160 *People's Daily* 1 March 1975, 1 April, 1975.
161 Wang Nianyi, *Dadongluan*, op. cit., p. 538.
162 *People's Daily*, 1 March 1975; a fortified village is a term used by Mao to describe the villages held by armed contingents organised by local authorities in the 1930s. *Selected Works of Mao*, vol. 4, p. 20.
163 Hao and Duan, op. cit., p. 645.
164 Yang Zhongwei, *Zhunyi Huiyi Yu Yannan Zhengfeng*, (The Zhunyi Conference and the Yannan Rectification Campaign), Hong Kong, Benma Press, 1988, p. 289.
165 Rodzinsky, op. cit., p. 194.
166 Gardner, op. cit., p. 106.
167 The poem reads: 'I have just drunk the waters of Changsha. And come to eat the fish of Wuchan.' *Mao Zedong Poems*, Beijing, Foreign Languages Press, 1976, p. 31.
168 Peng Cheng, op. cit., p. 50.
169 *San yao, san bu yao*: 'practice Marxism, unite, be open and above board; do not practice revisionism, do not split, do not intrigue and conspire').
170 Peng Cheng, op. cit., p. 51; Gardner, op. cit., p. 106.
171 Peng Cheng, p. 50.
172 Ibid.
173 Ibid. pp. 51, 56; see also Gardner, op. cit., p. 107.
174 Sabatier, op. cit., p. 196.
175 *People's Daily*, 4 September 1975.
176 Zhang Yufeng, op. cit., p. 7.
177 'Shui Hu' is a classical novel telling the story of a peasant revolt in the Song Dynasty, AD 960–1274. A group of rebels headed by Cao Gai established their base at Liangshan, from where they looted the rich and helped the poor. Song Jiang, a low-ranking

official of a local government and many others joined the rebels whose ranks became large enough to enable them to confront the government's army. After Cao Gai's death, Song became the leader of the rebels. He and another 107 rebel leaders swore to unite as brothers and to help the poor. When the emperor offered amnesty and enlistment of the Liangshan rebels, Song accepted and led his army to serve the imperial court.

178 Fu Bei, 'Mao Zedong Ping Shui Hu Zhenxiang' (the true story about Mao's comments on water margin), *Zhui Qiu (Pursuit)* no. 5, 1988.
179 Peng Cheng, op. cit., p. 57.
180 Xiu Ru, *1976 Nian Dashi Neimu (The Inside Story of the 1976 Events)*, Beijing, Oriental Press, 1989, p. 9.
181 Peng Cheng, op. cit., p, 57.
182 Gao and Yan, op. cit., pp. 553, 554.
183 *Chronology*, op. cit., p. 399; Dittmer, *Continuous Revolution*, op. cit., p. 131–2.
184 Joseph, William A., *The Critique of Ultra-Leftism, 1958–1981*, Standford, Standford University Press, 1984, p. 144.
185 Hao and Duan, op. cit., p. 649.
186 Ibid., p. 650; Onate, Andreas D., 'Hua Kuo-feng and the arrest of the gang of four', *The China Quarterly*, 75, 1978, pp. 54–65.
187 Zhang Yufeng, op. cit., p. 6.
188 Ibid.
189 Jia Sinan, op. cit., p. 376.
190 Ibid., p. 378.
191 *Chronology*, op. cit., p. 399.
192 Wang Nianyi, *Dadongluan*, op. cit., p. 560.
193 Ibid.
194 Hao and Duan, op. cit., p. 650.
195 Jin Chunming, op. cit., p. 173.
196 Sabatier, op. cit., p. 218; Ye Yonglie, Wang Hongwen, op. cit., pp. 462–6.
197 Wang Nianyi, *Dadongluan*, op. cit., p. 591.
198 *Chronology*, op. cit., p.401.
199 Ibid.
200 A reference to the role of Hungarian intellectuals in 1956 which Mao had repeatedly condemned. Ibid.
201 Xiu Ru, op. cit., p. 99.
202 Rodzinsky, op. cit., p. 198.
203 Dittmer, *Revolution*, op. cit., p. 133.
204 Rodzinsky, op. cit., p.199.
205 Xiu Ru, op. cit., p. 399.
206 Quan Yanchi, 'Zouxia Shengtan de Mao Zedong' ('Mao down from the shrine'), *Dangdai*, no. 3, 1989, pp. 53, 54.
207 Nixon, Richard, *In the Arena: a Memoir of Victory, Defeat and Renewal*, New York, Simon & Schuster, 1990, p. 362.
208 Zheng Derong, op. cit., p. 586.
209 Xui Ru, op. cit., p. 396.

NOTES

210 Gao and Yan, op. cit., p.671.
211 Wang Nianyi, op. cit., p. 601.
212 Xiu Ru, op. cit., pp. 403, 404.
213 Zheng Fulin, op. cit., p. 752.
214 Ibid.
215 Their official position were respectively: member of the Politburo; vice premier and head of the PLA political department; vice chairman of the Party; member of the Politburo.
216 Hua Guofeng was first vice chairman of the party; Chen Xilian, commander of the Beijing military region; Ji Dengkui, vice premier and political commissar of the Beijing military region; Wang Dongxing, head of the CC general office; Wu De, head of the Beijing municipal revolutionary committee; Chen Yongui, vice premier.
217 Zhou Ming, op. cit., vol. 1, p. 75.
218 Personal Notes.
219 Li and Hao, op. cit., pp. 155–7.
220 Ibid, p. 185.
221 Ye Yonglie, *Wang Hongwen*, op. cit., p. 492.
222 Dittmer, *Revolution*, op. cit., p. 135.
223 *Xinhua News Bulletin*, no. 11, 1980, p. 12; no. 12, 1980, pp. 58–61.
224 Xiu Ru, op. cit., pp. 404, 405.
225 Ye Yonglie, *Wang Hongwen*, op. cit., p. 480.
226 Gardner, op. cit., p. 111.
227 This was similar to the historical tradition of the defunct emperors' 'last edict' which bestowed special powers to its beholder.
228 Gao and Yan, op. cit., p. 694.
229 Gardner, op. cit., p. 112.
230 Liu Wusheng, op. cit., p. 433.
231 Ibid., p. 434.
232 Xui Ru, op. cit., p. 419.
233 Ibid., p. 420.
234 *Selected Works of Li Xiannian*, Beijing, People's Publishing House, op. cit., p. 158.
235 Dittmer, *Revolution*, op. cit., p. 136, note 70; Ye Yonglie, *Zhang Chunqiao*, op. cit., p. 319.
236 Xiu Ru, op. cit., p. 436.
237 Liu Wusheng, op. cit., p. 439.
238 Li Wusheng, op. cit., p. 439.
239 Ibid., p. 440.
240 Ibid.
241 *Chronology*, op. cit., p. 404.
242 Gao and Yan, op. cit., p. 703.
243 Zheng Derong, op. cit., p. 598.

NOTE ON CHINESE SOURCES

Since the end of the CR, academic enquiries into the CR were relatively rare in China. The reason for this was not a lack of interest in this area of recent Chinese history but rather a systematic discouragement by the Chinese authorities from researching and analysing this subject.

The first official analysis of the CR was published in 1981 in the form of a Central Committee resolution on the history of the Chinese Communist Party. According to the resolution, the main reason for the CR – which it considers as a disastrous event – was a misunderstanding of the political situation. It also attempts to analyse 'the complex social and historical causes' of the CR. But the analysis remains weak on these points. It reduces the causes of the CR to three elements: one, the lack of experience of the Party in establishing a socialist system; two, the excessive concentration of power in the hands of one person; and three, the cult of personality. The resolution, nonetheless, continued to regard Mao as a great Marxist, whose thought it considered as a valuable spiritual asset to the Party and as its principal guideline. The resolution implicitly suggested that a close examination of this period would be untimely and would have a disruptive effect on the unity of the Party. It was therefore discouraged.

Nonetheless, academic and public interest in the CR remained intense and widespread, not only because of its dramatic events, but also because of personal involvement. A host of literary fiction attests to this phenomenon. Former red guards described their disillusionment with the CR, intellectuals recounted their sufferings, and veteran revolutionaries wrote about their ordeals. This type of writing became known as the 'wounded literature'. With the progress of reform policies in the later part of the 1980s, a great number of publications – academic studies, reminiscences, biographies etc. – appeared on the book market, where it found a more widespread readership than any other political topic.

Academic studies

Gao Gao and Yan Jiaqi, at that time researchers at the Chinese Academy of Social Sciences, were the first to make a systematic study on the subject. Their 725-page-long book *A Ten-Year History of the Cultural Revolution (Wenhua Dageming Shinian Shi)*, though officially reserved for internal circulation (*neibu faxing*), became a bestseller and was printed twice in two years. The book, though containing a number of factual mistakes, provides a vast amount of data and concise descriptions of important events. Another of its weaknesses is the absence of an analytical approach to the subject. But this first attempt to break the official taboo on the subject is already of value in itself. Their work can be considered as a courageous effort by the authors to contribute their own version of the period.

Hao Mengbi and Duan Haoran, in their work on CCP history, allot considerable space to the Cultural Revolution, but they follow the official interpretation, attributing the causes of the CR to Mao's erroneous appraisal of the Party's and the state's internal situation. A more recent book by Hu Sheng, President of the Chinese Academy of Social Sciences, *Seventy Years of the CCP (Zhongguo Gongchandang De Qishinian)* – which also deals with the history of the CCP – contains authoritative presentations of major events during the CR.

Professor Wang Nianyi (professor at the PLA National Defence College), however, goes beyond the official interpretation. His *Years of Turmoil (Dadongluan De Niandai)* – published in 1988 as part of four volumes on the history of the People's Republic from 1949 to 1989 – is perhaps the most important work on this period. His approach mixes factual accounts with analysis, and relies on archival material to which he obviously had privileged access. The book contains very interesting passages about the problems Mao encountered with the CR, the means he used to solve them, and the unexpected consequences of his actions. Wang Nianyi emphasises that Mao's major goal was a thorough remoulding of the whole of Chinese society. This, he argues, can be gauged from the numerous writings and statements about this subject during the entire period of the CR. If the May 16 Circular and the '16 points' of August 1966 represent Mao's immediate goals, the CR, in Wang's view, can only be fully understood if one takes into consideration Mao's ultimate desire for a reformed society.

Two other authors, Hei Yannan and Tan Zongji – *A Decade of Turbulence* and *Critical Comments after Ten Years* (*Shinian Dongluan Shinian Houde Pingshou*) – also make the effort of going beyond the official views on the CR by analysing the period from many different angles. Tan Zongji's work, which is a collection of articles by teachers and researchers from the Central Party School, the National Defence College, and the CC research department on Party history, examine a series of problems such as the origins of the CR, Mao's theory of continuing revolution, and the migration of young people to the countryside.

Xiao Yanzhong's collection of articles entitled *Mao Zedong in his Later Years* (*Wannian Mao Zedong*), deal with a series of ideological and theoretical issues such as Mao's utopian socialism, his concepts and theories about class and class struggle, his political ethics, etc. There are only very few works dealing with specific aspects of the CR. One which does, is Li Ke's book on *The PLA in the CR* (*Wenhua Dageming Zhongde Renmin Jiefangjun*). It examines the role of the military in the CR.

A few other books which cannot be considered as academic studies but which provide useful information for the study of the Cultural Revolution, should be mentioned here. Peng Chen's *A Memorandum about the Chinese Political Situation* (*Zhongguo Zhengju Beiwanlu*) describes the relationship between Mao Zedong and Liu Shaoqi, Zhou Enlai and Deng Xiaoping during the CR. Xiu Ru's *Inside Story about the Events of 1976* (*1976 Nian Dashi Neimu*) and Fan Shuo's *Ye Jianying in 1976* (*Ye Jianying zai 1976*) complement each other, the first reporting about the infighting among top Party leaders prior and after Mao's death, and the second describing the planning and execution of the arrest of the 'gang of four'.

NOTE ON CHINESE SOURCES

Biographies

A second type of writing were biographies about major actors on the Chinese political scene. Among all the Chinese leaders active during the Cultural Revolution, it was Zhou Enlai who received the greatest attention. In recent years, more than ten titles have been published about him, among them are: Percy Jucheng Fang and Lucy Guinong J. Fang's *Zhou Enlai: a Profile*; Lin Qing's *Zhou Enlai's Premiership* (*Zhou Enlai He Tade Shiye*); Lu Xingdou, ed., *Zhou Enlai and his Cause; Zhou Enlai in the Cultural Revolution* (*Zhou Enlai Zai Wenhua Dageming Zhong*), edited by the CCP Party School; *Our Premier Zhou* (*Womende Zhou Zhongli*), edited by the Central Documentation Press, just to mention a few of these titles. A considerable number of contributions in these volumes were written by his close collaborators, including vice premiers, ministers and his personal secretaries providing a host of valuable information about the problems with which Zhou Enlai was confronted and how he handled them.

The life of Lin Biao, about whom four books were published in 1988, served as the second most frequently treated subject. The Party historian Lin Qingshan with his *Biography of Lin Biao* (*Lin Biao Zhuan*) focused on Lin Biao's activities during the period of the CR. One of Lin Biao's Secretaries, Zhang Yunsheng, in his book *A Factual Account About Maojiawan* (*Maojiawan Jishi*) provided interesting inside information about a series of events of the CR which were directly linked to Lin Biao. Its description of the power struggle between the Lin Biao and the Jiang Qing groups is revealing and unique in Chinese literature. Yu Gong's *The True Story about the Lin Biao Affair* (*Lin Biao Shijian Zhenxiang*) and Shao Yihai's *The Collapse of the Joint Fleet* (*Lianhe Jiandui De Fumie*) deal mainly with the period between the August 1970 Lushan conference and Lin Biao's death in September 1971. Both provide more data about the activities of Lin Biao's son Lin Liguo than about Lin Biao himself.

The two biographies *The Rise and Fall of Jiang Qing* (*Jiang Qing Chen Fu Lu*) and *Dream of an Empress* (*Nuhuangmeng: Jiang Qing Waizhuan*) about Jiang Qing published by Lin Qingshan and Zhu Zhongli respectively, both deal with her activities during the CR. Their value for research is negligible since both caricature Jiang Qing severely and provide hardly any factual information which cannot be obtained from other sources.

Lin Qingshan's and Zhong Kan's biographies of Kang Sheng, *An Unofficial Biography of Kang Sheng* (*Kang Sheng Waizhan*) and *A Critical Biography of Kang Sheng* (*Kang Sheng Pingzhuan*) although they also vilify their subject, contain valuable information about the politics of the CR. Ye Yonglie's (a Shanghai writer) biographies about Zhang Chunqiao, *The Rise and Fall of Zhang Chunqiao* (*Zhang Chunqiao Fuchen Shi*), Wang Hongwen, *The Vicissitudes of Wang Hongwen* (*Wang Hongwen Xingshuai Lu*), and Yao Wenyuan, *The Yaos, Father and Son* (*Yao Shi Fuzi*) are all well researched books providing useful information on several aspects of the CR, such as the series of events leading to the 'January Storm' or the power struggle among the leadership after the death of Lin Biao.

Another category of publications deals with the political and personal fate of a number of well-known personalities. Tie Zhuwei's *Marshall Chen Yi in the CR* (*Chen Yi Yuanshuai Zai Wenhua Dageming Zhong*) and Lin Qingshan's *Ten Years of Turmoil and Deng Xiaoping* (*Fengyun Shinian Yu Deng Xiaoping*) provide a record of Chen Yi's fate and Deng Xiaoping's conflicts with Jiang Qing after 1973. The six-volume work *Pondering about History* (*Lishi Zai Zheli Chensi*) by Zhou Ming, ed., examines the experiences of such well-known political figures as Liu Shaoqi, Luo Ruiqing, He Long, Tao Zhu, Deng Tuo, and of writers as Ba Jin, Fu Lie etc. Dong Baocun's *The Truth about the Yang-Yu-Fu Event* (*Yang Yu Fu Zhenxian*) deals exclusively with the purge of the three high-ranking generals and contributes greatly to the clarification of one of the most mysterious power struggles of the CR.

Qin Xiaoying's, ed., *A General Deprived of his Uniform* (*Buxu Chuan Janzhuang De Jiangjun*) contains the reminiscences of General Chen Zaidao who was deeply involved in the Wuhan crisis of July 1967, and provides an insider's view of the establishment of the alliance between Jiang Qing and Lin Biao which played a major role in the early years of the CR.

Articles

Articles in all forms about the CR proliferated during the last few years before the Tiananmen Square incident of 1989. They can be classified into the following categories:

NOTE ON CHINESE SOURCES

Studies about particular aspects of the Cultural Revolution

A series of studies pertaining to the duration of the CR, its origins and theoretical aspects, the personality cult of Mao, his thinking and behaviour in his later years, and the red guard movement were published in magazines such as *The Study of Party History (Dangshi Yanji)* and *Party Documentation (Dangde Wenxian)* – both bimonthly issued by the Department of Research on Party History under the Central Committee – and *Party School Forum (Dangxiao Luntan)*, a journal of the central Party school. Although they are official publications, many of their articles did not necessarily represent the official version about the CR as exemplified by the 1981 resolution on Party history. One example is an article by Xi Xuan (*The Study of Party History*, no. 5, 1988) who, in an examination of the origins of the CR, points out that the totalitarian system established by the Party, the personality cult as well as Mao's political thinking all contributed to the emergence of the CR. It is thus this writer's special merit to have reflected on the defects of the Party system as well as on individual responsibility. Xi Xuan emphasises the need to consider such questions as, how it was possible for Mao to concentrate so much power in his hands, how he was able to rule like an emperor, and how he managed to dominate the Party and society despite his frequently unpopular policies. Another example is Lu Zhenxiang's study on personality cult (*Party School Forum*, no. 2, 1989) and Huang Zhen's paper on Liu Shaoqi (*Party Documentation*, no. 5, 1988) are of particular interest.

Studies about personalities and events

Most of the articles available in other magazines are not academic studies. Many of them make, however, interesting reading, since they have been written by eye witnesses or by persons directly concerned with particular events. For example, an article by Luo Ruiqing's daughter, Luo Diandian, ('Mao Zedong and Luo Ruiqing', in: *Mao Zedong's Relations with Other People*) threw light on the life-long relationship between the two leaders and examines the reasons for Luo's purge; or the account about the United Action Committee organised by a group of red guards, which was written by two of its leaders and published in *Pursuit*, no. 5, 1986. Tao Zhu's meteoric rise and tragic death was recounted by his wife Zeng Zhi in *Encounter (Wenhui*, no. 9, 1986), whose revelations about the factional strife between radicals and moderates among the CCP leadership during the first year of the CR are particularly interesting. Mao's secretary, Zhang Yufeng, published an article entitled 'A few things about Mao Zedong and Zhou Enlai in their last years' in *Offspring of Emperors Han and Huang (Yan Huang Zisun)*, no. 1, 1989, which contains first-hand information about Mao's physical and mental condition after the shock of the Lin Biao affair, a subject which had been given rise to much speculation in China and elsewhere. Lin Biao, the official foe of the Chinese authorities after his death, became the subject of a number of publications many of which were by people who, at some time or another, had been directly involved with his activities. Xiong Xianghui reported about a private conversation he had with Mao about the Lushan conference of 1970, where Mao revealed his apprehension against Lin Biao (*New Observer, Xin Guancha*, October 1986). His would-be daughter-in-law, Zhang Ning, describes the confusion in Lin Biao's residence in the last few hours before his flight. Xu Wenyi, Chinese ambassador to Mongolia, wrote about his inspection on the site of the crash of Lin Biao's plane. (*World Affairs*, also reprinted in *Yu Gong*).

Shuai Dongbing's study – published in *Biography of Well Known Persons (Mingren Zhuanji*, nos 11–12, 1988) – about 'Peng Zhen on the eve of the storm' stands out among similar ones for its vivid description of the conflict between Peng Zhen and Mao regarding the problem of Wu Han's play *Hai Rui Dismissed from Office*.

The study of the Cultural Revolution in China had been well under way until the events of Tiananmen Square in June 1989, which dramatically changed the political atmosphere in the country. With the renewal of emphasis on the values of 'Chinese type of socialism' and the categorical rejection of 'Western influences' by the authorities, research in this field suddenly dried up, and even official institutions which had been engaged in the examination of this period, refrained from continuing their efforts to elucidate the complex nature of the Cultural Revolution. Nonetheless, the amount of material which had been produced before June 1989, undoubtedly contributed to the understanding of the period which, in Mao's words, was 'without precedence in history'.

BIBLIOGRAPHY

Chinese Sources

Books

CCP Party School, ed., *Zhou Enlai Zai Wenhua Dageming Zhong* (*Zhou Enlai during the Cultural Revolution*), Beijing, CCP Party History Publishing House, 1990.
Central Documentation Press, ed., *Womende Zhou Zhongli* (*Our Premier Zhou*), Beijing, 1990
Chen Boda Wenxuan (*Selected Works of Chen Boda*), Hong Kong, Historical Material Press, 1971
Cong Jin, *Quzhe Fazhande Suiyue* (*Years of Developments with Changing Directions*), Henan, Henan People's Press, 1989
Deng Xiaoping Wenxuan 1975–1983 (*Selected Works of Deng Xiaoping*), Beijing, People's Publishing House, 1983
Dong Baocun, *Yang Yu Fu Shijian Zhenxiang* (*The Truth About the Yang-Yu-Fu Event*), Beijing, PLA Press, 1987
Dong Baocun, *Zai Lishide Xuanwozhong,* (*In the Whirlpools of History*), Beijing, Chinese Foreign Culture Publishing Company, 1990
Dong Bian, *Mao Zedong He Tade Mishu Tian Jiaying* (*Mao Zedong and His Secretary Tian Jiaying*), Beijing, Central Documentation Press, 1990
Fan Shuo, *Ye Jianying Zai 1976* (*Ye Jianying in 1976*), Beijing, CCP Central Party School Press, 1990
Fang, Percy Sucheng and Fang, Lucy Guimong S., *Zhou Enlai a Profile*, Beijing, Foreign Languages Press, 1986
Gao Gao and Yan Jiaqi, *Wenhua Dageming Shinian Shi* (*A Ten-Year History of the Cultural Revolution*), Tianjin, Tianjin People's Publishing House, 1986
Guanyu Jianguo Yilai Dangde Ruogan Lishi Wenti De Jueyi Zhushiben, (*Annotated Resolution on CCP History*), Beijing, People's Publishing House, 1986
Guo Simin, ed., *Wo Yanzhong De Mao Zedong* (*Mao Zedong As I Saw Him*), Hebei, Hebei People's Publishing House, 1990

BIBLIOGRAPHY

Han Nianlong et al., *Dangdai Zhongguo Waijiao* (*Diplomacy of Contemporary China*) Beijing, Chinese Social Sciences Press, 1988

Hao Mengbi and Duan Haoran, *Zhongguo Gongchandang Luishinian* (*Sixty Years of the CCP*), Beijing, PLA Press, 1984

Hei Yannan, *Shinian Dongluan* (*A Decade of Turbulence*), Xian, International Culture Publishing Company, 1988

Hu Sheng, *Zhongguo Gongchandangde Qishinian* (*Seventy Years of the Chinese Communist Party*), Beijing, CCP History Publishing House, 1991

Jia Sinan, ed., *Mao Zedong Renji Jiaowang Shilu* (*Mao's relations with Other People*), Jiangsu, Jiang Literary and Arts Press, 1989

Jianguo Yilai Mao Zedong Wengao (*Mao Zedong Writings after the Founding of the People's Republic of China*), vols 1–5, Beijing, Central Documentation Publishing House, 1990

Jin Chunming et al., *Wenge Shigi Guaishi Guaiyu* (*The Absurdities of the Cultural Revolution*) Beijing, Qiushi Press, 1989

Li Ke and Hao Shengzhang, *Wenhua Dageming Zhongde Renmin Jiefangjun* (*The PLA in the Cultural Revolution*), Beijing, The CCP Historical Material Press, 1989

Li Tien-min, *Chou En-lai*, Taipei, The Institute of International Relations, 1974

Li Rui, *Lushan Huiyi Shilu* (*A Factual Record of the Lushan Conference*), Hunan, Spring and Autumn Press, 1988

Lin Biao, *Report to the Ninth Congress of the CCP*, Peking, Foreign Languages Press, 1969

Lin Qing, *Zhou Enlai Zaixiang Shengya* (*Zhou Enlai's Premiership*), Beijing, Great Wall Cultural Press, 1991

Lin Qingshan, *Fengyun Shinian Yu Deng Xiaoping* (*Ten Years of Turmoil and Deng Xiaoping*), Beijing, PLA Press, 1989

Lin Qingshan, *Lin Biao Zhuan* (*A Biography of Lin Biao*), Beijing, Knowledge Press, 1988

Lin Qingshan, *Jiang Qing Chen Fu Lu* (*The Rise and Fall of Jiang Qing*, Beijing, China News Press, 1988

Lin Qingshan, *Kang Sheng Waizhuan* (*An Unofficial Biography of Kang Sheng*), Beijing, China Youth Press, 1988

Liu Shaoqi Xuanji (*Selected Works of Liu Shaoqi*), Beijing, People's Publishing House, 1985

Liu Suinian and Wu Qunyan, *Wenhua Dageming Shiqi de Guomin Jingji* (*The National Economy During the Cultural Revolution*) Harbin, Heilongjiang People's Publishing House, 1986

Liu Suinian and Wu Qungan, eds., *China's Socialist Economy: an Outline History (1949–1984)*, Beijing, Beijing Review, 1986

Liu Wusheng, ed., *Zhonggong Dangshi Fengyunlu* (*Major Events in the CCP History*), Beijing, People's Publishing House, 1990

Liu Yan et al., *Zhou Enlai Yanjiu Wenxuan* (*Selected Articles on Zhou Enlai*) Tianjin, The Nankai University Press, 1987

Liu Yan et al., *Zhongwai Xuezhe Lun Zhou Enlai* (*Chinese and Foreign Scholars on Zhou Enlai*), Tianjin, The Nankai University Press, 1990

Lu Xingdou, ed., *Zhou Enlai He Tade Shiye* (*Zhou Enlai and His Cause*), Beijing, CCP Party History Publishing House, 1990

Mao Tsé-toung, *La Guerre Révolutionnaire*, Paris, Union Générale d'Editions, 1962

Mao Zedong Biography: Assessment, Reminiscences, Beijing, Foreign Languages Press, 1986

Peng Cheng, ed., *Zhongguo Zhengju Beiwanglu* (*A Memorandum on the Chinese Political Situation*), Beijing, The PLA Publishing House, 1989

Peng Dehuai, *Memoirs of a Chinese Marshal*, Beijing, Foreign Languages Press, 1984

The Polemic on the General Line of the International Communist Movement, Peking, Foreign Languages Press, 1965

Qin Xiaoying, *Buxu Chuan Junzhuang De Jiangjun* (*A General Deprived of his Uniform*), Beijing, Huaxia Press, 1988

Ren Jian, *Gongheguo Yuanshou Zhi Si* (*The Death of the Head of the Republic*), Hong Kong, Haiming Cultural Press

Selected Articles, Criticising Lin Biao and Confucius, vol. 1, Beijing, Foreign Languages Press, 1974, vol. 2, 1975

Selected Works of Mao Tse-tung, vols. 1–4, Beijing, Foreign Languages Press, 1965; vol. 5, Beijing, Foreign Languages Press, 1977

Shao Yihai, *Lianhe Jiandui De Fumie* (*The Collapse of the Joint Fleet*), Henan, Spring and Autumn Press, 1988

Sun Dengpan et al., *Zhongguo Gongchandang Lishi Jiangyi* (*A Textbook on the History of the CCP*), Jinan, Shandong People's Publishing House, 1985

Tan Zongji et al., *Shinian Houde Pingshou*, (*Critical Comments After Ten Years*), Beijing, Historical Materials Press, 1987

Tie Zhuwei, *Chen Yi Yuanshuai Zai Wenhua Dageming Zhong* (*Marshal Chen Yi in the Cultural Revolution*), Beijing, PLA Literary Press, 1986

Wang Nianyi, *Dadongluan De Niandai* (*Years of Turmoil*), Henan, Henan People's Publishing House, 1988

Wenzhai Xunkan (*Ten-day Digest*), Changchun, Jilin Daily, 1989

Wuchun Jieji Wenhua Dageming Shengli Wansui (*Long Live the Great Proletarian Cultural Revolution*), The Chinese People's University, Beijing, Xinhua Printing House, 1969

Xia Honggen, ed., *Dangshi Zhishi Zhengwenlu* (*Knowledge of Party History*), Beijing, PLA Press, 1988

Xiao Yanzhong, ed., *Wannian Mao Zedong*, (*The Last Years of Mao Zedong*) Beijing, Spring and Autumn Press, 1989

Xiu Ru et al., *1976 Nian Dashi Neimu* (*The Inside Story of the 1976 Events*), Beijing, Oriental Press, 1989

Yang Zhongmei, *Zhunyi Huiyi Yu Yanan Zhengfeng* (*The Zhunyi Conference and the Yanan Rectification Campaign*), Hong Kong, Benma Press, 1988

Ye Jianying Zhuanlue (*A Brief Biography of Ye Jianying*), Beijing, Military Science Press, 1987

Ye Yonglie, *Wang Hongwen Xingshuai Lu* (*The Vicissitudes of Wang Hongwen*), Changchun, Time Literary Press, 1989

Ye Yonglie, *Yao Shi Fuzi* (*The Yaos, Father and Son*), Dalian, Dalian Publishing House, 1989
Ye Yonglie, *Zhang Chunqiao Fuchen Shi* (*The Rise and Fall of Zhang Chunqiao*), Changchun, Time Literary Press, 1988
Yu Gong, *Lin Biao Shijian Zhenxiang* (*The True Story About the Lin Biao Affair*), Beijing, China Broadcasting and Television Press, 1988
Zhang Chungiao, *On Exercising All-Round Dictatorship over the Bourgeoisie*, Peking, Foreign Languages Press, 1975
Zhang Yunsheng, *Maojiawan Jishi* (*A Factual Account about Maojiawan*), Beijing, Spring and Autumn Press, 1988
Zheng Derong, *Xin Zhongguo Jishi, 1949–1984* (*Records of New China, 1949–1984*), Changchun, North East Normal University Press, 1986
Zheng Fulin, *Zhonggong Dangshi Zhishi Shouce*, (*Handbook of Party History*), Beijing, Beijing Press, 1985
Zhong Kan, *Kang Sheng Pingzhuan* (*A Critical Biography of Kang Sheng*), Beijing, Red Flag Publishing House, 1982
Zhongguo Gongchandang Liushinian Dashi Jianjie (*A Brief Account of Major Events of the 60-Year History of the CCP*), edited by the Party History Department of the Institute of Political Studies, National Defence University, Beijing, National Defence University Press, 1986
Zhonggong Dangshi Dashi Nianbiao (*Chronology of Major Events in the History of the CCP*), ed. by the CCP History Research Department, Beijing, People's Publishing House, 1987
Zhonggong Wenhua Dageming Zhongyao Wenjian Huibian (*Collection of Important CCP Documents on the Cultural Revolution*), edited by Journal of CCP Studies, Taipei, 1973
Zhongguo Renmin Jiefangjun Jiangshuai Minglu, (*Who is Who? Generals and Marshals in the People's Liberation Army*), Beijing, PLA Press, 1986
Zhou Enlai, *The Tenth National Congress of the Communist Party of China*, Peking, Foreign Languages Press, 1973
Zhou Enlai, *Report on the Work of the Government*, Beijing, Foreign Languages Press, 1975
Zhou Ming, *Lishi Zai Zheli Chensi* (*Pondering about History*), Beijing, Huaxia Press, 1986
Zhu Zhongli, *Nuhuangmeng: Jiang Qing Waizhuan* (*The Dream of an Empress: an Unofficial Biography of Jiang Qing*), Beijing, The Oriental Press, 1988
Ziliao Xuanbian (unpublished Speeches and Writings of Mao Zedong), Beijing, 1967

Articles

Chen Xuewei, 'Wenhua Dageming Shinian De Jingji Jianshe' ('Economic construction during the Cultural Revolution'), in Tan Jongji, *Critical Comments after Ten Years*
Chen Zaidao, 'Wuhan 7.20 Shijian' ('The Wuhan July 20th event'), in Peng Cheng, *Zhongguo Zhengju Baiwanglu* (A Memorandom on the Chinese Political Situation)

Fu Bei, 'Mao Zedong Ping Shui Hu Zhenxiang' ('The true story about Mao's comments on water margin'), *Zhui Qiu (Pursuit)*, no. 5, 1988

Gao Wenqian, 'Zai Zuihoude Rizili' ('In his last days'), in Gao Wenqian, *Pondering about History*

Gao Wenqian, 'Ji Wenhua Dageming Zhongde Zhou Enlai' ('Zhou Enlai in the Cultural Revolution'), in Gao Wenqian, *Pondering about History*

Gu Mu, 'Huiye Jingaide Zhou Enlai' ('In memory of the respected premier Zhou Enlai'), in *Our Premier Zhou Enlai*, Central Documentation Press, Beijing, 1990

Kong Jianmin, 'Zhongguo Da Sanxian Jianshe De Jiannan Licheng' ('The difficult path of China's third line construction'), *Zhui Qiu, (Pursuit)*, no. 1, 1989

Huang Zheng, 'Liu Shaoqi Yu Wenhua Dageming' ('Liu Shaoqi and the Cultural Revolution'), *Dang De Wenxian (Party Documentation)* Beijing, no. 5, 1988

Lin Qingshan, 'Sirenbang Zuge Meng De Pomie', ('The failure of the gang of four to seize power'), *Mao Zedong Sixiang Yanjiu (Study of Mao Zedong Thought)*, Sichuan Academy of Social Sciences, no. 3, 1988

Lin Qingshan, 'Mao Zedong Wannian De Yixiang Yingming Juece' ('A wise decision of Mao in his late years') *Yanhuang Zisun (The Offspring of Emperors Yan and Huang)*, no. 2 1988

Liu Pingping, Liu Yuan and Liu Tingting, 'Huainian Women De Baba Liu Shapqi' ('In memory of our father Liu Shaoqi'), in Gao Wenqian, *Pondering about History*

Lu Zhengxiang, 'Jianguohou Geren Chongbai Wentide Kaocha' ('A study of personality cult'), in *Dangxiao Luntan (Party School Forum)*, no. 2, 1989

Qiao Yi, 'Liandong Shijian', ('Liandong affairs') *Pursuit*, no. 5, 1986

Quan Yanchi 'Zouxia Shentan de Mao Zedong' ('Mao down from the shrine'), *Dangdai, (Contemporary Era)*, no. 3, 1989

Shao Yihai, 'Lin Biao Zhutao Zhenxiang' ('The truth about Lin Biao's flight'), *Pursuit*, no. 6, 1988

Shuai Dongbing, 'Peng Zhen Zai Baofengyu Qianye' ('Peng Zhen on the eve of the storm'), *Mingren Zhuanyi (Biography of Well-Known Persons)*, no. 11–12, 1988

Su Caiqing, 'Wenge Chuqi Jingji Zhanxian De Yanzhong Douzheng' ('Serious conflicts in the economic field during the early period of the Cultural Revolution'), in Tan Zongji, *Critical Comments Ten Years Later*.

Su Caiqing, 'Hongweibing Yundong' ('The red guard movement'), in *CCP History: a Textbook*.

Wang Nianyi, 'Guanyu Eryue Niliu De Yixie Ziliao' ('Some facts about the February Adverse Current'), *Dangshi Yanjiu Ziliao (Material on the Study of Part History)*, no. 1, 1990

Wang Nianyi 'Mao Zedong Tongzhi Fadong "Wenhua Dageming" Shi Dui Xingshide Guji' ('Comrade Mao Zedong's estimate of the situation when he launched the "Great Cultural Revolution" '), *Dangshi Yanjiu Ziliao*, no. 4, 1989

Wang Ruoshui 'Cong Pi Zuo Dao Xiang Fang You' ('From Criticising the left to opposing the right'), *Mingbao*, no. 3 1989

Xi Xuan, 'Guanyu Wenhua Dageming Qiyinde Tantao' ('The origins of the Cultural Revolution'), *Zhonggong Dangshi Yanjiu* (*Studies on the History of the CCP*), no. 4, 1988

Xiao Xiao, 'Lin Biao Nuer Dadan Pilu Fuqin Zhuzou Xiangqing' ('Lin Biao's daughter revealed the truth about his flight'), *Jingbao Yuekan* (*The Mirror Monthly*), no. 6, Hong Kong, 1988

Xiong Leiwen, 'Mao Zedong Tong Xiong Xianghui Tan Lushan Huiyi Wenti' ('Mao's talk with Xiong Xianghui about the Lushan Conference') *Xin Guancha* (*New Observer*), October 1986

Xiong Xianghui, 'Mao Zedong Dui Montgomery Tan Jichengren', ('Mao talks with Montgomery about his successor), *World Affairs*, no. 20, 1988

Xu Wenyi, 'Lin Biao Jihui Renwang Xianchang Ji' ('On-the-spot investigation of the crash of Lin Biao's plane'), in Yu Gong, *The True Story About the Lin Biao Affair*

Ye Yonglie, 'Wang Li Da Kewen' (Wang Li Interviewed), *Lianhe Bao* (*United Times*), Shanghai 23 December, 1988

Yu Nan, 'Lin Biao Jituan Xingwang Chutan' ('A study of the rise and fall of the Lin Biao group'), in Tan Zongji, Tan Jongji, *Critical Comments after After Ten Years*

Zeng, Zhi, 'Tao Zhu Zai Zuihoude Suiyueli' ('Tao Zhu in his last years'), *Wenhui* (*Encounter*), no. 9, 1986

Zhang Hua, 'Lun Zhishi Qingnian Shangshan Xiaxiang Yundong' ('On the movement of educated youth to go to the countryside'), in Tan Zongji, *Critical Comments After Ten Years*

Zhang Ning; 'Niuqu De Hong' ('A deformed rainbow'), in Gao Wemgian, *Pondering About History*, vol. 5, 1987

Zhang Yufeng, 'Mao Zedong Zhou Enlai Wannian Ersan Shi' ('A few things about Mao Zedong's and Zhou Enlai's last years'), *Yanhuang Zisun* (*The Offspring of Emperors Yan and Huang*), no. 1, 1989

II Western sources

Books and monographs

Ahn, Byung-joon, *Chinese Politics and the Cultural Revolution: Dynamics of Policy Processes*, Seattle, University of Washington Press, 1976

Aubert, Claude, Bianco, Lucien, Cadart, Claude, Domenach, Jean-Luc, *Regards froids sur la Chine*, Paris, Editions du Seuil, 1976

Barnett, Doak, *Communist China: The Early Years 1949–55*, New York, Frederick A. Praeger, 1964

Bauchau, Henri, *Mao Zedong*, Paris, Flammarion, 1982

Baum, Richard, *Prelude to Revolution: Mao, the Party, and the Peasant*

Question, 1962–66, Center for Chinese Studies, Research Monograph no. 2. Berkeley, 1968

Bennett, Gordon and Montapero, Ronald, *Red Guard: The Political Biography of Dai Hsiao-ai,* Garden City, N.Y., Doubleday and Co., 1971

Bergère, Marie-Claire, *La République populaire de Chine de 1949 à nos jours,* Paris, Armand Colin, 1987

Bergère, Marie-Claire, Bianco, Lucien, Domes, Jürgen, *La Chine au XXe Siècle,* Paris, Fayard, vol. 1, 1989, vol. 2, 1990

Bernstein, Thomas, *Up to the Mountains and Down to the Villages: The Transfer of Youth from Urban to Rural China,* New Haven, Conn., Yale University Press, 1977

Bettelheim, Charles, *Révolution Culturelle et organisation industrielle en Chine,* Paris, petite collection maspero, 1973

Bunce, Valerie, *Do New Leaders Make a Difference? Executive Succession and Public Policy under Capitalism and Socialism,* Princeton, Princeton University Press, 1981

Butterfield, Fox, *China: Alive in the Bitter Sea,* New York, Times Books, Quadrangle Publications, 1982

CCP Documents of the Great Proletarian Cultural Revolution, Hong Kong, Union Research Institute, 1969

Ch'en, Jerome, *Mao Papers,* London, Oxford University Press, 1970

Chang, Y. C., *Factional and Coalition Politics in China: The Cultural Revolution and Its Aftermath,* New York, Praeger, 1976

Chang, Parris H., *Power and Policy in China,* University Park, Pennsylvania State University Press, 1978

Chang, David W., *Zhou Enlai and Deng Xiaoping in the Chinese Leadership Succession Crisis,* London, University Press of America, 1984

Chen, Jack, *Inside the Cultural Revolution,* London, Sheldon Press, 1976

Chesnaux, Jean, *China, The People's Republic, 1949–1976,* New York, Pantheon Books, 1979

Chien, Yu-Shen, *China's Fading Revolution,* Hong Kong, Centre of Contemporary Chinese Studies, Army Dissent and Military Divisions, 1989

China, a Country Study, Area Handbook Series, Washington D.C., Headquarters of the Army, 1981

Chinese Communist Affairs: Facts and Features, vol. I, no. 3, 29 November 1967

Daubier, Jean, *Histoire de la Révolution culturelle prolétarienne en Chine,* vols 1 and 2, Paris, petite collection maspero, 1974

Dittmer, Lowell and Chen, Ruoxi, *Ethics and Rhetoric of the Chinese Cultural Revolution,* Berkeley, Center for Chinese Studies, Institute of East Asian Studies, University of California, no. 19, 1981

Dittmer, Lowell, *Liu Shao-ch'i and the Chinese Cultural Revolution, The Politics of Mass Criticism,* Berkeley, University of California, 1974

Dittmer, Lowell, *China's Continuing Revolution, The Post-Liberation Epoch 1949–1981,* Berkeley, University of California Press, 1987

Domenach, Jean-Luc, Richer, Philip, *La Chine, 1949–1985,* Paris, Imprimerie Nationale, 1987

BIBLIOGRAPHY

Domes, Jürgen, *China After the Cultural Revolution: Politics between Two Party Congresses*, Berkeley, University of California Press, 1975

Dumont, René, *Chine, La Révolution culturelle*, Paris, Editions du Seuil, 1974

Fairbank, John King, *The Great Chinese Revolution, 1800–1985*, New York, Harper & Row, 1986

Faligot, Roger, Kauffer, Remi, *Kang Sheng et les Servives secrets chinois, 1927–1987*, Paris, Robert Laffont, 1987

Franz, Uli, *Deng Xiaoping, China's Erneuerer, Eine Biographie*, Stuttgart, Deutsche Verlagsanstalt, 1987

Fraser, John, *The Chinese: Portrait of a People*, New York, Summit Books, 1980

Gardner, John, *Chinese Politics and the Succession to Mao*, London, The Macmillan Press, 1982

Glaubitz, Joachim, *Opposition Gegen Mao: Abendgespräche am Yanshan und andere politische Dokumente*, Olten, Walter Verlag, 1969

Goldman, Merle, *China's Intellectuals, Advice and Dissent*, Cambridge, Mass., Harvard University Press, 1981

Goodstadt, Leo, *China's Watergate: Political and Economic Conflict, 1969–1977*, New Delhi, Vikas Publications, 1979

Gottlieb, Thomas, *Chinese Foreign Policy Factionalism and the Origins of the Strategic Triangle*, New Delhi, Vikas Publications, 1979

Guillermaz, Jacques, *The Chinese Communist Party in Power, 1949–1975*, Boulder, Colorado, Westview Press, 1976

Guillermaz, Jacques, *Histoire du parti communist chinois*, vols 1 and 2, Paris, Petite Bibliothèque Payot, 1975

Han Suyin, *My House Has Two Doors*, New York, G. P. Putnam's Sons, 1980

Harding, Harry, *Organizing China: The Problem of Bureaucracy, 1949–1976*, Standford, Standford University Press, 1981

Harvard University Center for International Affairs and East Asian Research, *Communist China, 1955–1959*, Policy Documents with Analysis, 1962

Hinton, Harold C. *An Introduction to Chinese Politics*, 2nd edn, New York, Praeger, 1978

Hinton, Harold C., *The Bear and the Gate: Chinese Policy Making under Soviet Pressure*, Stanford, Hoover Institution Press, 1971

Ho, Ping-ti and Tsou, Tang, *China in a Crisis, China's Heritage and the Communist Political System*, vol. 1, Chicago, University of Chicago Press, 1968

Hollingsworth, Clare, *Mao*, London, Triad Paladin Grafton Books, 1987

Hsia, Adrian, *Die Chinesische Culturrevolution*, Neuwied, Herman, Luchterhand, 1971

Hsü, Immanuel, C. Y., *The Rise of Modern China*, 3rd edn, Oxford, Oxford University Press, 1983

Hu Chi-hsi, *Mao Tsé-toung et la construction du socialism*, Textes inédits, Paris, Editions du Seuil, 1975

Joseph, William A., *The Criticism of Ultra-Left in China, 1958–1981*, Stanford, Stanford University Press, 1984

Kaplan, Frederic M., *Encyclopedia of China Today*, New York, Eurasia Press, 1979

Kau, Y. M., *The Lin Biao Affair*, White Plains, New York, International Arts and Sciences Press, 1975

Ken Ling, *La vengeance du ciel: Un jeune Chinois dans la Révolution culturelle*, Paris, Robert Laffont, 1981

Kissinger, Henry, *The White House Years*, London, George Weidenfeld & Nicolson and Michael Joseph 1979

La Puissance militaire chinoise Paris, Bruxelles, Elsevier, 1980

Ladany, Laslo, *The Communist Party of China and Marxism, 1921–1985, A Self Portrait*, London, C. Hurst, 1988

Lee, Hong Yung, *The Politics of the Chinese Cultural Revolution: A Case Study*, Berkeley, University of California Press, 1978

Levenson, Joseph, *Confucian China and Its Modern Fate: A Trilogy*, Berkeley, University of California Press, 1968

Leys, Simon, *Les Habits neufs du Président Mao, Chronique de la 'Revolution culturelle'*, Paris, Editions Gérard Lebovici, 1987

Liang Heng and Shapiro, Judith, *Son of the Revolution*, New York, Alfred A. Knopf, 1983

Lieberthal, Kenneth and Dickson, Bruce, J., *A Research Guide to Central Party and Government Meetings in China, 1949–1986*, New York, M. E. Sharpe, 1989

Lifton, Robert Jay, *Revolutionary Immortality, Mao Tse-tung and the Chinese Cultural Revolution*, New York, Random House, 1968

Liu Guokai, *A Brief Analysis of the Cultural Revolution*, New York, M. E. Sharpe, 1987

Lo Fulang, *Morning Breeze: A True Story of China's Cultural Revolution*, San Francisco, China Books and Periodicals Inc., 1989

Louie, Kam, *Critiques of Confucius in Contemporary China*, Hong Kong, Chinese University of Hong Kong, Joint Publishers, 1979

MacFarquhar, Roderick, Cheek, Timothy, Wu, Eugene, *The Secret Speeches of Chairman Mao, From the Hundred Flowers to the Great Leap Forward*, Cambridge, Mass. The Council on East Asian Studies, Harvard University, 1989

MacFarquhar, Roderick, *Origins of the Cultural Revolution*, vol. I, New York, Columbia University Press, 1974; vol. II Oxford, Oxford University Press, 1983

Malraux, André, *Anti-Mémoires*, New York, Monthly Review Press, 1977

Maoism as It Really Is, A Collection, Moscow, Progress Publishers, 1981

Martin, Helmut, *Cult and Canon: The Origins and Development of State Maoism*, Armok, New York, M. E. Sharpe, 1982

Martin, Helmut and Bartke, Wolfgang, *Die Massesorganisationen der Volksrepublik China*, Hamburg, Institut für Asienkunde, Mitteilungen, no. 62, 1975

Meissner, Maurice, *Marxism, Maoism and Utopianism*, Madison, University of Wisconsin Press, 1982

BIBLIOGRAPHY

Mury, Gilbert, *De la révolution culturelle au X. Congrès du parti communist chinois*, Paris, Union Générale d'Editions, 1973

Myers, James, Domes, Jürgen, Von Groeling, Eric, *Chinese Politics – Documents and Analysis*, vols 1 and 2, Columbia, South Carolina, University of South Carolina Press, 1986

Nixon, Richard, *The Memoirs of Richard Nixon*, vols 1 and 2, New York, Warner Books, 1979

Nixon, Richard, *In the Arena; A Memoir of Victory, Defeat and Renewal*, New York, Simon & Schuster, 1990

Opletal, Helmut, *Die Informationspolitik der Volksrepublik China: Von der 'Kulturrevolution' zum Sturz der 'Viererbande' (1965–1976)*, Bochum, Studienverlag Brockmeyer, 1981

Pan, Stephen and Jaigher, Raymond J., *Peking's Red Guards: The Great Proletarian Cultural Revolution*, New York, Twin Circle Publishing Company, 1968

Pye, Lucien W., *The Mandarin and the Cadre: China's Political Cultures*, Ann Arbor, Centre for Chinese Studies, The University of Michigan Press, 1988

Robinson, Joan, *The Cultural Revolution in China*, Harmondsworth, Penguin Books, 1969

Robinson, Thomas, *The Cultural Revolution in China*, Berkeley, University of California Press, 1971

Robinson, Thomas, *A Political-Military Biography of Lin Biao, Part II. 1950–1971*, Santa Monica, RAND Corp., 1971

Rodzinsky, Withold, *The People's Republic of China, A Concise Political History*, New York, The Free Press, 1988

Sabatier, Patrick, *Le dernier Dragon, Deng Xiaoping . . . un siècle de l'Histoire de la Chine*, Paris, JC Lattès, 1990

Schram, Stuart, R., *Chairman Mao Talks to the People*, New York, Pantheon Books, 1974

Schram, Stuart, R., *Mao Zedong Unrehearsed*, Harmondsworth, Penguin, 1974

Schram, Stuart, R., *Mao Zedong, A Preliminary Reassessment*, Hong Kong, The Chinese University Press, 1983

Schram, Stuart, R., *The Thought of Mao Tse-Tung*, London, Contemporary China Institute Publications, SOAS, Cambridge University Press, 1989

Short, Philip, *The Dragon and the Bear, Inside China and Russia Today*, London, Abacus, 1982

Snow, Edgar, *The Long Revolution*, New York, Vintage Books, 1973

Spence, Jonathan D., *The Gate of Heavenly Peace, The Chinese and Their Revolution, 1895–1980*, Harmondsworth, Penguin Books, 1982

Spengler, Tilman, *Der Sturz von Lin Biao: Paradigm für militärischzivile Konflikte in der Volksrepublik China?* Hamburg, Institut für Asienkunde, Mitteilungen no. 76, 1976

Starr, John Bryan, *Continuing the Revolution: The Political Thought of Mao*, Berkeley, University of California Press, 1979

Teiwes, Frederick, C., *Leadership, Legitimacy, and Conflict in China: From a Charismatic Mao to the Politics of Succession*, Armok, N.Y., M. E. Sharpe, 1984

The Cambridge History of China, vols 14 and 15, Cambridge, Mass., Cambridge University Press, 1987, 1991

Tsou, Tang, *The Cultural Revolution and Post-Mao Reforms, a Historical Perspective*, Chicago, The University of Chicago Press, 1986

Wheelwright, E. L. and McFarlane, Bruce, *The Chinese Road to Socialism, Economics of the Cultural Revolution*, New York, Monthly Review Press, 1971

White III, Lynn T., *Policies of Chaos, The Organizational Causes of Violence in China's Cultural Revolution*, Princeton, Princeton University Press, 1989

Wilson, Dick (ed.) *Mao Tse-Tung in the Scales of History*, Cambridge University Press, 1977

Witke, Roxane, *Camarade Chiang Ch'ing*, Paris, Robert Laffont, 1978

Wu, Tien-wei, *Lin Biao and the Gang of Four: Counter-Confucianism in Historical and Intellectual Perspective*, Carbondale, Southern Illinois University Press, 1983

Yue Daiyun and Wakeman, Carolyn, *To the Storm, An Odyssey of a Revolutionary Chinese Woman*, Berkeley, University of California Press, 1985

Articles

'China and the Soviet Union, 1949–1984', *Keesing's International Studies*, Longman, 1985

Bartke, Wolfgang, 'Die politische Profilierung von Chiang Ching', *China Aktuell*, Hamburg, Institut für Asiankunde, February 1975

Bennet, Gordon, 'Military Regions and Provincial Party Secretaries: One Outcome of China's Cultural Revolution', *China Quarterly*, April–June 1973

Bernstein, Thomas P., 'Urban Youth in the Countryside: Problems of Adaptation and Remedies', *China Quarterly*, March 1977

Bridgham, Philip, 'The Fall of Lin Biao', *China Quarterly*, July–September, 1973

Bridgham, Philip, 'Mao's Cultural Revolution: The Struggle to Consolidate Power', *China Quarterly*, January–March 1970

Brugger, Bill, 'From "Revisionism" to "Alienation", from "Great Leaps" to "Third Wave" ', *China Quarterly*, December 1968

Burton, Barry, 'The Cultural Revolution's Ultraleft Conspiracy: The May 16 Group', *Asian Survey*, November 1971

Dittmer, Lowell, ' "Line Struggle" in Theory and Practice: The Origins of the Cultural Revolution Reconsidered', *China Quarterly*, December 1977

Dittmer, Lowell, 'The Structural Evolution of "Criticism and Self-Criticism" ', *China Quarterly*, October–December 1973

Domes, Jürgen, 'The Role of the Military in the Formation of Revolutionary Committees 1967–68', *China Quarterly*, October–December 1970

Domes, Jürgen, 'The "Gang of Four" and Hua Kuo-Feng: Analysis of Political Events in 1975–76', *China Quarterly*, September 1977

Field, Robert Michael, 'The Performance of Industry During the Cultural Revolution: Second Thoughts', *China Quarterly*, December 1986

Goldman, Merle, 'China's Anti-Confucian Campaign 1973–74', *China Quarterly*, September 1975

Gurtov, Melvin, 'The Foreign Ministry and Foreign Affairs During the Cultural Revolution', *China Quarterly*, October–December, 1969

Harding, Harry and Gurtov, Melvin, 'The Purge of Lo Jui-ch'ing: the Politics of Chinese Strategic Planning', *China Quarterly*, January–March 1972

Harding, Harry, 'Maoist Theories of Policy Making and Organisation', in: Robinson, Thomas, *The Cultural Revolution in China*, Berkeley, University of California Press, 1971

Joffe, Ellis, 'The Chinese Army after the Cultural Revolution: the Effects of Intervention', *China Quarterly*, July–September 1973

Knight, Nick, 'Mao Zedong's "On Contradiction" and "On Practice": Pre-Liberation Texts', *China Quarterly*, November–December 1984

Liao Kai-lung, 'Historical Experiences and our Road of Development', *Issues and Studies*, 17 October 1971

Munro, Robin, 'Settling Accounts with the Cultural Revolution at Beijing University, 1977–1978', *China Quarterly*, no. 82, 1980

Nelson, Harvey, 'Military Forces in the Cultural Revolution', *China Quarterly*, July–September 1972

Ouate, Andreas, 'Hua Kuo-Feng and the Arrest of the "Gang of Four"', *China Quarterly*, no. 75, 1978

Parish, William L., 'Factions in Chinese Military Politics', *China Quarterly*, October–December 1973

Pye, Lucian W., 'Reassessing the Cultural Revolution', *China Quarterly*, December 1986

Robinson, Thomas W., 'The Wuhan Incident: Local Strife and Provincial Rebellion during the Cultural Revolution', *China Quarterly*, July–September 1971

Ross, Robert, 'From Lin Biao to Deng Xiaoping: Elite Instability and China's US Policy', *China Quarterly*, June 1989

Schram, Stuart R., 'Mao Tse-tung and the Theory of the Permanent Revolution, 1958–69', *China Quarterly*, April–June 1971

Schram, Stuart R., 'From the "Great Union of Popular Masses" to the "Great Alliance"', *China Quarterly*, January–March 1972

Schram, Stuart R., 'The Limits of Cataclysmic Change: Reflections on the Place of the "Great Proletarian Cultural Revolution" in the Political Development of the People's Republic of China', *China Quarterly*, December 1986

Starr, John Bryan, 'Conceptual Foundations of Mao Tse-tung's Theory of Continuous Revolution', *Asian Survey*, June 1971

Tsou, Tang, 'Mao Tse-tung Thought, the Last Struggle for Succession, and the Post-Mao Era', *China Quarterly*, September, 1977

Wich, Richard, 'The Tenth Party Congress: The Power Structure and the Succession Question', *China Quarterly*, no. 58, 1974

Wang, James, 'The May Seventh Cadres School for Eastern Peking', *China Quarterly*, September 1976

Yahuda, Michael, 'Kreminology and the Chinese Strategic Planning, 1965–66', *China Quarterly*, January–March 1972

Documents

CCP Documents of the Great Proletarian Cultural Revolution, 1966–1967, Hong Kong, Union Research Institute, 19

Chinese Politics, Documents and Analysis, vols 1 and 2, Myers, James T., Domes, Jürgen, Von Groeling, Erik (eds), Columbia, University of South Carolina Press, 1986 and 1989

Chinese Law and Government, New York, International Arts and Sciences Press Inc., various issues

Classified Chinese Documents: A Selection, Taipei, Institute of International Relations, National Chengchi University, 1978

Important Documents on the Great Proletarian Cultural Revolution in China, Peking, Foreign Languages Press, 1970

The People's Republic of China, 1949–1979, Hinton, Harold C. (ed.), 5 vols, Delaware, Scholarly Resources Inc., 1980

The People's Republic of China, 1979–1984, Hinton, Harold C. (ed.), 2 vols, Delaware, Scholarly Resources Inc., 1986

Periodicals

Beijing Review (Peking Review)
China News Analysis (CNA), Hong Kong
China Aktuell Hamburg, Institut für Asiankunde
Issues and Studies, Taipei, Institute for International Relations
New China News Agency (NCNA), Hong Kong
Survey of China Mainland Press, Hong Kong
China Quarterly, London

GLOSSARY OF CHINESE NAMES

An Ziwen, member of the 8th Central Committee, head of the CC organisation department, 117, 185–6

Bo Yibo, alternate member of the Politburo of the 8th CC, vice prime minister, 117, 185–6

Cao Diqiu, mayor of Shanghai, 110–11

Cao Yion, Kang Sheng's wife, 73

Chen Boda, alternate member of the Politburo of the 8th CC, member of the Standing Committee of the Politburo of the 9th CC, 43, 47–50, 53, 60, 63, 65, 71, 75, 79, 82, 83–4, 86, 99, 102, 107–8, 121, 127, 130–1, 154, 165, 167, 177, 181, 189, 193–5, 197, 211–13, 216, 218–26, 230–1, 235, 243, 253

Chen Liyun, political commissar of the 5th army of the air force, 218, 231

Chen Pixian, alternate member of the 8th CC of the Shanghai Party Committee, 110, 111

Chen Shaomin, member of the 8th CC, vice president of All China Trade Unions, 174

Chen Shiju, member of the 9th and 10th CC, commander of the PLA engineering corps, 260

Chen Xilian, member of the Politburo of the 9th, 10th and 11th CC, commander of the Shenyang military region and later of the Beijing military region, 166, 177, 251, 286, 293

Chen Yi member of the Politburo of the 8th CC, vice prime minister and foreign minister; member of the 9th CC, 15, 117–19, 121, 130–1, 164–5, 168, 173, 175, 177, 201, 218–19, 228, 274

Chen Yonggui, member of the Politburo of the 10th CC, vice prime minister, 251, 293

Chen Yun, vice chairman of the 8th CC, member of the Standing Committee of the Politburo, vice prime minister, member of the 9th CC, 37–9, 43, 45, 82, 173

Chen Zaidao, commander of the Wuhan military region, 144–8

Cheng Shiqing, director of the Jiangxi revolutionary committee, political commissar of the Jiangxi military district, 231, 243
Chi Qun, secretary of the Qinghua university Party committee, 258, 271, 285–6, 293

Deng Liqun, head of the State Council policy research department, 279, 288
Deng Tuo, member of the secretariat of the Beijing municipal Party committee in charge of culture and education, 16–17, 19, 51, 56–7, 61–3, 88, 95
Deng Xiaoping, vice chairman of the 10th CC, vice prime minister, vice chairman of the military commission, general chief of staff, 26, 30, 32, 37–9, 42–3, 53, 55, 58, 74, 75, 77, 79, 82, 84–7, 101, 105, 115, 118, 122, 125, 132, 173, 175, 186, 193, 250, 269, 271–5, 278–80, 282–9, 292, 294
Deng Yingchao, member of the 8th, 9th, 10th, 11th and 12th CC, member of the Politburo of the 13th CC, Zhou Enlai's wife, 295
Deng Zihui, member of the 8th CC and head of the CC department for rural work, 39–40
Ding Sheng, member of the 9th and 10th CC, commander of the Guangzhou military region, later of the Nanjing military region, 238, 293
Dong Biwu, member of the Politburo of the 7th to the 10th CC, vice president of the PRC, 177, 215

Fan Wenlan, historian, 58, 226
Feng Youlan, philosopher, expert on Confucius, professor at Beijing University, 20, 26
Fu Chongbi, commander of the Beijing garrison, 148, 164–7, 170–1, 192, 196–7, 210, 227

Gao Gang, member of the Politburo of the 7th CC, vice president of the PRC, 27, 40, 45, 53
Geng Jinzhang, leader of the 2nd corps of the Shanghai workers' headquarters, 157
Gu Tongzhou, chief of staff of the Guangzhou military region air force, 235, 238
Gu Mu, head of the National Planning Commission, vice prime minister, 121
Gu Wengguang, deputy political commissar of the ocean liner *Feng Quing*, 270
Guan Feng, member of the CCRG, deputy chief editor of *Red Flag*, 20, 49, 58, 62, 141, 150, 154, 163, 165, 171, 192, 196, 224
Guan Guanglie, political commissar of the army division unit 0190, 236–7
Guo Moruo, president of the Chinese Academy of Science, vice chairman of the National People's Congress, 48, 261

GLOSSARY OF CHINESE NAMES

Han Aijing, leader of the 'Red Flag Militant Brigade' at the Beijing Aeronautical Engineering Institute, 103, 161
Han Xianchu, commander of the Fuzhou military region, 137, 205
Hao Liang, Beijing opera singer, vice minister of culture, 266
He Long, marshal, vice chairman of the military commission, vice prime minister, 69, 115, 166, 168, 177, 201, 209, 227, 274
Hu Ping, deputy chief of staff of the air force, 241
Hu Qiaomu, Mao's political secretary, vice minister of the CC propaganda department, 52, 279
Hu Sheng, historian, 279
Hu Yaobang, head of the Chinese Academy of Sciences, 125, 279, 288
Hua Guofeng, secretary of the Hunan provincial Party committee, later chairman of the CCP and the military commission, prime minister, 125, 249, 277, 286, 288–9, 291, 293–7
Huang Kecheng, general chief of staff of the PLA, 36, 68
Huang Shuai, a pupil in Beijing, 268
Huang Yongsheng, commander of the Guangzhou military region, later general chief of staff of the PLA, member of the Politburo of the 9th CC, 142, 151, 166, 171, 173, 200, 211, 221, 224, 226, 228, 235, 238–9, 241, 243

Ji Dengkui, member of the Politburo of the 10th CC, vice prime minister, 177, 225, 237, 293
Ji Pengfei, vice foreign minister, foreign minister, 122, 242
Jia Paofu, member of the 8th CC, secretary of the CC north-west bureau, 45
Jian Bozan, historian, professor at Beijing University, 18, 61
Jiang Qing, 1st deputy head of the CCRG, member of the Politburo of the 9th and the 10th CC, Mao's wife, 46–8, 51–4, 59–61, 71, 77, 81, 86–8, 102–3, 115–19, 121, 127, 132–4, 146, 148, 154, 164–7, 171, 173, 177, 181, 187, 191, 194, 197, 208–13, 219, 221, 225–6, 235, 247, 249, 251, 254–61, 263–5, 267–72, 274–7, 281–3, 285, 287, 289–91, 294–7
Jiang Guozhang, officer of the air force 4th army, 233
Jiang Tengjiao, secretary of the air force political department, political commissar of the Nanjing military region air force, 209, 236
Jiang Zemin, Secretary of the Shanghai Party Committee, 271
Jin Chunming, professor at the Central Party School, 197
Jin Zumin, member of the 9th and 10th CC, 271

Kang Sheng, adviser to the CCRG, member of the Standing Committee of the Politburo of the 9th and 10th CC, 43, 45, 47, 50, 53, 58, 60–1, 63–65, 71, 73, 74, 81–2, 87–8, 102–3, 117–18, 127, 132, 154, 165–7, 173, 177, 181, 185–7, 193–4, 197, 209–10, 213–14, 220, 225, 247, 251, 253
Ke Qingshi, member of the Politburo of the 8th CC, first secretary of the CC east China bureau and of the Shanghai Municipal Party Committee, 43, 54, 161
Kuai Dafu, leader of the 'Jinggangshan Red Guards Corps' at Quinghua University, 86, 103

Li Baohua, secretary of the Anhui provincial Party Committee, 136
Li Dazhao, Party leader in the early 1920s, professor at Beijing University, 189
Li Desheng, member of the Politburo, commander of the Beijing military region, later of the Shenyang military region, 177, 223, 225, 237, 241, 251, 292–3
Li Fuchun, vice prime minister, member of the Politburo of the 8th CC, 82, 117–19
Li Guotang, political commissar of the ocean liner *Feng Quing*, 270
Li Qi, head of the Beijing Party Committee's propaganda department, 57
Li Tianyu, deputy chief of staff of the PLA, 129
Li Weixin, deputy chief of the political department of the 7314 unit, member of the 'joint fleet', 233, 237
Li Wenpu, Lin Biao's security officer, 239
Li Xiannian, member of the Politbureau of the 8th and 9th CC, vice prime minister, 117–19, 177, 249, 271, 277, 292, 296
Li Xifan, literary commentator with the *People's Daily*, 53
Li Xiucheng, the 'loyal king' of the Taiping uprising, 18
Li Xuefeng, member of the 8th CC, alternative member of the 9th CC, political commissar and Party secretary of the Beijing military region, 70, 76–7, 223
Li Zhen, minister of public security, 197
Li Zuopeng, member of the Politburo of the 9th CC, political commissar of the navy, deputy chief of staff of the PLA, 133, 144, 177, 200, 217–18, 220–2, 235, 238, 241, 243
Liang Shuming, scholar, expert on Confucius, 261
Liang Xingchu, commander of the Chengdu military region, 204
Liao Mosha, 16, 19, 62–3, 88, 95
Lin Biao, vice chairman of the CCP and the military commission, member of the Standing Committee of the Politburo, vice prime minister and minister of defence, 32, 33, 37–8, 43–4, 51, 56, 59, 66–70, 82, 84–5, 93, 95, 115, 118, 123, 125–8, 130, 132–4, 137, 142, 146, 148, 153, 165–9, 173, 175–8, 181–2, 188, 191, 197, 199, 201–18, 220–35, 237–44, 247–8, 252–9, 262–6, 273, 275–6, 280–1
Lin Jie, researcher at the philosophy and social sciences department of the Chinese Academy of Sciences, 20
Lin Jieting, leader of the preparatory committee for the revolutionary committee in Sichuan, 164
Lin Liguo, Lin Biao's son, deputy chief of the air force operations department, 169, 216, 231, 233, 235–7, 240–1, 252
Lin Liheng, Lin Biao's daughter, associate editor in chief of the *Air Force Press*, 216, 231, 239, 244
Lin Qiangyun, vice governor of Guangdong province, 151, 187
Liu Bing, deputy secretary of the Qinhua University Party Committee, 285
Liu Bocheng, marshal, member of the Politburo of the 8th, 9th and 10th CC, vice chairman of the military commission, 177, 201, 275, 292

GLOSSARY OF CHINESE NAMES

Liu Feng, political commissar of the Wuhan military region air force, later of the Wuhan military region, member of the 9th CC, 146, 148, 243
Liu Lantao, Party secretary of the CC northwest bureau, 117, 185–6
Liu Lingkai, leader of the '616 red guards' of the Beijing foreign languages institute, 193
Liu Peifeng, section chief of the air force Party committee, member of the 'joint fleet', 240, 242
Liu Qingtang, ballet dancer, minister of culture, 266
Liu Shaoqi, vice chairman of the CCP, president of the PRC, 25–8, 30, 37–8, 40–5, 51, 55, 58, 64, 72–84, 89–93, 101, 103, 105–6, 108, 115, 117–20, 122, 132, 136, 140, 162, 172, 173–4, 179–80, 185–6, 193, 201, 209–10, 223–4, 228–9, 231, 245, 262, 275
Liu Shaotang, writer, 5
Liu Xiangping, minister of public health, Xie Fuzhi's wife, 251
Liu Xingyuan, member of the 8th, 9th and 10th CC, political commissar of the Guanhzhou military region, later the Nanjing military region, 238
Liu Yalou, member of the 8th CC, commander of the air force, 68
Liu Zhidan, veteran revolutionary from north Shaanxi, subject of a novel, 45, 53
Liu Zhijian, deputy head of the PLA department of general policies, head of the army cultural revolution group, 115, 126–7, 129–32, 168
Lu Di, teacher of classical Chinese, reader for Mao Zedong, 283–4
Lu Dingyi, alternate member of the Politburo of the 8th CC, member of the CC secretariat, head of the CC propaganda department, 46, 64, 66–7, 70–1, 88, 94, 186, 209
Lu Min, chief of the operations department of the air force, member of the joint fleet, 237
Lu Ping, president of Beijing University, 74
Lu Yang, deputy director of the Commission of Science and Technology for National Defence, 129
Lu Zhengcao, member of the 8th CC, minister of railways, 188
Luo Ruiqing, member of the 8th CC and the CC secretariat, general chief of staff of the PLA, general secretary of the military commission, 64, 67–71, 88, 94, 166, 168, 186, 203, 209, 227, 274

Ma Feng, writer, 22
Ma Tianshui, deputy director of the Shanghai revolutionary Committee, 250
Ma Wenbo, military representative to the foreign ministry, vice foreign minister, 198
Ma Wenrui, minister of labour, 45
Mao Yuanxin, political commissar of the Shenyang military region, Mao's nephew and liaison man with the Politburo, 267, 271, 287, 293, 295
Mao Zedong, chairman of the CCP and of the military commission, 1–5, 17–26, 28–9, 35–44, 46–8, 52–6, 58–61, 64, 66, 73–91, 93, 96, 99, 101, 108, 112–13, 118–20, 132, 136, 138, 143–4, 146, 149, 150, 153–5,

158–9, 160–3, 171–9, 181, 185–6, 189, 190, 192, 194–5, 199, 200–1, 205, 208–19, 214–16, 218, 220–2, 224–7, 230–3, 235–7, 241–2, 245–9, 251, 254–6, 259, 262–3, 268–78, 280–7, 289–92
Mao Zemin, Mao Zedong's brother, 189
Mi Jialong, political commissar of the Chinese civil aviation, 233
Mi Shiqi, Wang Hongwen's secretary, 294

Nie Rongzhen, marshal and vice prime minister, member of the 8th, 9th and 10th CC, 82, 116, 119, 130, 137, 173, 201, 208, 228, 295
Nie Yuanzi, party secretary of the department of philosophy at Beijing University, director of the revolutionary committee at Beijing University, 73–4, 80, 95, 103, 161

Pan Jingyin, pilot of the Trident of Lin Biao's flight, 242
Peng Dehuai, marshall, member of the Politburo of the 7th and 8th CC, vice premier and minister of defence, 10, 36–7, 39, 45, 52–3, 70, 199, 200, 262
Peng Shaohui, member of the 9th and 10th CC, deputy general chief of staff, 148
Peng Zhen, member of the Politburo of the 7th and 8th CC and of the CC secretariat, mayor and Party secretary of Beijing, 19, 44, 46, 53–60, 62, 64–67, 70–1, 88, 94, 166, 180, 186, 228–9, 281

Qi Benyu, member of the CCRG, 18, 20, 49, 58, 87, 89, 91, 120, 130, 132, 141, 154, 165, 171, 192, 196, 201, 220, 221
Qian Jun, leader of the Anhui military region, 151
Qiao Guanhua, vice foreign minister, foreign minister, 122, 271, 296
Qiu Huizuo, member of the Politburo of the 9th CC, chief of the PLA logistics department, 133, 177, 214, 217–18, 222, 235, 238, 243

Rao Shushi, member of the 7th CC, secretary of the east China bureau, head of the CC organisation department, 27
Ren Bishi, member of the Politburo of the 7th CC and of the CC secretariat, 26, 27

Shao Quanlin, Party secretary of the All China Writers Association, 22
Shen Shicai, governor of Xinjian province under the Guomindang Government, 188
Song Shilun, president of the Academy of Military Sciences, 295
Su Haidong, leader of the red guards of the Beijing Teachers' University, 193
Sun Yefang, economist, director of the institute of economics at the Chinese Academy of Sciences, 19
Sun Yuguo, deputy commander of the Shenyang military region, 293

Tan Houlan, leader of the 'Jinggangshan Militant Corps' of the Beijing Teachers' University, 103, 161
Tan Na, Jiang Qing's former husband, 209

GLOSSARY OF CHINESE NAMES

Tang Wensheng (Nancy Tang), Mao Zedong's interpreter, alternate member of the 10th CC, director of the American department in the foreign ministry, 263, 271–2, 287

Tan Zhenlin, member of the 7th and 8th CC, vice prime minister, member of the CC secretariat, 117–19, 121, 165, 250

Tao Zhu, member of the 8th CC, later member of its Politburo, head of the propaganda department, vice prime minister, 71, 82, 115, 127, 168, 173, 186, 194

Tan Zian, deputy commander of the Shenyang military region, 137

Ulanfu, alternate member of the Politburo of the 8th CC, chairman of the autonomous region of Outer Mongolia, 250

Wan Li, secretary of the Beijing municipal Party committee and vice mayor, 288

Wan Yi, army general operating in north east China in the 1940s, 188

Wang Bingzhang, deputy commander of the air force, minister of the 7th machine-building ministry and later of the commission of science and technology for national defence, 218

Wang Dabing, leader of the 'East is Red Commune' of the Beijing Institute of Geology, 103, 161

Wang Dongxing, director of the general office of the CC, member of the Politburo of the 10th CC, 144, 177, 218, 293, 296

Wang Fei, deputy chief of staff of the air force, director of the air force general office, member of the 'joint fleet', 236, 238

Wang Guangmei, Liu Shaoqi's wife, 40–1, 88, 91

Wang Hairong, Mao's grandniece, 242, 263, 296

Wang Hongkun, member of the 9th and the 10th CC, second political commissar of the navy, 212

Wang Hongwen, vice chairman of the CCP, member of the gang of four, 106, 110, 157–8, 231, 248–51, 255, 258, 259, 260, 263–4, 270–5, 277, 280, 283, 289, 291, 293–4, 296

Wang Zhao, secretary of the Qinghai provincial Party committee, 141

Wang Jiaxiang, member of the 8th CC, head of the CC international liaison department, 26, 250

Wang Li, vice minister of the CC international liaison department, member of the CCRG, 49, 58, 118, 122, 141–7, 154, 163–5, 171, 192, 196, 198, 213, 224

Wang Ming, leader of the CCP in the 1930s, 70, 118, 173, 223

Wang Nianyi, professor at the University of National Defence, 197

Wang Renzhong, secretary of the Hubei provincial Party committee, political commissar of the Wuhan military region, 115

Wang Ruoshui, deputy editor in chief of *People's Daily*, 254–5

Wang Weiguo, political commissar of the air force 4th army, alternate member of the 9th CC, member of the 'joint fleet', 218, 233, 236–7

Wang Xiuzhen, deputy director of the Shanghai revolutionary committee, 250

Wang Zhen, member of the 8th CC, minister of agriculture, 295

Wei Guoqing, member of the Politburo of the 10 CC, political commissar of the Guangzhou military region, 292
Wei Heng, secretary of the Shanxi provincial Party committee, 116
Wen Yucheng, member of the 9th CC, commander of the Beijing garrison, deputy commander of the Chendu military region, 171, 212
Wu De, member of the Politburo of the 10th CC, director of the Beijing municipal revolutionary committee, 71, 249, 251, 288–9, 293
Wu Faxian, member of the Politburo of the 9th CC, commander of the air force, 69, 132–3, 165–6, 169, 174, 177, 195, 200, 210, 215, 217–18, 220, 222, 226, 235, 238, 240
Wu Han, historian, vice mayor of Beijing, 16, 19, 46–7, 49, 51–2, 54–62, 65, 88, 95
Wu Lengxi, chief editor of *People's Daily*, director of the Xinhua News Agency, 46, 279

Xi Zhongxun, member of the 8th CC vice prime minister, 45
Xia Yan, vice minister of culture, 133–4, 167, 196
Xiao Hua, head of the PLA general political department, 134, 168, 205
Xie Fuzhi, member of the 9th CC, minister of public security, director of the Beijing municipal revolutionary committee, 81, 88, 105, 118, 145, 166, 177, 223, 195
Xie Jingyi, deputy secretary of the Qinghua university Party committee, 251, 271, 285–6
Xie Zichang, leader of a guerilla group operating in the Shaanxi-Gansu area in the 1930s, 45
Xiong Xianghui, ambassador, deputy department head at the general chief of staff, 226
Xu Jingxian, deputy director of the Shanghai revolutionary committee, 158
Xu Liqun, deputy minister of the CC propaganda department, 58, 60
Xu Shiyou, member of the Politburo of the 9th and 10th CC, commander of the Nanjing military region, later of the Guangzhou military region, 137, 166, 177, 231, 292
Xu Wenyi, ambassador to Mongolia, 242
Xu Xiangqian, member of the 7th and 8th CC, leader of the army cultural revolution group, 83, 116, 119, 122, 128, 130, 132, 137, 148, 168, 173, 201

Yan Hongyan, alternate member of the 8th CC, political commissar of the Kunming military region, Party secretary of Yunnan province, 116
Yan Weibin, Lu Dingyi's wife, 67
Yang Chenwu, alternate member of the 8th CC, acting general chief of staff, 137, 144, 164–5, 168–71, 192, 196–7, 203, 227, 229, 295
Yang Dezhi, member of the 9th and 10 CC, commander of the Jinan and later of the Wuhan military region, 166, 219
Yang Dezhong, official of the CC security bureau, 241
Yang Hansheng, writer, 18

GLOSSARY OF CHINESE NAMES

Yang Hucheng, leader of the north-west army of the Guomindang, 188

Yang Shangkun, member of the 8th CC, alternate member of the CC secretariat, director of the CC general office, 64, 70, 88, 94, 167, 209–10

Yang Xianzhen, president of the Central Party School, 19, 22, 45, 185–6

Yang Yi, Yang Chenwu's daughter, 169

Yao Dengshan, diplomat, 198

Yao Wenyuan, member of the Politburo of the 9th and 10th CC, member of the CCRG, 17, 49, 54–7, 59, 60–2, 110, 117–18, 141, 156–8, 177, 194, 211, 213, 219, 225, 249, 250–1, 254–6, 275, 281, 283–4, 289, 291, 293–7

Yao Zhen, deputy head of the CC propaganda department, 58

Ye Jianying, marshal, member of the Politburo of the 9th and 10th CC, minister of defence, vice chairman of the military commission, 58, 71, 82, 116–19, 127, 130, 137, 139, 168, 173, 177, 187, 201, 221, 228, 243, 249, 251, 271, 278, 286, 292, 295–6

Ye Qun, Lin Biao's wife, member of the Politburo of the 9th CC, director of Lin Biao's office, 67–9, 118, 130, 132, 134, 165, 169, 177, 201, 207–10, 213–16, 218, 222, 224, 229, 235, 238–9, 240–3

Yu Huiyong, composer, minister of culture, member of the 10th CC, 251

Yu Guanyuan, economist, 279

Yu Lijin, political commissar of the air force, 144, 164–7, 169, 170, 192, 196, 210, 227

Yu Pingbo, scholar, expert on the classical novel *A Dream of Red Mansions*, 53

Yu Qiuli, member of the 9th CC, vice prime minister, 117–19

Yu Xingye, deputy chief of the 1st section of the air force general office, member of the 'joint fleet', 233–4

Zhang Caiqian, member of the 9th and 10th CC, deputy general chief of staff, 225

Zhang Chunqiao, member of the Standing Committee of the Politburo, vice prime minister, director of the Shanghai revolutionary committee, director of the PLA department of general policies, 48–9, 54, 60, 65, 81, 86, 103, 110–11, 115, 118, 130, 141, 146, 156–8, 164, 177, 210, 211, 213–15, 219, 225, 233, 247, 248–51, 254–6, 263, 272, 275, 277, 280–1, 283, 291, 293, 295, 297

Zhang Guotao, a CCP leader in the 1930s, 118

Zhang Jianqi, leader of the 'Capital Red Guard May 16 Corps', 193–4

Zhang Linzhi, minister of coal industry, 116

Zhang Ning, dancer of the art troup of the Nanjing military region, Lin Liguo's fiancée, 239, 240, 244

Zhang Qinglin, medical doctor, Lin Liheng's fiancée, 239, 240

Zhang Tiesheng, student and hero of the campaign of 'going against the tide', 267

Zhang Wentian, alternate member of the Politburo of the 8th CC, vice foreign minister, 36, 275

Zhang Xiaochuan, officer of a PLA unit in Qinghai, 141
Zhang Xueliang, commander of the north east army of the Guomindang, 188
Zhang Xuesi, chief of staff of the navy, Zhang Xueliang's brother, 188
Zhang Yufeng, Mao's personal secretary, 245, 283–4, 290–1
Zhang Yunsheng, Lin Biao's assistant, 205
Zhang Yuqin, middle-school student in the campaign of 'going against the tide', 267
Zhang Zhixin, cadre of the Liaoning provincial Party committee, 191
Zhao Ruzhang, office director at the National Defence Commission, 102
Zhao Shuli, writer, 22
Zhao Yongfu, deputy commander of the Lanzhou military region, 139, 141
Zhao Ziyang, prime minister, general secretary of the CCP, 125, 244
Zhen Siyu, member of the 9th and 10th CC, commander of the Wuhan and later the Jinan military region, 148
Zheng Junli, film director, 209
Zheng Weishan, member of the 9th CC, commander of the Beijing military region, 223
Zhong Hanhua, second political commissar of the Wuhan military region, 145, 147–8
Zhou Enlai, vice chairman of the CCP, member of the Politburo Standing Committee, prime minister, 15, 27–8, 37–8, 43, 45, 56, 78, 82, 84, 87, 102, 113–19, 120, 122, 127, 130, 131, 144, 147–8, 160, 165, 167–8, 170, 172, 176–8, 181, 185–8, 192–4, 197, 201–2, 205, 220, 224, 226, 228, 238, 240–3, 247, 249–54, 262–5, 269, 270–3, 276–8, 280–1, 283, 285–9
Zhou Jiayu, vice minister, ministry of geology, 102
Zhou Lipo, writer, 22
Zhou Peiyuan, president of Beijing University, 253
Zhou Rongxin, minister of education, 279, 288
Zhou Xiaozhou, secretary of the Hunan provincial Party committee, 36
Zhou Yuchi, deputy director of the air force general office, member of the 'joint fleet', 231, 233, 235–8
Zhou Yang, deputy minister of the CC propaganda department, 46
Zhu De, member of the Politburo, chairman of the National People's Congress, 27, 37–8, 43, 82, 115, 168, 173–4, 177, 201, 239, 274, 289

INDEX

All Army CRG, 126, 129, 132, 140, 142, 148, 210
Anhui Event, 159
Anting Event, 106

Balluka, Begir, 186
Bhutto, Zulfikar Ali, 290

Cao Cao, King of Wei, 216
CCRG, 49, 71, 73, 79, 83, 86, 93, 103–4, 106–7, 113, 116–19, 121–2, 127, 129, 130–2, 136, 138, 140–50, 154–5, 159, 164–6, 170, 172, 177, 182, 192–6, 201–2, 210–13, 220, 223
Chang Guan Lou Event, 63

De-Stalinisation, 30
Diaoyutan, 170, 211, 235–6, 290

Eighth Party Congress (1956), 3, 4, 27, 30–2, 43–4, 107, 186
Eleventh Plenum, 78, 90, 96

Factionalism, 8, 100–2, 120, 123, 143, 155–9, 276
February Adverse Current, 115–21, 141–2, 164–5, 173, 175, 193
February Outline Report, 51, 58–9, 61, 64–5, 71, 115–16, 119
Feng Qing Event, 269–70
First and second line leadership, 35, 42

Five anti's, 14
Forum on literature and art, 58–9
Four cleanings, 14, 40
Fourth National People's Congress, 269, 274

Gang of four, 282, 289–7
Gao Zu, Han emperor, 17
General headquarters of Shanghai revolutionary rebels, 111, 107, 110–13, 157
Great Leap Forward, 7–12, 15–16, 19, 33, 35–6, 45, 48, 52, 63
Group of five, 22, 51, 58, 64
Guomindang, 89, 150, 170, 180, 184, 188, 200, 223

Hundred Flowers movement, 4–6, 61

Inner Mongolian People's Revolutionary Party, 187–87

January storm, 89
Joint fleet, 231, 223

Kissinger, H., 226
Khrushchev, N., 13, 23, 30, 34, 42, 72, 118

Leadership structure, 25, 27, 44–5, 82–3, 176–8, 200, 250–1, 292–3
Lee Kuan Yew, 290

367

Lushan conference (1959), 10, 36–7, 53
Lushan conference (1971), 179, 199–200, 213–14, 217–22, 229–30, 238

Malton, 290
Mao Zedong personality cult, 26, 28–35, 53, 169
Mao Zedong Thought, 2, 5, 24, 26–7, 30–1, 33–4, 44, 66, 107; on class struggle, 6, 7, 10, 12–15, 38, 64–5, 179; on contradictions, 5–7, 18; on intellectuals, 7, 20; on literature and art, 19–22, 58–60; on the purpose of the CR, 22; on revisionism, 13, 16–17, 282
Maojiawan, 170, 205–6, 211
May 16 Circular, 51, 65, 71–2, 76, 78
May 16 Group, 154, 190, 192–8
May 13 Event, 133–4
Meissner, Maurice, 34
Montgomery, 37

Ninth Party Congress, 163, 171–8, 185, 199, 200, 222, 230
Nixon, R. 290

Ondorhaan, 242
One Million Heroes, 144–8

People's Communes, 8, 9, 12, 15, 36, 39
PLA, 32, 44, 66, 123–52, 156, 184, 200–1, 203–4, 208–9, 211
Political campaigns: against empiricism, 291–2; against the May 16 group, 192–8; against Lin Biao, 243; against Lin Biao and Confucius, 247, 255–62, 276, 281, 283; against the Liu-Deng line, 81–92; against renegades, 180, 185–91; against ultra-leftism, 252–5; against *Water Margin*, 283–5; against Zhou Enlai, 262–67, 276; anti-rightist campaign (1959), 39; 'going against the tide', 267–8; 'one smash and three anti's', 190; to purify class ranks, 178–90; to study Marxism-Leninism, 281

Qin Shihuang, 28–9
Quotations, 33

Red guards, 87, 93–105, 109, 120, 122, 154, 159, 161, 164, 179
Revolutionary rebels, 105–8, 110, 122, 159, 179
Revolutionary committees, 120, 150–1, 153, 156, 159, 160–3, 178, 201, 276

Seizure of power, 108–15, 157, 179
Seven thousand cadres conference (1962), 17, 37–8
Seventh Party Congress (1945), 26–7, 186
Shanghai People's Commune, 158
Shanghai revolutionary rebels' committee of great alliances, 157
Shanghai workers' scarlet guards defending Mao Zedong Thought, 107, 111
Sino-American relations, 228
Sino-Soviet border clashes, 91
Sino-Soviet border talks, 214
Sino-Soviet conflict, 13
Sino-Soviet relations, 228
Snow, Edgar, 34, 227
Soviet Union, 13, 42, 191, 244
Stalin, 30–2, 42
Struggle-criticism-transformation, 82, 89, 123–4, 178
Sun Quan, King of Wu, 216

Tenth Party Congress (1973), 249–50
Twentieth Congress of the Soviet Communist Party, 5, 13

INDEX

Ulan Baatar, 242

Work teams, 40, 75–80, 102, 129
Workers' propaganda teams, 162
Wuhan Event, 122, 139, 143–50

Wuhan workers' general headquarters, 140

Xiang Yu, ruler of Western Chu, 17